Praise for
# A MAN FOR ALL M

"In *A Man for All Markets*, Thorp delightfully recounts his progress (if that is the word) from college teacher to gambler to hedge-fund manager. Along the way we learn important lessons about the functioning of markets and the logic of investment."

—*The Wall Street Journal*

"Compelling . . . For anyone who's even remotely interested in finance or investing, or just enjoys reading about fascinating people, I can't recommend Thorp's book enough. It's a riveting read and one you won't soon forget."

—The Motley Fool

"Thorp gives a biological summation (think Richard Feynman's *Surely You're Joking, Mr. Feynman!*) of his quest to prove the aphorism "the house always wins" is flawed. . . . Illuminating for the mathematically inclined, and cautionary for would-be gamblers and day traders."

—*Library Journal*

"Ed Thorp takes us on an incredible journey as we learn how to beat blackjack, roulette, and then Wall Street; stop off to have dinner with a young Buffett; unmask Madoff before anyone else; and so much more. More important, it's all fun, fascinating, and filled with lessons we can all use to be more successful in business and life. Learn and enjoy; I did!"

—JOEL GREENBLATT, author of the *New York Times* bestseller *The Little Book That Beats the Market*

"An extraordinary autobiography that reads like a novel and contains insights into what has gone wrong with the financial system along the way."

—JOHN KAY, author of *Other People's Money: The Real Business of Finance*

"What makes a good investor? To gauge from this amiable account by math whiz, professor, gambler, hedge fund manager, and investor Thorp (*The Mathematics of Gambling,* 1984, etc.)—one of the early "quants," as brokers call number nerds—much hinges on being curious and being willing to do the work necessary to satisfy that curiosity. . . . His account of making a broker blanch with a daring hedge maneuver during the height of the October 1987 crash is an exercise in learned derring-do, with the upshot that while the S&P dropped by a quarter, he at least broke even during the worst of it and gained in the long term. It's the kind of thing any would-be investor, to say nothing of casino cowboy, ought to read. Thorp's in-the-trenches account of gaming the system(s) is a pleasure—and instructive, too."

—*Kirkus Reviews*

"An amazing book by a true icon; Thorp launched revolutions in Vegas and on Wall Street by turning math into magic, and here he weaves his own life lessons into a page-turner as hot as a deck full of aces. Loved it!"

—BEN MEZRICH, *New York Times* bestselling
author of *Bringing Down the House* and
*The Accidental Billionaires*

"Whether you are an aspiring professional player, a casual gambler, or an occasional visitor to Las Vegas, you can feel the impact of Professor Ed Thorp's intellect on that desert city. In 1962, Thorp published the classic book *Beat the Dealer.* The text was based on Thorp's original research that stemmed from his curiosity about the game of 21 and was billed as a "how-to book" for the layperson to beat the casinos at blackjack. And, simply stated, it changed everything. . . . *A Man for All Markets* chronicles Thorp's hero-like arc from his humble beginnings growing up in a family that struggled to get by—first in the cold winters of Chicago and later in the sun-soaked cities of southern California, where he excelled in a variety of high school science courses and ultimately earned a scholarship for his exceptional talents in physics—through his professional career as a gaming guru, and ultimately to his amazing success in a stock market–centered career, where he would take his knowledge and understanding of games of chance and apply them to the biggest casino in the world: Wall Street. *A Man for All Markets* chronicles Thorp's personal journey in navigating the unexpected and sometimes dangerous obstacles that come along with challenging the status quo of a wealthy corporate adversary."

—NICHOLAS G. COLON, professional advantage gambler and managing director of Alea Consulting Group, a casino gaming consulting firm

"What a CV! Figure out how to win at blackjack using card counting? Check. Build the world's first wearable computer? Check. Find the formula for valuing financial options but use it to make money rather than win a Nobel Prize? Check. This book is in part the gripping story of how one man's genius and dedication has solved so many problems in diverse fields. But more important, it's a fascinating insight into the thought processes of someone with little interest in fame, who has mostly stayed under the radar, but who has followed his inquisitive mind wherever it has led him, and reaped the resulting rewards. There is nothing more crucial than knowing how to think clearly. Read this book and learn from a master."

—PAUL WILMOTT, founder, *Wilmott* magazine

BY EDWARD O. THORP

*A Man for All Markets*
*Beat the Dealer*
*Beat the Market*
*Elementary Probability*
*The Mathematics of Gambling*

# A MAN
# — *for* —
# ALL MARKETS

*From Las Vegas to Wall Street,
How I Beat the Dealer and the Market*

## *Edward O. Thorp*

RANDOM HOUSE

NEW YORK

2018 Random House Trade Paperback Edition

Published in the United States by Random House, an imprint and
division of Penguin Random House LLC, New York.

RANDOM HOUSE and the HOUSE colophon are registered
trademarks of Penguin Random House LLC.

Originally published in hardcover in the United States by
Random House, an imprint and division of
Penguin Random House LLC, in 2017.

LIBRARY OF CONGRESS CATALOGING-IN-PUBLICATION DATA
Names: Thorp, Edward O., author.
Title: A man for all markets : from Las Vegas to Wall Street,
how I beat the dealer and the market / Edward O. Thorp.
Description: New York : Random House, [2017] | Includes index.
Identifiers: LCCN 2016026545 | ISBN 9780812979909 | ISBN 9780812998740 (ebook)
Subjects: LCSH: Thorp, Edward O. | Investment advisors—United States—Biography. |
Mathematicians—United States—Biography. | Gambling systems. | Investments. |
Finance—Mathematical models.
Classification: LCC HG4928.5.T54 A3 2017 | DDC 332.6092 [B]—dc23
LC record available at https://lccn.loc.gov/2016026545

Printed in the United States of America on acid-free paper

8th Printing

*Book design by Christopher M. Zucker*

*To Vivian and to our children and their families: Raun,*
*Brian, and Ava;*

*Karen, Rich, Claire, Christopher, and Edward;*

*Jeff, Lisa, Kylie, and Thomas.*

# CONTENTS

# PREFACE

Join me in my odyssey through the worlds of science, gambling, and the securities markets. You will see how I overcame risks and reaped rewards in Las Vegas, Wall Street, and life. On the way, you will meet interesting people from blackjack card counters to investment experts, from movie stars to Nobel Prize winners. And you'll learn about options and other derivatives, hedge funds, and why a simple investment approach beats most investors in the long run, including experts.

I began life in the Great Depression of the 1930s. Along with millions of others, my family was struggling to get by from one day to the next. Though we didn't have helpful connections and I went to public schools, I found a resource that made all the difference: I learned how to think.

Some people think in words, some use numbers, and still others work with visual images. I do all of these, but I also think using models. A model is a simplified version of reality, like a street map that shows you how to travel from one part of a city to another or the vision of a gas as a swarm of tiny elastic balls ceaselessly bouncing against one another.

I learned that simple devices such as gears, levers, and pulleys follow basic rules. You could discover the rules by experimenting and, if you got them right, could then use the rules to predict what would happen in new situations.

Most amazing to me was the magic of a crystal set—an early primitive radio made with wire, a mineral crystal, and headphones. Suddenly, I heard voices coming from hundreds or thousands of miles away, carried through the air by some mysterious process. The notion that things I couldn't even see followed rules I could discover just by thinking—and that I could use what I discovered to change the world—inspired me from an early age.

Because of circumstances, I was largely self-taught and that led me to think differently. First, rather than subscribing to widely accepted views—such as *you can't beat the casinos*—I checked for myself. Second, since I tested theories by inventing new experiments, I formed the habit of taking the result of pure thought—such as a formula for valuing warrants—and using it profitably. Third, when I set a worthwhile goal for myself, I made a realistic plan and persisted until I succeeded. Fourth, I strove to be consistently rational, not just in a specialized area of science, but in dealing with all aspects of the world. I also learned the value of withholding judgement until I could make a decision based on evidence.

I hope my story will show you a unique perspective and that *A Man for All Markets* will help you think differently about gambling, investments, risk, money management, wealth-building, and life.

# FOREWORD

Ed Thorp's memoir reads like a thriller—mixing wearable computers that would have made James Bond proud, shady characters, great scientists, and poisoning attempts (in addition to the sabotage of Ed's car so he would have an "accident" in the desert). The book reveals a thorough, rigorous, methodical person in search of life, knowledge, financial security, and, not least of all, fun. Thorp is also known to be a generous man, intellectually speaking, eager to share his discoveries with random strangers (in print but also in person)—something you hope to find in scientists but usually don't. Yet he is humble—he might qualify as the only humble trader on planet Earth—so, unless the reader can reinterpret what's between the lines, he or she won't notice that Thorp's contributions are vastly more momentous than he reveals. Why?

Because of their simplicity. Their sheer simplicity.

For it is the straightforward character of his contributions and insights that made them both invisible in academia and useful for practitioners. My purpose here is not to explain or summarize the book; Thorp—not surprisingly—writes in a direct, clear, and engaging way. I am here, as a trader and a practitioner of mathematical finance, to show its importance and put it in context for my community of real-world scientist-traders and risk-takers in general.

That context is as follows. Ed Thorp is the first modern mathematician who *successfully* used quantitative methods for risk taking—and most certainly the first mathematician who met financial success doing it. Since then there has been a cohort of such "quants," such as the whiz kids in applied mathematics at SUNY Stony Brook—but Thorp is their dean.

His main and most colorful predecessor, Girolamo (sometimes Geronimo) Cardano, a sixteenth-century polymath and mathematician who—sort of—wrote the first version of *Beat the Dealer*, was a compulsive gambler. To put it mildly, he was unsuccessful at it—not least because addicts are bad risk-takers; to be convinced, just take a look at the magnificence of Monte Carlo, Las Vegas, and Biarritz, places financed by their compulsion. Cardano's book *Liber de ludo aleae* ("Book on Games of Chance") was instrumental in the later development of probability, but, unlike Thorp's book, was less of an inspiration for gamblers and more for mathematicians. Another mathematician, a French Protestant refugee in London, Abraham de Moivre, a frequenter of gambling joints and the author of *The doctrine of chances: or, a method for calculating the probabilities of events in play* (1718) could hardly make both ends meet. One can easily count another half a dozen mathematician-gamblers, including greats like Fermat and Huygens—who were either indifferent to the bottom line or not particularly good at mastering it. Before Ed Thorp, mathematicians of gambling had their love of chance largely unrequited.

Thorp's method is as follows: He cuts to the chase in identifying a clear *edge* (that is something that in the long run puts the odds in his favor). The edge has to be obvious and uncomplicated. For instance, calculating the momentum of a roulette wheel, which he did with the first wearable computer (and with no less a coconspirator than the great Claude Shannon, father of information theory), he estimated a typical edge of roughly 40 percent per bet. But that part is easy, very easy. It is *capturing* the edge, converting it into dollars in the bank, restaurant meals, interesting cruises, and Christmas gifts to friends and family—

that's the hard part. It is the dosage of your betting—not too little, not too much—that matters in the end. For that, Ed did great work on his own, before the theoretical refinement that came from a third member of the Information Trio: John Kelly, originator of the famous Kelly Criterion, a formula for placing bets that we discuss today because Ed Thorp made it operational.

A bit more about simplicity before we discuss dosing. For an academic judged by his colleagues, rather than the bank manager of his local branch (or his tax accountant), a mountain giving birth to a mouse, after huge labor, is not a very good thing. They prefer the mouse to give birth to a mountain; it is the perception of sophistication that matters. The more complicated, the better; the simple doesn't get you citations, H-values, or some such metric *du jour* that brings the respect of the university administrators, as they can understand that stuff but not the substance of the real work. The only academics who escape the burden of complication-for-complication's sake are the great mathematicians and physicists (and, from what I hear, even for them it's becoming harder and harder in today's funding and ranking environment).

Ed was initially an academic, but he favored learning by doing, with his skin in the game. When you reincarnate as practitioner, *you want the mountain to give birth to the simplest possible strategy*, and one that has the smallest number of side effects, the minimum possible hidden complications. Ed's genius is demonstrated in the way he came up with very simple rules in blackjack. Instead of engaging in complicated combinatorics and memory-challenging card counting (something that requires one to be a savant), he crystallizes all his sophisticated research into simple rules: Go to a blackjack table. Keep a tally. Start with zero. Add one for some strong cards, minus ones for weak ones, and nothing for others. It is mentally easy to just bet incrementally up and down—bet larger when the number is high, smaller when it is low—and such a strategy is immediately applicable by anyone with the ability to tie his shoes or find a casino on a map. Even while using wearable computers at the roulette table, the detection of edge was simple, so simple that one can get it while standing on a balance ball in the gym; the fanciness resides in the implementation and the wiring.

As a side plot, Ed discovered what is known today as the Black-Scholes option formula, before Black and Scholes (and it is a sign of economics public relations that the formula doesn't bear his name—I've called it Bachelier-Thorp). His derivation was too simple—nobody at the time realized it could be potent.

Now money management—something central for those who learn from being exposed to their own profits and losses. Having an "edge" and surviving are two different things: The first requires the second. As Warren Buffet said: "In order to succeed you must first survive." You need to avoid ruin. At all costs.

And there is a dialectic between you and your P/L: You start betting small (a proportion of initial capital) and your risk control—the dosage—also controls your discovery of the edge. It is like trial and error, by which you revise both your risk appetite and your assessment of your odds one step at a time.

Academic finance, as has been recently shown by Ole Peters and Murray Gell-Mann, did not get the point that avoiding ruin, as a general principle, makes your gambling and investment strategy extremely different from the one that is proposed by the academic literature. As we saw, academics are paid by administrators via colleagues to make life complicated, not simpler. They invented something useless called utility theory (tens of thousands of papers are still waiting for a real reader). And they invented the idea that one could get to know the collective behavior of future prices in infinite detail—things like correlation, that could be identified today and would never change in the future. (More technically, to implement the portfolio construction suggested by modern financial theory, one needs to know the entire joint probability distribution of all assets for the entire future, plus the exact utility function for wealth at all future times. And without errors! [I have shown that estimation errors make the system explode.] We are lucky if we can know what we will eat for lunch tomorrow—how can we figure out the dynamics until the end of time?)

The Kelly-Thorp method requires no joint distribution or utility function. In practice, one needs the ratio of expected profit to worst-case return—dynamically adjusted (that is, *one gamble at a time*) to avoid ruin. That's all.

Thorp and Kelly's ideas were rejected by economists—in spite of their practical appeal—because of economists' love of general theories for all asset prices, dynamics of the world, etc. The famous patriarch of modern economics, Paul Samuelson, was supposedly on a vendetta against Thorp. Not a single one of the works of these economists will ultimately survive: Strategies that allow you to survive are not the same thing as the ability to impress colleagues.

So the world today is divided into two groups using distinct methods. The first method is that of the economists who tend to blow up routinely or get rich collecting fees for managing money, not from direct specula-tion. Consider that Long-Term Capital Management, which had the crème de la crème of financial economists, blew up spectacularly in 1998, losing a multiple of what they thought their worst-case scenario was.

The second method, that of the information theorists as pioneered by Ed, is practiced by traders and scientist-traders. Every surviving specu-lator uses explicitly or implicitly this second method (evidence: Ray Dalio, Paul Tudor Jones, Renaissance Technologies, even Goldman Sachs!). I said *every* because, as Peters and Gell-Mann have shown, those who don't will eventually go bust.

And thanks to that second method, if you inherit, say, $82,000 from uncle Morrie, you know that a strategy exists that will allow you to dou-ble the inheritance without ever going through bankruptcy.

Some additional wisdom I personally learned from Thorp: Many success-ful speculators, after their first break in life, get involved in large-scale structures, with multiple offices, morning meetings, coffee, corporate in-trigues, building more wealth while losing control of their lives. Not Ed. After the separation from his partners and the closing of his firm (for reasons that had nothing to do with him), he did not start a new mega-fund. He limited his involvement in managing other people's money. (Most people reintegrate into the comfort of other firms and leverage their reputation by raising monstrous amounts of outside money in order to collect large fees.) But such restraint requires some intuition, some self-knowledge. It is vastly less stressful to be independent—and one is never independent when involved in a large structure with powerful clients. It is hard enough to deal with the intricacies of probabilities, you need to avoid the vagaries of exposure to human moods. True success is exiting some rat race to modulate one's activities for peace of mind. Thorp certainly learned a lesson: The most stressful job he ever had was running the math department of the University of California, Irvine. You can detect that the man is in control of his life. This explains why he looked younger the second time I saw him, in 2016, than he did the first time, in 2005.

Ciao,
Nassim Nicholas Taleb

# A MAN
*— for —*
# ALL MARKETS

*Chapter 1*

---

# LOVING TO LEARN

My first memory is of standing with my parents on an outdoor landing at the top of some worn and dirty wooden steps. It was a gloomy Chicago day in December 1934, when I was two years and four months old. Even wearing my only set of winter pants and a jacket with a hood, it was cold. Black and leafless, the trees stood out above the snow-covered ground. From inside the house a woman was telling my parents, "No, we don't rent to people with children." Their faces fell and they turned away. Had I done something wrong? Why was I a problem? This image from the depths of the Great Depression has stayed with me always.

I next recall being taken at age two and a half to our beloved family physician, Dr. Dailey. My alarmed parents explained that I had yet to speak a single word. What was wrong? The doctor smiled and asked me to point to the ball on his desk. I did so, and he asked me to pick up his pencil. After I had done this and a few more tasks he said, "Don't worry, he'll talk when he's ready." We left, my parents relieved and a little mystified.

After this, the campaign to get me to talk intensified. About the time of my third birthday, my mother and two of her friends, Charlotte and Estelle, took me along with them to Chicago's then famous Montgomery Ward department store. As we sat on a bench near an elevator, two women and a man got off. Charlotte, keen to tempt me into speech, asked, "Where are the people going?" I said clearly and distinctly, "The man is going to buy something and the two women are going to the bathroom to do pee-pee." Charlotte and Estelle both blushed deeply at the mention of pee-pee. Far too young to have learned conventional embarrassment, I noticed this but didn't understand why they reacted that way. I also was puzzled by the sensation I had caused with my sudden change from silence to talkativeness.

From then on I spoke largely in complete sentences, delighting my parents and their friends, who now plied me with questions and often received surprising answers. My father set out to see what I could learn.

Born in Iowa in 1898, my father, Oakley Glenn Thorp, was the second of three children, with his brother two years older and sister two years younger. When he was six his family broke up. His father took him and his brother to settle in the state of Washington. His mother and sister remained in Iowa. In 1915 my grandfather died from the flu, three years before the Great Flu Pandemic of 1918–19, which killed between twenty and forty million people worldwide. The two boys lived with an uncle until 1917. Then my father, at age eighteen, went to France to join World War I as part of the great American Expeditionary Force. He fought with the infantry in the trenches, rose from private to sergeant, and was awarded the Bronze Star, the Silver Star, and two Purple Hearts for heroism in places like Château-Thierry, Belleau Wood, and the Battles of the Marne. As a very small boy I remember sitting in his lap on a humid afternoon examining the shrapnel scars on his chest and the minor mutilation of some of his fingers.

Following his discharge from the army after the war, my father enrolled at Oklahoma A&M. He completed a year and a half before he had to leave for lack of funds, but his hunger and respect for education endured and he instilled them in me, along with his unspoken hope that I would achieve more. Sensing this and hoping it would bring us closer, I welcomed his efforts to teach me.

As soon as I began to talk, he introduced me to numbers. I found it easy to count first to a hundred, then to a thousand. Next I learned how to increase any number by adding one to get the next number, which meant I could count forever if I only knew the names of the numbers. I soon learned how to count to a million. Adults seemed to think this was a very big number so I sat down to do it one morning. I knew I could eventually get there but I had no idea how long it was going to take. To get started, I chose a Sears catalog the size of a big-city telephone book because it seemed to have the most things to count. The pages were filled with pictures of merchandise labeled with the letters *A, B, C . . .*, which I recall appeared as black letters in white circles. I started at the beginning of the catalog and counted all the circled letters, one for each item, page after page. After a few hours I fell asleep at something like 32,576. My mother reported that when I awoke I resumed with "32,577 . . ."

A trait that showed up at about this time was my tendency not to accept anything I was told until I had checked it for myself. This had consequences. When I was three, my mother told me not to touch the hot stove because it would burn me. I brought my finger close enough to feel the warmth, then pressed the stove with my hand. Burned. Never again.

Another time, I was warned that fresh eggs would crack if they were squeezed just a little bit. Wondering what "a little bit" meant, I squeezed an egg very slowly until it cracked, then practiced squeezing another, stopping just before it would crack, to see exactly how far I could go. From the beginning, I loved learning through experimentation and exploration how my world worked.

After teaching me counting, my father's next project for me was reading. We started with See Spot, See Spot Run, and See Jane. I was puzzled and disoriented for a couple of days; then I saw that the groups of letters stood for the words we spoke. In the next few weeks I went through all of our simple beginner books and developed a small vocabulary. Now it got exciting. I saw printed words everywhere and realized that if I could figure out how to pronounce them I might recognize them and know what they meant. Phonics came naturally, and I learned to sound out words so I could say them aloud. Next was the reverse process—hear a word and say the letters—spelling. By the time I turned five I was reading at the level of a ten-year-old, gobbling up everything I could find.

Our family dynamics also changed then, with the birth of my brother. My father, fortunate to be employed in the midst of the Great Depression, worked longer hours to support us. My mother was fully occupied by the new baby and was even more focused on him when, at six months of age, he caught pneumonia and nearly died. This left me much more on my own and I responded by exploring endless worlds, both real and imagined, to be found in the books my father gave me.

Over the next couple of years I read books including *Gulliver's Travels, Treasure Island,* and *Stanley and Livingstone in Africa.* When, after an eight-month arduous and dangerous search, Stanley found his quarry, the only European known to be in Central Africa, I thrilled to his incredible understatement, "Dr. Livingstone, I presume," and I discussed the splendor of the Victoria Falls on the Zambezi River with my father, who assured me (correctly) that they far surpassed our own Niagara Falls.

*Gulliver's Travels* was a special favorite, with its tiny Lilliputians, giant Brobdingnagians, talking horses, and finally the mysterious Laputa, a flying island in the sky supported by magnetic forces. I enjoyed the vivid pictures it created in my mind and the fantastical notions that spurred me to imagine for myself further wonders that might be. But at the time Swift's historical allusions and social satire mostly escaped me, despite explanations by my father.

From Malory's story of King Arthur and the Knights of the Round Table, I learned about heroes and villains, romance, justice, and retribution. I admired the heroes who, through extraordinary abilities and resourcefulness, achieved great things. Introverted and thoughtful, I may have been inspired to mirror this in the future by using my mind to overcome intellectual obstacles, instead of my body to defeat human opponents. The books helped establish lifelong values of fair play, a level playing field for everyone, and treating others as I myself wish to be treated.

The words and adventures were largely in my head; I didn't really have anyone to discuss them with, except sometimes my tired father after work or on weekends. This led to an occasional unique pronunciation. For instance, for a couple of years I thought *misled* (*miss-LED*) was pronounced *MYE-zzled,* and for years afterward when I saw the word in print I would hesitate for a beat as I mentally corrected my pronunciation.

When I was reading or just thinking, my concentration was so complete that I lost all awareness of my surroundings. My mother would call me, with no response. Thinking I was willfully ignoring her, the shout would became a yell, then she would bring her flushed face right up to me. Only when she appeared in my visual field did I snap back into the here and now and respond. She had a hard time deciding whether her son was stubborn and badly behaved or was really as unaware as he claimed.

Though we were poor, my parents valued books and managed to buy me one occasionally. My father made challenging choices. As a result, between the ages of five and seven I carried around adult-looking books and strangers wondered if I actually knew what was in them. One man put me to an unexpected and potentially embarrassing test.

It happened because my parents became friends with the Kesters, who lived on a farm in Crete, Illinois, about forty-five miles from our home. They invited us out for two weeks every summer, starting in 1937 when I was turning five. These special days were what I most looked forward to each year. For a city boy from the outskirts of Chicago, it was sheer joy to watch "water spiders" scoot over the surface of a slowly meandering creek, to play hide-and-seek in the fields of tall corn, to catch butterflies and display them arrayed and mounted on boards, and to wander through the fields and among the cottonwood trees and orchards. The Kesters' oldest boy, strapping twentysomething Marvin, would carry me around on his shoulders. My mother, along with the women of the household, Marvin's pretty sister Edna Mae, their mother, and their aunt May, would preserve massive quantities of fruits and vegetables. In our basement back home my father built racks for the rubber-sealed mason jars of corn, peaches, and apricots that we brought back.

Then there were the rows of fruit jellies, jams, and preserves in glasses sealed with a layer of paraffin on top. This cornucopia would last us well into the next year.

My father helped Marvin and his father, Old Man Kester, with the work of the farm, and sometimes I tagged along. One sunny forenoon during the second summer of our two weeks in Crete, my father took me to pick up supplies at a local store. I was just turning six, tall and thin with a mop of curly brown hair, lightly tanned, pants too short, the bare ankles ending in a pair of tennis shoes with frayed laces. I was carrying *A Child's History of England* by Charles Dickens.

A stranger chatting with my father took the volume I was holding, written at the tenth-grade level, thumbed through it, then told my father, "That kid can't read this book." My father replied proudly, "He's already read it. Ask him a question and you'll see."

With a smirk the man said, "Okay, kid, name all the kings and queens of England in order and tell me the years that they reigned." My father's face fell but to me this seemed to be just another routine request to look into my head to see if the information was there.

I did and then recited, "Alfred the Great, began 871, ended 901, Edward the Elder, began 901, ended 925," and so on. As I finished the list of fifty or so rulers with "Victoria, began in 1837 and it doesn't say when she ended," the man's smirk had long vanished. Silently he handed me back the book. My father's eyes were shining.

My father was a sad and lonely man who didn't express his feelings and who rarely touched us, but I loved him. I felt that this stranger was using me to put him down and I realized that I had stopped it. Whenever I remember my dad's happiness at this, it echoes in me with a force that still seems undiminished.

My unusual retention of information was pronounced until I was about nine or ten, when it faded into a memory that is very good for what I'm interested in and, with exceptions, not especially remarkable for much else. I still remember facts from this time such as my phone number (Lackawanna 1123) and address (3627 North Oriole; 7600 W, 3600 N) in Chicago and Chicago's seven-digit population (3,376,438), cited in the old green 1930 *Rand McNally Atlas and Gazetteer* that's still on my bookshelf.

Between the ages of three and five I learned to add, subtract, multiply, and divide numbers of any size. I also learned the US version of the prefixes million, billion, trillion, and so on, up to decillion. I found that I could add columns of figures quickly by either seeing them or hearing them. One day when I was five or six I was in the neighborhood grocery store with my mother and overheard the owner calling out the prices as he totaled up the customer's bill on his adding machine. When he announced the answer, I said no, and gave him my number. He laughed good-naturedly, added the numbers again, and found I was right. To my delight he rewarded me with an ice-cream cone. After that I dropped by when I could and checked his totals. On the rare occasions when we disagreed, I was usually correct and would get another cone.

My father taught me to compute the square root of a number. I learned to do it with pencil and paper as well as to work out the answer in my head. Then I learned to do cube roots.

Before the advent of writing and books, human knowledge was memorized and transmitted down the generations by storytellers; but when this skill wasn't necessary it declined. Similarly, in our time with the ubiquity of computers and hand calculators, the ability to carry out mental calculations has largely disappeared. Yet a person who knows just grammar school arithmetic can learn to do mental calculations comfortably and habitually.

This skill, especially to make rapid approximate calculations, remains valuable, particularly for assessing the quantitative statements that one continually encounters. For instance, listening to the business news on the way to my office one morning, I heard the reporter say, "The Dow Jones Industrial Average [DJIA] is down 9 points to 11,075 on fears of a further interest rate rise to quell an overheated economy." I mentally estimated a typical (one standard deviation) DJIA change from the previous close, by an hour after the open, at about 0.6 percent or about sixty-six points. The probability of the reported move of "at least" nine points, or less than a seventh of this, was about 90 percent, so the market action was, contrary to the report, very quiet and hardly indicative of any fearful response to the news. There was nothing to worry about. Simple math allowed me to separate hype from reality.

Another time, a well-known and respected mutual fund manager reported that Warren Buffett, since he took over Berkshire Hathaway, had compounded money after taxes at 23 to 24 percent annually. Then he said, "Those kind of numbers will not be achieved in the next ten years—he'd own the world." A quick mental estimate of what $1 grows to in ten years compounded at 24 percent gave me a little over $8. (A calculator gives $8.59.) Since, at the time, Berkshire had a market cap of about $100 billion, this rate of growth would bring the company to a market value of roughly $859 billion. This falls far short of my guesstimate of $400 trillion for the present market value of the world. The notion of a market value for the whole world reminds me of a sign I saw on an office door in the Physics Department of the University of California, Irvine. It read EARTH PEOPLE, THIS IS GOD. YOU HAVE THIRTY DAYS TO LEAVE. I HAVE A BUYER FOR THE PROPERTY.

Just after I turned five I started kindergarten at Dever Grammar School in northwest Chicago. I was immediately puzzled by why everything we were asked to do was so easy. One day our teacher gave us all blank paper and told us to draw a copy of an outline of a horse from a picture she had given us. I put little dots on the picture and used a ruler to measure the distance from one to the next. Then I reproduced the dots on my piece of paper, using the ruler to make the distance between them the same as they were on the picture and with my eye estimating the proper angles. Next, I connected up the new dots smoothly, matching the curves as well as I could. The result was a close copy of the original sketch.

My father had shown me this method and also how to use it to draw magnified or reduced versions of a figure. For example, to draw at double scale, just double the distance between the dots on the original drawing, keeping angles the same when placing the new dots. To triple the scale, triple the distance between dots, and so on. I called the other kids over, showed them what I had done and how to do it, and they set to work. We all handed in copies using my method instead of the freehand sketches the teacher expected, and she wasn't happy.

A few days later the teacher had to leave the room for a few minutes. We were told to entertain ourselves with some giant (to us) one-foot-sized hollow wooden blocks. I thought it would be fun to build a great wall so I organized the other kids and we quickly assembled a large terraced mass of blocks. Unfortunately my project totally blocked the rear door—and that was the one the teacher chose when she attempted to reenter the classroom.

The last straw came a few days later. I sat on one of the school's tiny chairs meant for five-year-olds and discovered that one of the two vertical back struts was broken. A sharp splintered shard stuck up from the seat where it had separated from the rest of the strut, so the whole back was now fragilely supported only by the one remaining upright. The hazard was obvious, and something needed to be done. I found a small saw and quietly cut off both struts flush with the chair's seat, neatly converting it into a perfect little stool. At this, the teacher sent me to the principal's office and my parents were called in for a serious conference.

The principal interviewed me and immediately recommended that I be moved up to first grade. After a few days in my new class, it was clear that the work there also was much too easy. What to do? Another parent–teacher conference. The principal suggested skipping me again into second grade. But I had barely been old enough to qualify for kindergarten: I was a year and a half younger on average than my first-grade classmates. My parents felt that skipping another grade would leave me at an extreme social, emotional, and physical disadvantage. Looking back on twelve years of pre-college schooling, where I was among the smallest and always the youngest in my class, I think they were right.

As we were barely managing on my father's Depression-era wages, an academically advanced private school was never an option. We were fortunate that he had found work as a security guard at the Harris Trust and Savings Bank. His battlefield medals from World War I may have helped.

The Depression permeated every facet of our lives. Living on my father's $25-a-week salary, we never wasted food, and we wore our clothes until they fell apart. I treasured objects such as the Smith Corona typewriter my father had won in a writing contest and the military binoculars he used in World War I. Eventually both became part of my tiny collection of possessions and followed me for the next thirty years. For the rest of my life I would meet Depression-era survivors who retained a compulsive, often irrational frugality and an economically inefficient tendency to hoard.

Money was scarce and no one scorned pennies. Seeing the perspiring WPA workers in the streets (created by presidential order in 1935, "Works Progress Administration" was the largest of FDR's New Deal programs to provide useful work for the unemployed), I borrowed a nickel and bought a packet of Kool-Aid, from which I made six glasses that I sold to them for a penny each. I continued to do this and found that it took a lot of work to earn a few cents. But the next winter, when my father gave me a nickel to shovel the snow from our sidewalk, I hit a bonanza. I offered the same deal to our neighbors and, after an exhausting day of snow removal, returned home soaked in sweat and bearing the huge sum of a couple of dollars, almost half of what my father was paid per day. Soon lots of the kids were out following my lead and the bonanza ended—an early lesson in how competition can drive down profits.

The Christmas I was eight, my father gave me a chess set. A friend of his made the board by gluing squares of light and dark wood on a piece of felt, so I could fold the board in half or even roll it up. The pieces were the classic Staunton-style, the kind I have ever after preferred, with ebony-black chessmen opposing a pine-colored white force. After I had learned the basics from my father, our neighbor across the back alley, "Smitty" Smittle, decided to entertain himself by playing against me. I was often at his house to use his pool table, having recently been granted the privilege. Smitty won our first two chess games easily, but then it got tougher. A few games later, I won. Smitty never won again, and after increasingly one-sided routs, he abruptly refused to play me. That evening my father told me I was no longer welcome at Smitty's pool table.

"But why?" I asked.

"Because he's afraid you'll tear the felt with the cue."

"But that makes no sense. I've been playing there for a while and he can see how careful I've been."

"I know, but that's what he wants."

I was disappointed and indignant at this treatment. In my world of books, ability, hard work, and resourcefulness were rewarded. Smitty should have been pleased that I was doing well, and if he wanted to do better, he should practice and study, rather than penalize me.

Before another Christmas, this miniature war on the chessboard would be followed by the United States' entry into the already raging World War II.

My last prewar spring of 1941 I got the measles. As it was widely believed that bright light could ruin my eyes, I was confined in a shaded room. To keep me from straining my eyes, books were removed. Not allowed to read, and bored, I discovered an atlas that had been mistakenly left in the room. For the next two weeks I studied the maps, read the write-ups on all the individual countries, and gave myself an education in geography and a facility with maps that would serve me well for a lifetime. Then I used the atlas to follow the battles around the world. I became interested in the military strategy of the antagonists. How were they deploying their forces? Why? What were they thinking? From daily radio and newspaper reports of the fighting, I used a pencil to shade in on the maps, step by step, the frightening, ever-expanding area under Axis control. I did this throughout the war, using an eraser when the Allies reclaimed territory.

That summer while we wondered whether the United States would, as we expected, enter the war, my mother's brother Edward came to visit. Chief engineer on a ship in the merchant marine, he was classically tall, dark, and handsome with his uniform, his mustache, and a slight Spanish accent giving him the persona and appearance of a Latin Clark Gable. My parents and teacher thought I spent too much time in my head (I'm afraid I still do), and that it would be healthy for me to learn to do things with my hands. After initial resistance on my part, I was lured with Uncle Ed's help into the world of model airplanes, and we spent several wonderful weeks making our own air force.

The boxed kits came with lots of fragile balsa-wood sticks and some sheets with other plane parts to be carefully cut from outlines. We taped the large sheet of plans onto a piece of cardboard and glued balsa-wood pieces together after laying them on the plan and holding them in place with pins. When we had completed the wings, the fuselage top, bottom, and sides, and the tail sections, we assembled them into a completed skeleton and covered it by gluing on tissue paper. I remember the pervasive acetone smell from drying glue, like that of some brands of nail polish remover. My first propeller-driven planes, powered by rubber band motors, didn't fly well. They were too heavy because I had used excessive amounts of glue to be sure everything would hold together. When I learned to use glue more judiciously, I had some satisfying flights. The skills from model building and using tools were a valuable prequel to the science experiments that would occupy me during the next few years, and my introduction to planes helped me follow the details of the great air battles of World War II. I was sorry to see Uncle Ed go and worried about what would happen to him if war came.

Later in that pre–Pearl Harbor summer of 1941 my parents bought their first car, a new Ford sedan, for $800. We drove "America's mother route," historic Highway 66, from Chicago to California, where we visited friends from the Philippines who had settled in the picturesque art colony of Laguna Beach. Each year they had mailed us a little box of candy oranges, which my brother and I eagerly awaited. Now we saw groves of real orange trees.

Then the great world war that was consuming Europe and Asia struck the United States. Late on the morning of Sunday, December 7, 1941, we were listening to music on the radio and decorating our Christmas tree when an authoritative voice broke in: "We interrupt this program to bring you a special announcement. The Japanese have just bombed Pearl Harbor." A frisson ran through me. Suddenly the world had changed in a momentous way for all of us.

"The president will address the nation shortly. Stay tuned."

The next morning (California time), Franklin Delano Roosevelt addressed the nation asking Congress to declare war, uttering the phrase that electrified me, and the millions of others listening, "a date which will live in infamy . . ." When we had recess at school the next day, I was astonished to see the other children playing and laughing as usual. They seemed wholly unaware of what was to come. As I had been following the war closely, I stood alone off to one side, silent and grave.

Our immediate concern was for my mother's family in the Philippine Islands. My mother's father had left Germany and gone to work as an accountant for the Rockefellers in the Philippines. There he met and married my grandmother. They, along with six of my mother's siblings and their children, were trapped in Manila when the Japanese invaded the islands just ten hours after the attack on Pearl Harbor. We heard nothing further from them. As the eldest of five sisters and three brothers, all fluent in both English and Spanish, my mother was a life-of-the-party extrovert. She was a head-turner, too, as evidenced by a picture I found decades later of her aged forty, with a black one-piece bathing suit showing off her dark hair and five-foot-two, 108-pound movie-star figure against the background of the Pacific Ocean. Her parents, along with the other siblings and their families, except for Uncle Ed, were living in Manila, the capital. We would not learn their varied fates for more than three years, until after the islands were liberated near the end of the war in the Pacific. Meanwhile, my nine-year-old eyes followed in detail the Battle of Bataan, reports of the horrors of the Bataan Death March, and the heroic resistance by the island fortress of Corregidor in Manila Bay.

For this I had my own father as a living guide. He had been stationed on Corregidor as a member of the Philippine constabulary, which the United States created, and he accurately foretold that Corregidor would fall only when the troops, weapons, ammunition, and food were exhausted. It became a twentieth-century version of the Alamo. After leaving Oklahoma A&M in order to support himself, my father went back to the Pacific Northwest, where he worked as a lumberman and became a member of the International Workers of the World, or IWW. Fleeing the fierce persecution of that union, he went to Manila, where his military credentials led him to join the constabulary. While there he met and married my mother. Fortunately they moved to Chicago in

1931, so my younger brother and I were born in America and our family spent the war in safety, unlike many among my mother's family, who we later learned spent it in Japanese prison camps.

The war drastically transformed the lives of everyone. The Great Depression's twelve years of persistent widespread unemployment, peaking at 25 percent, were suddenly ended by the greatest government jobs program ever, World War II. Millions of fit young men went off to war. Mothers, wives, sisters, and daughters poured from homes into factories, building planes, tanks, and ships. The "arsenal of democracy" would eventually build ships faster than U-boats could sink them and fill the skies with planes on a scale never known before and not foreseen by the Axis powers. To support our troops and allies, gasoline, meat, butter, sugar, rubber, and much else was rationed. Lights were blacked out at night. Neighborhoods were patrolled by air raid wardens and warned of possible danger with sirens. Barrage balloons, which were tethered blimps, were anchored over critical regions such as oil refineries to deter attacks by hostile aircraft.

Our earlier trip to Southern California made it easier for our family to move there after the United States went to war; my parents hoped to find jobs in the expanding war industries. While we spent a few weeks with our friends in Laguna Beach, I hung out on the seashore watching artists paint, examining tide pools and marine life, and marveling at the heaps of abalone shells (today an endangered species) in the front yards of so many of the beach cottages.

My parents soon bought a house in the small town of Lomita, located at the base of the Palos Verdes Peninsula. My mother was a riveter on the swing shift (4 P.M. until midnight) at Douglas Aircraft. Diligent and dexterous, she was nicknamed "Josie the riveter" by her co-workers after famous World War II posters of the bandanna-clad heroine. Meanwhile, my father worked the graveyard shift at Todd Shipyards in nearby San Pedro as a security guard. My parents were usually gone or sleeping, seldom seeing us or each other. They left my brother and me to raise ourselves. We served ourselves cereal and milk in the mornings. I stuffed peanut butter and grape jelly sandwiches into brown bags for our lunches.

I enrolled in the sixth grade at the Orange Street school. As I was a year and a half younger than my classmates and had also missed the first half of the school year, I was condemned to repeat the sixth grade the following year. My new school was at least two grade levels behind my school in Chicago. Faced with the horror of years of boredom, I protested. My parents met with the principal and as a result I was asked to take a supervised test one afternoon after school. Unaware of the purpose of the test and eager to play, after answering most of the 130 questions, I looked at the last twenty True–False questions and simply drew a line through the Trues so I could leave earlier. When I later learned that this was a test to see if I could avoid repeating grade six I was very upset. Yet after the test was scored, there was no further problem. Although an achievement test was appropriate, showing that I was at grade level, I eventually found out that, oddly, I had instead been given the California Test of Mental Maturity, an IQ test. Years later, I learned why I was allowed to proceed to grade seven. It was the highest score they had ever seen, one that the high school I would enter could statistically expect from a student less than once in a hundred years.

Although they were behind scholastically, my California classmates were bigger than their Chicago contemporaries and much more athletic. As a smaller, thinner, brainy kid, it looked like I might be in for hard times. Luckily I hit it off with the "alpha dog" and helped him with his homework. He was the biggest, strongest kid in our class, as well as the best athlete. Under his protection, I safely finished the sixth grade. Decades later I especially appreciated the 1980 movie *My Bodyguard*.

I started grade seven at nearby Narbonne High School in the fall of 1943. Over the next six years I'd face the difficulties of coping with being an extreme misfit at a school where muscles were important and brains were not. Fortunately, my test score attracted a gifted and dedicated English teacher, Jack Chasson, who would become a mentor and act in loco parentis. Jack was twenty-seven then, with wavy brown hair and the classic good looks of a Greek god. He had a ready, warm smile and a way of saying something that boosted the self-esteem of everyone he met. With a background in English and psychology from UCLA, he was an idealistic new teacher who wanted his students not only to suc-

ceed but also to work for the social good while respecting the achieve-
ments of the past. He was my first great teacher, and we would remain
friends for life.

As there was no spare money, my parents encouraged me to save
some so I could go on one day to college. So in the fall of 1943, at age
eleven, I signed up to become a newspaper boy. I rose every morning
between two thirty and three and pedaled my used bike (one speed was
all we had then) about two miles to an alley behind a strip of stores. I and
the classmate who told me about the job, along with a few others, would
throw ourselves onto a pile of baling wire left over from previous bun-
dles of newspapers and talk. When the *Los Angeles Examiner* truck finally pulled up and dumped a dozen packets of a hundred newspapers
each onto the ground, we each took one, folding the papers individually
for throwing and stuffing them into canvas saddlebags carried on racks
over the rear wheels of our bikes.

Because of the wartime blackout the lights were out and the darkness
was complete except for the headlights of an occasional early-morning
driver. As we were at the base of the Palos Verdes Peninsula just a few
miles from the ocean, on many nights, especially in winter, a marine
layer of overcast blotted out the moon and stars, intensifying the blackness and seeming to mute the tiny background sounds from nature. As I
floated along the streets, a lonely ghost tossing papers from my bicycle,
the one sound I heard was the soft cooing of pigeons. Forever after, the
gentle voices of the pigeons in the dark of early morning evoke memories of those paperboy days.

Getting about five hours of sleep each night, I was perpetually tired.
One morning, rolling down a steep thirty-foot hill near the end of my
route, I fell asleep. I awoke in pain sprawled on a front lawn, papers
scattered everywhere, my bike bent, and a mailbox, its four-by-four
wooden post snapped off by my impact, askew on the grass nearby. I
gathered my papers and managed to make the bike ridable. Aching and
bruised, I finished my route and headed for school.

About a quarter mile beyond our backyard was the Lomita Flight
Strip, a small municipal airport that had become a military base. Lock-
heed P-38 Lightning twin-engine fighter-bombers routinely buzzed our

treetops as they landed. Since I was given a couple of extra papers for contingencies—a poor throw might land a paper on a roof or in a puddle—I took to biking over to the base to sell my extras for a few cents apiece. Before long I was invited to join the soldiers for breakfast in the mess. I stuffed the bounty of ham, eggs, toast, and pancakes into my skinny frame while the soldiers read the papers I sold them. They often gave them back, encouraging me to sell them again. But selling papers on the base was too good to last. After a few weeks, the base commander called me into his office one morning and explained, sadly and considerately, that because of wartime security I was no longer allowed entry. I missed the satisfying hot breakfasts, the camaraderie with the soldiers, and the extra income.

The base, which later became Torrance Airport, was dedicated as Zamperini Field for Louis Zamperini, while he was a Japanese war prisoner. He grew up just a couple of miles from where I lived. The famous Torrance High School and Olympic track star, hero of Laura Hillenbrand's bestseller *Unbroken,* had gone to war as a B-24 bombardier just a couple of months before my family arrived in adjacent Lomita.

Each newspaper route had about a hundred stops, for which we were paid about $25 per month. (Multiply by fourteen to convert to 2016 dollars.) This was an astonishing amount of money for an eleven-year-old. However, our take-home pay was usually less, because we had to collect payment from our customers and any shortfall was deducted from what we received. Since subscriptions were something like $1.25 or $1.50 per month, and there were deadbeats who moved away owing money, others who refused to pay, and some who paid only part because of missed papers, our pay was often reduced significantly. We collected after school in the afternoons and early evenings and often had to come back many times for people who weren't home or didn't have the money. I gave most of what I earned to my mother so she could buy savings stamps for me at the post office. My booklets, when they reached $18.75, were exchanged for war bonds that would mature in several years for $25 each. As my pile of bonds grew, college began to seem possible. But then my area supervisor gradually cut our paper-route wages so he could keep more for himself.

We understood when we signed on that if we continued to do our jobs well, we would get our full pay and eventually maybe get a small raise. Now the boss was taking part of our pay simply because he could get away with it. This was unfair but what could a bunch of kids do? Would King Arthur's Knights of the Round Table tolerate this? No! We took action.

My friends and I went on strike against the *Examiner.* Our supervisor, an ever-perspiring obese man of about fifty, with thinning black hair and rumpled clothing, was forced to deliver newspapers to ten routes in his aging black Cadillac. After a few months of this, his car wore out, papers were not delivered, and he was replaced. Meanwhile, I had already signed on with the *Los Angeles Daily News.* Unlike the *Examiner,* it was an afternoon paper, so I could start catching up on my years of sleep deprivation. As I was delivering newspapers on the beautiful summer afternoon of Tuesday, August 14, 1945, people suddenly erupted from their houses, cheering wildly. World War II had ended. It was my thirteenth birthday and that was its only celebration.

*Chapter 2*

---

# SCIENCE IS MY PLAYGROUND

I n the 1940s, graduates of Narbonne High School were not expected to go on to college. The course requirements reflected this. In the seventh and eighth grades, though hungry for academic learning, I was required to take practical subjects, including wood shop, metal shop, drafting, typing, print shop, and electric shop.

I wanted to pursue my interest in radio and electronics, which was sparked a couple of years earlier when I got one of the first simple radios, a crystal set. Made with a rectifier of galena, which was a shiny black crystal, a wire called a cat's whisker for touching it in the right spot, and a coil of wire, it had earphones, an antenna wire, and a variable capacitor for tuning in different stations. Then like magic: Through my earphones came voices from the air!

The mechanical world of wheels, pulleys, pendulums, and gears was ordinary. I could see, touch, and watch it in action. But this new world was one of invisible waves that traveled through space. You had to figure out through experiments that it was actually there and then use logic to grasp how it worked.

It was no surprise that the required course that caught my interest was electric shop, where we each had to build a small operational electric motor. The teacher, Mr. Carver, was a universally liked, plump, avuncular man whom the other teachers called Bunny. I suspect that Jack Chasson had a word with him, for somehow he learned of my interest in electronics and told me about the world of amateur radio. At that time there already was a web of do-it-yourselfers who built or bought their own radio transmitters and receivers and talked night and day by voice or by Morse code all over the globe. It was in effect the first Internet. With less electricity than it takes to power a lightbulb, I could talk to people around the world. I asked Mr. Carver how I could be part of it. He told me that all I needed to do was pass what was then a rather difficult examination.

In those days the exam began with a series of written questions on radio theory. Next was a test on Morse code. That hurdle, since relaxed, was a major obstacle for most, and Mr. Carver warned me about the long, tedious hours of practice needed for proficiency. We had to copy code as well as send it with a telegrapher's key at an error-free rate of thirteen words per minute. A *word* meant any five characters, so this was sixty-five characters a minute, or a little faster than one per second. I thought about it, then went out and bought a used "tape machine" for what was then the enormous sum of $15, almost three weeks' income from delivering newspapers. The machine looked like a stubby black shoe box. The lid unclipped to reveal two spindles. It came with a collection of reels of pale-yellow paper tapes. These tapes had short holes for the "dots" and long holes for the "dashes." You could look at them and read off the code for letters, and thus "read" the tape. The machine wound the tape from one spindle to the other, like the old reel-to-reel high-fidelity music tape players and the later cassette-tape machines. For power, you simply wound up the machine with a crank. It was simple, low-tech, and effective. When a hole moved past a spring contact, the circuit closed for the length of time its journey took. Long holes gave dashes, and short holes gave dots. The box was hooked to a simple device, an "audio oscillator," that emitted a fixed tone such as the piano middle C. As the tape ran, the contact in the box switched the oscillator alternately on and off, sending dots and dashes.

The great thing about the machine as a teaching aid was that its speed was adjustable, from the slow rate of one word per minute up to fast rates like twenty-five words per minute. My plan was to understand every tape at a slow rate, then speed the tapes up slightly and master them again. To motivate our class and give us a benchmark, Mr. Carver showed us a chart of the rate of progress of World War II army trainees in radio code. These students were at least a few years older than we were and under wartime pressure to learn quickly. Previous classes found it a difficult standard to match. So did our class—but my plan worked for me. I drew a graph of the hours I spent versus my speed and found that using my method I learned four times as fast per hour spent as did the army trainees.

I brought my code speed up to twenty-one words a minute to give myself a margin of safety. The American Radio Relay League, an organization of amateurs, provided guidance on preparing for the theory part of the exam. Feeling ready, I signed up for the test and, one summer Saturday morning, took the twenty-mile bus ride to a federal building in downtown Los Angeles. A twelve-year-old in an old flannel shirt and worn jeans, I nervously joined a group of about fifty adults. We sat at long wooden tables on hard chairs in a room with bare painted walls. Closely supervised and monitored, we worked for two hours in library-like silence, broken only by the sounds of Morse code during that part of the exam. On the bus ride home, as I ate my bag lunch, I speculated that I probably had passed but, not knowing how harshly they graded, couldn't be sure.

For the next few weeks I expectantly checked the mail until, a few days after the war ended, I got an official government envelope with the results. I was now amateur radio operator W6VVM. I was one of the youngest amateurs, or "hams," the age record at the time being eleven years and some months. There were then about two hundred thousand amateurs in the United States and a comparable number in the rest of the world. I was thrilled to know that I could talk to people in this web who might be anywhere on earth.

Meanwhile American troops had liberated the survivors of my mother's family from a Japanese prison camp in the Philippines. Now my grandmother, my mother's youngest brother, and two of her sisters and their families came over from the Philippines to stay with us. They told us that my aunt Nona and her husband had been beheaded in front of their children by the Japanese and that my grandfather had died painfully of prostate cancer in the camp just a week before liberation. My uncle Sam, a pre-med student before the war, told us how he could do nothing but offer comfort to my dying grandfather, denied both medicine and surgical facilities.

To house everyone, my father, in between graveyard shifts at work, built out the attic, adding two bedrooms and a stairway. I shared one bedroom with my brother, James (Jimmy); the other was Sam's. Having ten extra residents packed into the house along with our family of four brought difficulties in addition to overcrowding and the economic burden of supporting them. One aunt, with her husband and three-year-old son, had contracted tuberculosis while they were prisoners of the Japanese. To protect the rest of us from catching the disease, they ate from a separate set of tableware, with possible severe penalties for us if they made a mistake. Of course, we shared the same air, so we still risked infection from their coughs and sneezes. Decades later, my first lung X-rays showed a small lesion, which remained stable. My doctor thought it came from my earlier tuberculosis exposure.

The other aunt staying with us brought her spouse and three children. The husband, a fascistic martinet who abused his compliant wife, required that she and the children obey his every command. It may have been this, as well as everything the family experienced at the hands of the Japanese, that turned the oldest boy into what I viewed as a sociopath. He told my brother that he wanted to kill me. I had no clue then or later as to why. Though Frank, as I'll call him, was older and larger, I had no intention of backing down if we had a confrontation. As a precaution, I kept with me a squirt bottle of full-strength household ammonia, the most benign of my array of chemical weapons. We never met again after his family moved out, but our relatives told me he later went to war in Korea. They said he enjoyed killing so much that he reenlisted. Another first cousin who saw him years later with his seven-year-old son was shocked to see the little fellow ordered about in military fashion.

When Frank died in 2012, his obituary mentioned that he had become a well-known practitioner and teacher of martial arts.

Seeing what World War II had done to my relatives, and how World War I plus the Great Depression had limited my father's future, I determined to do better for myself and the children I hoped to have.

Despite the horrors my relatives suffered it never occurred to me, then or later, to blame or discriminate against Japanese Americans. I only became aware of the US government's treatment of them after they were interned in isolated special camps, their land and homes expropriated and sold by the authorities, their children disappearing from my classes. Jack Chasson educated my close friends Dick Clair and Jim Hart and me, along with other students and faculty, about this injustice. After the war, when some of the imprisoned students returned to school, Jack told me about one whose IQ score was 71, ranking him in the lowest 3 percent. But Jack, who had a degree in psychology, said he could see that this student was unusually smart, attributing his low score to difficulty understanding English. Would I tutor him during lunch hours? Of course. He was retested after a semester and scored 140, extremely gifted, in the upper 1 percent, and well above the threshold for the IQ society Mensa.

My focus on science developed rapidly as I used some of my paper-route money for electronic parts to build ham radio equipment, to buy chemicals by mail and from the local druggist, and to purchase lenses to build a cheap telescope from cardboard tubes.

Then, in November 1946, as a high school sophomore, I saw an advertisement by the Edmund Scientific Company for war-surplus weather balloons. Ever since I had been building model airplanes I had been thinking about ways to achieve my fantasy of a personal flying machine. One of my ideas was to construct the tiniest possible airplane, small, compact, and yet able to carry me. I also thought about building a little blimp, a one-person helicopter, and its variant, the flying platform. My plan was to build scale models as an easy and less costly way both to prove feasibility and to solve some of the practical problems. All this was beyond my financial capability, but flying with balloons was not. I visualized how to complete every step needed to succeed.

Imagining myself drifting up into the sky, I ordered ten balloons, each eight feet tall, for a total cost of $29.95, which is like $360 today. I knew, from the chemistry I was teaching myself, that each eight-footer, filled with hydrogen, would lift about fourteen pounds. Since I weighed 95 pounds, eight of the balloons, with a total lifting power of 112 pounds, should carry me plus a harness and ballast. I didn't know how to get the hydrogen I needed at a price I could afford, so I turned to the family stove: It was powered by natural gas, whose main constituent was methane, with a little less than half the lifting power of hydrogen. If my tests succeeded I could always buy more balloons. I imagined myself tethered to sixteen or more eight-foot balloons, slowly ascending over my house and looking out first over my neighborhood and then miles in all directions over Southern California. I planned to carry bags of sand to use as ballast. When I wanted to go higher, I'd just lighten up by spilling a little sand, which wouldn't injure anyone below. If I wanted to go lower or land, I had designed a valve system for each balloon that would let me release its gas in a controlled manner.

After a wait that seemed endless, but was only a couple of weeks, the balloons arrived and I set to work. One quiet Saturday when my family wasn't around, I connected the gas line for the stove to my balloon and blew it up to about four feet in diameter, which was the largest size I could squash through the kitchen door to get it outside. As predicted, it had a lifting power of nearly one pound. I went to an open field and sent the balloon up to about fifteen hundred feet tethered to strong kite string. Everything was working as expected, and I enjoyed watching a small plane from the nearby local airport "buzz" my balloon. About forty-five minutes later the plane returned, flew near my balloon, and then the balloon suddenly popped. The plane appeared to have shot it down, although I had no idea how or why.

This gave me pause. I pictured myself tied to a flock of eight-foot balloons, making an irresistible target, and being shot down by the local kids who owned air rifles (then known as BB guns). Too risky, I decided. However, that original balloon ad must have been wonderfully successful, for I saw it many times down through the years and it was still running under the banner PROFESSIONAL WEATHER BALLOONS fifty-four years later, with much the same wording. Almost forty years after my experiment, "Lawnchair Larry" tied a cluster of four-foot helium-filled balloons to a chair and ascended several thousand feet.

Disappointed, I wondered what else I could do with the balloons. The first idea came one day when my father brought home some wartime parachute flares from surplus lifeboats. They came in metal canisters that looked like shell casings, and could be fired high into the sky by a special gun. The blazing flare illuminated a large area as it slowly drifted down on its parachute. One night I attached a homemade slow-burning fuse to one of these flares. Then I hung the flare with its fuse on one of my giant balloons and went to a quiet intersection near our house. I lit the fuse and sent the gas-filled balloon up on several hundred feet of cord. I loosely noosed the cord around a telephone pole so, as the balloon rose, the noose slid up the pole, causing the apparatus to be tethered from the top, well out of reach. Then I backed off a block or so and waited. In a few minutes the sky lit up with a dazzling brilliance. A crowd gathered and police cars converged on the telephone pole. A few minutes later the light in the sky went out. The police cars left, the crowd dispersed, and all was as before. A second slow-burning fuse then severed the cord, releasing the balloon, so the evidence leapt into the sky, traveling off to I know not where.

Pranks and experiments were part of learning science my way. As I came to understand the theory, I tested it by doing experiments, many of which were fun things I invented. I was learning to work things out for myself, not limited by prompting from teachers, parents, or the school curriculum. I relished the power of pure thought combined with the logic and predictability of science. I loved visualizing an idea, and then making it happen.

In the upstairs bedroom I shared with my brother, I set up a two-meter (wavelength) amateur radio station, complete with a rotating directional beam antenna in the area not filled with beds. I also had created a laboratory space at the far end of a narrow laundry room attached to the rear of the garage. This was where I did many of my investigations in chemistry, some of which went awry. For instance, having read that hydrogen gas would burn in air with a pale-bluish flame, I decided to see for myself. To generate the gas, I poured hydrochloric acid onto zinc metal in a glass flask, sealing it with a rubber stopper that had a tube through it from which the gas would be emitted. I hoped there would be so much hydrogen produced that it would "wash" all the air out of the system before I attempted to ignite the hydrogen coming out the end of the tube. Otherwise—boom. With safety goggles and protective clothing, I was just attempting to ignite the hydrogen as my brother burst in. Unable to stop my hand with the match I screamed "DOWN" as he ducked and the apparatus blew apart. After this, I painted a white "no trespassing" line across the floor to mark off my zone, about five feet wide and ten feet long, lined with shelves I built and stocked with chemicals and glassware. The frequent fumes and explosions ensured voluntary compliance.

I had plenty of other enthusiasms. For instance, at thirteen I was seriously exploring explosives. My experiments had begun a couple of years earlier when I found a recipe for gunpowder in an old Funk and Wagnalls encyclopedia. The ingredients were a mixture of potassium nitrate (commonly known as saltpeter), charcoal, and sulfur (which we were told to put in our dog's food to make his coat shiny). A batch ignited accidentally while I was working on it, burning the skin of my entire left hand to a gray-black, brittle crust. My father soaked my hand in cold tea, after which I wore a tea-soaked bandage for a week. The healing liquid worked: When we removed the bandage and the crusted skin came off, I was overjoyed to see total recovery.

With my well-stocked homemade chemistry lab as a base, I made large quantities of gunpowder and used it either to launch homemade rockets or to shoot model rocket cars down the street in front of my house. The cars had balsa-wood bodies, lightweight wheels from a hobby shop, and a "motor" that consisted of a carbon dioxide or $CO_2$ cartridge like the ones used nowadays to carbonate drinks or power air rifles. These cartridges were being discarded as war surplus, so my father brought them home from the shipyard. Only I didn't use the $CO_2$ to propel my cars. I drilled out the seal at the end of the cartridge, to the rush of escaping gas. A cold white powder of solid $CO_2$ would collect as the gas expanded and cooled. Once emptied, I filled the cartridge with my homemade gunpowder, inserted a fuse, and tucked my new super-motor into a slot in the back of the tiny vehicle. As the motors sometimes exploded, casting shrapnel, I wore safety goggles and kept myself and the neighborhood kids well back. When it all worked, the cars were astonishingly fast. One moment they would be there, then they weren't, reappearing after a second or so a couple of blocks away. Noting the motors' tendency to blow up, I built and tested bigger versions designed to explode, bombs made from short lengths of steel plumbing pipes, which I used to blow craters in cliff faces at the nearby undeveloped Palos Verdes Peninsula.

The next challenge was guncotton, or nitrocellulose. It's the basis for the so-called smokeless powder. The encyclopedia again gave me the recipe: Slowly add one part of cold concentrated sulfuric acid to two parts of cold concentrated nitric acid. Whenever the mixture becomes warm, chill everything before continuing. Into the brew I added ordinary surgical cotton, again chilling the mixture as it became warm. Then I let it stew in our refrigerator with a DON'T TOUCH sign attached. By now my family knew such signs meant serious business, so I could rely on them to keep away from my projects. After twenty-four hours I removed the cotton, rinsing and drying it. I verified that it was no longer ordinary cotton by dissolving some in acetone. I continued to make more guncotton in my refrigerator "factory" and began a series of experiments. Guncotton explodes, but not easily, and typically requires a detonator. I didn't have one, so I put a small wad on the sidewalk and whacked it with a sledgehammer. There was a *whum-m-p* and the sledgehammer leapt up and back over my shoulder while I hung on. The sidewalk now sported a palm-sized crater. After blowing a few more craters in the sidewalk, I used guncotton in rockets and pipe bombs, where it was more predictable and more effective than gunpowder.

Finally I felt ready to try "the big one," nitroglycerine. The recipe and procedure followed that for guncotton, with just one seemingly minor change, the substitution of ordinary glycerine for the cotton. The result was a pale, almost colorless liquid that floated on top, which I removed carefully, since it was a violent and treacherous explosive that had killed many people in the past.

One quiet Saturday I bundled myself up, put on a safety visor, and moistened the tip of a glass tube with nitro. Using far less than a drop, surely a safe amount, I heated it over the gas flame and suddenly there came a *CRACK!*—with a duration much shorter than and violently different from all my other slower-acting explosives. Tiny bits of glass were embedded in my hand and arm, blood seeping from the myriad holes. I picked the bits out with a needle over the next few days as I found them. Next I put some nitro on the sidewalk and used the sledgehammer to blow another crater. But nitroglycerine's dangerous instability worried me and I discarded the rest of my stockpile.

Where did a fourteen-year-old get such powerful and dangerous chemicals? From my local pharmacist, who sold them to me privately at a nice markup. My parents worked long hours and when they were home they were either seeing to the needs of the ten refugee relatives who were staying with us, taking care of household logistics, or falling into an exhausted sleep. I and my brother were left to manage on our own. I didn't volunteer any information about my experiments. If they had realized the full extent of what I was up to, they would have shut it down.

By the time I took chemistry in the eleventh grade, I had been doing experiments for a couple of years. Enjoying the theory as well as having fun, I read a high school chemistry book from cover to cover. I fell asleep at night mentally reviewing the material, a habit that proved, both then and later, remarkably effective for understanding and permanently remembering what I had learned. Our teacher was Mr. Stump, a short bespectacled man in his fifties. He loved his subject and wanted us to learn it properly. Moreover, he had always longed to produce a student good enough to be one of the fifteen winners in the annual Southern California American Chemical Society high school chemistry contest. This was a three-hour examination given in the spring, and typically attracted about two hundred of the top high school chemistry students from all over Southern California. But after twenty or so years at our academically impoverished working-class school—that year it ranked thirty-first out of the thirty-two schools in the Los Angeles district on standardized achievement tests—he had given up hope of ever realizing his dream.

Among the thirty or so students that showed up for class, Mr. Stump saw a thin younger student with dark curly hair who volunteered to answer every question. He had heard about this kid before from other teachers—the smart ones who enjoyed him and the dull ones whom he filled with dread. Sure, the kid might have picked up a little chemistry and could answer the easy questions during the first couple of weeks, but Mr. Stump had seen others start strong and quickly fade. He warned us about the first exam and how hard it was going to be. When he returned our tests the other students' scores ranged from zero to thirty-three out of one hundred. My score was ninety-nine. I had his attention now.

I went to talk to him about the chemistry contest. Mr. Stump had saved every old exam for the last twenty years. I wanted to borrow them to study for the contest. He was reluctant to give them up and pointed out the huge odds against me: I was taking the exam in my junior year, whereas most others waited until they were seniors. I'd skipped a grade, which meant I'd be a fifteen-year-old up against a field of seventeen- and eighteen-year-olds. And I had only five months to prepare. Besides, our school's facilities were inferior and I had no peers to study with or to push me to a higher level. Few from our school had ever been audacious enough to enter and none of them had placed. "Why not wait a year?" suggested Mr. Stump.

But I was determined. The winners usually got scholarships to the California college or university of their choice. An academic life was becoming my dream. I liked all the science experiments I was doing and the knowledge they led to. If I could have a career continuing this kind of playing, I would be very happy. And the way to have that kind of life was by joining the academic world where they had the laboratories, the kinds of experiments and projects I enjoyed, and maybe the chance to work with other people like me. But I couldn't afford the education I needed for an advanced degree. Here was a way.

After Mr. Stump talked with English teacher Jack Chasson, he agreed to lend me ten of the tests from alternate years, from which I could determine their range and difficulty, and any trend toward changes that had occurred over the years. Mr. Stump held back the other ten so he could check my level of preparedness.

Alongside my high school chemistry book, I worked through two college chemistry texts. When a concept wasn't clear in one of them, it was generally clarified in another. With my background in experiments and my previous reading, the subject sang to me. Every night I spent an hour on theory, then fell asleep mentally reviewing the periodic table, valences, allowable chemical reactions, Gay-Lussac's law, Charles's law, Avogadro's number, and so on. I also continued my experiments—and my pranks.

One great trick began when I read about a powerful dye called aniline red. It turned water a deep blood color in the astonishing ratio of six million grams of water for each gram of dye! I obtained twenty grams of the dye for experiments.

My homemade chemistry lab, as I've mentioned, was located in the laundry room tacked onto the back of our garage, which in turn opened onto our backyard. And in the middle of that yard was our kidney-shaped goldfish pool, about ten feet by five feet and a foot deep. That's a little less than one and a half cubic meters. Now, one gram of this dye would color six cubic meters of water a deep red, so a mere pinch, one-quarter of a gram of dye, ought to do the job on the pool.

To be sure, I put in four times that much, a whole gram, stirring the water vigorously as I scattered it, and the goldfish pool turned a satisfying blood red. The color was so dense that plants could no longer be seen except where they broke the surface. The only sign of the fish was when they stuck their mouths up to feed.

I returned to work in my lab. Several minutes passed before I heard my mother scream and scream and scream. She thought someone, probably me, was in the pool bleeding to death. It took a long time to calm her down.

I was sorry to have scared my mother, but it gave me an idea. Eight miles away in the city of Long Beach was an enormous swimming pool open to the public. The Long Beach Plunge was part of the Long Beach

Pike, an old established amusement complex. A World War II "orphan" who more or less raised myself while my parents toiled in war factories, I had bused to the pike and had used the plunge many times.

The largest heated indoor pool in Southern California, it was 120 feet long and 60 feet wide, with an average depth of 5 feet. That's a volume of about a thousand cubic meters. My remaining nineteen grams of aniline red would intensely color only about an eighth of that. I decided to go ahead anyhow. To help me with my plan, I picked a thin, pale, nerdy classmate with thick glasses and a shock of straight light-blond hair who liked to hang out during my experiments. Making a pouch out of waxed paper and filling it with all of the dye, I sealed it with candle wax and fastened two strings to the top in such a way that when they were pulled in opposite directions the pouch would open into a flat sheet and dump out all the dye.

On a beautiful summer Saturday morning we boarded a bus for Long Beach. Arriving at the plunge, we bought our tickets and went to our lockers, changed into our suits, then made our way to the pool, with the dye pouch hidden under my bathing trunks. A hundred or so swimmers were already enjoying themselves in and around the pool.

I put the pouch in the water, then we each took a string. We walked to opposite ends of the pool and drew the lines tight, but not so tight as to release the dye. Whimsically, I wanted a swimmer to do that for us. Soon one obliged. He hit a string unawares. The pouch opened, released the dye, and created a tiny red cloud no bigger than a man's hand.

All was quiet. We raced to our lockers and changed. With alarm my "assistant" noted a red dye smudge that somehow had appeared on his bathing suit: evidence of the crime. As we sped to the viewing balcony above the main pool and deck, I urged him not to worry.

Now the opaque red cloud was the size of a basketball. It was still quiet. Then another swimmer churned it up to about three feet in diameter. The deep blood-red irregular cloud was still so thick you could not see into it. Then the first scream came, followed by cries of alarm and more screams. A hero dove into the cloud, stirring it and expanding it.

The pool emptied in a panic. Within minutes everyone was out. They were given free passes to return. Entranced by the commotion, we neglected to collect ours. As the plunge employees searched through the crimson cloud, it eventually grew large enough to become semi-transparent. Meanwhile, someone held up the waxed paper and strings, looked puzzled, and discarded it as meaningless debris.

That afternoon, after a pleasant day in the surrounding amusement park, we checked the plunge from the viewing balcony. About half of it was the color of strawberry Kool-Aid. A few swimmers had returned and it was quiet—quieter than usual, because so few people wanted to swim in the red water.

The next day the Long Beach paper carried a small article: "Unknown Pranksters Dye Long Beach Plunge Red." Sixty years later my son-in-law, Judge Richard Goul, was chatting about local history with a retired judge who happened to mention reading about that incident at the time, never knowing of Rich's current relation to "the perp."

With ten weeks to go before the American Chemical Society exam, as I practiced taking old tests, I was scoring 990 or more out of 1,000. I told Mr. Stump I was ready to try the ten he had held back. I got over 99 percent on the first two of these as well, so we went directly to the exam from the previous year, on which I did equally well. I was ready.

On the day of the exam my father drove me twenty miles to the El Camino Junior College, where I followed the crowd among the one-story barracks-like buildings to the test room. We had been told that slide rules would be allowed for the first time this year but that they weren't necessary. As an afterthought I brought along a ten-cent toy slide rule—all I felt I could afford—thinking I could always do a quick rough check of my calculations if I had any extra time.

As I worked through the test I knew every answer. But then the last section of the test was distributed. This part of the exam required many more calculations than I could do by hand in the time allowed. My cheap tiny slide rule was worthless. Out came the full-sized well-machined slide rules all around me. Surprise! Slide rules were not merely optional—they were necessary for anyone who wanted to win. There was no credit given for showing the correct method, only credit for a numerical answer, to a specified level of "slide rule accuracy." I was sickened by the realization I would likely not place high enough to get the scholarship I needed and unhappy with myself for not preparing by purchasing a hard-to-afford top-of-the-line slide rule. It seemed so unfair to convert a test about chemistry into one about slide rule arithmetic.

Be that as it may, I set to calculating by hand as quickly as I could. In the end, I was only able to complete 873 of the entire exam's 1,000 points' worth of questions, so this was the most I could possibly score. I knew the top winner typically got 925 to 935, so I had no chance at first place.

When my father picked me up I was forcing myself not to cry and could barely talk. In class Mr. Stump could see that I was chastened and obviously had done badly. We didn't talk about it. I wrote the episode off to my own naïveté. But I did go out and buy the best slide rule I could afford. A couple of weeks after the test, Mr. Stump called me aside to tell me the results. My score was 869 points out of the 873 points I had answered. First place was far ahead at about 930, but second and third place were just a few points ahead of my fourth-place finish. With a good slide rule I could have been first. Expecting to win, I had no backup plan for getting the rest of the money I needed for college. Although I had the satisfaction of confirming to myself my judgment of my ability, I was devastated.

Mr. Stump, on the other hand, was elated. After twenty frustrating years of teaching chemistry at one of the academically worst high schools in Los Angeles, finally he had a winner. Ashamed at how poorly I had done, I tried to beg off attending the awards dinner, explaining I had no transportation all the way to Los Angeles, but Mr. Stump insisted on taking me himself. At the dinner, the winners, in order of their finish, picked from a list of scholarships offered, one from each, by various colleges and universities. As I expected, numbers one and two picked Caltech and UC–Berkeley. As I believed them to be the two best places for science in the state back then, these were the only schools I wanted. It would have been wise to have a backup school in mind when my turn came, but I didn't know enough to choose, so I passed. The winners' high schools were the same elite clubby list that won every year: Beverly Hills, Fairfax, Hollywood, and so on. My evening brightened a little when they were startled at the mention of my "nobody" high school, Narbonne. Sadly, I learned that I was not allowed to take the test again the next year.

About this time I became interested in the measurement of intelligence, wanting to see how I stacked up. One Saturday morning I took the twenty-mile bus ride from Lomita to the Los Angeles Public Library to browse and learn about interesting topics (as people do now with Google or Wikipedia). I discovered several IQ tests along with answer keys, so, to measure myself, I took one test on each of nine different Saturdays, then graded them to get my scores.

Pleased with the results, I was curious to see how I had done years earlier when a test, which I now knew was an IQ exam, had allowed me to avoid repeating the sixth grade. The school wouldn't disclose this information, so I decided on self-help. I noticed that a flat L-shaped metal measuring tool that I had at home ought to allow me to open all the locked doors in the school. Late one night I rode over, hid my bike in the bushes, and nervously approached a locked entry door. Sliding my flat angled device through the crack between the door and the jamb, I hooked it behind the curved tongue of the lock and pulled. The bolt slid back and I entered the strangely darkened and deserted hallways of my high school. As the building creaked spookily and I worried about whether there was a night watchman to fear, I tiptoed silently up the stairs to the second-floor office of the school psychologist. Easily opening all the additional locks I encountered using the same technique, I was soon searching by flashlight through the records of the IQ tests for me and my classmates. I spent hours scanning hundreds of scores. Mostly I verified what I had already guessed, including the fact that the girl I found most talented and interesting in school had an IQ of 148.

Narbonne High School then had about eight hundred students spread over grades seven through twelve. It also had a class social structure that became more entrenched as the grades advanced. About 20 percent of the students were "sochies" who held all the class and student government offices, and planned all the dances and proms to their own satisfaction. These insiders included most of the better athletes, the prettier cheerleaders, and students from the wealthier families. Since the surrounding cities of Lomita and Harbor City were mostly working-class people, "wealthier" meant small-business owners. The "ins" could afford to buy lunch and eat together in the cafeteria. The brown-baggers like me were "outs," and ate lunch wherever. The "ins" had access to cars, which they were eligible to drive at sixteen; many of them were already driving in the tenth grade. I wouldn't be old enough to drive until my senior year and then wouldn't be able to afford a car. Car access was a must for dating, beach parties, and travel to athletic events.

With my own tiny circle of "outs," I launched a chess club, and the ever-helpful Mr. Chasson found a room where we could play during lunch. I also started a science club that attracted a few of the academically inclined. I spent some lunches at handball, hitting old tennis balls off outdoor wooden backboards, or playing keep-away. When I had the ball, pursued by a horde of bigger kids, I was hard to catch, partly because of my strong legs from lots of biking and partly from alarm at what would happen if they caught me.

I viewed everyone I met as my equal, due the same respect I wanted, unless their behavior showed me otherwise. Many of the "ins," on the other hand, believed they and their clique were due special treatment by everyone else. From their entitled perch, the "outs" were to be excluded and ignored.

My clash with the "ins" began when I got a B in ninth-grade physical education (PE). To my astonishment, I learned that my grades in this academically irrelevant subject would be counted when I applied for college. Further investigation showed that those who went out for a sport like football or track got an automatic A in PE. This used up the quota of A's, leaving the others, like me, with B's, C's, or worse. I was fast for my age but physically a year and a half younger. Track was a stretch and football was out. What to do?

At Jack Chasson's urging, I took tennis for my physical education requirement, which meant I was automatically trying out for the team. The so-called coach was a history teacher who knew nothing about tennis and simply organized and monitored us. There was no instruction, so I learned by playing. I somehow was chosen for the junior varsity, and then I was advanced to the varsity for my junior and senior years.

One of the school's star football players, an "in," of course, expressed what several of the "sochies" thought of this effrontery: "Tennis is a sissy sport." I invited the hero to show me on the courts after school. He was better than I expected, and could return the ball fairly consistently if I hit it to him, so I ran him from side to side until, after about twenty minutes, he quit from exhaustion.

Shortly after this, in the spring of my junior year, and after the ill-fated chemistry exam, my irritation with the "ins" led me to a plan, inspired by excitement over the concurrent 1948 presidential campaign (Truman versus Dewey and Wallace). I recruited about a dozen others, including my pals Dick Clair and Jim Hart, and formed the Student Betterment Committee. Our goal was to make student government more than ceremonial—to work for the best interests of the students and to structure activities so they would include all the students, not just the "ins." The plan was to run a slate of candidates for every student body office; the family of one of our Japanese members had a lettuce farm with a one-room building where we met in the evenings to organize and strategize.

The night before the election we hoisted two huge banners over the school saying VOTE STUDENT BETTERMENT COMMITTEE. The signs were carried aloft by my weather balloons, which in turn were attached to inaccessibly high branches of trees using the telephone pole loop trick that had worked so well for me the evening I hoisted the aerial flare. Overnight winds moved the balloons around somewhat, leaving the banners droopy but still clearly readable when day broke.

As students streamed into the auditorium to hear the candidates speak, we handed them literature explaining our platform and sample ballots showing votes for our candidates. It was the first organized student political party that anyone could remember in the twenty-five-year history of the school. Taken by surprise, the "ins" had no time to counterpunch. A couple of their candidates realized I must be behind it and spent their campaign speech time attacking me personally. The social clique had always run student government. They were entitled. Change meant I was a troublemaker, a radical, a threat to the status quo. Though I narrowly lost my bid for student council, when the ballots were counted we had swept thirteen of fifteen positions. My friend Dick Clair was elected student body president.

Forty-six years later, when I stopped by our high school reunion for a couple of hours, the "ins" seemed the same as they had so long ago, only older and mellower. High school had been the apex of their lives. Many had married one another and lived locally ever since, whereas for me high school was a launching pad for life's great adventure.

In the summer of 1948, following my junior year at Narbonne, I sat on the beach and read my way through a list of about sixty great novels, mostly from American literature, by authors such as Thomas Wolfe, John Steinbeck, Theodore Dreiser, John Dos Passos, Upton Sinclair, Sinclair Lewis, Ernest Hemingway, and F. Scott Fitzgerald. There were foreign authors as well, such as Dostoyevski and Stendhal. Jack Chasson had given me the list and lent me the books from his personal library. I punctuated my hours of reading with body-surfing and with thoughts about who I was and where I was going.

That summer, three years after the war ended, was especially difficult for me. My parents filed for divorce. At the time I thought the household stress of the past few years was the cause. Working different shifts during the war, probably so one of them would, even though sleeping, be nominally present at the house, they drifted apart. In addition, the little village packing our house was often filled with conflict during the three years it took for the last of our ten guests to move out.

My father moved to Los Angeles. During my senior year in high school, I saw him only on Sunday mornings. He drove the twenty miles from Los Angeles and parked a block or so away, where I could see him from my second-story bedroom. I'd come out and spend several hours with him, practicing for my driving test, going to lunch, talking, whatever. Meanwhile my mother was preparing to sell the house when I left for the university, although I didn't know it at the time. The situation with the divorce was confusing, as neither parent offered any explanation. What was going on only became clear years later. My mother had been carrying on an affair with the husband of the family with whom we had originally stayed when we visited California for the first time during the summer before Pearl Harbor. Only recently did I learn from my brother that the affair started then, and that when my father eventually discovered it, this led to the divorce.

As my senior year began I still faced the problem of how to scrape together the money I needed to attend a university. I hadn't gotten the scholarship I expected to win from the chemistry exam and I couldn't expect help from home. I learned that the Physics Teachers Association had an all–Southern California high school physics test similar to the chemistry exam. But I hadn't studied physics intensely yet and had only a few months to prepare. Our physics teacher was an athletics coach who babysat the class and knew nothing of the subject. I taught myself. With no old tests to practice on, all I had to judge the exam by was a brief printed announcement. However, my experiments with electricity, mechanics, magnetism, and electronics over the years helped me with the theory. And of course, learning these subjects my way, I devised new pranks.

As part of my study of optics and astronomy, I bought some cheap mail-order lenses from Edmund Scientific (my balloon supplier) and made a refracting telescope. Besides the stars, I noticed that there was a direct view from my second-story window to a hilltop about half a mile away where teenagers often parked at night to neck. Coincidentally I acquired an old twelve-volt auto headlight, which I used as a compact and powerful searchlight.

The idea was immediate: mount the headlight on my telescope so it could illuminate whatever the telescope pointed at. I lined up the scope on "Lover's Lookout" and waited for nightfall. Once several cars had been parked for a while, I looked through the eyepiece and hit the switch. Blam! The cars were brightly lit and the stunned teenagers, caught in various states of entanglement, drove away in a panic. Since I didn't want to be identified, I kept the light on only for seconds at a time. I tried this trick just a couple of times, stopping once I realized the distress it must have caused the courting couples.

The day of the great physics exam came, but seemed anticlimactic after the chemistry test. I knew how to answer questions worth about 860 of the 1,000 points and, with my new super slide rule, rolled through the calculations. But two questions, together worth about 140 points, came from material I hadn't covered. Was I doomed again to fourth place? I asked myself, *What can I do about this?* In the time left, I used a notion called dimensional analysis to reason out what I hoped was the correct formula for solving one of them, and made a stab at the other. As with the chemistry exam, the fifteen top scorers attended an awards banquet. Again, the finalists came mainly from the top academic schools in the Los Angeles city school system. There was general astonishment when the top spot went to someone from where? Narbonne High School? Some trade school out in the sticks? The scoring pattern of the chemistry exam was repeated, only this time I was first with 931 points. The second-place winner was fifty or sixty points behind. Surpassing the smug and privileged, I had first pick of the scholarships that were offered, wavering between Caltech and UC–Berkeley. Caltech, my first choice, offered full tuition, but I did not have an extra $2,000 per year for the dormitories and expenses. Pasadena was expensive and I knew of no place nearby within my budget. I simply couldn't afford Caltech.

My UC–Berkeley scholarship, the largest they then gave, was for $300 a year. Tuition, which was $70 a year, was covered separately for me by a scholarship for children of World War I veterans. Berkeley also had low-cost room and board just off campus. Cheaper yet was the Student Cooperative Housing Association, with room and board for $35 per month and four hours of work a week. When I picked Berkeley, I consoled myself with the hope that at least there would be plenty of girls and my social life might bloom.

Some years earlier, my interest in radio and electronics came to the attention of Mr. Hodge, a retired electrical engineer whose spacious California property, with its subtropical garden, palm trees, Spanish-style stucco and tile, and elaborate goldfish-filled pools, adjoined our back fence. From twenty-five feet up in my tree house, which consisted of a board platform I nailed onto a huge horizontal forked branch, I peered through a stand of bamboo and saw a mysterious tower. The slim conical building, wrapped in green asphalt roofing material, had once supported a windmill. One day Mr. Hodge invited me inside, where we ascended thirty feet on a tiny central spiral staircase. As we passed each level, I saw new treasure troves of radio components. Wisely, Mr. Hodge let me choose as a gift from him just one item that I could use, a magnificently crafted air spaced variable capacitor. This device was an essential part of the radio receivers and transmitters of the time. Built with a set of fixed metal plates, it had a dial to bring another set of moving plates nearer to or farther from them, changing the frequency to which the radio responded. Incorporating this into my homemade radio allowed me to tune in stations sharply and crisply. Every few weeks Mr. Hodge fed my hunger with another of his treasures. As my facility with, and interest in, radio grew, I began to speculate about what I thought were possible remarkable technological future uses.

One idea was about how I could open or close a door just by thinking that it be so. I could use the fact that thought was known to produce electrical activity in the brain and faint but detectable electrical currents in the scalp. I considered shaving my scalp and attaching wires to pick up these currents. I expected to be able to vary the currents by varying my thoughts. Feeding these currents into a radio transmitter I wore would cause the appropriate signal to be sent to a radio receiver by the door, in turn activating motors to open or close the door. In principle, I could send information that was equivalent to the dots and dashes of Morse code (or, more up to date, the zeros and ones of binary code) and so send instructions of any degree of complexity. I never built this gadget, but the idea of a wearable electronic device with which I could wirelessly control objects stayed with me.

Mr. Hodge also bought me a subscription to a magazine called *Science News-Letter* (now *Science News*), and told me about the annual Westinghouse Science Talent Search. (Later it was sponsored by Intel and then by Regeneron.) No one in my high school had ever heard of this contest, including the teachers. Along with more than sixteen thousand high school students from all over the United States, I entered the Eighth

Annual Search in 1949, my senior year. We all took a written exam in science, and the knowledge I gained from *Science News-Letter* was valuable preparation.

In addition to teachers' recommendations, I needed to submit an essay on science. With no guidance available, I went to the library and began a scholarly write-up on the metal beryllium. It was drudgery. I stopped and thought about the fun things I had figured out for myself. Choosing from them gave me my essay: "Some Original Calculations." In the first of these, I showed how to approximate the positions of the planets in the sky by assuming their orbits were circles instead of the more exact Keplerian ellipses. My second calculation showed how to find the index of refraction of a glass prism (and hence the relative speed of light in it) merely by moving it on a tabletop until it half reflected, half transmitted light at its lower face. A few simple measurements with a meter stick and trigonometry then gave the answer.

I believed I did well on the test, but the teachers' letters and the essay were of major importance and I had no sense of how I rated on either of these. As weeks passed with no word, I figured I was an also-ran and would find that out once the winners were announced.

Having put the talent search out of mind I was astonished one spring morning to find a telegram at our doorstep. Not realizing it was for me, I brought it inside. As we had never received a telegram, thinking it might be an emergency, I opened it.

It was from Westinghouse. Excited and astonished, I read, "Congratulations, you are one of forty finalists." A few weeks later I took my first train trip, traveling together with the two other finalists from California, for a five-day all-expenses-paid trip to Washington, DC, where we joined the rest. The forty of us were treated to an audience with Nobel Prize–winning physicist I. I. Rabi and a visit to the local sixty-inch cyclotron. No one was allowed to wear magnetizable material when entering the cyclotron room, for the device's electromagnet was so powerful it would rip loose watches, buttons, and belt buckles, turning them into deadly missiles flying to the device.

At a public evening exhibition, we each presented some aspect of our scientific work. These exhibits would play an important role in ranking the forty of us for cash awards. I displayed the small radio station I had built, complete with a remote-controlled rotating antenna. Unfortunately, as there was no electric power for our booths, my planned live demonstration became a collection of lifeless objects. The top ten finalists got cash awards ranging from $10,000 to $1,000, according to the rankings by the judges. The remaining thirty of us got $100 each. Nonetheless, we were all sought after by science departments of leading universities. As a highlight we were greeted in the White House Oval Office by President Harry S. Truman. I remember the feel of his hand as we shook: firm, compact, and with the sensation of a leather chair lightly dusted with talcum powder.

Throughout high school no one else had much of an interest in the physical sciences, so I studied and experimented on my own, teaching myself. But I shared other interests with my friends. Dick Clair, Jim Hart, and I were especially close from the eighth grade on. We talked about school politics and discussed national and world issues, among them elections, the Cold War, the rebuilding of Western Europe, and racial discrimination. We read literature and pondered morality and ethics. Jim was a poet, writer, and gifted cartoonist. Dick was a writer and philosopher. Though we led very different lives, we would stay in touch for a lifetime.

The only game I played was chess. At this point, I had no interest in or experience with cards or gambling. However, one of the physics ideas I thought about briefly during this year was the analogy between a circling roulette ball and an orbiting planet. Since planetary positions were accurately predictable, I thought I might be able to forecast the outcome of a roulette spin. I was over at Jack Chasson's house for dinner just after he and his wife had come back from a trip to Las Vegas. When he said that there was no way to beat the casinos, I said with rash teenage hubris, encouraged by my idea about roulette, that someday I was going to do just that. Jack said, "Oh, come on, Eddie," and I let it drop.

But the idea lay dormant, waiting to come to life.

# Chapter 3

# PHYSICS AND MATHEMATICS

I n August 1949, as I was turning seventeen, I went off to the Berkeley campus of the University of California. Now divorced, my mother sold our house, moved away, and installed my twelve-year-old brother in military school. It would be several years before I saw much of either parent again, an echo of my father's experience, as he was without parents and on his own from age sixteen. He had joined the army, and I went off to university. Like him, I was on my own from then on.

I found room and board a few blocks south of the campus. Shortly before leaving for college, I learned that my mother had cashed the war bonds I had paid for with my paper route and spent the money. Her unexpected betrayal was an emotional blow that estranged us for years, and whether I could support myself at the university was now in doubt. I survived with scholarships, part-time jobs, and $40 a month for my first year from my father. I got by on less than $100 a month, including everything: books, tuition, food, shelter, and clothes. On Sundays, when my boardinghouse did not provide meals, I visited church open houses, where I consumed large quantities of free hot chocolate and doughnuts.

The campus was overflowing with returning veterans on the GI Bill. Basic science courses such as physics and chemistry were taught in classrooms of several hundred, but the best professors were lecturing and quality was high. In chemistry, my major, I was one of fifteen hundred students. We were split into four lecture sections of almost four hundred each. The course was taught by a famous professor, and we were using his book. As he was then preparing a revision, he offered 10 cents per misprint to the first student to report it. I set to work and soon brought him a list of ten errors to see if he would pay. He gave me my dollar. Encouraged, I came back with a list of seventy-five more mistakes. That netted me $7.50 but he wasn't happy. When I returned a few days later with several hundred he explained that they needed to be errors, not mere misprints. Despite my objections, he disqualified nearly all of them. This unilateral retroactive change in the deal, which I would later encounter often on Wall Street, done by someone for their benefit just because they could get away with it, violated my sense of fair play. I quit reporting additional corrections.

As the semester wound to a close, I had missed only a single point out of the hundreds given out for the written exams and the lab work, ranking me number one. After my unfortunate experience with the chemistry exam in high school, this was vindication. Part of our grade came when we were asked each week to chemically analyze a sample that was not known to us. After hearing that some students might sabotage others by secretly changing these unknowns, I made a practice of holding back part of mine so that, if this were done to me, I could prove that I had correctly analyzed whatever I had. On the very last sample given us to evaluate that semester, I was told I got it wrong. I knew better, and to prove it I asked that the part I had saved be tested. The decision on my appeal was left to the teaching assistant for my lab sections, who refused to act. The points I lost caused me to end the term in fourth place rather than first. Outraged, I did not enroll in chemistry the second semester and changed my major to physics. Thus I missed organic chemistry, the study of carbon compounds, and the basis for all living things. It is fundamental for biology.

This rash decision, which led me to change my school and my major subject, would change my whole path in life. In hindsight, it turned out for the best, as my interests and my future were in physics and mathematics. Decades later, when I wanted to know some organic chemistry to explore ideas for extending healthy human longevity, I learned it as I needed to.

Although it wasn't as good a school then in math and physics as Berkeley, I transferred at the end of the year to UCLA. For one thing, I hadn't made any close friends at Berkeley, so it seemed cold and lonely, whereas Southern California was familiar. My teacher Jack Chasson, almost a substitute parent, along with my two best friends from high school, Dick Clair and Jim Hart, added emotional support and a sense of belonging. Also, my living arrangements up north were horrible. The second semester I lived in the student co-op. It was by far the cheapest room and board. As I recall, it was a building called Cloyne Court. Being a new member, I got the worst room, with multiple entrances, and shared by five people. There was traffic in and out, day and night. You couldn't get anything done there. You couldn't sleep.

Crucially, my UC scholarship was transferable to UCLA. Once there, I moved into the University Cooperative Housing Association, another independent student living group. Part of the national co-op movement, like the Berkeley co-op, it was a miniature United Nations, with students from all over the world. This branch, which then had two buildings, Robison Hall and Landfair House, was founded in the Depression by a few students who pooled their resources in order to attend UCLA. When I came it had grown to 150 members.

One of the first people I met in that fall of 1950 was Vivian Sinetar. She was slim, blond, and pretty, majoring in English literature. Best of all, she was very smart. She had also transferred to UCLA as a sophomore, coming from Los Angeles City College. We got to know each other through a student group that advocated fair treatment for people of all religious beliefs, ethnic groups, and political affiliations. We both liked to write so we volunteered to produce a newspaper for the group.

One injustice affecting students was that no barber in the area would cut the hair of our black friends; another was that the upper-division UCLA course on the Civil War was taught by a senior professor who claimed the southern slavocracy was just one happy welfare state for underprivileged blacks. Together Vivian and I distributed hundreds of copies of our broadside against what we argued was an outrageous distortion of history. The enraged professor spent an entire lecture defending himself and denouncing the authors as anonymous cowards. The authors saw no point in identifying themselves and risking expulsion.

During the evenings we spent working on the paper, Vivian and I talked about everything, and learned how much we had in common. Each of us would be the first in our families to graduate from a university. We also shared a sense of justice and fair play. Hers came partly because her parents were immigrant Hungarian Jews who, along with their very large extended families, had experienced centuries of persecution in Europe. Many of her relatives perished in concentration camps during World War II, and they continued to face anti-Semitism in America. But fair play was also a very personal issue for Vivian. She was the oldest of three children, with a sister who was born a little more than a year later, followed by a brother in two years. Her sister aggressively demanded her way and, Vivian felt, as much more than her share as she could get. Vivian's mother, partly unwilling to tangle with her sister and partly in admiration of her chutzpah, prevailed on Vivian, as the oldest, to make peace by always giving in. Partly from that came her deep conviction that everyone deserved a level playing field, a feeling I shared.

Cautious and choosy about dating, Vivian tried the patience of her matchmaking mother and sister. One evening as I picked her up to work on the paper, they took her aside and asked, "What's wrong with this one?" I think she answered (correctly), "He's too young." I was just eighteen when we met, and she was nearly twenty-one. As she was much more mature for her age than I was for mine, neither of us thought of the other as someone to date. She majored in literature, and though my major was in physics, I chose some of her classes for my electives. We became good friends. The years passed and we dated others, while I slowly became less young.

With smart attractive coeds everywhere, the whole world of women was opening up for me. After almost a year of going out with many different girls, I was at a party one night when, across the room, my attention was caught by a stunning girl. A tall brunette with the figure of a fashion model, "Alexandra" was a classic beauty with high cheekbones and large brown eyes, her face framed by Cleopatra-styled hair. We were immediately attracted to each other and dated exclusively and constantly for the next two years. As a theater arts major, she got me a one-line part in a play she was in. I spent most of the time standing at attention in a Roman legionnaire's outfit thinking the acting life was not for me.

My academic career almost ended during my junior year. It was often 2 A.M. by the time I got home from dates with Alexandra and I was working long hours to support myself. I was frequently tired and irritable, especially when I arrived at my 8 A.M. physics class.

The professor, the son of a famous physicist, was himself a mediocrity. Because he was insecure and afraid of questions from the class, he copied his lectures from a stack of note cards onto the board, turning his back to the class to discourage interaction. Then we recopied them into our notebooks. He had been doing this for years, and the content seldom changed. This seemed stupid to me. Why not just hand out copies so we could read them in advance and come to class with intelligent questions? Of course, he was afraid someone might ask him a question he couldn't answer.

Bored, I began to read UCLA's student newspaper, the *Daily Bruin,* in class. This damaged his self-esteem, which, as I came to understand later, is an absolute no-no in human relationships unless you don't mind creating an inveterate enemy. He was piqued enough to periodically interrupt his copying to suddenly ask me a question at a moment when I appeared to be totally absorbed in my reading. I would give the correct answer and return to my newspaper.

Matters came to a head one morning. I had been out late with Alexandra and then stayed up during the early-morning hours completing a lengthy but simple homework assignment due before the start of class. I rushed down the stairs of the lecture hall to turn in the assignment and as I handed it to the professor, the first of eight chimes marking the hour reverberated. He looked at me and said, "Uh-uh." I threw my work on the table and shouted, "What do you mean, uh-uh?" I went on to tell him what I thought of his teaching, while a frightened class looked on. I took my seat, all was quiet, and the class went on as before. Looking back, I realize that I had always been irritated by what I viewed as petty, rigid mediocrities. Later I would understand the stupidity of butting heads with them. I would learn to avoid them when I could and finesse them when I couldn't.

A week later I was summoned by the dean of students. He told me that as a result of my disrespectful behavior, various options were being considered, including expulsion. This would not only ruin my academic career but, as it was 1951 and the Korean War was under way, end my 1S student deferment from the draft. It would convert my status to 1A, the first group to be drafted. I would almost undoubtedly be in the military within weeks. As it was, the draft board near UCLA was mostly filled with students holding 1S deferments. The few 1A's had been called ahead of them and were already gone. Now the 1S students were going to war. Each week a few more disappeared from the seats around me. Fortunately my draft board was for the area where my father now lived, in a part of Los Angeles with lots of 1A registrants and very few students. There, as a 1S, I would be among the last to be called. This meant as long as I was enrolled at UCLA, my 1S status was likely to keep me in school.

My case was referred for discipline to the assistant dean of students. By this time the full consequences of my immaturity and bad behavior were becoming evident to me. At my conference with the assistant dean, who was surprisingly sympathetic, we worked out a deal. I would personally apologize to the professor. I would be on probation for the rest of the academic year. I would be on my best behavior from now on. I would not run for any student body office. This last requirement puzzled me until I learned the dean of students was concerned about politically independent and outspoken students and, in the period of McCarthyism and loyalty oaths, wanted to limit possible embarrassment to the administration from student government officials.

By the time I met with the professor in his office to apologize, I realized I had behaved stupidly and rudely, and told him truthfully that what I did was improper and I regretted my actions. But there was still the more serious matter of what I had said about his teaching. I had damaged his self-esteem. He would never forgive this unless he felt I retracted what I had said. My own values and sense of self-worth made me unwilling to grovel and tell lies, despite the personal stakes. I had to find another way. I explained that I had come to realize that his teaching methods were unique and that students, though they may not always appreciate it, rarely encounter a professor of his caliber. What I said was true but allowed more than one interpretation. He picked the one I expected him to choose. He was beaming when I left, my career was saved, and I would become a better-behaved and somewhat more mature person.

My grades had suffered during this, my junior year, and though they rebounded when I was a senior, I also had been put on probation, so my election to Phi Beta Kappa came as a surprise. I was lucky to come off no worse than I did. None of this would have happened if, as I wish I had done, I had asked myself beforehand, *If you do this, what do you want to happen?* and *If you do this, what do you think will happen?* I wouldn't have liked either answer. These two questions became valuable guides for me in the future.

Alexandra's parents were upper-middle-class Jews with a successful plastics business. They were gracious and polite when I visited but had higher aspirations for their daughter than a penniless nondenominational student without prospects. During our senior year, a few months before Alexandra and I graduated, with me still too young, immature, and unready to offer any girl security or permanence, we tearfully ended our romance. I was so depressed that I skipped my graduation ceremony. There was no one close to share it with. Vivian, a casual friend of Alexandra's, went to her graduation party. I wasn't invited. My friends graduated and dispersed.

As a reward to myself for getting my degree, I took six weeks off and, with a friend, drove to Manhattan in my old inexpensive sedan. We slept in it while on the road, and I had the loan of an apartment for the four weeks we spent in New York. We got by cheaply, spending mainly on gas and food.

Beginning our drive across the country, we arrived in Las Vegas around midnight and wondered where we could sleep in the car without being harassed by the police. Finding a spacious and apparently deserted park, we parked by the bathrooms. Needing showers, we stripped, drew water from a hose bib, and scrubbed ourselves, lit up by the headlights of my car. Then we heard voices—lots of them. The park was filled with the homeless, many of them families, and as we learned the next morning, most had lost their money gambling. Fortunately for them the summer nights were balmy. Before leaving the next day we adventurously hung out poolside at one of the strip casinos, where we met a group of three girls. They gave us nickels to play the slot machines, which I did with some apprehension as—not yet twenty-one—I wasn't legally permitted to do so. I promptly hit a small jackpot. Bells rang, lights flashed, and a few dollars' worth of nickels poured into the machine's tray. We spent the bounty on food and drink for the five of us.

This was the first time I had seen Las Vegas and it left me with conflicting, but vivid, images. The glitter and glamour of the strip, with its promise of easy unearned riches, contrasted with the crowd of homeless in the park, victims of the dark side of the dream. It was a memory that stuck: a glitzy playground where suckers were induced to gamble at games that, I knew from mathematics, they must collectively lose. The winners were celebrated as poster-people to draw more suckers while a greater number, betting too much or too often, were impoverished and sometimes even ruined. At the time I didn't realize I would someday turn the tables for some of them.

The friend traveling with me was one of a group of weight lifters with whom I'd begun exercising a year earlier. It started one evening when, as I walked by the basement furnace room behind the co-op, I heard the sound of iron clanking. Curious, I ventured inside and found three muscular residents hoisting barbells. When I suggested that this seemed like a lot of work for who knew how much gain, they bet me a milkshake that if I worked out with them for one hour, three times a week, for a year, it would double my strength. Though I wasn't the ninety-eight-pound weakling of the famous advertisements by Charles Atlas, I accepted their challenge. When the year ended, just before my drive to New York, I had more than doubled what I could lift and gladly paid off the bet. This was the beginning of a lifelong interest in fitness and health.

After the trip, it was back to working and studying. During my first graduate year, 1953–54, I applied for and got a graduate fellowship in physics at Columbia University. All I needed to do was come up with enough money to live in New York. Unable to do so, I had to decline and continued on at UCLA. One Sunday afternoon the following year, working on my master's degree, I was taking tea in the co-op dining area as a break from studying, along with a few others. Someone who had been to Las Vegas was explaining how no one could beat the casinos. This was the consensus view of the group. It was also the view of the world in general, backed up by the painful experience of generations of gamblers.

The Martingale system, or doubling-up system, is one of the many betting schemes that gamblers had devised in an attempt to win. It was often used at roulette for bets with even-money payoffs, such as "red" or "black." The standard American wheel has eighteen red numbers, eighteen black numbers, and two green numbers for a total of thirty-eight. With an even-money payoff, for each thirty-eight spins, you can expect to win a bet on red or a bet on black on average eighteen times and lose twenty for a net loss of two. In an attempt to get around this disadvantage, you start the Martingale by betting $1 on, say, red. After each loss, bet twice as much on the next spin of the wheel, always on red. Eventually you win—red has to come up sometime—and that win covers the previous string of losses, plus a profit of $1. Then start again by betting $1 and repeat the whole process, netting another $1 profit each time when you finally win. The catch is that after many doublings, your required bet can be so large that either you have run out of money or the casino won't allow it.

With an infinite number of possible sequences of outcomes in a gambling game, it was impossible to ever know through trial and error whether any particular betting system worked. To analyze each scheme mathematically, one at a time, was hopeless as well, as there was always a new one to test. One of the triumphs of mathematics had been to prove with a single theorem that all such systems must fail. Under fairly general assumptions, no method for varying the size of your bets could overcome the casino's advantage.

Recalling my old high school ideas for the physical prediction of roulette, as I sipped my tea I argued with the others at the table that, despite all the math to the contrary, you could beat roulette. Using what I had learned from six additional years of physics, I explained that friction would gradually slow the orbiting ball in its circular track until finally gravity would be enough to cause it to spiral down and in toward the center. I argued that an equation could forecast the ball's position during this process. Although the descending ball crosses onto the rotor, which spins in a direction opposite to the ball, a second equation could also specify the position of the rotor. Limiting the predictive power of my equations were random irregularities that can't be forecast, what mathematicians and physicists call noise. Conventional wisdom said the noise was enough to ruin the prediction. I didn't think so and decided to find out.

Fortunately, I didn't know at the time that one of the greatest mathematicians of the previous hundred years, Henri Poincaré, had "proven" that physical prediction at roulette was impossible. His proof was sound, only assuming a modest and plausible randomness in predicting the final resting place of the ball.

At this point I had done all the course work for my PhD in physics and passed the written exams. Under the direction of Professor Steven Moskowski I was halfway through the final obstacle, my thesis (an original research paper) on the shell structure of atomic nuclei. All that remained was to finish the work and pass a final oral exam on it, but I needed to learn much more mathematics in order to complete the complex quantum mechanical calculations. Physics students at UCLA at that time were required to take very little mathematics, and my background in the subject was skimpy. Quantum mechanics in particular requires advanced math, and I found that I needed to learn so much for my research that I could equally well get a PhD in mathematics. It appeared to me that I could finish in mathematics as soon as or sooner than in physics, an especially tempting choice, since UCLA PhD candidates in physics then frequently took ten years or more to finish.

Engrossed in graduate physics, I had drifted out of touch with Vivian, as well as with most of my other friends. Then Vivian sent me a Christmas card with the note "Don't be such a stranger." I called Vivian, and our first date, a few weeks later, was at a little art theater in Hollywood where we saw Jean Renoir's film *The River*. Despite the rave reviews, it seemed dreary and endless. As we left, we each thought this date might be a disaster. But during a light meal afterward, as we talked we found our old camaraderie and something new. By now we both had enough experience dating others to realize how well suited we were. As in one of the Jane Austen books she loved, we at last realized we wanted to be together. Luckily for me, despite family pressure to marry, Vivian was still single because she would have the right person or no one.

We had a lot in common. We both were avid readers and enjoyed plays, movies, and music. As we both very much wanted children, we also agreed on the principles for raising them. We planned to give them all the education they wanted, teach them to think for themselves rather than simply accept received wisdom from experts and authority, and encourage them to choose their own calling in life. Both somewhat introverted, I more so, we looked forward to an academic life with its collection of smart educated people, teaching, research, and travel. There wouldn't be a lot of money but it would be enough. What was important to us was how we spent our time and the people, family, friends, and colleagues, with whom we shared it.

Though we shared many interests, we also had differences that were enriching. Vivian enjoyed literature, people, psychology, art, and drama, rather than math and science. But she had a good scientist's clear and logical way of thinking, which she applied to people and society. I offered a rational and scientific understanding of the natural world, and she would help expand my insights about the human world. I would teach her about things and she would teach me about people.

Vivian's parents, Al and Adele Sinetar, met in the 1920s in New York. As Jewish immigrants, starting in America with no money and little education, they worked hard in their new country, running successful businesses and rising to middle-class comfort. They also contributed for decades to the success of many relatives who also came to the United States, including about ten siblings on each side plus parents and their eventual children. Vivian was the first in her large extended family to graduate with a university degree, and now she was again breaking new ground: She would be the first to marry outside the Jewish faith. Fortunately, both her parents liked me.

Al and Adele were welcoming and accepting of me, but it may have been a dinner at their house one night that closed the deal. Adele was a legendary cook who served bountiful portions of borscht with sour cream, chicken paprikash, stuffed cabbage, potato latkes with more sour cream, and on and on. Having lived for years in the student co-op, where the ultimate entrée was blue-veined oddly sweet-tasting horse meat, and canned peaches for dessert, I was perpetually hungry. As she always did for everyone at meals, Adele urged me to take additional helpings. Struggling between politeness and the temptations of culinary heaven, I said yes often. Then, when I thought dinner was over, Adele brought out a large platter of something I had never seen before called cheese blintzes. I ate the two she offered and waited. Sure enough, two more were offered. And again. And again. I finally stopped at . . . twenty, pretty much wiping out the family reserves.

I got my MA in physics that June and shortly thereafter asked Vivian to marry me. Vivian said yes, and her parents were willing to accept a son-in-law who would be forever poor on an academic salary. However, we had to have a Jewish wedding or the family would be scandalized. We agreed but still had a problem: What rabbi would marry us? Finally we found the man for the job: a young Reform rabbi named William Kramer. Five years earlier he had been chaplain of the US Senate. Later, in 1960, he would perform the ceremony for the black entertainer Sammy Davis, Jr., and the Swedish actress May Britt—a wedding so politically polarizing that JFK himself asked them (unsuccessfully) to wait until after the election. The marriage outraged conservatives in America.

Davis had lost an eye in an auto accident a few years earlier. He also had converted to Judaism. While they were playing golf one day, Jack

Benny said to Sammy, "What's your handicap?" Davis famously replied, "My handicap? I'm a one-eyed Negro Jew."

A generation later, when Rabbi Kramer performed marriage ceremonies for each of my daughters, he said at the first of the two weddings, "I appreciate the repeat business, but please don't wait another thirty-four years."

All was well afterward at our wedding reception until a favorite high school teacher whom I had invited proclaimed repeatedly and loudly, "I always knew he would marry a landsman!" (In this usage, *landsman* is a Yiddish term referring to a fellow Jew, especially one from the same region.) Fortunately, the older relatives feigned hearing loss and once again all was well.

Luckily, my in-laws didn't see the possessions I brought to the marriage. My worn clothing fit into a single suitcase with a broken clasp. Having been washed regularly together, the colors shared a dishwater-gray commonality with hints of purple, beige, and yellow. A couple of years earlier my roommate and I had for $40 jointly purchased a Harris Tweed jacket, which we would alternately use on dates. He gave me his half as a wedding present. I did have boxes and boxes of books along with my own improvised bookcases, the shelves consisting of planks separated by concrete blocks, a student standard in those days.

After our marriage in January 1956, I began taking courses in mathematics. Vivian supported my bold gamble, which was to skip the upper-division math courses I needed as background and jump directly into graduate work, sink or swim, filling in the gaps as best I could. When summer came, even though Vivian was working to support us, we badly needed the extra income I could provide from three months of full-time work. An engineering student and friend from the co-op, Tom Scott, said that National Cash Register (NCR) was hiring. I filled out the forms, passed the interview, and was offered a job at $95 a week! (Multiply by eight for the 2016 equivalent.) My job was to teach upper-division modern algebra to the employees, using a text of my choice. The book I picked, *A Survey of Modern Algebra* by Birkhoff and MacLane, was legendary in the education of mathematicians. Each day I learned the material, then lectured on it the next.

Vivian and I were invited to a house party by one of Tom Scott's female friends from NCR. We were introduced to her boyfriend, Richard Feynman, who was sitting in an alcove, playing the bongo drums. A thirty-eight-year-old professor at Caltech, he was already regarded as one of the world's most brilliant physicists. Feynman later won a Nobel Prize and subsequently commanded national attention when he publicly explained the tragic *Challenger* disaster that killed seven astronauts, using a glass of ice water and a rubber ring.

I had been told this story about Feynman and roulette in Las Vegas: Watching a man placing $5 bets on red or on black, Feynman told him betting against the casino was a losing proposition and that he, Feynman, would be happy to play the part of the casino. The two of them wandered from wheel to wheel with the gambler betting against Feynman by calling out "red" or black" before the spin, paying Feynman when he lost and getting paid in turn when he won. As it happened, even with a disadvantage, the gambler was lucky enough to get ahead by $80, at which point Feynman quit. Though he was acting as the casino and would eventually come out ahead, he wasn't willing to risk further losses. Feynman was like a casino that only had an $80 bankroll, one likely to be wiped out by a customer's lucky run. Assuming the truth of the story, even one of the world's greatest physicists may not have realized that he needed a much larger bankroll to cover the risk he was taking. Understanding and dealing correctly with the trade-off between risk and return is a fundamental, but poorly understood, challenge faced by all gamblers and investors.

If anyone knew whether physical prediction at roulette was possible, it should be Richard Feynman. I asked him, "Is there any way to beat the game of roulette?" When he said there wasn't, I was relieved and encouraged. This suggested that no one had yet worked out what I believed was possible. With this incentive, I began a series of experiments.

One evening not long after we married, Vivian's parents arrived for dinner and I wasn't there. Their brief search found me in our bedroom with a funny V-shaped wooden trough. One end was raised above the floor and I was releasing marbles from a marked spot on the higher end and letting them roll down the trough and across the floor, marking where each one stopped. I explained this was an experiment to predict roulette. What had this contraption to do with roulette? Imagine the circular track on the roulette wheel "unfolded" so it is straight, then rotated so it is a "trough." Now raise one end and release a marble (the ball) from a measured height. The amount the marble drops corresponds to a "push," in this case from gravity rather than from a hand. The marble rolling across the floor gradually slows from friction just as the roulette ball is slowed as it orbits in its circular track. What I wanted to know was how closely I could predict where the marble would stop. The results from this crude test were encouraging to me but not so much to my in-laws. They had hoped their daughter would marry "our son-in-law the doctor" or "our son-in-law the lawyer." *What have we here?* they mused.

A year or so later a wealthy older student whom I was tutoring, knowing of my interest, gave me a new half-scale replica of a roulette wheel. With Vivian's help I made movies of the spinning ball and included a stopwatch graduated in hundredths of a second in each film to provide an accurate time for every frame. The predictions were not good enough but the wheel and ball had lots of defects; if these—as I expected—were not present on casino wheels, it would allow me to win. Vivian was remarkably tolerant of my roulette experiments, seeing as they diverted time from finishing my thesis and getting a full-time job. Yet for me it was science play, just as when I was younger. It was relaxing, much as others might find a book or a movie. I certainly wasn't motivated by the hope of making big money. What drew me was the chance of doing something people thought wasn't possible, to be a bit prankish—the fun of just pulling it off.

While my roulette experiments continued during bits of spare time, I focused on my PhD thesis in mathematics. For my adviser, I was fortunate to choose Angus Taylor, who was both a distinguished mathematician and a gifted teacher. His coauthored book on calculus, known in the math world as Sherwood and Taylor, had been widely used since its initial publication in 1942. I got to know him first as a student in his advanced calculus course and then as a reader (paper grader) for the class. A Scotsman with a twinkle in his eye and an honest forthright way with people, he gave lectures that were models of clarity, striking a balance among theory, examples, and problems.

The time came for me to apply for a teaching assistantship in the Mathematics Department, and I asked for three letters of recommendation from my teachers. When I borrowed my file from a department secretary a few days later to check a detail, the letters were accidentally included. Two of them were full of extravagant praise, but the one from Taylor was measured. He mentioned that it took a while before I did everything to his complete satisfaction, adding that I was mentally very quick but not always wholly accurate. As I told Vivian, I was worried now that I would fail to get this appointment.

At my interview with the department chairman to learn how I had fared, he said that two of my letters of recommendation were excellent, as were my qualifications, but it was the third, the one from Professor Taylor, that left no question as to whether I should be awarded the assistantship. I felt sick. And then he continued that rarely, if ever, had Professor Taylor written a letter that was so positive. I was reminded of my father, a good man but also spare with praise, who would ask, when I got ninety-nine on an exam, "Why didn't you get one hundred?" Thriving under Taylor, I finished my thesis earlier than expected but too late in the spring of 1958 to apply for a postdoctoral position elsewhere.

The Mathematics Department kept me on as an instructor for a year while I applied for a job. This is how it happened that, partly to study real casino wheels, Vivian and I spent the UCLA Christmas break later that year in Las Vegas. While there, I looked at several roulette wheels and found that, at least as far as I could tell without getting my hands on them, they were well maintained, were more or less level, and didn't show obvious imperfections. These casino wheels convinced me more than ever that prediction was possible. All I needed, I thought, was a full-sized wheel and some good laboratory equipment.

*Chapter 4*

# LAS VEGAS

Vivian and I decided to spend some of our Christmas holidays in Las Vegas because Las Vegas, to attract gamblers, had turned itself into a bargain vacation spot. As a twenty-six-year-old with a PhD in mathematics, I was earning too little at UCLA to treat money casually. I also believed then, as I do now after more than fifty years as a money manager, that the surest way to get rich is to play only those gambling games or make those investments where I have an edge. Since I knew of no one who had ever found a way to beat the casinos, gambling in Vegas wasn't on my list of priorities.

Seeing Las Vegas back in 1958, I did not imagine today's glittering strip of giant high-rise hotels, jammed together helter-skelter, fronted at all hours by multi-lane, gridlocked traffic. Legendary casinos such as the Sands, Flamingo, Dunes, and Riviera are gone, the mob and cash-skimming operations replaced by multibillion-dollar public companies. Back then the long, straight, uncrowded highway had a dozen or so one-story hotel-casino complexes scattered on either side with hundreds of yards of sand and tumbleweeds separating them.

Just before we left for our vacation, my colleague Professor Robert

Sorgenfrey told me about a new strategy for playing blackjack that claimed to give players the smallest house edge of any casino game. Next best was baccarat, with a house advantage as low as 1.06 percent, and then craps, with some bets costing just 1.41 percent. The new figure of 0.62 percent for the house edge in blackjack was so close to even that I planned to risk a few dollars for fun. Devised by four mathematicians during their time in the army, the strategy covered several hundred possible decisions a player might face. I condensed its main features onto a card that fit into the palm of my hand. My only experience in a casino had been my earlier adventure putting a few coins in a slot machine.

After settling into our hotel room, we headed for the casino. Weaving past drinkers, smokers, and slot machines, I found two rows of blackjack tables, separated by an aisle or "pit" complete with reserves of chips, extra cards, and cocktail waitresses who offered alcoholic nirvana to the marks, or suckers, all of whom the pit boss monitored closely. It was early afternoon and the few open tables were busy. Managing to get a seat, I plunked down my entire stake—a stack of ten silver dollars—on the green felt table behind my "betting spot." I didn't expect to win, since the odds were slightly against me, but as I expected to build a device to successfully predict roulette and had never gambled before, it was time to get casino experience. I knew virtually nothing about casinos, their history, or how they operated. I was like a person who had glanced at recipes but never been in a kitchen.

The game I was about to play, blackjack, or twenty-one, was basically the same as the Spanish game of twenty-one, referred to as early as 1601 in a story by Cervantes. During the mid-eighteenth century, as part of the European gambling craze of that time, the French called it vingt-et-un. Later, when the game was introduced in the twentieth century to US gaming establishments, bonuses were sometimes offered for special combinations of cards, among them a ten-to-one payoff if a player's first two cards were the Ace of Spades plus one of the two black Jacks, a "blackjack." Though the bonus was soon rescinded, this name for the game stuck, and any two-card total of 21—that is, any Ace plus any Ten-value card—is now called blackjack as well.

The action starts when the players place their bets on "spots" in front of them, after which the dealer gives two cards to everyone and also two cards to himself. The first of the dealer's cards is dealt faceup for everyone to see, and the second is placed facedown under it. Then, starting with the player on his left, the dealer asks each participant in turn how he wants to play his hand.

The player may draw cards so long as his total does not exceed 21. Anyone who does so "busts" and immediately loses. Aces count as either 1 or 11 at the option of the player. Ten, Jack, Queen, and King all count as 10, the so-called Tens or Ten-value cards. The other cards, 2, 3, and so on through 9, count as their face value. The dealer typically must draw until he has a total of 17 or more, then he must stop or "stand." A player may stand at any time. The dealer's edge is that the player must risk busting first, losing immediately, even if the dealer later also goes over 21, though in effect they have tied. Because he loses when they both bust, a player who follows the dealer's strategy for his hands has a disadvantage of about 6 percent.

On the other hand, the dealer has fixed rules to follow and the player doesn't, giving the player more choices than the dealer, and this flexibility to choose a different way to play his cards can have a remarkable impact. Among these choices, before drawing or standing, a player with two cards of the same value, such as a pair of 9s (9, 9), may split them into two new hands, adding another bet equal to his original one. He then plays out the two hands one at a time, beginning with the rightmost one. Not all pairs should be split. Splitting a pair of 8s, for example, usually turns out to be good, but splitting Ten-value cards does not. Alternatively, the player can elect to turn his first two cards faceup, double his bet, and get exactly one more card. This is called doubling down. Unlike the dealer, the player is also free to draw or stand on any total of 21 or less.

When I sat down, the players at my table had been losing heavily and continued to do so. I worried about consulting the tiny strategy card in my palm. Would I be kicked out? Forbidden to use the card? Instead, ridicule was the problem. When I held up the game by consulting my strategy card, the dealer made patronizing "helpful" suggestions on how to play my hand and indicated to the crowd that he was dealing to (and with) someone just in from the farm. Snickering at my unorthodox bets, onlookers wondered who would split a pair of lowly 8s, doubling the amount of money at risk, when the dealer's upcard was the powerful Ace? What fool would stand on a piteous total of 12 against a dealer's weak upcard of 4? Surely my ten silver crumbs would soon be swept away by the dealer. Or would they?

Playing with unhurried deliberation, I managed to keep my stack of chips even. Then a strange thing happened. I was dealt an Ace and a 2, and since Aces can be counted as either 1 or 11, my total was either 3 or 13. Next, I drew a 2, and then a 3. I now had Ace, 2, 2, 3, for a total of 8 or 18. The dealer had a 9 up, and might or might not have had a Ten hidden for a total of 19, but 18 was a pretty good hand. Surely only a fool would draw again and risk the destruction of such a good hand. The strategy said to ask for another card. I did. It was with no little satisfaction and several *tsk-tsks* that the amused onlookers saw me get a 6. Now I had to value the Ace in my hand as a 1, for a total of 14! "Serves him right," said a bystander. For my sixth card, I drew an Ace, which brought my total to 15. "You deserved to bust," muttered a kibitzer. Now I drew my seventh card. It was a 6! I now held Ace, 2, 2, 3, 6, Ace, 6 for a seven-card total of 21. This is a rare event.

After a moment of shock, several people in the crowd said I had a $25 bonus coming. The dealer said no—it was paid at only a few places and those were in Reno. Unaware that any casino even had such a rule, I thought it might be amusing to create the impression that I had indeed sacrificed my 18 because I foresaw the seven-card 21. And who knows. They might even pay me. Of course they did not. But the amusement and patronizing attitude of some bystanders changed to attentiveness, respect, and even awe.

Fifteen minutes later, I had lost $8.50 of my $10 stake and quit. But now, to Vivian's dismay, I was hooked on blackjack—though not in the usual sense. The atmosphere of ignorance and superstition surrounding the blackjack table that day had convinced me that even good players didn't understand the mathematics underlying the game. I returned home intending to find a way to win.

Had I been more knowledgeable about the history of gambling and the centuries of effort devoted to the mathematical analysis of games, I might not have tackled blackjack. To anyone who observes the glittering Las Vegas Strip and the gambling boom that has brought lotteries and casinos to most US states, clearly a lot of people are losing a lot of money—tens of billions annually. Furthermore, for most casino gambling games, mathematicians had proved no system of varying bets could blunt the casino's edge. Generations of gamblers had been seeking the impossible. Players are confused about the inevitability of losing in the long term because they each play for a comparatively short time, which allows some of them to be lucky winners.

This is true for any game where you can compute the edge and the payoff does not depend on the results of previous bets or the wagers of other players. Coin tossing, craps, keno, roulette, and the money wheel are examples, provided you don't have, for instance in the case of wheels, the help of a prediction device. Horse racing and the stock market are different, because you can't compute the probabilities and because other players' bets affect the payoffs.

The belief that casinos must come out ahead in the long run was supported by conventional wisdom, which argued that if blackjack could be beaten, the casinos would have to either change the rules or drop the game. Neither had happened. But, confident from my experiments that I could predict roulette, I wasn't willing to accept these claims about blackjack. I decided to check for myself if the player could systematically win.

*Chapter 5*

---

# CONQUERING BLACKJACK

t wasn't the money that drew me to blackjack. Though we could certainly use extra dollars, Vivian and I expected to lead the usual low-budget academic life. What intrigued me was the possibility that merely by sitting in a room and thinking, I could figure out how to win. I was also curious to explore the world of gambling, about which I knew nothing.

Back from Las Vegas, I headed for the section in the UCLA library where the mathematical and statistical research articles were kept. Grabbing from its shelf the volume containing the article with the strategy I had played in the casino, I stood and began to read. As a mathematician, I had heard that winning systems were supposed to be impossible; I didn't know why. I did know that the theory of probability had begun more than four hundred years earlier with a book on games of chance. Attempts to find winning systems over the following centuries stimulated the development of the theory, eventually leading to proofs that winning systems for casino gambling games were, under most circumstances, impossible. Now I benefited from my habit of checking it out for myself.

As my eyes gobbled up equations, suddenly I saw both why I could beat the game and how to prove it. I started with the fact that the strategy I had used in the casino assumed that every card had the same chance of being dealt as any other during play. This cut the casino's edge to just 0.62 percent, the best odds of any game being offered. But I realized that the odds as the game progressed actually depended on which cards were still left in the deck and that the edge would shift as play continued, sometimes favoring the casino and sometimes the player. The player who kept track could vary his bets accordingly. With the help of a mental picture based on ideas from an advanced mathematics course, I believed the player edge must often be substantial. Moreover, and this also was new, I saw how the player could condense and use this information in actual play at the table.

I decided to begin by finding the best strategy to use when I knew which cards had already been played. Then I could bet more when the odds were in my favor and bet less otherwise. The casino would win more of the small bets, but I would win a majority of the big wagers. And if I bet enough where I had an advantage, I should eventually get ahead and stay ahead.

I left the UCLA library and went home to figure out the next steps. Almost at once, I wrote to Roger Baldwin, one of the four authors of the blackjack article, asking for details about the calculations, telling him I wished to extend the analysis of the game. He generously sent me the actual computations a few weeks later, consisting of two large boxes of lab manuals filled with thousands of pages of calculations done by the authors on desk calculators while they served in the army. During the spring of 1959, wedged in between my teaching duties and research in the UCLA Mathematics Department, I mastered every detail, my excitement mounting as I strove to speed up the enormous number of calculations that lay between me and a winning system.

The Baldwin strategy was the best way to play the game when nothing was known about which cards had already been played. Their analysis was for a single deck because that was the only version played in Nevada at the time. The Baldwin group also showed that the advice of the reigning gambling experts was poor, unnecessarily giving the casinos an extra 2 percent advantage.

Any strategy table for blackjack must tell the player how to act for each case that can arise from the ten possible values of the dealer's up-card versus each of the fifty-five different pairs of cards that can be dealt to the player. To find the best way for the player to manage his cards in each of these 550 different situations, you need to calculate all the possible ways subsequent cards can be dealt and the payoffs that result. There may be thousands, even millions of ways each hand can play out. Do this for each of the 550 situations and the computations just for the complete deck become enormous. If you are dealt a pair, the strategy table must tell you whether or not to split it. The next decision is whether or not to double down, which is to double your bet and draw exactly one card to the first two cards of a hand. Your final decision is whether to draw more cards or to stop ("stand"). Once I had figured out a winning strategy, I planned to condense these myriad decisions onto tiny pictorial cards, just as I had with the Baldwin strategy. This would allow me to visualize patterns, making it much easier to recall what to do in each of the 550 possible cases.

The Baldwin group's calculations for the full deck were approximate because the exact calculations could not be done with desk calculators in a human lifetime. The work I faced in 1959 was much more extensive as I had to deduce the strategy for each of the millions of possible partially played decks. To see what I was up against, suppose, as was standard practice then, the dealer begins by "burning" one card. This means taking it from the top of the deck and placing it on the bottom faceup as a signal not to deal it later, leaving fifty-one cards still in play. There are ten cases to analyze, corresponding to the ten different card values of the missing card: Ace, 2 . . . 9, 10. What if, as often happens, we see the burned card and want to use the knowledge that it's gone? We could apply the Baldwin analysis for each of these ten cases and make a strategy table for each of 550 playing situations. We would then have eleven strategy tables, one for the full deck and one each for the ten possibilities where one card is missing.

Next, suppose we identify two missing cards, so only fifty cards are left to play. How many different such fifty-card decks can arise? As there are forty-five ways to take out two cards with different values

[(A, 2), (A, 3) . . . (A, 10); (2, 3), (2, 4) . . . (2, 10); et cetera] and ten ways to take out two cards of the same value [(A, A), (2, 2) . . . (10, 10)], the total is fifty-five. This leads to fifty-five more calculations, and fifty-five more strategy tables, each of which could take twelve man-years if done on desk calculators as per the Baldwin group. We could continue in this way to develop strategy tables for every such partial deck. For one deck of fifty-two cards there are about thirty-three million of these partially played decks, leading us to a gigantic library of thirty-three million strategy tables.

Facing four hundred million man-years of calculations, with a resulting railroad car full of strategy tables, enough to fill a Rolodex five miles long, I tried to simplify the problem. I predicted that the strategies and player's edge for partly used decks depended mainly on the fraction—or, equivalently, the percentage—of each type of card remaining rather than on how many there were.

This turned out to be true, and it meant, for example, that the effect of 12 Tens when, say, forty cards were left to be played, was about the same as 9 Tens with thirty cards left, and 6 Tens with twenty left, as all three of these decks have the same fraction, 3/10, or 30 percent, of Ten-value cards. In counting cards, it's mainly the fraction remaining that matters, not the number.

I started by looking at how the player's strategy and edge changed when I varied the percentage of each card. I planned to take out all four Aces, do the calculations, and see what happened, then repeat this by removing only four 2s, then only the four 3s, and so forth.

I began this work during the spring semester of 1959. I was teaching then at UCLA for the year after I received my PhD in June 1958. That happened because I had gotten my degree sooner than either I or my adviser, Angus Taylor, had expected. As a result I hadn't applied for a postdoctoral teaching position, thinking it would be another year before I was available. Professor Taylor arranged for my interim appointment at UCLA and then helped me find possible positions for the following year. The offers I liked best were a C. L. E. Moore Instructorship at the Massachusetts Institute of Technology (MIT), and a job at the General Electric Corporation in Schenectady, New York. At GE I would be using my physics background to do orbital calculations for space projects. This sounded like it would be interesting for a while, but I didn't think I would have the freedom I expected to find in academia to follow my interests wherever they led. Expecting that kind of life as a professor in a university, I chose MIT as a first step.

We moved to MIT in June 1959. To get there, I purchased a used black Pontiac sedan for $800 at a police auction and drove it across the country towing a two-wheeled U-Haul trailer loaded with our household goods. We were expecting our first child in two months, so Vivian stayed with her parents in Los Angeles while I went to Cambridge, Massachusetts, to set up our apartment and do mathematics research on a summer grant. As I was obliged under the terms of the grant to work at MIT until mid-August and the baby was due a few days later, I was very nervous about whether I would get back in time. Vivian and I spoke almost daily that summer over the phone. Fortunately, the results of her checkups were always excellent.

Two Japanese mathematicians who were visiting at UCLA needed a ride to New York. I was happy to take them, in return for their sharing the driving. But on a deserted highway somewhere in Ohio, I was startled from a sound sleep about 1 A.M. as the brakes squealed and the car shuddered. We stopped just feet from a large brown-and-white cow meandering placidly across the road. Since the only set of brakes we had were on the car, and the loaded trailer doubled our mass, it also doubled our stopping distance. I had explained this carefully before we left, but apparently without success. Fighting fatigue, I drove the rest of the way.

Once I reached Cambridge, I had a lot to think about. I had never been to the Boston area and didn't know anyone there. Most of the regular staff and faculty were away for the summer but the department did arrange a marvelous rental, the first floor of a grand old three-story family home in Cambridge. Having taken it sight unseen, I was pleasantly surprised at how large it was and at the graciousness of my landlady, an Irish widow who lived there with the two youngest of her five sons.

By day I did academic research in mathematics, but after dinner I'd walk through the nearly deserted buildings to the calculator room. Once there, I would pound the Monroe calculators every night from eight o'clock until shortly before dawn. These were noisy electromechanical beasts about the size of a very large typewriter. They could add, subtract, multiply, and divide and were equivalent in this to today's simplest cheapest handheld digital devices. As there was no air-conditioning, I worked shirtless, my fingers flying over the clacking keyboard, the calculator whirring and rumbling in the humid Cambridge summer nights.

One morning about three o'clock, I came out to find my car was missing from the spot where I regularly parked it. When I went back inside to call the police, a friendly night owl graduate student told me that the officers of the law might themselves be the problem. I phoned the police station and learned my car had been towed. When I pointed out that it had been legally parked, the officer on duty explained that since it was seen in the same spot every night, they assumed it was abandoned. I hurried downtown to night court where the judge to whom I appealed screamed and threatened to fine me $100 on the spot if I said another word. The friendly student, who had driven me there, explained that the police had an arrangement with the tow yard and that the impound charges for my car were going to go up quickly if I pressed my case. The next morning I ransomed my car at the tow yard for about $100. This was a week's pay. Welcome to Boston. Fortunately my new hometown was also a beautiful one, rich in science, education, culture, and the arts.

The weeks wore on and the calculations piled up. However, even though I had introduced shortcuts and efficiencies and was very fast, I was making little progress. My hand calculations were going to take hundreds, perhaps thousands of years. At that point I learned that MIT had an IBM 704 computer and, being a faculty member, I could use it. Using a book from the computer center, I taught myself to program the machine in its language, FORTRAN.

In August 1959 I flew to Los Angeles four days before the birth of our first child. Knowing we were having a girl, we agonized over name choices for weeks, finding many we liked but none that was a first choice for both of us. We enlisted the help of Vivian's brother, Ray, a speech major at UCLA with a gift for the English language, who would go on to a distinguished legal career. He invented the name Raun, with its uplifting rhyming images, like dawn and fawn. None of us had ever heard of it but we loved it and the search was over.

I was back at MIT a month later with Vivian and our new baby, beginning my teaching and research duties. MIT then, as now, had one of the best mathematics departments in the world, and much was expected of its young faculty members. I taught two classes each semester, which meant six hours per week in the classroom, preparation that could run another twelve to fifteen hours a week, additional hours in my office to meet with and help students, plus the giving and grading of homework and exams. We were also expected to conduct and publish our own original research in scholarly journals. When this was submitted, it was reviewed by anonymous experts, known as referees, as a precondition of acceptance. Rejections were common. Those of us who wanted to succeed in the academic hierarchy all knew the mantra "Publish or perish." Despite all this, I also continued to work on my "arbitrary subsets" blackjack program for the IBM 704 computer, testing and correcting the computer code for one module (or "subroutine") at a time.

The 704 was one of the early mainframe electronic computers, one of a series of increasingly powerful models developed by IBM. In those days, users entered instructions via punched cards roughly the size of a $1 bill. A card had eighty columns with ten oblong vertical marks in each column. I put cards, one at a time, in a keypunch and typed as I would on a typewriter; each time I hit a key the machine punched holes in a vertical line and shifted to the next column. The pattern of holes represented the letter, number, or symbol on that key.

I left batches of punched cards bound with a rubber band in the inbin at the computer center, where they were collected and read as instructions to be carried out by the IBM 704. It took several days for me to get the results, because MIT shared the computer with thirty New England universities (such as Amherst, Boston College, and Brandeis).

The work went more quickly as I mastered the strange new language. I had divided the problem of writing the computer program into sections, or subroutines, each of which I tested, corrected, and then crosschecked. Weeks passed, then months, as I completed one part after another. Finally, early in 1960, I put them together and submitted the complete program. The first results indicated that the casino advantage, when you played as perfectly as possible without keeping track of the cards that have been played, was 0.21 percent. The game was virtually even for anyone. It wouldn't take much in the way of card counting to give the player an edge! However, because even the IBM 704 was unable to do all the necessary calculations in the available time, I used approximations for some parts of the calculations. I knew that the results using these shortcuts were slightly pessimistic. This meant that the real game was even better for the player than my computer results indicated.

As computers became more powerful, my approximations were removed step by step. Twenty years later, around 1980, computers had finally become powerful enough to show that the final figure for one deck using the blackjack rules as given in the book I would go on to write, *Beat the Dealer,* was +0.13 percent in favor of the player. Players using my strategy had had, all along, a small edge over the casino even without keeping track of the cards. But the real power of my method was that I could analyze the game not only for the complete deck, but for any collection of cards. I could explore the impact on the game as the cards were used during play.

Now I instructed the computer to venture into the unknown: Analyze the game when all four Aces were missing. Comparing the results with those I already had for the full deck, I would see the effect Aces had on the game. With anticipation I picked up my rather thick deck of punch cards a few days later from the out-bin. (It occurred to me that I was using cards to evaluate a card game.) The IBM 704 had done a thousand man-years of hand calculations in just ten minutes of computer time. I looked at these results with great excitement, for they would very likely either prove I was right or dash my hopes. The result was a player disadvantage of 2.72 percent with all the Aces gone—2.51 percent worse than the overall 0.21 percent casino edge. Although this was a huge shift in favor of the casino, it was actually great news.

It proved conclusively what I believed in that Eureka moment back in the UCLA library when I thought I could beat the game, namely, that as cards were played there would be huge shifts in the edge, back and forth, between the casino and the players. The math also showed me that if removing a specific group of cards from the deck shifted the odds in one direction, adding an equal number of the same cards instead would move the odds the other way about the same amount. This meant that with an Ace-rich deck rather than an Ace-poor deck, the player should have a big advantage. For instance, with twice the usual proportion of Aces, which happens when all four Aces remain among the last twenty-six cards (half the deck), the player ought to gain roughly 2.51 percent over his initial 0.21 percent disadvantage, for a net edge of about 2.30 percent.

Every two or three days I went to the computer center and picked up another completed calculation, each of which would have taken a thousand man-years by hand. I now knew the impact of removing any four cards of one type from the deck. Taking out four Aces was worst for the player, and removing four Tens was next worst, adding 1.94 percent to the house edge. But taking out the "small" cards, which are 2, 3, 4, 5, and 6, helped the player enormously. Removing four 5s was best, changing the casino edge of 0.21 percent to a huge player edge of 3.29 percent.

Now I could design a great variety of winning strategies based on keeping track of the cards. My analysis using MIT's IBM 704 had produced the basic results that gave me the Five-Count System, most of the Ten-Count System, and the ideas for what I called the ultimate strategy. The latter assigned a point value to every card, proportional to its effect on the game, with Aces each counted as −9, 2s counted as +5, and so on, down to Tens counted as −7. Though this was too difficult for almost anyone to keep track of mentally, many simpler counting systems worked quite well. One of the best compromises between ease of use and profitability was to count the small-value cards (2, 3, 4, 5, 6) as +1 as they are seen during play, intermediate cards (7, 8, 9) as 0, and large-value cards (10, J, Q, K, A) as −1. From the results of my computer runs anyone could work out the details of nearly all the blackjack card counting systems in use today.

Intuitively, these results make sense. For instance, when the dealer has a total of 16 he has to hit. He loses if he draws a big card that puts his total over 21 and survives if he draws a small card. A 5 gives him 21, best of all. So he benefits when the deck is richer in small cards and poorer in big cards. On the other hand, when the deck has a higher percentage of Aces and Tens, there will be more two-card totals of 21, or blackjacks. The player and the dealer each win with a blackjack about 4.5 percent of the time but the player gets paid 1.5 times his bet for this while the dealer gains only the player's bet, for a net benefit to the player.

Keeping track of the 5s leads to a very simple winning system. Suppose the player bets small whenever any 5s are left and bets big whenever all the 5s are gone. The likelihood of all the 5s being gone increases as fewer cards remain. When twenty-six cards are left, this will happen about 5 percent of the time, and if only thirteen cards are left, 30 percent of the time. Since the player then has a 3.29 percent edge on his bets, if these are very big compared with his other bets he wins in the long run.

For actual casino play, I built a much more powerful winning strategy based on the fluctuation in the percentage of Ten-value cards in the deck, even though my calculations showed that the impact of a Ten was less than that of a 5, since there were four times as many Tens. The larger fluctuations in "Ten-richness" that resulted gave the player more and better opportunities.

During our family drive from Boston to California in the summer of 1960, I persuaded a reluctant Vivian to stop briefly in Las Vegas so I could test the Tens strategy. We sat down to play blackjack in one of the casinos downtown on Fremont Street. I had a $200 bankroll (worth about $1600 in 2016) and a palm-sized card with my new strategy. I hoped not to use the card and so avoid drawing attention to myself. This card was unlike anything before it. Not only did it tell me how to play every hand versus each dealer upcard, but it also showed how much to bet and how the playing decisions changed as the percentage of Tens varied. Specifically, the complete deck had 36 non-Tens and 16 Tens, so I started counting "36, 16," which gives a ratio of non-Tens to Tens of $36 \div 16 = 2.25$.

Vivian and I sat down together, with her betting 25 cents a hand to keep me company. As play progressed and I kept track of the non-Tens and Tens that were used, I reduced the totals for those remaining. Whenever I had to place a bet or make a decision on how to play my hand, I used the current totals to recalculate the ratio. A ratio below 2.25 meant the deck was Ten-rich, and when a ratio hit 2.0 the player had an edge of about 1 percent. For ratios of 2.0 or less, which meant advantages of 1 percent or more, I bet between $2 and $10 depending on the size of my edge. Otherwise I bet $1.

Vivian watched nervously as I gradually lost $32. At this point my dealer said hostilely, "You'd better take out some more money, because you're going to need it." Smelling a rat, Vivian said, "Let's get out of here." Even though I lost, I was satisfied because I had shown that I could play the Ten-Count System at casino speed without looking at the strategy card. The $32 loss was well within the range of possible outcomes predicted by my theory, so it didn't lead me to doubt my results. With nothing more for me to learn that day, I left, poorer once again but, I hoped, wiser.

Mathematical friends at MIT were astounded that fall when I told them of my discovery. Some thought I should publish quickly to establish priority before someone else either rediscovered my idea or stole it and passed it off as his own. I needed little prompting, since I had already been burned once. While I was at UCLA, my PhD thesis adviser, Angus Taylor, suggested that I send some of my mathematical work to a well-known California mathematician for his comments. I got no response. But eleven months later at a Southern California meeting of the American Mathematical Society, Taylor and I heard the great man talk. The subject was my discovery, in detail, presented as part of his original work, and it was also about to appear under his name in print, in a well-known mathematical journal. Both of us were stunned. Taylor, who would later become academic vice president of the entire University of California system, was an ethical and experienced mathematician to whom I looked for guidance, but he didn't know what to do. So neither of us did anything.

It is also common in science for the time to be right for a discovery, in which case it is made independently by two or more researchers at nearly the same time. Famous examples include calculus by Newton and Leibniz, and the theory of evolution by Darwin and Wallace. Five years before I did my blackjack work, it would have been much more difficult to accomplish. Five years afterward, with the increasing power and availability of computers, it was clearly going to be much easier.

Another reason to publish quickly is the well-known phenomenon that it is typically much easier to solve a problem if you know it can be solved. So the mere fact that the news was spreading through word of mouth meant others would repeat my work, sooner rather than later. This point was made in a science-fiction story I had read earlier in college. A professor at Cambridge University has by far the most brilliant class of graduate physics students ever. He divides the twenty of them into four teams of five and assigns his hardest homework problems. Since the class knows he has the answers, they persist until they can answer every question. Finally, to stump them, he says, untruthfully, that the Russians have discovered how to neutralize gravity, and their job is to show how it's done. A week later two of the four groups present solutions.

To protect myself from this happening with my work on blackjack, I settled on *Proceedings of the National Academy of Sciences,* as it was the quickest to publish of any journal I knew, taking as little as two or three months, and was also very prestigious. This required a member of the academy to approve and forward my work, so I sought out the only mathematics member of the academy at MIT, Claude Shannon. Claude was famous for the creation of information theory, which is crucial for modern computing, communications, and much more.

The department secretary arranged a short appointment with a reluctant Shannon at noon. However, she warned me that Shannon was going to be in for only a few minutes, that I shouldn't expect more, and that he didn't spend time on topics or people that didn't interest him. A little in awe but feeling lucky, I arrived at Shannon's office to find a thinnish alert man of middle height and build, somewhat sharp-featured. I told the blackjack story briefly and showed him my proposed article.

Shannon cross-examined me in detail, both to understand the way I analyzed the game and to find possible flaws. My few minutes turned into an hour and a half of animated dialogue, during which we grabbed lunch in the MIT cafeteria. He pointed out in closing that I appeared to have made the big theoretical breakthrough on the subject, and that what remained to be discovered would be more in the way of details and elaboration. He asked me to change the title from "A Winning Strategy for Blackjack" to "A Favorable Strategy for Twenty-One," as this title was more sedate and acceptable to the academy. Space in the magazine was tight, and each member could submit only a limited number of pages per year, so I reluctantly accepted Shannon's suggestions for condensation. We agreed that I'd send him the revision right away to forward to the academy.

As we returned to the office he asked, "Are you working on anything else in the gambling area?" I hesitated for a moment then decided to spill my other big secret, explaining why roulette was predictable, and that I planned to build a small computer to make the predictions, wearing it hidden under my clothing. As I outlined my progress, ideas flew between us. Several hours later, as the Cambridge sky turned dusky, we finally parted, excited by our plans to work together to beat the game.

Meanwhile, I was planning to present my blackjack system at the annual meeting of the American Mathematical Society in Washington, DC. I submitted an abstract of my talk titled "Fortune's Formula: The Game of Blackjack" for the program booklet (*The Notices*), where it would appear amid a large collection of typically technical and abstruse summaries of presentations.

When the screening committee received my abstract, their near-unanimous reaction was to reject it. I learned this later from John Selfridge, a number theorist whom I had known at UCLA and a member of the committee. For a while, he held the world's record for finding the largest known prime number. (A prime is a positive whole number greater than one which is divisible only by itself and one. The first few are 2, 3, 5, 7, 11, 13 . . .) Fortunately, Selfridge persuaded them that I was a legitimate mathematician and that if I said it was true, it likely was.

Why would the committee reject my talk? Professional mathematicians regularly receive claims that the sender has solved some famous problem, claims that almost always turn out to be from cranks, from the mathematically uneducated unaware of what's already been done, or that include proofs containing simple errors. The so-called solution often is to a problem that has long ago been proven to be impossible, such as a method for trisecting (dividing into three equal angles) any angle whatsoever with compass and straightedge alone. On the other hand, students of plane geometry learn a simple method for bisecting an angle this way. A small change in the problem, from dividing an angle into two equal parts, to splitting it into three equal parts, transforms an easy problem into an impossible one.

The situation then was similar for gambling systems, since mathematicians had proved that a winning system was impossible for most of the standard gambling games. And obviously, if the casinos could be beaten they would either change the rules of the game or go out of business. No wonder the committee was inclined to reject my abstract. Ironically, their reason for doing so—that mathematicians had apparently proven that winning gambling systems were impossible—was my strongest motivation for showing it could be done.

Two evenings before I left for the meeting, I was surprised by a call from Dick Stewart of *The Boston Globe,* inquiring about my upcoming talk. Meanwhile, the newspaper sent out a photographer. I explained the basic ideas of my system on the phone. The next morning my picture and Stewart's article were on the front page. Within hours the news services released the story and more photos to scores of papers across the country. As I left for the airport Vivian was wearily logging an incoming wave of hundreds of messages and, before long, our baby daughter, Raun, cried each time the telephone rang.

## Chapter 6

# THE DAY OF THE LAMB

I flew into Washington, DC, with its leaden wintry skies and the first snow flurries of what would become a gigantic storm. The city was still packed with people after the recent inauguration of the new president of the United States, John F. Kennedy.

The meeting of the American Mathematical Society was held in the old Willard Hotel. Instead of the anticipated scholarly audience of forty or fifty, I found an animated standing-room-only crowd of hundreds. Scattered among the mathematicians were others who were sporting sunglasses, gaudy oversized pinkie rings and cigars, as well as reporters with cameras and notepads. In the manner of mathematics meetings, I had prepared a matter-of-fact talk, which I began with an explanation of how to win by counting 5s. I went on to mention that counting Tens was much better, and then hinted at the cornucopia of additional counting systems revealed by my methodology. My terse technical presentation didn't deter my audience. I finished and placed a woefully inadequate fifty copies of my speech on the table in front of me. The group surged toward them like carnivores competing for fresh meat.

Responding to requests, the officials in charge of the meeting arranged a press conference for me following my talk, after which I was televised by a major network and interviewed on several radio programs. The scientists and technical types generally understood and believed the winning strategy I described, but the casinos and some of the press did not. In a cynical editorial, *The Washington Post* said there was a mathematician in town claiming to have a winning gambling system, which reminded them of this ad: Send $1 for a surefire weed killer. Back comes a note saying "Grab by the roots and pull like hell." One casino spokesman mockingly claimed they sent cabs to the airport to meet players with systems. (I've waited over fifty years now for those cabs.) Another told of how I had sent a detailed questionnaire asking about the precise blackjack rules used in his gaming house. He stated that I was so ignorant, I didn't even know the rules of the game. When starting my calculations a couple of years earlier, I had, in fact, sent just such an inquiry to twenty-six Nevada casinos. My object was to learn how the rules varied from one establishment to another, in particular to see if some places had rules even more favorable than usual. Thirteen of the twenty-six casinos were kind enough to reply to an ignorant academic.

A young reporter for the *Post* named Tom Wolfe followed up after my talk with an interview. The *Post* ran his story, "You Can So Beat the Gambling House at Blackjack, Math Expert Insists." He was curious rather than skeptical, sympathetic but probing. Wolfe later became one of America's most famous authors.

By this time, Washington's airports were buried in two feet of snow, so I boarded a train for Boston. During the long ride back I wondered how my research into the mathematical theory of a game might change my life. In the abstract, life is a mixture of chance and choice. Chance can be thought of as the cards you are dealt in life. Choice is how you play them. I chose to investigate blackjack. As a result, chance offered me a new set of unexpected opportunities.

Ever since my first meeting with Claude Shannon in September, we had been working on the roulette project approximately twenty hours a week. Meanwhile, I was teaching courses, doing research in pure mathematics, attending department functions, writing up my blackjack research, and adjusting to being a new father. Following a roulette work session at the Shannons', Claude asked me at dinner if I thought anything would ever top this in my life. My thoughts then were much like I expected his to have been: that acknowledgment, applause, and honor are welcome and add zest to life but they are not ends to be pursued. I felt then, as I do now, that what matters is what you do and how you do it, the quality of the time you spend, and the people you share it with.

Meanwhile, the national AP wire service ran Tom Wolfe's story, causing thousands of letters and phone calls to pour into the MIT Math Department. The secretaries were busy for weeks, trying the patience of everyone. I decided it was wiser not to answer some of my correspondence. For instance, one writer sent me an elaborate twenty-five-page "proof" that he was the reincarnation of Ponce de León. Although I did not write back, there followed another lengthy recitation of "connections" among him, me, and Ponce de León demonstrating that I played a crucial role in his story. He claimed it was my duty to get involved!

Another man offered to be my bodyguard, assuring me that I was going to need one if I went out to beat the casinos. When I didn't answer him he sent a hostile letter outlining his military and firearms skills, assuring me that he could "put a bullet between your eyes at 25 yards" with a .45-caliber automatic, and that he would work free just for the privilege of learning what he could from being around me. This was followed by a final letter warning that when I learned, to my sorrow, that I needed his protection, he wouldn't be there. He expressed bitterness that I "was just like all the rest of them" to whom he had offered his services.

The greatest number of letters asked for copies of my paper and for detailed instructions on "how to do it." I manufactured and sent out hundreds of copies of the talk and paper, in the academic spirit of freedom of information, courtesy of the MIT Mathematics Department until, overwhelmed, I gave up.

Before I gave my talk at the meeting, I hadn't envisioned the clamor and publicity that would follow. Instead, I'd expected scholars to look at my work, be very surprised at the results, and eventually agree that it was correct. But rather than this happening in a quiet, slow-paced academic way, I was besieged by strangers all wanting a piece of me. This kind of "fame" I didn't need.

Offers to back a casino test of my system ranged from a few thousand dollars to $100,000. The decision was being thrust upon me as to whether or not to prove my academic theory would really work at the tables. I finally decided to go to Nevada, partly to silence that irritating jeer often leveled at academics, "Well, if you're so smart, why aren't you rich?" As a matter of personal pride and honor I felt that I owed my readers proof that the theory really worked, despite scoffs from casinos that my claims were ridiculous. The clincher was the casino spokesman on television who, speaking of my system said, "When a lamb goes to the slaughter, the lamb might kill the butcher. But we always bet on the butcher."

The most promising offer came from two New York multimillionaires whom I called Mr. X and Mr. Y when I wrote about them later. After repeated phone calls from Mr. X and much hesitation on my part about the dangers of risking a bankroll provided by strangers in a place about which I knew little, I finally agreed to a meeting.

It was a wintry February afternoon outside our Cambridge apartment, framed by stark leafless trees against a gunmetal-gray sky. Wooden multistory houses lined the street, the pores of their wood sides and stoops permeated with coal dust and a sooty crust covering the new snow. By 4 P.M. the light was fading and our visitor was overdue. Then a midnight-blue Cadillac pulled up with two good-looking young blondes inside, one visible through the front passenger window and another who stepped out from behind the wheel. I thought, *Who are these people? Where is Mr. X?* While the passenger-side blonde held the door for him, a short white-haired man in a long black cashmere overcoat emerged. They rang our bell and we realized this must be Mr. X. He introduced himself as Emmanuel "Manny" Kimmel, then about sixty-five, and said he was a wealthy businessman from Maplewood, New Jersey, who knew his way around the gambling world. He explained that the two mink-coated beauties were his nieces. I took this at face value, although I could see from Vivian's expression that she had a different view.

Kimmel dealt blackjack to me for a couple of hours and quizzed me about my research. Off to the side, Vivian, with our eighteen-month-old daughter, talked to the "nieces." At one point, just as the younger niece was naïvely volunteering personal information, the other niece whispered out of the side of her mouth, "Cool it."

After our discussion, Manny was ready to plan a trip to Nevada. We agreed to go as soon as I was free, which was during MIT's one-week spring break in April. As they were leaving he drew out a tangled handful of pearl necklaces from a pocket of his overcoat and offered a strand to Vivian. The pearls stayed in the family and still, more than fifty years later, are worn by Raun.

Vivian was both apprehensive and supportive about the casino test. On the one hand, though the math details were incomprehensible to her and almost everyone else, she knew that I generally didn't make claims I couldn't back up, especially in math and science. Even though it was all calculations and reasoning so far, she believed I would win in a fair fight. But this was going to take place in the real world, not a world of symbols and equations. Would the casinos play fair or might they somehow cheat or render me incompetent, perhaps with drugs or violence? What about those supposed nieces who she saw clearly weren't? I'd be entering a world of easy money and easy women, and who knew what other perils. What about my backers? Were they competent to protect me against any casino funny business? Could they last through the temporary losses we were bound to incur sometime early in the play?

In my view, after the whole country had heard my claims, backing down would appear to validate the retorts that I was full of baloney. I was certain that I was right. There was no way I would let my family, friends, and colleagues think otherwise. Even though the Goliath I was challenging had always won, I knew something no one else did: He was nearsighted, clumsy, slow, and stupid, and we were going to fight on my terms, not his. The clincher was that Vivian, despite her reservations and her preference that I play it safe, thought I could do it.

In preparation for our foray, I flew from Boston to New York every Wednesday, a day I had no classes to teach. I'd arrive in Manny's Manhattan penthouse; he dealt while I played the Ten-Count. Although I had several card counting methods to offer, Kimmel fixated on the Ten-Count and would hear of nothing else. Meanwhile, that suited me because I had already worked out the strategy tables for the Ten-Count but hadn't done so yet for the others. The Ten-Count raises bets when the remaining deck is rich in Aces and Tens. After a couple of hours Manny's butler served lunch as we continued playing. At the end of each session Kimmel would give me $100 or $150 to cover expenses and, curiously, a salami. These salamis added an unmistakable aroma to the cabin during my return flight.

Kimmel's friend and co-backer for our venture, Mr. Y, came to some of the sessions. One of the nieces sometimes watched as well. Mr. Y was Eddie Hand, a wealthy businessman from upstate New York. He was fortyish, dark-haired, and of medium stature; he spoke with a curious mix of gruff complaint and humor. As the weeks passed, the chips piled up on my side of the table and Manny became more and more enthusiastic. After half a dozen sessions, we were ready for our Nevada adventure.

There were two main approaches we could adopt when we sat down to play in the casinos. One, which I call wild, involved betting the table limit whenever the advantage to the player exceeded some small figure, say 1 percent. This typically wins the most money, but fluctuations in wealth may be violent, and a large bankroll is required to ride out big losses. Kimmel and Hand said that they would put up $100,000, and more if necessary. (This was worth $800,000 in 2016 dollars, as the inflation conversion table in appendix A indicates.)

I was not in favor of this strategy, since there was too much that I did not know about the gambling world. Could they cheat or swindle me somehow? And how would I react if I were to get behind $50,000, each minute having to continue betting more than my monthly salary? Would Kimmel and Hand stay the course if we lost this much? If they were to quit at that point, it would mean we really had only a $50,000 bankroll but didn't know it beforehand and so should have been betting more conservatively from the start. Besides, my goal was more to test my system than to make big money for my backers. To better achieve this, I went for a nearly certain moderate win rather than taking on more risk of loss to try for a big payout. I planned to play conservatively, betting twice my lowest bet when the advantage for me became 1 percent, four times as much with a 2 percent edge, and finally leveling off at ten times my small bets when the game was 5 percent or more in my favor. Varying bets from $50 to $500, the highest casino maximum then generally available, I felt $10,000 should be an adequate stake.

Manny reluctantly agreed. During the MIT spring break we met at the airport in New York on a cold April afternoon. We chatted for an hour, then boarded our plane. At midnight, as we approached Reno, a garish patch of light appeared ahead in the otherwise Stygian blackness. As we circled to land I got my first view of a city that looked like a bloody reddish neon spider spread over the landscape. I wondered apprehensively about what would happen to me over the next week. Vivian was more alarmed than I was about my flight into the unknown and wanted me to call every day. It relieved me to know I was connected to her and, through her, to my familiar world. In those days long-distance calls were expensive. To save money I called collect if everything was okay, asking for "Edward __. Thorp," the middle initial being a code we had devised to tell how many thousands of dollars we were ahead or, if the initial came before "Edward," how many behind. The idea was simple: The initial $A$ meant less than $1,000, $B$ meant between $1,000 and $2,000, $C$ between $2,000 and $3,000, and so on up to $Z$, which covered $25,000 to $26,000. After hearing the name of the person being called, Vivian would politely tell the operator that Mr. Thorp "wasn't here at the moment."

After a few hours of sleep, we met for breakfast in the hotel. Sandy-eyed and tired, I fortified myself with eggs Benedict and orange juice accompanied by lots of black coffee, and the three of us headed for the tables. At our first casino, situated outside of town, I started small, betting from $1 to $10, planning to increase my bet size as I became more comfortable with the level of risk. Eventually I would bet $50 to $500. Before the trip I insisted on only a $10,000 bankroll, but I knew that Manny favored bets ten times as big—$500 bets whenever we had a 1 percent edge—backed by a $100,000 bankroll. I insisted on warming up by betting $1 to $10. I had explained carefully to Manny that I needed to work up to big bets at my own pace, but he couldn't stand watching and waiting while I did it. Growing ever more agitated, Manny's pale complexion eventually flushed bright red, a startling contrast with his full head of white hair. I learned later that he typically won or lost tens of thousands of dollars at casinos in the United States and in Cuba before the communist takeover.

I won a few dollars in an hour or so of play, but then the establishment closed for three hours because of Good Friday. Returning to downtown Reno, we chose a casino with very favorable rules. They dealt to the last card and allowed players to double down on any hand, and split any pair. If the dealer's first card, always dealt faceup, was an Ace, some casinos, including this one, allowed the player to "take insurance" against the dealer's second card being a 10 or a face card (giving him a "natural," namely, a two-card total of 21) by making an additional bet equal to one-half of his original stake. If the dealer has a natural, the insurance bet pays 2:1.

After a lavish dinner and a rest, I continued playing for fifteen or twenty minutes at a time and then resting for a few minutes. When I sat down again, as usual I chose the table with the fewest players. Playing slowly, I paused for thought and stared at all the cards played. Management thought I was using one of the many fallacious betting systems. These featured patterns of betting that were supposed to somehow overcome the house edge. There are infinitely many of them. None work. Such players, common in the casinos, are welcomed as long as they are losing. Whatever I was doing, playing at the betting level of from $1 to $10, I gradually fell further behind until I was $100 in the hole. All this had taken eight hours, during which time Manny became in turn frantic, disgusted, excited, and finally close to giving up on me as his secret weapon.

It was now 3 A.M. and during the last couple of hours most of the players in the room had left. I was able to get a table completely to myself. My new dealer was unfriendly, and I was tired and irritable. After a sharp exchange of words, she dealt as rapidly as she could. Annoyed and feeling that I was experienced enough to raise my bets, I moved up to the $2 to $20 range. Coincidentally, the deck turned favorable, and I won the next several hands. I recouped my losses and finished a bit ahead. I was exhausted so I stopped and went off to bed. It was 5 A.M. but it could have been any time. Casinos don't have clocks and generally lack windows so the gamblers don't notice day changing to night and back to day. Perhaps the best clue as to where you are in the dismal diurnal cycle of this detached surreal world is the people as they ebb and flow like the tides.

Still tired, I awoke about noon and called Vivian collect. Using our code I asked for Edward A. Thorp, meaning "Everything is okay and we are ahead but by no more than a thousand dollars." I was buoyed by the tone of relief in my wife's voice as she told the operator that Mr. Thorp was not available.

After breakfast Manny and I again visited the casino outside of town. Within minutes, now playing $10 to $100, I won two or three hundred dollars. Then with me counting for both of us, my excitable backer decided he wanted to play as well. After two hours, we had accumulated $650 and the house began to "shuffle up"—that is, they would reshuffle the entire pack after dealing only a few rounds. Since favorable situations come more often toward the end of the deck, early reshuffling sharply reduces the rate of profit. We decided to go elsewhere.

My play was becoming fast and smooth, equal to any dealer's speed. I was also growing more comfortable with raising the stakes. Moving up to $25 to $250 at the next gaming establishment we visited, after an hour I raised the bets to the $50-to-$500 range. I had calculated this to be the highest we could bet safely with our $10,000 bankroll. This plan, of betting only at a level at which I was emotionally comfortable and not advancing until I was ready, enabled me to play my system with a calm and disciplined accuracy. This lesson from the blackjack tables would prove invaluable throughout my investment lifetime as the stakes grew ever larger.

Eddie Hand arrived Saturday evening, in time for the three of us to visit the famous Harold's Club in downtown Reno.

Starting with a floundering bingo parlor in the 1930s, owner Harold Smith, Sr., had built it into the most famous casino in the United States. In addition to twenty-three hundred road advertisements on America's highways and promotion overseas by servicemen who had been well treated, Smith had introduced the innovations of women dealers, twenty-four-hour operation, and customer service directed at the every-day gambler. The strategy was enormously profitable, and the club was a destination for high-stakes gamblers as well. Twenty years earlier, when my family drove to California from Chicago, I had been intrigued as a ten-year-old by all the roadside signs proclaiming HAROLD'S CLUB, RENO, OR BUST. Now here I was.

Manny, Eddie, and I walked into the ground floor of Harold's Club, which was light and spacious compared with the typical gaming establishment. Passing rows of slot machines, I sat down to warm up at $25 to $250, as Manny and Eddie watched closely. My backers then asked if we could get our own $500-limit game to be free of the nuisance of players dropping in to make small bets. At this point the pit boss invited us to the private area upstairs for higher-stakes players. There I had my own dealer and one of the three tables entirely to myself. I couldn't have asked for better playing conditions. But after about fifteen minutes, when I was ahead a mere $500, owner Harold Smith, Sr., with his son Harold Smith, Jr., in tow, slipped in from a side door and came up behind our dealer. Looking back, I believe that they knew who Manny and Eddie were and, in light of their high-rolling history, were concerned that they had some scheme that could prove costly to the casino. Pleas-antries and politenesses were exchanged, but they made their point: The deck would be shuffled as often as necessary to prevent me from doing whatever it was that I might be doing.

The owners instructed our dealer to shuffle with twelve to fifteen cards left in the deck. I still won. They shuffled halfway through the deck. Finally, the cards were shuffled after only two hands had been played. I squeezed out another $80 and we left.

At our next stop, the maximum was only $300, but the rules were excellent. Players could insure, split any pair, and double down on any set of cards. Even so, the cards ran badly, I lost steadily, and after four hours I was behind $1,700 and discouraged. Of course, I knew that just as the house can lose in the short run even though it has the advantage in a game, so a card counter can fall behind and this can last for hours or, sometimes, even days. Persisting, I waited for the deck to become favorable just one more time.

It happened a few minutes later as the deck suddenly produced a 5 percent advantage. I made the maximum bet of $300, which took all my remaining chips. Thinking about whether to quit or buy more chips if I lost this one, I picked up my hand and found a pair of 8s. They must be split. Why? Because 16 is a terrible hand. Draw and you probably bust, or stand and the dealer probably beats you with 17 or more. But if you split, you start each of your two new hands with an 8—a so-so first card. I flung three $100 bills from my wallet onto the second 8. On one of the 8s the second card I received was a 3. Doubling down was the right move, so I dropped another $300 onto this hand and was dealt one more card. Nine hundred dollars, the largest bet I'd yet made, was now lying on the table.

The dealer, showing a 6 up, had a Ten under and promptly busted, so I won both hands for a gain of $900, leaving me only $800 down. This deck continued to be favorable, calling for big bets, and the next deck quickly became good as well. In a few minutes I had wiped out my losses and went ahead $255. Then we quit for the evening.

For the second time, the Ten-Count System had shown moderately heavy losses mixed with "lucky" streaks of the most dazzling brilliance. I learned later that this was a characteristic of a random series of favorable bets. And I would see it again and again in real life in both the gambling and the investment worlds.

The next afternoon the three of us visited the casino outside of town again. Before sitting down at the table, I called Vivian. When I came back my friends told me the casino had barred us from play, but would be only too happy to pick up our meal tab. I asked the floor manager what this was all about. He explained, in a friendly and courteous manner, that they had seen me playing the day before and were puzzled at my steady winning at a rate that was large for my bet sizes. He said that they decided that a system was involved.

I later read that Nevada casinos were able to bar players without cause because—incredible as it sounds—they were considered to be private clubs, not offering themselves to the general public, and so could exclude whomever they pleased. Skin color was among the criteria once used by some gaming establishments.

The next afternoon, we drove to Stateline, Nevada, at the south end of Lake Tahoe. The town was jammed against the Nevada side of the border with California. Across the line, California looked normal, with motels, coffee shops, and residential areas. But in Nevada, where gambling was legal, casinos and hotels crowded as close to California as possible, to better their chances of luring the tourists entering Nevada.

Amid the glitter and congestion, we arrived about 6 P.M. at a large, brightly lit gambling factory. It was jammed. I was barely able to get a seat at the blackjack tables.

I placed $2,000 worth of chips on the table, and Manny, unable anymore to bear simply watching, insisted on playing beside me, with me calling his plays and attempting to control the size of his bets. This was a bad idea because he didn't know the strategy and, playing the cards the way he was used to doing, he lost the advantage. I was unable to correct him at the table without making what we were doing obvious. Meanwhile, besides playing my cards and trying to quietly instruct him, I was counting cards and determining how much we each should bet. Excitable and a bad listener under normal circumstances, he paid little attention to me, misplayed hands, and bet too much for our $10,000 bankroll. Soon I had won $1,300. Betting wildly, Manny won $2,000. Then a drooling pit boss invited us to dinner and the show. Passing on the show, we enjoyed filet mignon and champagne. Within hours, Destiny would present us with the bill. The charge? Eleven thousand dollars in lost profits.

After dinner we strolled over to the new glittering high-rise that housed one of the biggest casinos, Harvey's Wagon Wheel. It had evolved from a one-room log cabin built in 1944 by Sacramento meat wholesaler Harvey Grossman and his wife, Llewellyn, on the Nevada side of the border with California. The name came from the wagon wheel they had nailed over the door. Now the site held the first tower on the south shore, featuring a casino within a 197-room, twelve-story hotel. I bought $2,000 in chips from the cashier's cage and made my way to an empty table. Soon I was plagued by $1 bettors who came and went, slowing the game and concealing cards, which made it harder to count.

Betting $50 to $500, I pointedly reduced my minimum bet to $1 whenever another player arrived. After a few minutes the pit boss got the message and asked if I would like a private table. I said it would transport me with ecstasy. He explained that the club didn't like the psychological effect of a private table on the other customers, but with a trace of a smile he added that a $25-minimum game could be arranged and wondered if that would be satisfactory. Indeed it would, and when the sign was posted it cleared the table of all customers but me. A small crowd gathered. They were quiet, perhaps anticipating the imminent slaughter of their fiscally plump fellow lamb.

After I had won a few hundred dollars, Manny once again jumped in. He had agreed not to do this after the last time. Again he wouldn't listen; I tried to make the best of it. I kept the count and again directed the play of the hands for both of us. I tried to be subtle and he wasn't paying close attention, but he did know to follow me in moving his bet size up and down. Since this is more important than exact play of the cards, he still had an edge. After thirty minutes we emptied the table's money tray—the blackjack version of breaking the bank. No longer smiling, the pit boss was scared.

The employees began to panic. Our dealer begged her higher-up boyfriend, who had been attracted by the commotion, "Oh, help me. Please, help me." The pit boss was trying to explain away our win to a nervous knot of subordinates. While the money tray was being restocked, the crowd swelled. They began to cheer their David on against the casino Goliath.

We played another two hours and broke the bank again. The great heaps of chips in front of us included more than $17,000 in profits. I won $6,000, and Manny, again overbetting wildly, had added $11,000 to his stake. I was tiring from the aftereffects of our huge dinner, the increased effort in managing Manny's hand along with my own, and the fatigue from the previous few days. It was getting harder to count properly and my partner was also wilting. Insisting that we quit, I headed for the cashier. Stuffed with chips, my pockets bulged like saddlebags. My bounty did not go unnoticed. Along the way, I was startled to meet three or four lovely ladies wandering back and forth across my path smiling affectionately.

I cashed out and wended my way back to the tables to watch horror-stricken as Manny, feeling lucky and refusing to stop, poured back thousands of dollars. For me blackjack was a game of math, not luck. Any luck, good or bad, would be random, unpredictable, and short-term. In the long run it would be unimportant. Manny didn't see it that way. When I tried to dislodge him he cried excitedly, "I . . . will . . . not . . . leave . . . this . . . place!" In the forty-five minutes or so that it took to pry him loose, he lost back the entire $11,000 that he had won. Even so, when we returned to our hotel that evening with my winnings, we were ahead $13,000 so far on the trip. My daily calls to Vivian had shown her that we were winning more each day. Now came the best call of all: I asked dramatically for Edward M. Thorp (ahead between $12,000 and $13,000). In a relieved and buoyant voice she told the operator I wasn't home.

On our last day we returned to the club where I had first practiced. I put $1,000 in chips on the table and began to win. Word had spread and within minutes the owner was on the scene. In a panic, he gave the dealer and the pit boss instructions. If I changed my bet size, the dealer was to shuffle the entire deck before the next deal. Whenever I varied the number of hands I took (I could now play from one to eight hands at a time, and faster than the best dealers could deal), the cards were shuffled. The dealer whom I had last played against in my little practice session was standing in the background saying over and over, in reverent tones, how much I had advanced in skill since the other night. When I happened to scratch my nose, the dealer shuffled! Incredulous, I asked her whether she would shuffle each time I did so. She said she would. I tested with a few more scratches. She meant what she said. I asked if any unusual act, no matter how minute, would cause her to shuffle. Again she said, "Yes."

I was now playing merely even with the house, as shuffling all the cards and starting each deal with a full deck destroyed my advantage. I asked for larger chips—$50 or $100—as all I had were twenties. The owner stepped forward and said that the house would not sell them to us. He then had a brand-new deck of cards brought in. The dealer carefully spread it facedown, then again faceup. I asked why they spread them facedown. Although this practice is common, casinos seldom examine the backs of the cards but now they did, for a full two minutes. Even though I wear glasses, the dealer explained that they believed I had unusually acute vision, and could distinguish tiny blemishes on the backs of the cards. This let me know what cards would appear next. I scoffed, but the panicky owner brought in four fresh decks in five minutes.

Changing decks didn't matter to me, so they gave up on that. In whispers, they formulated a new theory. I asked them what they now thought my secret was. The dealer claimed I could count every card as it was played, so I always knew exactly which cards had not yet appeared. It is well known to students of mnemotechny (the science of memory training) that you can learn to memorize in proper order a deck of cards as it is dealt. However, I am familiar enough with the method involved to know that the information, when so memorized, cannot be used quickly enough for play in blackjack. So I challenged the dealer by rashly claiming that no one in the world could watch thirty-eight cards dealt quickly off a pack and then tell me quickly how many of each type of card remained.

She claimed the pit boss, standing next to her, could do just that. I offered $5 for a demonstration. They both looked down sheepishly and wouldn't answer. I made my offer $50. They remained silent and ashamed. Eddie Hand, who had been watching throughout, increased the offer to $500. There was no response. We left in disgust.

Spring break was ending at MIT, so our trip also was at an end. In thirty man-hours of medium-to-large-scale play, our $10,000 grew to $21,000. At no point did we have to go into our original capital further than $1,300 (plus expenses). Our experiment was a success, and my system performed at the tables just as the theory predicted. I was satisfied. Future blackjack trips, if any, would have to fit in around my academic schedule and my family life. I made no plans for another trip with Manny and Eddie, and simply left the possibility open.

On the plane back to Boston, I remembered the casino spokesman who, upon hearing my claim that I could beat blackjack, scoffed, "When a lamb goes to the slaughter, the lamb might kill the butcher. But we always bet on the butcher."

The day of the lamb had come.


Some thirty years later, author and investigative journalist Connie Bruck filled me in on Manny Kimmel's background when she called to interview me for her book *Master of the Game*. The book details the story of how Steve Ross "took his father-in-law's funeral business and a parking lot company and grew them into the largest media and entertainment company in the world, Time Warner." The parking lot company was Kinney Service Corporation, started in 1945 by a hidden partner, Emmanuel Kimmel. Kimmel allegedly made his fortune in the 1920s and '30s from bootlegging and the numbers racket, in company with Abner "Longie" Zwillman (chronicled in the book *Gangster #2* by Mark Stuart), the don of New Jersey and supposedly the second most powerful mobster in the United States in 1935. Knowing this now, I'm glad I decided to play with a $10,000 bankroll for an almost sure moderate win, rather than with a $100,000 bankroll and any risk whatsoever of a serious loss. It also makes me reflect on my own past naïveté, and the greater wisdom of my wife, Vivian, in these matters.

Manny's friend Eddie Hand was also a source for Connie Bruck. At the time of our trip his company "shipped all the cars and trucks for Chrysler." Based in Buffalo, New York, he was battle-toughened through conflict with the Teamsters Union. A few years later he sold his company to Ryder Industries. During my stock market years I learned that he received Ryder warrants that, on the day I checked their price, were worth $47 million. Once when he, Kimmel, and I were flying from Reno to Las Vegas, Eddie Hand suddenly became nostalgic while reading the "Milestones" column in *Time* magazine. The vignettes mentioned the upcoming marriages of two ladies with whom he had been romantically involved. One was a Chilean copper heiress and the other was tennis player "Gorgeous Gussy" Moran, who scandalized Wimbledon by presenting herself for play in lace panties.

According to Bruck, Manny Kimmel died in Florida in 1982 at the age of eighty-six, leaving a young widow named Ivi, the older of the two nieces who had, with her younger sister and Manny, visited us so long ago on that dreary winter afternoon in Boston. Manny told me he met her while she worked in a jewelry store. They married after the death of his wife. In 2005, the History Channel featured Vivian and me in a one-hour program about my blackjack story. Ivi, who also appears on the program, still had a copy of a letter I'd written Manny in 1964 with some of my new discoveries about baccarat. When I last spoke with him, Eddie Hand was prospering in the wealthy enclave of Montecito in Southern California. Later he retired to the south of France.

Meanwhile, blackjack had still more to teach me, about both investing and how the world worked.

## Chapter 7

# CARD COUNTING
# FOR EVERYONE

Back at the Massachusetts Institute of Technology, I attracted attention in the cafeteria when, once a week, I cashed yet another $100 bill from my casino winnings. With the way our currency has depreciated since 1961, the impact then was almost the same as if I were to pay today with $1,000 bills.

Meanwhile, my two-year appointment at MIT would end June 30, just three months away. The department chairman, W. T. "Ted" Martin, encouraged me to stay a third year at MIT and told me how highly I was regarded by institute professor Shannon. There was a chance this could lead to a permanent position either then or at a later date. Whether to try for this was a difficult decision. MIT had become one of the world's great mathematics centers, following its transformation by projects for the government during World War II from a technical school to a scientific powerhouse. Simply walking down the hall, I would chat with people like the prodigy Professor Norbert Wiener (cybernetics) and the future Abel Prize winner Isadore Singer. The C. L. E. Moore Instructorship program, of which I was part, had brought in new PhDs like John Nash, who later won the Nobel for economics, and future Fields

Medal winner Paul Cohen. Though there's no Nobel Prize for mathematics, the Fields and the Abel prizes have that status. Cohen had left a few days before I arrived; his name was just being scraped off his door.

I finally decided not to stay on. From a career standpoint, I thought I had the talent to keep up with the big boys but I felt I needed more mathematical background. I also hadn't collaborated on research with a senior faculty mentor or other colleagues in my area of specialty, and such work with others often is key to advancing in an academic department. Instead, I had spent much of my time working on blackjack and on building a computer with Professor Shannon to predict roulette. However, my work with Shannon wasn't part of any academic field. It wasn't mathematics per se and had no constituency and no name. It couldn't help my academic career. Ironically, thirty years later MIT had become a world leader in the development of what would be called wearable computers, and the time line placed on the Internet by its Media Lab credited Shannon and me with building the first one.

New Mexico State University was bidding for bright young faculty members and subsidizing an incoming supply of good graduate students. They had just received a $5 million post-Sputnik Centers of Excellence Grant from the National Science Foundation, an amount equivalent to more than $40 million today, with a mandate to build a PhD program over the next four years. They proposed to jump my pay, from the $6,600 that both MIT and the University of Washington offered, to $9,000 a year and promote me to associate professor with tenure. I would also have a six-hour-a-week teaching load consisting of my choice of graduate courses. It provided the opportunity I wanted to expand my mathematical background, learning through teaching, doing my own research, directing doctoral theses, and collaborating with my students.

The position in New Mexico seemed to me to be the best next career step, even though my colleagues regarded it as an ill-advised gamble at what had been a mathematical backwater. Most important, a move to New Mexico would take Vivian and baby Raun to a much better climate and closer to our families.

As I was making this decision I agreed to write a book about blackjack. This came about after I mentioned my successful casino test to a few of my friends. The MIT grapevine did the rest. Yale Altman, representing the academic publisher Blaisdell (then a subsidiary of Random House), invited me to propose a book. I gave him the ten chapter headings from an outline I was already sketching, and he accepted it enthusiastically.

My working title was *Fortune's Formula: A Winning Strategy for Blackjack.* Then Random House took the project away from Blaisdell, over the strenuous protest of its president. They wanted to distribute the book directly as a trade book, and proposed the new title *Beat the Dealer.* It would appear in November 1962, giving me time to exploit my strategies in the Nevada casinos before publication, after which I expected to be given a hard time whenever I showed up to play blackjack.

During the next few months I wrote the book. Vivian and I packed up with Raun and spent that summer of 1961 in Los Angeles. It was a fury of writing, doing mathematics research, going to Nevada on another blackjack trip, preparing to move in the fall to New Mexico State University, working twenty hours a week on roulette with Claude Shannon, and getting ready for the birth of our second child, Karen. Looking back I don't see how Vivian and I did it all.

In August I traveled from Los Angeles to Las Vegas to play blackjack at the invitation of "Junior." I was writing my book and wanted to learn more about the tactics casinos might use to prevent my readers from winning. Junior (also known as Sonny) was a Harvard law student who had contacted me while I was at MIT. He started playing casino blackjack on his twenty-first birthday, using a method called end play, a system discovered and exploited by a few early players. The basic idea was to play single-deck games that were dealt all the way down. Even though players of that era with their imperfect strategies usually had the worst of it, sometimes the deck toward the end would get very rich in Aces and Tens. Canny players would then make huge favorable bets. They needed enormous bankrolls to withstand the wild fluctuations in capital that followed. Although the casinos might win big, they also might lose a lot, so they did not like these players. Junior, for instance, had been widely barred, cheated, or reshuffled on, so he went to a Hollywood makeup artist who recast him to look Chinese. With his hair dyed black and his hairline carefully revised with a razor, he sat down at a Las Vegas blackjack table. Wearing a bulky body shell under his Chinatown outfit, he looked like a different person. Then the pit boss pointed at him, laughed, and said, "Look at Junior, all dressed up like a Chinese."

Vivian had helped me train for this trip by dealing hands at high speed, blowing cigarette smoke at me, and engaging me in complicated conversations. Meanwhile, I was keeping track of the cards, calculating the percent advantage and my bet size, then playing out my hand using strategies that varied depending on the count. The key was to take it one step at a time, adding a new difficulty only after I became comfortable and relaxed with what I was already doing. What had seemed daunting finally became easy.

Junior backed my play with a modest $2,500 bankroll, equivalent to about $20,000 today. He followed me around Vegas with one eye open for cheating and another eye on his bankroll. While I was playing in the Sands, a pit boss who knew Junior told his friends that the kid was in town. Casino management saw that whenever Junior was around, I was playing nearby. Then my dealers stepped up the reshuffling and cheating. There was so much crooked dealing that I worried about playing on my own in the future without an expert to watch for it and warn me off. After a modest win, I returned to Los Angeles. The following month, September 1961, Vivian, Raun, and I moved to Las Cruces, New Mexico, where I began my duties at New Mexico State.

Although I learned from Junior that cheating was a serious problem and could make me a loser instead of a winner, he didn't show me how it worked or how to spot it. Meanwhile I was writing a book that might send thousands of gamblers to the tables thinking they could win. If dishonest dealers wiped them out, it would be a slaughter. I had to understand how the cheating was done and explain it to my readers so they would have a chance to spot and avoid it. That's what led to my next visit to Nevada.

The opportunity arose because I had been corresponding with Russell T. Barnhart, a magician and gambling scholar, who contacted me after my Washington, DC, talk in January 1961. We became acquainted while I was still at MIT and met in his apartment near Columbia University to talk about gambling and magic. As a treat Russell invited Persi Diaconis, a seventeen-year-old prodigy. Persi astounded me with card sleight of hand for an hour or so, then at Russell's suggestion we talked about Persi's future. What did I think about an academic career in mathematics as a professor versus being a professional magician? What advice would I give?

I told of the glories of the life of the mind, to be able to think about interesting problems as much as you wanted, as long as you wanted, to interact with intellectually challenging colleagues and students, to learn about any subject you chose, to have a lot of discretionary time with summers to travel and do research. Whether or not our conversation influenced Diaconis, he eventually became a full professor of mathematics at Harvard and also was awarded a MacArthur Foundation "genius" grant. He studied the theory of card shuffling, and the popular press widely reported his conclusion that seven fairly thorough shuffles was enough for practical purposes to randomize any deck of cards.

After the trip with Junior, when I told Russell of my problem with casino dishonesty, he proposed that I take him and his friend Mickey MacDougall on a blackjack foray. Mickey was perfect, being both a magician and a well-known card detective. His book *Danger in the Cards* describes his adventures detecting swindles in private games. He also had worked as a special consultant to the Nevada Gaming Control Board for several years. This led to the board citing several small casinos for cheating. Russell solved the bankroll problem by raising $10,000 from anonymous backers, with any profit—after our expenses had been paid—to be shared.

We met in Las Vegas in January 1962, during the year-end academic break at New Mexico State. Russell was a high-strung thirty-five-year-old bachelor and Mickey, a sixtyish fun-loving extrovert.

When we picked a casino and I found a seat I liked at the blackjack tables, our plan was for me to bet modestly until I got the go-ahead from Mickey. Following this, I would raise the scale of my betting and play for an hour, stopping sooner if I was warned off by Mickey or Russell. Stopping after an hour gave me a break during which I moved to another casino. Changing casinos after each session and varying the shifts on which we returned limited the time we were observed by any one casino employee. To further avoid notice, I stopped playing in any session before my wins became large, and I also stopped after a moderate loss to limit the impact in cases of cheating that we hadn't detected. Mathematically, interruptions didn't matter, because my lifetime of playing was just one long series of hands, and chopping it into sessions and playing them at various times and in various casinos should not affect my edge, nor the long-run amount I could expect to win. This principle applies in both gambling and investing.

When Mickey and Russell signaled that I had been cheated, I quit and went off with them for a lesson in how it was done. Mickey would demonstrate, first slowly then at casino speed. When I could see it or, more typically, infer it from what poker players call tells, we would return to the same dealer and resume play, briefly and for low stakes, so I could get better at spotting the crooked dealing at the table.

I saw this done with great skill at what had become my favorite strip hotel casino. We had several winning sessions on this trip, bringing my lifetime total to fifteen winning rounds, no losses. As I began session number sixteen, the pit boss walked up and asked us how we were doing. Mickey replied, "Up and down, like an elevator." Twenty minutes later, a man hurried through the front door of the hotel, rushed to the table, and replaced our dealer. Suspicious, I reduced my bets to the minimum, lost a couple of hands, and was signaled by Mickey to leave. Back in our rooms, Mickey showed me the virtually undetectable peek and second-card dealing that the new man had used.

This, a common technique, was to peek at the next card to be dealt, the so-called top card. Then, if that card was good for the player, deal the card just below it instead, the second card, in the likelihood it was worse. On the other hand, if the dealer was giving a card to himself, he would take the top card if it was good for him, and otherwise deal himself the second. The dealer who does this is a heavy favorite to beat the player. An expert cheat or magician does this so well that even when you are told in advance and are watching close up, you can't see. It's also nearly impossible to prove it ever happened. Cheating was so relentless during those days in Las Vegas that I spent as much time learning about the many ways it was being done as I did playing. Everywhere we went, we reached a point where we were cheated, barred from play, or the dealer reshuffled the cards after every hand.

For the last couple of days, we flew to the Tahoe-Reno area, where we visited Mickey's contact at the Nevada Gaming Control Board. Invited to tell our story, we recounted for two hours the litany of second dealing, stacked decks, missing or marked cards, and more.

We named dozens of casinos and described the dealers and their methods. Of course, our accusations ranged in authority from "dead certain" down to "circumstantial but strongly suggestive." Although the gaming control board official repeatedly invited us to guess or speculate, we made clear which statements were facts and which inferences. I had the uncomfortable feeling that we were being encouraged to speak carelessly and make exaggerated claims. I wondered at the time if this might be natural impatience with my academic habit of being careful and precise, or whether the board official was trying to get evidence to discredit what was in effect our damning indictment of the board itself.

After hearing our marathon account of rampant cheating, Mickey's contact at the board claimed he wanted to talk about additional consulting work, and suggested that in the meantime I take the opportunity to play blackjack. For some reason Russell didn't come with me. When I balked at playing without my cheating protectors, Mickey's contact assigned one of the gaming control board's agents to watch over me. Mickey thought this was a good idea, and had told me earlier that the dealers knew all the people the board used, so whenever they showed up the cheating stopped until they left.

I started at the Riverside Hotel in downtown Reno (years later the casino addition where I played was demolished, to my silent cheers), betting a cautious $5 to $50. It was uncrowded and I sat down alone in the middle of an empty table. My "protector," pretending not to know me, wandered in a minute later and sat down to play also. Our dealer, a young woman with a low-cut blouse and heavily freckled skin, won the first few hands against each of us. On the next hand I was dealt a "stiff" (10, 6) versus a dealer's upcard of 9 or 10. I hit and, to my amazement the card meant for me emerged from the deck and stuck twanging, held by its edge between the top card and the rest of the deck. The dealer froze and blushed bright red from cheeks to décolletage. The pit boss, watching the action from the end of the table to my left, literally asked me if I wanted the top card or the second! I could see that the second was a face card, which would bust me like it was supposed to. So that the gaming control board agent could hear me even if he were nearly deaf, and blind as well, I said loudly and distinctly, "The second busts me so I'll take the top card." It was an 8 and busted me anyhow. I cashed in my chips and left.

As my protector followed me outside, I said, "Did you ever see a second card like that before?" He replied, "Second? What second?" This agent had been sitting just three feet from the dealer. He saw everything and pretended to see nothing. Realizing he was there to finger me for the casinos, I used the restroom excuse to lose him and went to play at another casino. I was doing well and a small crowd gathered, but eventually my dealer, and only my dealer, was replaced. Looking around, I saw my now unwanted escort in the crowd. I played hide-and-seek with him for another two and a half hours.

The following morning, it was time to go home. The three of us barely escaped from Reno. Heavy snow closed the local airport, but there was a plane leaving from a nearby air force base runway that was still open. We caught it, learning later that it was the last plane out for eleven days. Afterward I learned that our backers were William F. Rickenbacker, one of two adopted sons of the famous flying ace Eddie (who, as the first man to drive faster than a mile a minute, was the original "Fast Eddie"), and other staff members of the *National Review*.

This trip taught me that while playing well, even with experts to warn me of dirty dealing, I could no longer openly win a significant amount. On future visits, I would need to change my appearance, be low-key, and generally avoid drawing attention to myself. Mickey Mac-Dougall told the gaming control board that he saw more cheating in Nevada casinos while watching my eight days of play than he had seen in all his previous five years of working for the board. After his damning report he was never again asked to consult by them. Russell Barnhart became fascinated with gambling and went on to write several books on the subject.

I was beginning to realize Las Vegas had a scary underside. It has evolved over the years. In 1947 mob elements, reportedly unhappy with his management of the Flamingo casino, gunned down fellow gangster Bugsy Siegel in Southern California. In 1960, the El Rancho Vegas mysteriously burned to the ground two weeks after a well-known mobster was forcibly ejected. When I played in the early 1960s, tens of millions of dollars in cash were being taken from the counting rooms without being tallied. The hidden profit avoided taxes and funded mob operations throughout the nation.

Not long after I played, as numerous card counters began to appear, they were jailed on pretexts, their money was taken, and some were beaten in back rooms. A gang of employees at one strip casino robbed drunks in their spare time. The 1970s weren't as bad but, as portrayed in the nonfiction book *Casino,* by Nicholas Pileggi—later a movie of the same name—they were bad enough.

Since then, Nevada has been dramatically transformed from mobster Bugsy Siegel's dream of a Disneyland for the mafia to a mainstream entertainment destination run by corporations. Las Vegas now enshrines the old days with a mob museum open to the public. The current consensus among professional blackjack experts seems to be that cheating has become rare in the older established areas like Nevada and Atlantic City, but players should be careful in the smaller, less regulated, and more remote casinos in the United States and abroad.

*Beat the Dealer* came out in November 1962. It sold briskly to favorable reviews, and continued to show strong, steady sales, with a spurt after minor bits of publicity. Readers were excited and enthusiastic. I believed that it might really take off if there were some way to publicize it more widely.

Ralph Crouch, chairman of the Mathematics Department at New Mexico State University, knew the science editor at *Life* magazine, and suggested they do a story. A mathematical system for beating blackjack had both scientific and public interest, and they enthusiastically agreed on a piece. But the story was evergreen, meaning not time-sensitive, so they had no schedule. Meanwhile David Scherman at Time Life's associated publication *Sports Illustrated* got permission to do a piece in advance of the *Life* article.

As time passed, blackjack players faced escalating casino countermeasures in Nevada. Management watched us through the "eye in the sky," a system of one-way mirrors above the tables. Our faces were checked against a book of photos of undesirables. Honest card counters were treated like player cheats and other criminals. When a casino spotted an undesirable, it passed the word around.

Countermeasures included reshuffling the pack of cards by the time half or fewer of them had been played. This not only limits the card counter's chances to make favorable bets, but is also costly for the casino because it slows the game down, fleecing the ordinary players more slowly and reducing casino profits. If one likens a casino to a slaughterhouse for processing players, then more time spent shuffling means less efficient use of plant capacity.

Cheating, on the other hand, not only makes money faster but can capture profits the house would otherwise miss. I saw this happening one night when I walked into the lounge of a packed Las Vegas Strip hotel casino about 10 P.M. Louis Prima, a famous musician of that era, and his lead singer, new wife Gia Maione, were entertaining, and the adjacent blackjack tables were packed, with crowds of players waiting. I had come to play blackjack and as I checked all the tables, hoping to get a seat, I noticed that the players at every table were losing at an astonishing rate. The dealers were all wearing glasses with the same yellow-orange tint, through which they could see identifying marks on the backs of the cards. If the card on top was good for the player, the dealer dealt him the next card, or "second," instead. Since players were wiped out faster, with their vacated seats being immediately refilled, profits soared. As a result, many who would have been discouraged by the wait and taken their money elsewhere left it at this casino instead.

Often, a suspected card counter was simply barred from playing blackjack. Apparently this was legal under Nevada law. Ironically, many innocent non-counters found themselves barred, along with incompetent would-be card counters. To get around this, I experimented with disguises, including contact lenses, sunglasses, a beard, and drastic changes of wardrobe and table behavior. This bought me extra playing time. Once, when I returned from a trip still in my disguise, my children didn't recognize me. Frightened by the bearded stranger, they burst into tears. Though just five and three at the time, Raun and Karen still remember this. It didn't bother baby Jeff, who was only a year old.

I tested one such disguise in Reno, where I had arranged through mutual friends to meet a couple who would keep an eye on me in the casinos in return for the fun of watching me play. We had never met and they didn't know what I looked like. When I introduced myself at dinner, they saw a bearded fellow wearing a brightly patterned Hawaiian shirt, wraparound sunglasses, and jeans. Afterward, we headed for one of the big hotel casinos, where I settled into a higher-limit table on the quieter second floor. I chose the best seat for a card counter, known as third base, which is farthest to the left as viewed from the player's side of the table.

Sitting there, I was the last to act, so I would benefit by having seen more cards when it was time to play my hand. Flashing a roll of bills, I bought a heap of chips. Seeing the money, my dealer, an attractive young woman, found me interesting. As we chatted and the casino offered drinks, which I accepted not to relax me but to relax them, she told me her shift was over at 2 A.M. and maybe we could "do something" afterward. Meanwhile, my steady winnings attracted the attention of the pit boss. He eventually decided I was a card counter, after which a parade from management came to watch. By 1 A.M. they had had enough and told me, to the astonishment and disappointment of my dealer, that I was no longer welcome at the tables. They evidently spread the word. Wearing the same disguise, I was barred from play the next day at several casinos.

That afternoon, I decided to put my disguise to the acid test. Before meeting my companions for dinner, I shaved off the beard, replaced the prescription sunglasses with contact lenses, and combed my hair differently. A sports jacket and tie—cocktail attire—completed the transformation. Opening their door to my knock, my companions, showing no signs of recognition, said, "Yes-s-s?" Their astonishment was my delight.

After dinner, I went to the same casino and took the same seat I had the night before. The same dealer looked up as I put a few chips from my pocket on the table in front of me. She saw no cash roll and I was now wearing a wedding ring—not a person of interest. To avoid being given away by my voice, I didn't talk. When the cocktail waitress offered me a drink, I said in a barely audible hoarse whisper, "Milk." I won again and all was well—for a while.

Then the pit boss came to watch as before, followed by the same management parade as on the previous night. But instead of me, they were focused on a player cheat who—worse luck—was seated next to me. After betting and receiving his first two cards, if he liked his chances he would add to his wager, and take some of the bet back if he didn't. For an hour or so, they scolded him repeatedly, and when he wouldn't either stop cheating or leave, they escorted him out. With my pile of chips growing steadily, I played on undisturbed. The next day I had no problem playing in the establishments that had barred my bearded self just the day before.

It was becoming clear that there was more to beating blackjack than counting cards and keeping cool as your bankroll went up and down. The green felt table was a stage and I was an actor on that stage. A card counter who wanted to be allowed to continue playing had to put on an effective act and present a nonthreatening persona. There are as many ways to do this as there are to portray characters in the theater. You can be the drunken cowboy from Texas or the wildly animated lady from Taiwan who can't wait to get her next bet down. You can be Caspar Milquetoast, the nervous accountant from Indianapolis who has already lost too much down the street. Or Miss Spectacular, who draws all the attention to herself, not to how she bets and plays.

Dave Scherman's full-length piece, "It's Bye! Bye! Blackjack" appeared in the January 1964 issue of *Sports Illustrated*—and *Beat the Dealer* sold out everywhere. Two months later *Life* ran a nine-page story and the book moved onto the *New York Times* bestseller list.

The publicity brought both expected and unexpected consequences. For me, it was the pleasure of seeing my father's silent pride in my fulfilling some of his hopes for me. In addition, there was a contact from my father's younger sister, who had vanished from his life in 1904 along with his mother when their parents divorced. The *Life* story led his sister to him through me and he arranged to visit her in Iowa where she, her five children, and numerous grandchildren now lived. Separated when he was six and she was four, my father had dreamed for a lifetime that he would somehow find her again. But he never saw her. He died of a heart attack shortly before the trip.

After reading the articles, thousands of counters and would-be counters headed for Las Vegas. The Nevada Resort Hotel Association met in a secret emergency session. Twenty-nine years later, here is how long-time casino executive Vic Vickrey described that meeting.

"How the heck do I know how he does it? I guess he's got one of them mathematical minds or photographic memories, or something."

This was Cecil Simmons, the casino boss at the Desert Inn, talking on the phone with Carl Cohen, the Sands casino manager. It was the mid-1960s and they were discussing a book that would have a most profound impact on Las Vegas casinos and their approach to the game known as 21 or blackjack.

"All I know," Simmons roared, "is he wrote a book that teaches everyone how to win every time they play blackjack. I'm just telling you, this book-learning SOB has ruined us . . . we're out of the blackjack business." . . .

Thorp's book was the main topic of conversation whenever and wherever casino bosses gathered back during the '60s . . .

. . . A meeting was called [to find] a solution . . .

We . . . gathered in . . . the Desert Inn. I still today do not know why the boys from Back East thought we had to be so damned secretive . . . I reminded them that this meeting was not exactly the same as their Appalachia meeting in up-state New York that had been raided by the feds years earlier.

... They could all have passed for actors who had just left an old George Raft movie set. They began talking out of the side of their mouths at the same time, with each one shouting out his remedy to the problem.

Hard-Knuckle Harry's solution was quite simple: "Break a few legs . . ."

"No, Hard-Knuckles, no," our chairman almost shouted. "We're all legit now and we gotta think like legit businessmen."

... It was finally agreed that a number of rule changes must be implemented . . . to thwart these card counters.

On April 1, 1964, April Fool's Day—the Association announced the result: for the first time ever, it was changing the rules of blackjack. Pair splitting and doubling down would be restricted and the entire pack of cards would be reshuffled after just a couple of deals.

As part of an orchestrated PR follow-up, a *Las Vegas Sun* editorial of April 3, 1964, assured us that "Anybody who has been around Nevada very long knows that [casinos welcome] players with a system." "Edward O. Thorp . . . obviously doesn't know the facts of gambling life. There has never been a system invented that overcomes . . . the advantage the house enjoys in every game of chance." And for the clincher: " 'Dr. Thorp may be qualified at mathematics, but he is sophomoric on gambling,' is the way Edward A. Olsen, Gaming Control Board chairman, put it." In a nonconfrontational vein, Gene Evans of Harrah's Club explained that ". . . the club believes the player may have a better chance when the deck is shuffled every time, because all the Aces and face cards could come up on each deal."

I told the press that the changes would hurt business badly and that skilled counters would still win. As Vic Vickrey reported, "Our regular 21 players who were not attempting to count cards . . . rebelled to such a degree that our 21 play began to decline at an alarming rate. [After several weeks] We had no choice but to reinstate the original rules which were more favorable to the player." The casino bosses understood what their apologists denied. The mocking from a few weeks earlier was replaced by headlines like these: "Vegas Casinos Cry Uncle, Change Rules—Players Too Smart," and "How Wizard of Odds Beat Las Vegas Cards."

From a mathematical idea in my head, I forged a system for beating the game. Then I was ridiculed by the casino beast, which said that it sent cabs for fools like me. Thinking they played fair and that I was taking my secret weapon, a brain, to a sporting event, I found myself barred, cheated, betrayed by a representative of the gaming control board, and generally persona non grata at the tables. I felt satisfaction and vindication when the great beast panicked. It felt good to know that, just by sitting in a room and using pure math, I could change the world around me.

Rather than quit the field, I launched an army with *Beat the Dealer*. Thus continued the great blackjack war between the casinos and the players that still rages, more than fifty years after the invention of card counting.

*Chapter 8*

# PLAYERS VERSUS CASINOS

After my book appeared, legions of blackjack players hit the tables in Nevada. Anyone could bring the book's palm-sized strategy cards and find a game with rules good enough to let them play on level terms with the casino, even without counting cards. Then there were the card counters and would-be card counters. Many were good and some would go on to make their living from blackjack, but for the majority the effort and persistence required to practice card counting, the restraint and discipline needed, to say nothing of the temperament, were obstacles to success.

Still, the fact that blackjack could be beaten led to an upsurge in play. As a result, during the next few decades blackjack displaced craps as the dominant table game. However, the casinos were in a bind: Should they let the minority of players who were counters beat them in return for the vastly increased revenues from the great majority of players who couldn't or wouldn't count, or should they try to choke off the card counters with countermeasures, even if this would slow the boom in blackjack play?

When the casinos first tried a rules change and lost more in revenues than they gained in benefits, they went back to the old rules. Next, they brought in dealing boxes known as shoes, which allowed the use of four, six, or even eight decks. This was supposed to make card counting more difficult. But for those who used the High–Low System, it wasn't much harder. That was because the correct play of the hand was pretty much the same for various numbers of decks and because the High–Low System already adjusted for the number of unused cards, whether the game was played with one or several decks. The good players, who were getting better with practice, continued to win.

The most widely used photo gallery of undesirables was developed for the casinos by Griffin Investigations, Inc., a private detective agency founded in 1967 by Beverly and Robert Griffin. The usual collection of criminals, player cheats, and public nuisances was rapidly expanded by the addition of ever more card counters. They were barred on sight, and their descriptions were shared among the casinos. However, dealers and pit bosses often couldn't figure out who was counting and who wasn't. Non-counters who inadvertently aroused suspicion were, to their bafflement, forbidden to play. Players were cheated and beaten in back rooms. Eventually the Griffin agency was successfully sued by two top card counters, one of whom was James Grosjean, a member of the Blackjack Hall of Fame, and the firm filed for bankruptcy in 2005.

Card counters formed informal networks and developed new and improved techniques. *Beat the Dealer* had introduced the idea of a team. Suppose several players, say five, each with a $10,000 bankroll, are playing separately, winning at an average rate of 1 percent or $100 an hour. Then the five players together will gain an average of $500 an hour. If instead they pool their money into one $50,000 bank, when one of them plays he can bet five times as much as he could safely risk on his own $10,000. Consequently he expects to win five times as much, namely, 1 percent of $50,000 or $500 per hour, rather than $100. But it gets better. The four other players can all be playing, too, typically at different tables or casinos, acting as though they each have a $50,000 bankroll, so the group makes $2,500 per hour when all are playing whereas, playing without pooling their bankrolls, they would make collectively only $500 an hour.

The next step was obvious. Entrepreneurs went into the blackjack business by recruiting and training players, providing a bankroll, and sharing the profits between the players and the financier. Notable teams include Tommy Hyland's and the now famous MIT group, chronicled in the book *Bringing Down the House,* which inspired the 2008 movie *21.* Al Francesco pioneered the creation of blackjack teams, and the idea was well publicized by one of his recruits, Ken Uston (1935–87). Uston's books *Million Dollar Blackjack* and *The Big Player* inspired the formation of other teams as well as intensified casino efforts to stop them. Ken Uston was one of the more colorful characters in blackjack history. One-quarter Asian, with a Japanese grandfather, he was born Kenneth Senzo Usui. Starting his career in the securities business, he became the youngest senior vice president ever at the Pacific Stock Exchange. Drawn by the allure of blackjack he then left the securities industry to play professionally.

Card counters wish to bet as little as possible when the casino has the edge, then make a large bet when the cards favor them. Ideally, a player with a bankroll large enough to allow $1,000 bets when the deck is favorable would bet the table minimum, say $5, when it isn't. Such a wide betting spread of 200:1 is a red flag to casino personnel. But to bet $1,000 on good situations with a narrower betting spread of, say, 4:1 requires $250 bets when the deck is unfavorable. This cuts back the overall gain.

The remedy was to use what was called a Big Player. Teams placed members at several blackjack tables to track the deck, meanwhile betting the minimum. When a deck became favorable they signaled the Big Player, who seemed to wander randomly from table to table, putting down sizable bets erratically. Since he hadn't been at the table before he bet, he couldn't be counting. All this was disguised with an act. The Big Player might appear to be a drunken flamboyant high-roller, often with a beautiful companion.

Meanwhile, the blackjack community was exploring and developing the various possible counting methods. These followed directly from my original computations showing the effects of removing various cards from the deck. A counting system assigns points to each card that reflect the card's impact upon removal. The closer these points correspond to

the actual effects of the cards, the more accurately that particular counting method estimates the player's current edge.

To illustrate this basic idea I presented what I called the ultimate
strategy, which assigned a whole number value to each card in close proportion to its impact on the odds. The numbers in table 1 are from the
1962 edition of *Beat the Dealer.* The second line shows the change in the
player's edge upon removing one card. The third line, obtained by multiplying by 13 and rounding to the nearest whole number, gives the point
count for the ultimate strategy, a good approximation to a perfect point
count. Because of the diverse point values, I expected this system to be
used by computers, not people. I intended it only to illustrate the basic
principle for constructing point-count systems—the closer the point as-
signments were to the effects of the corresponding cards, the more powerful the system. On the other hand, the more diverse the point values
used for a particular card counting system, the harder that count was to
use.

**Table 1: Effect of Removing One Card from One Deck and
the Ultimate (Point-Count) Strategy**

| Card | 2 | 3 | 4 | 5 | 6 | 7 | 8 | 9 | 10 | A |
|------|---|---|---|---|---|---|---|---|----|---|
| Change In Edge | 0.36 | 0.48 | 0.59 | 0.82 | 0.47 | 0.34 | 0.03 | -0.23 | -0.54 | -0.68 |
| Points | 5 | 6 | 8 | 11 | 6 | 4 | 0 | -3 | -7 | -9 |

Perhaps the best compromise between power and simplicity is the
High–Low, or the Complete Point Count, which appears in the 1966
revised edition of *Beat the Dealer.* Still used today by top professionals,
this is the simplest possible point count in that cards get values of –1, 0,
or +1 only. You start with the count at 0. As the "small" cards 2, 3, 4, 5, 6
are used, they each add +1 to the cumulative count. The intermediate
cards 7, 8, and 9 are counted as 0 so their appearance doesn't affect the
total count. Big cards—Aces and Ten-value cards—count as –1 so they
each reduce the total by one.

Suppose the player using the High–Low count sees these cards in the first round of play: A, 5, 6, 9, 2, 3. Then the count, which started with zero, becomes $-1 + 1 + 1 + 0 + 1 + 1 = +3$. With this count in a one-deck game—and with reasonably favorable rules—the player has an edge on the next deal. As cards are dealt, the count goes up and down around zero. When the count is positive the player benefits, and when it is negative it helps the casino. The impact of any particular value of the count is greater when fewer cards are left. Good players simply estimate this by seeing how many cards are in the discard tray.

How hard is it to keep the point count? A typical test is to shuffle the deck, remove one to three cards facedown, then count through the rest of the deck. The player declares the result, then the missing card or cards are turned over to see if he is right. For example, suppose after one card has been set aside without its face being shown, the count for the rest of the deck is zero. Then, since the total count must come out to zero (as you may have already noticed, the complete point count has 20 negative points and 20 positive points in each fifty-two-card deck), the unseen card must be a 0-point card, namely, a 7, 8, or 9. This can lead to some surprises.

One night I was playing in Puerto Rico with the comedian and TV personality Henry Morgan, who was well known in the 1950s and '60s. I had been losing for an hour or so. At the end of a two-deck shoe, my dealer had a Ten up. As the casino betting limit was $50 per hand, I could get more money on the table and keep out other players by betting on all seven spots. I was using the variation of the point count where the cards 2, 3, 4, 5, 6, 7 are +1, 8 is 0, and 9, 10, A are −1, as they appear. The cards had run out on the deal, and the point count was zero. Therefore the one unseen card, which was the dealer's hole card, had to be a 0. So the dealer had an 8 in the hole for a total of 18. The deck was reshuffled so I could finish playing my seven hands. Since I had several hands of hard 17 that I alone knew were to be sure losers if I did nothing, I hit them. This is a disastrous choice unless you know the dealer's hole card, and that he has you beat. Unlucky, I busted every one of them.

The dealer looked up scornfully, saying to me with a laugh, "So you count the cards, amigo. Why, I'll bet you even know what I've got." As the other dealers grinned, I said, "Why, you have an 8 under there." The dealer laughingly summoned several other dealers and the pit boss. He explained contemptuously that the Americano expert said that he had an 8 in the hole. A babble of uncomplimentary remarks in Spanish passed back and forth.

I was tired and ready for a break. I had made an occasional counting error over the last hour. There was a chance I would be wrong (better for me if I was, probably). Then the dealer turned over his hole card. It was an 8. The torrent in Spanish raged anew.

How hard is it to count? The more I practiced, the better my times, and I found that if I was able to count one deck in twenty to twenty-five seconds I could easily keep up in any game I was in, so I simply checked to be sure I was up to this standard each time before I played. One of the members of the Blackjack Hall of Fame impressed the professionals by counting two decks in thirty-three seconds. But the most amazing performance I have seen was at the third World Game Protection Conference at the Paris Hotel in Las Vegas. A highlight of one evening's entertainment was a card counting contest. The choice of technique for handling the cards was crucial for attaining really low times. The winner, among scores of contestants from the casino industry, had the fastest time I ever saw, 8.8 seconds.

The casinos introduced technology to stop the counters. Cameras and observers followed the action through one-way mirrors above the tables. Currently, this is automated, incorporating face-recognition software. RFID chips keep track of a player's bets, and machines can track the cards and check the play of the hands, searching for patterns characteristic of counters. Machines that continually reshuffle the cards proved to be a perfect defense without slowing the game down, but the casinos pay fees to the vendors of the machines.

Meanwhile the card counters were developing more techniques for winning. One of these methods was based on the fact that the players are dealt two cards each and the dealer also typically receives two cards, the first faceup and the second facedown and hidden under the first. If the dealer's top card is an Ace or Ten-value card (K, Q, J, 10) then the dealer checks his hidden card to see if he has a natural, or a blackjack, in which case he shows it and all bets are settled at once. A dealer blackjack beats all player hands except another blackjack. A dealer making this hole-card check would typically bend up the corner of his two cards to see what was hidden underneath. Eventually the Aces and Tens would get slightly warped. If the dealer was especially careless or if decks weren't changed often enough, the savvy player could spot the warps before they were dealt and know where the Aces and Tens were, a huge advantage.

Mining the same ore were the so-called spooks, confederates strategically placed to see the hole-card of a dealer who was careless in checking it. If the dealer does not have blackjack, the play of the hands continues and a player whose spook tells him the value of the dealer's hidden card gets a huge edge. Some casinos prevent players from using spooks and warps by having the dealer wait to draw his second card until after all the players finish playing their hands. Then the dealer's second card can be dealt faceup.

In the 1970s, several people developed concealed computers to play blackjack. The casino industry's response was to have the Nevada legislature pass a law in 1985 outlawing devices that assisted players in calculating odds. But the ingenious players weren't done yet. When one deck of cards or a multideck pack of cards is shuffled, the shuffling may not be thorough enough to randomize the deck. A deck that isn't well shuffled may have predictable patterns that can be exploited.

This was a natural evolution from my early thoughts about nonrandom shuffling back in 1961 and 1962. I realized that the type of shuffle that was used could substantially affect the odds of many games. I designed a two-pronged attack: I would build mathematical models to approximate real shuffling, and do empirical studies of real shuffling.

As a first simple approach for exploiting this, I came up with a way to locate the Aces in single-deck blackjack. To see how this works, shuffle the deck and spread it faceup. To track the Ace of Spades, for example, notice the card just ahead of it. Suppose it is the King of Hearts (KH). You are going to shuffle and cut the deck and follow what happens to the pair of cards. Just to help you keep track, turn over the Ace of Spades and the card just ahead of it so they are faceup in the otherwise facedown deck. Now cut and shuffle once. One or more cards may get in between the Ace and the card that was just ahead, which we're taking to be the King of Hearts, separating them. But if you were to play black-jack now with this deck, as soon as you saw the King of Hearts you would know that the Ace of Spades was likely to be close behind. As you successively cut and shuffle, still more cards crowd between the two cards. Sometimes, because the deck is cut for each shuffle, the order reverses and the Ace of Spades will appear first, in which case there is no prediction. If the deck is not shuffled well, the player can frequently tell that the corresponding Ace has a more-than-average chance of appearing soon. Applied to all four Aces, this is a powerful advantage.

Ace-locating led to the notion of following where groups of cards ended up after shuffling. Casinos typically use standardized shuffling techniques, which can be analyzed. Players, often with the aid of computers, learned to keep track of where chunks of cards rich in Aces and Tens were redistributed in the deck. The advantage gained from this could be substantial. The camouflage was effective as well since shuffle-trackers frequently found an advantage at the start of the first deal, betting big before having seen any cards. Other times, they raised their bets when the count was bad if they knew the next cards to be dealt had more than their share of Aces and Tens.

In 1997 Vivian and I went to St. George, Utah, where I ran in their annual marathon. On the way there and also coming back, we passed through Las Vegas. My friend Peter Griffin (no relation to the Griffin agency or its founders) of *The Theory of Blackjack* fame arranged with Joe Wilcox, who was then the casino manager at Treasure Island, to pay for ("comp") our stay there. Joe agreed, if in return I would not play blackjack in any of Steve Wynn's casinos. Joe was a gracious host and the room, food, and shows were excellent. He mentioned that the casinos were losing significant amounts to the shuffle-trackers and indicated that no one seemed to have found a shuffle that gave effective protection. After watching the dealers at Treasure Island and at two other casinos, and seeing what was wrong, with a little math I found a new shuffle that prevented tracking. I kept it to myself.

The players and the casinos fought not only at the tables and in the back rooms, but also in the courts. Nevada casinos were permitted to bar players, whereas New Jersey–ruled casinos could not. In both states, gaming establishments could always protect themselves by making the rules of the game more favorable to themselves or by reshuffling the cards at will. As to whether card counting was cheating, the statutes in Nevada clearly defined cheating as "to alter the selection of criteria which determine: (a) the result of a game; or (b) the amount or frequency of payment in a game"; using your brain to play well is clearly allowed. Introducing loaded dice would be cheating under clause (a), and adding or subtracting chips after you see your cards in blackjack would be cheating according to clause (b).

As the war between casinos and counters has evolved, so Las Vegas itself has been transformed. The early mob-dominated period was described in the bestselling 1964 book *The Green Felt Jungle*. Mob control gave way during the corporate transformation of the 1980s, the subsequent rise of the corporate gambling billionaires, and the ongoing expansion of gaming worldwide. Today the best players still thrive, but opportunities are increasingly limited and newcomers find success much more difficult.

The professional players share their stories each year at a private gathering in Nevada known as the Blackjack Ball. Hosted by professional card counter Max Rubin and sponsored by the Barona Casino, which is located hundreds of miles away in Southern California, many of the past and present best players in the world gather. Members of the Blackjack Hall of Fame are honored attendees. They also are featured in a picture gallery at the Barona, where they can stay for free but not play. The Barona benefits from the ball because any expert who attends must pledge never to play blackjack there—one of the most profitable investments ever by a casino.

My children, Raun, Karen, and Jeff, attended the ball with me in 2013, mixing with pseudonymous legends like James Grosjean, the Harvard mathematics graduate who has continued to develop and use new methods for "advantage play." We spoke with the Holy Rollers, a card counting team of young Christians whose Robin Hood–like mandate is to transfer money from the casinos ("bad") to their church ("good") and themselves. Among the 102 guests, nearly half had net professional winnings of more than $1 million. The rest were family, spouses, and significant others. One of the champions was Blair Hull, who parlayed a fortune from running a blackjack team into several hundred million dollars at the Chicago Board Options Exchange. Bill Benter used his blackjack winnings to bankroll and build a billion-dollar worldwide business betting on horse races. A cheerful Taiwanese wearing the name tag B. J. TRAVELER sat down next to me with a shopping bag full of books he had written for the Chinese public about his adventures. He had played in sixty-four countries over six years, netting almost $7 million. Most amazing was that he survived a year in Moscow dodging thieves as he carted money from the casinos.

The next day, I had lunch on the strip with John Chang, a star of the MIT team featured in the movie *21,* and an expert friend of his. After-ward, at a nearby casino, the three of us asked to have our picture taken in front of a blackjack table. Not allowed. So we sat down to play a hand or two at a $100-minimum/$10,000-maximum table with good rules. Chang and his friend whipped out rolls of $100 bills, peeled off $5,000 each, and bought in. "Our pockets are our banks," they said. Our dealer, a friendly older woman from Eastern Europe, with no clue as to who was seated at her table, thought some of John's unorthodox plays were beginner's errors. When she advised him as to how to play correctly, he thanked her politely for her help and indicated a willingness to improve. Twenty minutes later, the casino was a few thousand dollars poorer and we had an employee take photos for us by the entrance.

Can an ordinary player still beat the game? My answer is a qualified yes. Many blackjack games have rules that have been changed enough so they are hard to beat. For instance, never play at a table where the payoff for getting a two-card 21, or blackjack, has been changed from the orig-inal 3:2 to lesser amounts like 6:5 or 1:1. There are newsletters and ser-vices that currently rate the games, and tell which ones are still good.

When I was the keynote speaker at the third World Game Protection Conference in Las Vegas in 2008, I was asked whether, when I wrote *Beat the Dealer,* I foresaw the magnitude and duration of its impact on the casino industry. I said that I didn't know in 1962 if it would last five years or fifty, but now we know it has continued to this day.

*Chapter 9*

# A COMPUTER THAT PREDICTS ROULETTE

The modern form of roulette seems to have first appeared in Paris in 1796. It became the favored high-stakes game of the rich and the royal, enshrined in Monte Carlo in the nineteenth century, and celebrated in story and song. With its high stakes, splendid settings, and runs of extreme luck, which were sometimes good but more often bad, it was a target for those with systems attempting to overcome the casino's advantage. These systems were too complex for gamblers to analyze precisely, but they had plausible features that inspired hope.

A favorite was the Labouchère, or cancellation, system. This was used in roulette for bets that paid even money, where you win or lose an amount equal to your bet. Among the even-money bets in roulette are wagers on red or on black, each of which has eighteen chances in thirty-eight of winning. To start the Labouchère, write down a string of numbers, such as 3, 5, and 7. The total of these, 15, is what you try to win. Your first bet is the total of the first and last numbers in the string, 3 + 7, or 10. If you win, cross off the first and last numbers, leaving only 5. Your next bet is 5, and if you win you have reached your goal. If you lose, add 10 to the string so it becomes, 3, 5, 7, 10 and then bet 3 + 10 or 13. In any case, each time you lose you add one number to the string, and each time you win you cross off two numbers. Therefore, you need to win only a little over a third of the time to reach your goal. What can go wrong? Gamblers, trying systems like the Labouchère, were baffled when they never seemed to prevail.

However, using the mathematical theory of probability, it was proven that if all roulette numbers were equally likely to come up, and they appeared in random order, it was impossible for any betting system to succeed. Despite this, hope flared briefly at the end of the nineteenth century when the great statistician Karl Pearson (1857–1936) discovered that the roulette numbers being reported daily in a French newspaper showed exploitable patterns. The mystery was resolved when it was discovered that rather than spend hours watching the wheels, the people recording the numbers simply made them up at the end of each day. The statistical patterns Pearson detected simply reflected the failure of the reporters to invent perfectly random numbers.

If betting systems don't work, what about defective wheels where, in the long run, some numbers will come up more than others? In 1947, two graduate students at the University of Chicago, Albert Hibbs (1924–2003) and Roy Walford (1924–2004), found a roulette wheel in Reno that seemed to favor the number 9. They increased an initial stake of $200 to $12,000. The next year they found a wheel at the Palace Club in Las Vegas on which they made $30,000. They took a year off and sailed the Caribbean, then went on to distinguished careers in science. Among many accomplishments, Hibbs became director of space science for Caltech's Jet Propulsion Laboratory, and Walford became a UCLA medical researcher who showed that caloric restriction in mice could more than double their maximum life span. Hibbs later wrote, "I wanted to conquer space, and my roommate, Roy Walford, decided that he would conquer death."

Feynman must have known about biased wheels when he told me there was no way to beat the game, because Hibbs got his PhD in physics under Feynman at Caltech the previous year. In any case, biased wheels at big casinos were likely a thing of the past, as gambling houses took better care of their equipment.

So this was the setting when Claude Shannon and I, in September 1960, set to work to build a computer to beat roulette. The key fact was that casinos allowed players to bet for a few seconds while the ball was spinning.

As it was the last year of my two-year appointment at MIT, we had to complete the task in nine months. We spent twenty hours a week at the Shannons' three-story wooden house. Dating from 1858, it was sited on one of the Mystic Lakes, a few miles from Cambridge. The basement was a gadgeteer's paradise, with perhaps $100,000 worth of electronic, electrical, and mechanical items. There were thousands of mechanical and electrical components—motors, transistors, switches, pulleys, gears, condensers, transformers, and on and on. As someone who had spent much of his boyhood building and experimenting in electronics, physics, and chemistry, I was now happily working with the ultimate gadgeteer.

We purchased a reconditioned regulation roulette wheel from a company in Reno for $1,500. From the labs at MIT we borrowed a strobe light, and a large clock with a second hand that made one revolution per second, the latter recapitulating the role the stopwatch had in my earlier movie experiments. The dial was divided into hundredths of a second and we could interpolate still-finer time divisions. We set up shop in the billiard room, where a massive old slate table made a solid base on which to mount the wheel.

Our wheel was typical, carefully machined with an elegant design and beauty that added to the appeal of the game. It consisted of a large stationary piece, or stator, with a circular track around the top, where the croupier starts each play of the game by launching a small white ball. As the ball orbits, it gradually slows until finally it falls down the sloped conelike inside of the stator and crosses onto a circular centerpiece, or rotor, with numbered pockets that the croupier previously set spinning in a direction opposite to that in which he spun the ball.

The motion of the ball is complicated by having several different phases, making it so daunting as to discourage analysis. We followed my original plan, which was to divide the motion of ball and rotor into stages and analyze each separately.

We began by predicting when and where the orbiting ball would leave the outer track. We did this by measuring the time it took for the ball to make one revolution. If the time was short, the ball was moving fast and would go relatively far. If the time was longer, the ball was traveling slower and would soon fall from the track.

To measure the speed of the ball, we hit a microswitch as the ball passed a reference mark on the stator. This started the clock. When the ball passed the same spot the second time we hit the switch again, stopping the clock, which then showed how long it took for the ball to go around once.

Simultaneous with starting and stopping the clock, the switch triggered the flash of a strobe whose very short pulses of light were like those in a disco. We dimmed the lights in the room so the strobe flashes "stopped" the ball each time the switch was hit, allowing us to see how much the ball was ahead or behind the reference mark. This showed us how much we were off in hitting the timing switch. From this we corrected the times recorded by the clock for one revolution of the ball, making the data more accurate. We also got from this a numerical measure of our errors in hitting the switch as well as direct visual feedback. As a result we learned to become much better at timing. With practice, our errors fell from values of about 0.03 second to about 0.01 second. We were able to retain this level of accuracy later when we concealed everything for casino play, having trained our big toes to operate switches hidden in our shoes.

We found that we could predict, with a high degree of accuracy, when and where the ball would slow enough to fall from the circular track. So far so good. Our next step was to determine the time the ball would take and the distance it would travel as it spiraled down the conical inside of the stator to reach the spinning rotor. Most wheels had vanes or deflectors in this region—typically eight—that the ball would frequently hit. The effect was to randomize the ball's behavior. Its path could be shortened or lengthened, depending on whether and how it hit one of these deflectors. We found that the uncertainty this introduced into our prediction was too small to ruin our advantage. The deflectors also gave us a handy choice of reference points for timing the ball and rotor.

Finally, after the ball crossed onto the moving rotor, it would bounce around among the individual numbered pockets, introducing yet another uncertainty into our forecast.

The total prediction error was the sum of many effects, including our imperfect timing, the spattering of the ball on the rotor pocket dividers (frets), the deflection of the ball by metal obstacles as it spiraled down the stator, and the possible tilt of the wheel. Assuming the total error was approximately normally distributed (the Gaussian or bell-shaped curve), we needed the standard deviation (a measure of uncertainty) for the error of prediction around the actual outcome to be sixteen pockets (0.42 revolution) or less to get an edge. We achieved the tighter estimate of ten pockets, or 0.26 revolution. This gave us the enormous average profit of 44 percent of the amount we bet on the forecast number. If we spread our bet over the two closest numbers on each side, for a total of five numbers in all, we cut risk and still had a 43 percent advantage.

Using physics to win at roulette brings to mind the bizarre game of Russian roulette. You cannot win, but physics may help you survive. The name appears to have originated in a 1937 story by Georges Surdez:

> "Did you ever hear of Russian Roulette?" [. . .] With the Russian army in Romania, around 1917, some officer would suddenly pull out his revolver, put a single cartridge in the cylinder, spin the cylinder, snap it back in place, put it to his head and pull the trigger . . .

The spinning of the revolver's cylinder is reminiscent of the roulette wheel's whirling rotor. With six chambers, only one of which is loaded, the chance of firing the cartridge would seem to be one in six. But for a properly lubricated and maintained weapon held upright with the cylinder parallel to the ground, gravity and the weight of the cartridge will cause the full chamber to tend to end up near the bottom, provided the cylinder is allowed to stop on its own. If the cylinder is then relatched, the player has shifted the odds in his (women are too smart to play) favor. The effect of gravity on the final resting position of an unevenly weighted cylinder varies, depending on the orientation of the gun. My younger daughter, an assistant deputy district attorney for more than two decades, tells me that modern forensic scientists are aware of this.

Shannon, with his treasury of intriguing information and ingenious ideas, was a joy to work with. Discussing our need for secrecy, he mentioned that social network theorists studying the spread of rumors and secrets claimed that if you pick two people at random in, say, the United States, then they are usually connected by a chain of three or fewer acquaintances or "three degrees of separation." An obvious way to test this when you meet strangers is to ask what famous people they know. It is likely that a famous person they know shares an acquaintance with a famous person you know. Then the steps are (1) you to your famous person, (2) your famous person to their famous person, and (3) their famous person to them. The two famous people connecting you give "two degrees of separation."

As is my lifelong habit, I tested this claim, often with remarkable results. Once on a train from Manhattan to Princeton, New Jersey, I noticed that the pleasant, well-dressed, motherly-looking lady sitting beside me seemed agitated. She didn't understand English, French, or Spanish but she responded to my elementary German, telling me her problem was knowing when to get off in Philadelphia. After I had helped her, I learned she was a Hungarian economic official from Budapest on her way to a meeting. I decided to play my "degrees of separation" game.

"Do you know anyone in Budapest named Sinetar?" I asked.

"Of course. They are a famous family," she replied. "There's Miklos, the film producer, as well as an engineer, and a psychologist."

"Well," I said, "they are relatives of my wife."

Me, to Vivian, to a Budapest Sinetar, to my economist seatmate. Two degrees of separation. So far, I've never needed more than three to connect with a stranger.

The concept entered popular culture as "six degrees of separation" after John Guare's 1990 play of that name. The notion of degrees of separation was well known as early as 1969 among mathematicians as the

Erdös (*ERR-dosh*) number, linking them via other mathematicians to the prolific and peripatetic Hungarian mathematician Paul Erdös, using the relation "coauthored a paper with." If you coauthored a paper with Erdös your Erdös number is one. If your number isn't one but you coauthored with someone who had Erdös number one, then your number is two, and so forth.

The few steps that connect strangers explain how rumors spread rapidly and widely. If you have a good investment idea, you might want to keep it secret. In 1998 a *New York Times* Science Times article said that mathematicians had discovered how networks might "make a big world small" using the equivalent of the famous person idea, and attributed the concept of six degrees of separation to a sociologist in 1967. Yet all this was known to Claude Shannon in 1960.

He loved to build ingenious gadgets. One of these would flip a coin end over end a specified number of revolutions and have it land—at his choice—either heads or tails. He also ran a cable from his workshop (the "toy room") to his kitchen. When Claude pulled on the cable, a finger, attached to it and set up in the kitchen, would silently and jokingly summon his wife, Betty.

During our work breaks, Claude taught me to juggle three balls, which he did while riding a unicycle. He also had a steel cable tied between two tree stumps and walked along it, encouraging me to learn with the aid of a balance bar. He could do any two of the three tricks together: juggle three balls, ride the unicycle, and balance on the tightrope, and his goal was to be able to do all three at once. One day I noticed two huge pieces of Styrofoam that looked as if they could be worn like snowshoes. Claude said they were water shoes that enabled him to "walketh upon the water," in this case the Mystic Lake in front of his house. The neighbors had been astounded to see Claude moving upright above the surface of the lake. I tried the water shoes but found it difficult to keep from toppling over.

We got along so well because, from an early age, science was play for both of us. Tinkering and building things was part of the fun, as was letting our curiosity range freely.

In American roulette, the wheel has thirty-eight pockets for the ball to fall into. Thirty-six of these, numbered from 1 to 36, are either red or black, with eighteen of each. The green pockets, 0 and 00 (zero and double-zero), are opposite each other on the rotor and thus split the other thirty-six into two groups of eighteen. A winning bet on a single number pays 35:1, meaning you get back your stake plus a profit of thirty-five times the amount you bet. If there were no 0 or 00, this payoff would make the game even, because on average, for each $1 bet, the player wins $35 one time in thirty-six spins and loses $1 thirty-five times in thirty-six, for no net gain or loss. However, with the addition of 0 and 00, on average the bettor who has no ability to predict will win $35 one time in thirty-eight and lose $1 thirty-seven times in thirty-eight, for a net loss of $2 per thirty-eight bets. The casino edge for him on single-number bets then is $2 ÷ $38 or 5.26 percent. European roulette is typically more generous, having just the single zero.

For bet sizing in favorable games, Shannon suggested I look at a 1956 paper by John Kelly. I adapted it as the guide for bets in blackjack and roulette, and later in other favorable games, sports betting, and the stock market. For roulette, the Kelly strategy showed that it was worth trading a little expected gain for a large reduction in risk by betting on several (neighboring) numbers, rather than a single number.

The croupier begins play by spinning the rotor. With our roulette computer, we then time one revolution of the rotor, after which our device knows where it is in the future, until the time comes when the croupier once again gives it a push. Our computer then sends out a repeating sequence of eight increasing pitched numerical tones, do, re, mi . . . Think of it as a piano scale: (middle) C, D, E . . . C (next octave) and repeat. We chose to time the ball when it had between three and four revolutions remaining. The closer to the end we made our measurements, the more accurate our predictions, and three revolutions to go still gave us enough time to place our bets. The computer's timing switch was hit when the orbiting ball first passed a reference mark on the wheel. When this happened, the tone sequence shifted and played faster. When the timing switch clocked the ball as it passed the reference mark again, after having made one revolution, the tones stopped. The last tone heard named the group of numbers on which to bet. If the person doing the timing misjudged the number of ball revolutions that were left, the tones did not stop and we placed no bets, except for camouflage. When the prediction was sent, it was simultaneous with the last input. The compute time was zero!

Claude and I were doing this work while I went to Nevada with Manny and Eddie to test my blackjack system, which gave me the opportunity to check roulette wheels and confirm that they behaved like our lab wheel. I saw that many were tilted, which we had already discovered could further improve prediction because it tended to limit the zones of the track from which the ball could fall. I reported to Claude that half-chip and even one-chip tilts were common. In our lab we had experimented by putting a coin half the thickness of a casino chip (a "half-chip tilt") under one of the three feet of the wheel and found that this amount of tilt gave us a nice boost in advantage.

Months of experiments with a wide range of designs led us to a final version of the system. We split our equipment into parts, requiring a team of two. One of us wore the computer, which had twelve transistors and was the size of a pack of cigarettes. Data was input with switches hidden in the wearer's shoes and operated by his big toes. The computer's forecast was transmitted by radio, using a modification of the inexpensive, widely available equipment ordinarily used to remotely control model airplanes. The other person, the bettor, would wear a radio receiver, which played the musical tones telling him on which group of numbers to bet. We two confederates would act like strangers.

The person placing the bets heard musical output through a tiny loudspeaker pushed into one ear canal and connected by very thin wires to the radio receiver, which was concealed under his clothing. So the wires wouldn't be noticed, we stuck them on with transparent spirit gum and painted them to match the wearer's skin and hair. The fragile copper wires, only the diameter of a hair, broke constantly. Claude suggested that we find ultrathin steel wires to replace the copper. After an hour of telephoning we located a supplier in Worcester, Massachusetts, that had what we needed.

We worked feverishly through April and May 1961 to complete the computer because I would be leaving MIT the following month for Los Angeles with Vivian and our not-quite-two-year-old daughter, Raun, and then on to New Mexico State University in the fall. As we hadn't quite finished when Vivian, Raun, and I left, a couple of weeks later I took a red-eye back from Los Angeles to Boston, showing up on the Shannons' country doorstep about 7 A.M. on a sunny summer morning. I lived there for three weeks while Claude and I worked furiously to finish the project. Finally, after more tuning and testing, we were ready. The wearable version of the computer was operational at the end of June 1961.

Returning to Los Angeles, I told Vivian that the roulette computer was ready, and Claude and I wanted to test it. Vivian and I met Betty and Claude in Las Vegas in August. After we settled in adjoining hotel rooms with our equipment, we headed out to locate suitable wheels. Our machine could beat all the wheels we saw, so we chose one for the next day where we liked the casino ambience. Then it was on to dinner and plans for the morrow.

The next morning we wired ourselves up. Claude wore the computer and the radio transmitter and would use his big toes to operate switches hidden in his shoes. I wore the radio receiver with the new steel wires going up my neck to the speaker in my right ear canal. As I stood ready to leave for the casino, Claude cocked his head and with an elfish smile asked, "What makes you tick?"

Claude was jokingly referring to the strange sounds (actually these were musical tones) he would be sending from the computer he was wearing to my ear canal, once we went into action at the roulette table. As I look back now from the future, seeing myself wired up with our equipment, I stop that moment in time and I think about a deeper meaning to the question of what makes me tick.

I was at a point then in life when I could choose between two very different futures. I could roam the world as a professional gambler winning millions per year. Switching between blackjack and roulette, I could spend some of the winnings as perfect camouflage by also betting on other games offering a small casino edge, like craps or baccarat.

My other choice was to continue my academic life. The path I would take was determined by my character, namely, *What makes me tick?* As the Greek philosopher Heraclitus said, "Character is destiny." I unfreeze time and watch us head for the roulette tables.

The four of us arrive in the casino, with Vivian and Betty Shannon strolling and chatting, while Claude and I are strangers to them and each other. Lacking my casino experience, the others are nervous but fortunately don't show it. Claude stands by the wheel and times the ball and rotor; as misdirection for what he is really doing, he writes down the winning number after each roll of the ball, looking like just another doomed-to-fail system player. Meanwhile, I take my seat at the far end of the layout, some distance from both Claude and the wheel.

Claude waits for the croupier to give the rotor a push to keep it spinning. As the green zero on the rotor goes by a reference point on the stator, which Claude has chosen to be one of the ball-deflecting vanes, his big toe hits one of the silent mercury switches hidden in his shoe. Contact. The soundless equivalent of a click! When the green 0 comes around again, click. The elapsed time is the duration of one rotation. After the second click, an eight-tone musical scale—do, re, mi, and so on—begins to play in my ear, repeating each time the rotor turns once. Now the computer knows not only how fast the rotor is turning but also where it is in relation to the stator. The rotor will gradually slow down even though it is suspended on a very low-friction jeweled bearing. The computer also corrects for that. Claude will have to retime the rotor every few minutes when the croupier gives it another push to offset its gradual loss of speed.

I get ready to bet. The croupier launches the ball. As it speeds around the track inside the top of the stator, Claude watches each time it passes the reference point. When he thinks it has more than three but less than four revolutions left, he clicks with the other big toe. The pace of the repeating musical scale speeds up. Finally, as the ball completes the next revolution, Claude's toe hits the switch again. *Click!* The musical tones stop. The last tone I hear tells me the group of numbers on which to bet. As it is only a test, I bet 10-cent chips. Within a few spins, the computer works its magic, turning a few dimes into a heap as yet another bet scores. I bet each time on a group of five numbers that are adjacent on the rotor. This is common in Europe, where the French call a group like this a *voisinage,* or "neighborhood."

We have divided the numbers on the wheel into eight such groups of

five, with 0 and 00 appearing twice, as our groups included forty numbers and the wheel has only thirty-eight. We've called these groups of
five "octants." The average player who bets $1 on each of five numbers
will win about five times in thirty-eight or just over one-eighth of the
time and lose all five bets otherwise, with an overall rate of loss that
turns out to be $2 for each $38 worth of bets, a 5.3 percent disadvantage.
However, using our computer, our bet on five numbers won a fifth of the
time, giving us a 44 percent edge.

But we had issues. Well into one winning session, a lady next to me
looked over in horror. Knowing I should leave, but not why, I raced to
the restroom and there in the mirror saw the speaker peeking out from
my ear canal like an alien insect. More seriously, though we frequently
turned small piles of dime chips into large ones, we had a problem that
prevented us on this trip from moving to large-scale betting. This had to
do with the wires to the ear speaker. Even though they were steel, they
were so fine that they broke frequently, leading to long interruptions
while we returned to our rooms and went through the tedious process of
doing the repairs and then rewiring me.

But when it was up and running, the computer was a success. We
knew we could solve the wire problem by using larger wires and growing hair to cover both our ears and the wire running up our neck. We
also considered persuading our reluctant wives to "wire up," concealing
everything under their fashionable longer hair.

While I was betting, no one watching had any idea that what Claude
and I were doing was in any way unusual, nor did they realize the connections among the four of us. Even so, I realized that if the casinos figured out what we were doing, they had an easy way to stop us. All they
had to do was say "No more bets" before the ball was spun, instead of
waiting as they customarily did until the ball had almost completed its
rotations around its track. To prevent them from catching on and doing
this, we would need to put on an act to divert attention from our winning. I already knew how much effort this would take, based on my
experience with blackjack. Neither I nor Vivian, Claude, and Betty
would want to go through the rehearsed theatrics, disguises, and misdirection needed, and with all the blackjack publicity I was becoming too

conspicuous to go unrecognized for long. It also wasn't the way any of the four of us wanted to spend what would inevitably involve a very large amount of our time. So, with some ambivalence, we put the project aside. I have always thought it was a good decision.

The MIT Media Lab lists our device as the first of what would later be called wearable computers, namely, computers that are worn on the body as part of their function. In late 1961 I built the second wearable computer, a knockoff to predict the wheel of fortune or money wheel. As in the roulette computer, my device used the toe-operated switch for input, the speaker for output, and just a single unijunction transistor; it required only one person. Matchbox-sized, it worked well in the casinos, but the game had too little action to conceal the spectacular consequences of my late bets. Several times when I placed bets on 40:1 as the wheel was spinning, the croupier would give the wheel an extra push.

Finally in 1966, I publicly announced our roulette system because it was clear by then that we weren't going to exploit it. I published the details later. When a mathematician from UC–Santa Cruz phoned me, I explained the method to him. UCSC was where the *Eudaemonic Pie* group of physicists would use the more advanced technology of the next decade to build their own roulette computer. Like us they found a 44 percent advantage and, like us, were frustrated by hardware problems. Later, groups using roulette computers reportedly won large amounts.

Shannon and I had also discussed building a wearable blackjack computer. Using the program I had used to analyze blackjack, such a computer could count the cards and play a perfect game, winning at up to double the rate of the best human card counters. This was an early instance, perhaps the first, of a computer that could outplay any human at a game. Later, computers went on to play perfect checkers and to beat the world's best at chess, Go, and Jeopardy. Subsequently, others built and marketed wearable blackjack computers. At the time, Nevada law, in particular the statutes on cheating, did not forbid their use. However, as hidden computers in blackjack and roulette increasingly cut into casino profits, the Nevada devices law was passed as an emergency measure on May 30, 1985. It banned use or possession of any device to predict outcomes, analyze probabilities of occurrence, analyze strategy for playing or betting, or keep track of cards played. The penalty: fines and imprisonment. This broadly drawn legislation even seems to outlaw the palm-sized strategy cards that are part of every copy of *Beat the Dealer*. When, in 2009, an entrepreneur wrote a popular iPhone application to count cards and recommend plays for blackjack, casinos reminded users that it was a crime to do so at the tables.

Claude and I corresponded at intervals for a few years, initially about roulette, until it became more and more clear that we didn't want to take it further. The last letter I remember writing was in late 1965 or early 1966, where I recalled our discussions about the stock market triggered by my seeing on his blackboard the figure $2^{11}$, which equals 2048, representing the amount \$1 becomes if it is doubled eleven successive times, an investing goal he was contemplating. I told him in my letter that I had found an extraordinary method for investing in a small niche in the stock market, which I thought could make 30 percent per year. Given time, I could surpass the $2^{11}$ figure. He never said what he thought of this hubris. And hubris it was, as the actual rate of profit would turn out to be closer to 20 percent.

We met for the last time in 1968, at a math meeting in San Francisco. His poignant last words to me were, "Let's get together again before we're both six feet under."

After Claude's death in 2001, Betty donated many of his papers and devices to the MIT museum, including the roulette computer. It was lent by the museum to the Heinz Nixdorf Computer Museum in Paderborn, Germany, for an exhibit in the spring of 2008 where thirty-five thousand people viewed it in the first eight weeks.

When Claude walked up to the Las Vegas roulette wheel in August 1961, he was using something no one but the four of us had ever seen before. This was the world's first wearable computer. To me, a wearable computer is just what the name indicates: a computer that is worn by a person in order to fulfill its intended function. Though our device had little impact on later developments, wearable computers, such as my Apple Watch, are everywhere today.

After blackjack and roulette, I wondered: Could other casino games be beaten?

## Chapter 10

# AN EDGE AT OTHER GAMBLING GAMES

In September 1961, a month after our test of the roulette computer in Las Vegas, Vivian, Raun, and I moved to Las Cruces, New Mexico, where I began my duties as a professor in the Mathematics Department at New Mexico State University. Then a town of thirty-seven thousand people, located in the high desert about four thousand feet above sea level, Las Cruces was established near a principal source of the state's water, the Rio Grande. Towns were widely spaced in the desert expanse, and the nearest population center was El Paso, Texas, about forty-five miles to the south. After the University of New Mexico in Albuquerque, some two hundred miles to the north, NMSU was the next most important campus in the state university system. When I arrived it was being transformed from an agricultural college to a university. Just to the east of the campus was "A" mountain, a large hill with an enormous white *A* for "Aggies." Some claimed that when the football team learned the first letter of the alphabet, it would be changed to *B*.

Our four years in New Mexico were memorable. Our younger daughter, Karen, was born there and our son, Jeff, was born in nearby El Paso. About twenty miles away was White Sands Proving Ground and National Monument, where we found some relief from summer heat, as the sun's rays were efficiently reflected away by the white gypsum "sand."

I followed up on my childhood interest in astronomy, enjoying New Mexico's dark skies through a small telescope. The astronomical highlight was a private lunch with Las Cruces resident and fellow NMSU professor Clyde Tombaugh (1906–97), who became world famous in 1930 when, at the Lowell Observatory in Flagstaff, Arizona, he discovered the planet Pluto (recently demoted to a "dwarf planet"). My student William E. "Bill" Walden, who worked at Los Alamos, arranged for me to spend an afternoon there with Stanislaw Ulam (1909–84), one of the twentieth century's greatest mathematicians. Ulam, part of the Manhattan Project that developed the atomic bomb, later supplied crucial ideas for the hydrogen bomb—the Ulam-Teller concept for thermonuclear weapons.

While teaching graduate courses and doing mathematical research at NMSU, I wondered whether what I had learned so far would enable me to beat other gambling games. One of the casino games I noticed on my Nevada blackjack trips was baccarat, which James Bond plays both in Ian Fleming's book *Casino Royale* and in the dramatic beginning of the original version of the movie of the same name. Long played in Europe for high and sometimes unlimited stakes, this Continental favorite had been introduced in a slightly modified form by a few Las Vegas casinos. With similarities to blackjack, baccarat was a natural target for my methods. Fortunately, Bill Walden, a computer scientist with an interest in applying mathematics, was happy to be recruited. We began our analysis of baccarat in 1962, with the goal of finding to what extent we might be successful using my card counting methods.

Nevada-style baccarat was dealt from eight decks, totaling 416 cards. These have the same values as in blackjack, except only the last digit counts. Thus Aces are 1, 2s through 9s are their numerical value, and 10s, Jacks, Queens, and Kings count as 0, not 10. The game begins after the cards are shuffled and a blank "cut card" is inserted into the pack of cards faceup near the end. The 416 cards are then put into a wooden dealing box known as a shoe. The first card is exposed, its value noted, and this number of cards is discarded, or "burned." If the exposed card is a 10 or a face card, then ten cards are burned.

A casino table had twelve seats, occupied by an assortment of customers and shills (house employees who bet money and may pretend to be players in order to attract customers). There are two main bets on the layout: Banker and Player.

After the players place their wagers, the croupier deals two cards each facedown to a betting spot on the table layout labeled BANKER and another spot called PLAYER. Then the croupier turns the hands faceup. As with individual cards, only the last digit of a total counts. For example, 9 + 9 = 18 counts as a total of 8. If the first two cards of a hand total 8 or 9, termed a natural 8 or a natural 9, as the case may be, all bets are settled without any further cards being dealt. If neither the Player spot nor the Banker spot receives a natural, each hand, starting with the Player's, either receives one more card from the croupier or stands according to a set of rules. The high hand wins. If there is a tie the bettors get their money back.

Our analysis of baccarat followed the same approach I had used for blackjack because of the similarities between the two games. To begin, we calculated, for the first time ever, the correct values for the house advantage in the Nevada version of baccarat for the two bets, Banker and Player. For the Banker, it was 1.058 percent of all bets placed; it was 1.169 percent if ties were not included. For the Player bet it was 1.235 percent, or 1.365 percent omitting ties. These figures assume that the player does not keep track of the cards that have been used. The casino edge is different for the two bets, Banker and Player, because the rules for drawing a third card differ and also because winning bets on Banker have to pay the casino 5 percent.

What if a player does count cards?

To find out, Bill Walden and I proved what we called the Fundamental Theorem of Card Counting, which says, in a precise mathematical way, that the advantage from card counting becomes better as more cards are seen. This means the best situations come toward the end. We found that even those were tiny and rare.

The reason baccarat does not have enough opportunities is because the impact of removing one card from the pack in baccarat is about one-ninth what it is in blackjack, so the effect on the house edge is correspondingly smaller. Also, the house edge to be overcome is greater, being more than 1 percent.

However, in addition to the main bets of Banker and Player, the baccarat layout had four separate side bets: Banker natural 9, Player natural 9, Banker natural 8, and Player natural 8. Banker natural 9 won if the first two Banker cards totaled 9, in which case the bet paid 9:1, meaning that a winning $1 bet was paid a $9 profit. The other three side bets had the same payoff.

For the non-counter these bets were terrible, with a house edge of 5.10 percent for each of the two bets on natural 9 and 5.47 percent for natural 8. But we discovered that although a card counter couldn't beat the Banker and Player bets, he could beat these side bets! As I predicted by reasoning and we verified by computation, the edge on the side bets varied widely as cards were used. About one-third of the way through the shoe, good opportunities appeared, and things got better as more cards were played.

We devised a practical card counting system, which used the fact that when the remaining cards had a big excess of 9s, the natural 9 bet favored the Player. An 8-rich deck did the same for bets on Player natural 8.

For a casino test, I recruited the chairman of the Mathematics Department, Ralph Crouch. We practiced counting down the eight-deck pack. This required a running tally of the number of unseen cards, as well as the number of 8s and 9s among them. Counting was harder than in blackjack because eight decks have 416 cards, including thirty-two 9s and thirty-two 8s, and we would track all three quantities.

Ralph was unlike any other math department chairman I have ever encountered. Of middle height, florid-faced, bubbly, and chatty, he was an extreme extrovert. This set him apart from the typical introverted mathematician. A well-known joke is, "How do you tell whether a mathematician is an introvert or an extrovert?" Answer: "If he looks at his shoes when he talks to you, he's an introvert. If he looks at your shoes, he's an extrovert." The life of the party, Ralph promoted departmental get-togethers fueled by "Las Cruces Punch," a concoction made in a huge bowl with two or more gallons of Bacardi rum along with frozen orange juice, pineapple juice, and lemonade. Vivian and I evaded as many of these parties as we could and made brief polite appearances when we did go. Years later, when my daughters came across the recipe and the proportions—mostly rum—they wondered how anyone remained vertical.

I am often asked what it takes to be a successful card counter. I've found that an academic understanding is not enough. You need to think quickly, be disciplined enough to follow the system, and have a suitable temperament, including the ability to switch your mind into the here and now and stay focused on the cards, the people, and your surroundings. Better still is to have an "act" or persona that makes you seem like a type of player with which casinos are familiar.

I thought Ralph would be perfect, along with his male golfing buddy Kay Hafen, the controller of the university, for my proposed baccarat team. Kay was low-key, levelheaded, and unflappable. In the practice sessions I held with them, both learned to count well. Our wives came, too, and Vivian, who hadn't been on the various blackjack trips, was relieved to be able to monitor my safety firsthand. When we weren't playing, the six of us planned to enjoy ourselves around town.

We drove to Las Vegas during the university's 1963 spring break. We arrived at the Dunes shortly before their baccarat game started at 9 P.M., and acted as though we didn't know one another. Velvet ropes separated the baccarat alcove from the rest of the casino floor. The imposing raised table had six chairs at each horseshoe-shaped end. Several female shills were already seated when I sat down. Despite my publicity from blackjack, I went unnoticed by the casino people. At least at first.

As play began, a crowd gathered outside the velvet rope to watch what could become a high-stakes game. Betting limits were $5 to $2,000 on the main bets and $5 to $100 on the side bets, equivalent to about ten times as much in 2016.

Then someone cried out, "There's the guy who wrote the book." The baccarat supervisor's eyes popped open and he ran to a nearby phone. One of the wives, eavesdropping on the call upstairs, saw the man's concern change to reassurance and then amusement. Beating blackjack is one thing; baccarat is another. Our spy heard, "Ha, ha. Let him play!" And so play we did.

Our first night was pleasant. With the newly shuffled pack of 416 cards, all bets favored the house, so I started with the smallest allowed bets on Banker, $5, while I tracked the number of 8s, 9s, and total cards that remained, and waited for favorable situations. I set the size of our big bets to give a win rate of $100 per hour, hoping that would be low enough to keep us from being barred.

It took about forty-five minutes to play through a shoe. After playing two of them, I rested while Ralph and Kay played the next one. They split the work, with Ralph monitoring the natural 8 bets, while Kay counted and bet for the natural 9s. This was easier because they each had only two separate card totals to keep track of, rather than three. After one shoe they rested and I played two more sessions. We continued this pattern. When the game shut down at the usual time of 3 A.M., we were ahead five or six hundred dollars, about what we expected.

The next night, as I sat down for the start of the game, the atmosphere had changed. The casino crew was distant and unfriendly—and the shills did something strange. On the previous night the game began with me, another player or two, and half a dozen female shills spread among the twelve seats. Soon other players were attracted to this falsely busy scene and joined the action. When all seats were filled, one shill popped up, leaving just a single seat vacant for the maximum power to draw bettors: *Just one seat left—grab it while you can.* As soon as a new player was drawn to that seat, yet another shill popped out of hers. This dance of shill-in, shill-out, leaving exactly one seat empty, had continued through the evening. But on this, our second night, the shills on each side of me remained parked, watching closely. At the time I had a bronchial tickle that triggered frequent strident coughs. Our undercover wives were amused when the shills assigned to me became concerned for their health, rebelled, and had to be ordered to stay at their posts.

As we continued to win, other players starred in their own human dramas. Vivian noted a bleached-blond Asian lady with long magenta fingernails. Heavily made up and bejeweled, she was betting the $2,000 limit on each hand and losing. She owned a chain of supermarkets and in a couple of hours she lost one of them. Baccarat is a game favored by big bettors. By 1995 baccarat in Nevada accounted for half as much casino profit as did blackjack, yet with only one-fiftieth as many tables. A baccarat table was twenty-five times as profitable as a blackjack table.

The game shut down again about 3 A.M. on this second night. After we counted our winnings, Ralph and Kay returned to the bar for a drink. The pit boss and a couple of men from the casino were there with the baccarat shoe and the eight decks of cards. They were muttering and examining the cards one by one, looking for bends, crimps, markings, and any other clues as to how we were winning.

The third night began with obvious hostility toward me by all the employees in the pit. They conspicuously watched my every move. To mislead them, I frequently touched my thumb behind my ear, as though I were a cheat marking the cards with "daub," a nearly invisible Vaseline-like substance easily seen through special glasses. I hoped they would waste another night examining every card, looking for what wasn't there. On the first two evenings they had repeatedly offered me drinks, but I had chosen coffee with cream and sugar instead. Tonight it was war and they didn't offer me anything. We won again.

When I sat down to play on the fourth night, the atmosphere had again changed, drastically. The pit boss and his minions were smiling and relaxed. They seemed pleased to see me. Then they volunteered "coffee with cream and sugar, just the way you like it." I was deep into the first shoe happily winning and drinking my coffee when suddenly I couldn't think. I could no longer keep the count. I was shocked because I had managed well enough through noise, smoke, conversation, the pressure of high-speed play, the excitement of losing or winning, and the impact of alcoholic beverages. Something unexpected had taken place. I took my chips and left, replaced on the next shoe by Ralph and Kay.

The wives saw that my pupils were hugely dilated. Bellamia Hafen, who was a nurse, said that she had seen this often when people who had used drugs were admitted to her hospital. I wanted to collapse into sleep but Vivian, Isobel Crouch, and Bellamia plied me with black coffee and walked me for several hours until the effects began to wear off. Ralph and Kay played through the evening until night four ended. We won again.

After considerable discussion among us, I took my seat for the start of the game on night five. No longer smiling, the boys again offered me coffee with cream and sugar. I said, "No thanks. Just bring me a glass of water." The rest of my group groaned silently. It took a suspiciously long time and when the water came I expected it to have something extra. To find out, I carefully put only a single drop on my tongue. Ugh! It tasted as if a box of baking soda had been emptied into the glass. But that single drop was enough to flatten me again. I wondered what a swallow would have done.

With numb brain and dilated pupils I left and repeated the black-coffee-and-walking routine. Meanwhile Ralph and Kay were asked to leave, permanently, and the same went for all of their friends.

There was one more baccarat game with the side bets and it was at the Sands casino. After a day of R&R, I went there with our bankroll and took a seat at the table. I revised our target from $100 an hour to $1,000, figuring that the Dunes would have contacted the Sands so I would soon be barred. After two and a half hours I was ahead $2,500. Then Carl Cohen, part owner of the Sands and the person in charge, paid me a table-side visit. Carl had previously disciplined Frank Sinatra for making a commotion in the casino. When Sinatra persisted, Cohen saw to it that he didn't return, even though Sinatra was a minor part owner. It was Cohen who now told me not to play at his casino anymore. I asked why and he said, "No reason. We just don't want you to play here." He was accompanied by the largest security guard I had yet seen. Discussion was pointless. I left.

During our six nights of play, we had proven the system at the tables. We validated the theoretical mathematical calculations and demonstrated yet another application of the Kelly system for betting and investing. But our trip would have an unnerving postscript.

The six of us left Las Vegas the next morning to drive back to Las Cruces. I was at the wheel as we went down a mountain road in northern Arizona. We were going sixty-five miles an hour when the accelerator pedal suddenly jammed. The steep downhill and the wide-open throttle were too much for the brakes. The car sped up to eighty miles an hour and the turns in the road became unmanageable.

With little time to think and my foot pressing as hard as I could on the brakes, I also set the emergency brake, downshifted so the engine would help slow the car, and cut off power by turning off the ignition. I finally managed to stop in a turnout. A Good Samaritan who understood cars pulled over to help us. Opening the hood to see why the accelerator jammed, he found a part that had come unscrewed from a long, threaded rod, something he had never before seen happen and found baffling. He fixed it and we continued on our way, alive, relieved, and sobered.

We had proven the system worked at the tables like it did in theory. As a result, both the Dunes and the Sands removed the natural 8 and natural 9 bets.

While at New Mexico State, I invested money from book royalties and gambling winnings in stocks. But I was ignorant of the market as well as unlucky. The results were poor. I wanted to do better. Investments presented a new type of uncertainty, but the theory of probability might help me make good choices.

Things came together when I realized that there was a far greater casino than all of Nevada. Could my methods for beating games of chance give me an edge in the greatest gambling arena on earth, Wall Street? Ever curious, I decided to find out. I began to teach myself about the financial markets, lighting my way with an unusual lamp, the knowledge I had gained from gambling games.

*Chapter 11*

---

# WALL STREET: THE GREATEST CASINO ON EARTH

ambling is investing simplified. The striking similarities between the two suggested to me that, just as some gambling games could be beaten, it might also be possible to do better than the market averages. Both can be analyzed using mathematics, statistics, and computers. Each requires money management, choosing the proper balance between risk and return. Betting too much, even though each individual bet is in your favor, can be ruinous. When the Nobel Prize winners running the giant hedge fund Long-Term Capital Management made this mistake, its collapse in 1998 almost destabilized the US financial system. On the other hand, playing safe and betting too little means you leave money on the table. The psychological makeup to succeed at investing also has similarities to that for gambling. Great investors are often good at both.

Relishing the intellectual challenge and the fun of exploring the markets, I spent the summer of 1964 educating myself about them. I haunted the big Martindale's bookstore then in Beverly Hills. I read stock market classics like Graham and Dodd's *Security Analysis,* Edwards and Magee's work on technical analysis, and scores of other books and periodicals ranging from fundamental to technical, theoretical to practical, and simple to abstruse. Much of what I read was dross but, like a baleen whale filtering the tiny nutritious krill from huge volumes of seawater, I came away with a foundation of knowledge. Once again, just as with casino games, I was surprised and encouraged by how little was known by so many. And just as in blackjack, my first investment was a loss that contributed to my education.

A couple of years earlier, when I knew nothing at all about investing, I heard about a company whose stock was allegedly selling at a bargain price. It was Electric Autolite, and among their products were automobile batteries for Ford Motor Company. The story on the business page of my newspaper said we could expect a great future: technological innovations, big new contracts, and a jump in sales. (The same forecasts for battery makers were being made forty years later.)

As I finally had some capital from playing blackjack and from book sales, I decided to let it grow through investing while I focused on family and my academic career. I bought one hundred shares at $40 and watched the stock decline over the next two years to $20 a share, losing half of my $4,000 investment. I had no idea when to sell. I decided to hang on until the stock returned to my original purchase price, so as not to take a loss. This is exactly what gamblers do when they are losing and insist on playing until they get even. It took four years, but I finally got out with my original $4,000. Fifty years later, legions of tech stock investors shared my experience, waiting fifteen years to get even after buying near the top on March 10, 2000.

Years later, discussing my Electric Autolite purchase with Vivian as we drove home from lunch, I asked, "What were my mistakes?"

She almost read my mind as she said, "First, you bought something you didn't really understand, so it was no better or worse than throwing a dart into the stock market list. Had you bought a low-load mutual fund [no-load funds weren't available yet] you would have had the same expected gain but less expected risk." I thought the story about Electric Autolite meant it was a superior investment. That thinking was wrong.

As I would learn, most stock-picking stories, advice, and recommendations are completely worthless.

Then Vivian remarked on my second mistake in thinking, my plan for getting out, which was to wait until I was even again. What I had done was focus on a price that was of unique historical significance to me, only me, namely, my purchase price. Behavioral finance theorists, who have in recent decades begun to analyze the psychological errors in thinking that persistently bedevil most investors, call this anchoring (of yourself to a price that has meaning to you but not to the market). Since I really had no predictive power, any exit strategy was as good or bad as any other. Like my first mistake, this error was in the way I thought about the problem of when to sell, choosing an irrelevant criterion—the price I paid—rather than focusing on economic fundamentals like whether cash or alternative investments would serve better.

Anchoring is a subtle and pervasive aberration in investment thinking. For instance, a former neighbor, Mr. Davis (as I shall call him), saw the market value of his house rise from his purchase price of $2,000,000 or so in the mid-1980s to $3,500,000 or so when luxury home prices peaked in 1988–89. Soon afterward, he decided he wanted to sell and anchored himself to the price of $3,500,000. During the next ten years, as the market price of his house fell back to $2,200,000 or so, he kept trying to sell at his now laughable anchor price. At last, in 2000, with a resurgent stock market and a dot-com-driven price rise in expensive homes, he escaped at $3,250,000. In his case, as often happens, the thinking error of anchoring, despite the eventual sale price he achieved, left him with substantially less money than if he had acted otherwise.

Mr. Davis and I used to jog together occasionally and chat about his favorite topics, money and investments. Following my recommendation, he joined a limited partnership that itself allocated money to limited partnerships, so-called hedge funds, which it believed were likely to make superior investments. His expected rate of return after paying his income taxes on the gains was about 10 percent per year, with considerably more stability in the value of the investment than was to be found in residential real estate or the stock market. I advised him to sell his house at current market just after the 1988–89 peak. He would have received perhaps $3,300,000 and then, as was his plan, moved to a $1,000,000 house. After costs and taxes he would have ended up with an additional $1,600,000 to invest. Putting this into the hedge fund he had already joined at my recommendation, the money would have grown at 10 percent per year for eleven years, becoming $4,565,000. Add that to the $1,000,000 house, whose market price would have declined, then recovered, and Mr. Davis would have had $5,565,000 in 2000 instead of the $3,250,000 he ended up with.

I've seen my own anchoring mistake repeatedly made by real estate buyers and sellers, as well as in everyday situations. As I was driving home one day in heavy traffic, an SUV forced its way in front of me, giving me a choice of yielding or "maintaining my rights" and having a fender bender. Since I receive these invitations daily, I saw no need to accept this one for fear I would miss out. The SUV was in "my" space (anchoring: I've attached myself to an abstract moving location that has a unique historical meaning to me, and am allowing it to dictate my driving behavior). We were now lined up about seventy cars deep in the most notoriously slow left-turn lane in Newport Beach. Ordinarily the road is two lanes wide, but construction had narrowed it to one, and the complex sequence of light changes allowed only about twenty cars through on each two-minute cycle. What if, when we finally got to the signal, the evil SUV was the last one through the yellow? Since it was really "my" space, was I justified in risking an accident by rolling through on the red? Otherwise, the time thief gains two minutes at my expense. The temptation may sound as foolish to you as it does in cold print to me, but I see this kind of behavior regularly.

Having learned the folly of anchoring from my investment experience, I have seen that it can be equally foolish on the road. Being a more rational investor has made me a more rational driver!

Two "expert" longtime insurance investors from Dallas drew me into my next adventure in the market. They claimed to have become rich investing in life insurance companies. According to their figures the A. M. Best AAA index of the average price of such companies had gone up in each of the last twenty-four years, and they had plausible arguments that this would continue. Sure enough, the amazing winning streak they had identified ended just after my purchase, and we all lost money.

Lesson: Do not assume that what investors call momentum, a long streak of either rising or falling prices, will continue unless you can make a sound case that it will.

Thinking about momentum led me to wonder whether past prices could somehow be used to predict future prices. To test this, I looked at charting, the art of using patterns in the graphs of stock (or commodity) prices to forecast their future changes. I was introduced to this by Norman, a Canadian resident living in Las Cruces, while I was teaching at New Mexico State University. After months of examining his data and predictions, I was unable to find anything of value. As Vivian said at the start, "This is going to be a waste of time. Norman's been doing this for years and you can tell he's barely getting by. Just look at his worn-out shoes and shabby clothes. And you can tell from the quality of his wife's old and dated outfits that they were once better off."

I still owed more tuition to Mr. Market for his introductory course in investment mistakes. Mr. Market is an allegorical character famously introduced by Benjamin Graham to illustrate the excessive market price swings above and below the actual underlying business values of quoted securities. Some days he's manic and prices are high. Other days he's gloomy and shares can be bought well below what Graham called their "intrinsic value." In the early 1960s the demand for silver was exceeding supply and I expected prices to spurt sharply. The value of the silver extracted from melting everyday coins was eventually expected to exceed the face value by enough to pay costs and give a profit. Bill Rickenbacker, who backed my blackjack trip with Mickey MacDougall and Russell Barnhart, had by then purchased US silver dollars and stored them in a vault while he waited for this to happen.

The further price rise of silver would slow somewhat as a new supply came from melting coins. Also some five billion ounces of silver could potentially be extracted from the vast pool of jewelry in India. Once demand absorbed these new supplies, prices would jump even more. When the price of silver actually did pass $1.29 per ounce, those US coins that contained 90 percent silver were worth more as metal than as legal tender. Coins were skimmed from circulation and melted to extract their silver. After the US government banned this, the coins were hoarded and bought and sold in sixty-pound bags via dealers.

Believing this economic supply and demand analysis was correct, I opened a Swiss bank account to buy silver, with the help and encouragement of local promoters who got a commission for making the arrangements. They recommended doing this on 33⅓ percent collateral. That means that for each dollar's worth of silver I bought, I had to deposit only 33⅓ cents in my account. The promoters arranged for my friendly Swiss bank to loan me the rest. Of course, when I borrowed to buy three times as much silver as I could have with cash alone, they got triple the commissions, and the bank was happy to collect interest on the loan and charge me monthly storage fees.

Silver rose as predicted and the promoters recommended using the profits together with more bank loans to buy yet more silver. When the commodity reached $2.40 an ounce my account had a lot more of the metal than when I started, and I had a large profit on all of my purchases. However, as I had reinvested my profits on the way up, $1.60 of that $2.40 an ounce was owed on my loan from the bank. It was like buying a house with one-third down. Then the price of silver dropped. When this happened some people sold to capture their profit. This drove down the price still further until others, who had borrowed to an even greater extent than I had, were sold out by their lenders as their accounts threatened to go underwater—meaning there wouldn't be enough left to pay off the loan. These sales pushed the price down even more, forcing more sales by the remaining borrowers, causing silver to drop rapidly to a little below $1.60, just enough to wipe me out, after which it resumed its upward path. I learned from this that even though I was right in my economic analysis I hadn't properly evaluated the risk of too much leverage. For a few thousand dollars I learned from this to make proper risk management a major theme of my life for more than fifty years thereafter. In 2008 almost the entire world financial establishment didn't understand this lesson and had overleveraged itself.

I also learned from my losing silver investment that when the interests of the salesmen and promoters differ from those of the client, the client had better look out for himself. This is the well-known agency problem in economics, where the interest of the agents or managers don't coincide with those of the principals, or owners. Shareholders of companies that have been pillaged by self-serving CEOs and boards of directors are painfully familiar with this.

After these lessons from Mr. Market, I was tempted to believe that the academics were right in claiming that any edge in the markets is limited, small, temporary, and quickly captured by the smartest or best-informed investors. Once again, I was invited to accept the consensus opinion at face value, and once again I decided to see for myself.

In June 1965, I began a second summer of self-education in economics, finance, and the markets. The thin pamphlet on common stock purchase warrants that I'd ordered had just come in the mail. I settled into a lawn chair, curious to find out how these securities worked. It was a revelation.

The pamphlet explained that a common stock purchase warrant is a security issued by a company that gives the owner the right to buy stock at a specified price, known as the exercise price, on or before a stated expiration date. For instance, in 1964 a Sperry Rand warrant entitled the holder to purchase one share of common stock for $28 until September 15, 1967. On this final day, if the stock trades above that price, you can use one warrant plus $28 to buy one share of stock. This means the warrant is worth the amount by which the stock price exceeds $28. However, if the stock price is below $28, it is cheaper to buy the stock outright, in which case the warrant is worthless.

A warrant, like a lottery ticket, was always worth something before it expired even if the stock price was very low, if there was any chance the stock price could move above the exercise price and put the warrant "into the money." The more time left, and the higher the stock price, the more the warrant was likely to be worth. The prices of these two securities followed a simple relationship regardless of the complexities of the balance sheet or business affairs of the underlying company. As I thought about this I formed a rough idea of the rules relating the warrant price to the stock price. Since the prices of the two securities tended to move together, the important idea of "hedging" occurred to me, in which I could use this relationship to exploit any mispricing of the warrant and simultaneously reduce the risk of doing so.

To form a hedge, take two securities whose prices tend to move together, such as a warrant and the common stock it can be used to purchase, but which are comparatively mispriced. Buy the relatively underpriced security and sell short the relatively overpriced security. If the proportions in the position are chosen well, then even though prices fluctuate, the gains and losses on the two sides will approximately offset or hedge each other. If the relative mispricing between the two securities disappears as expected, close the position in both and collect a profit.

A few days after I had the idea of hedging warrants versus common stock, we packed up our possessions and moved from New Mexico State University to Southern California, where I became a founding faculty member of the Mathematics Department of the new Irvine campus of the University of California (UCI). During our four years in Las Cruces, I had learned much more mathematics, directed the PhD dissertations of talented students, and published my research as a series of professional articles in mathematics journals. But we wanted to live in Southern California where our children would see their grandparents and our own siblings and their families, and we would be near old friends. I also liked the fact that UCI purposely was starting out emphasizing collaboration between faculty and students from different subject areas.

On my first day in my new teaching position at UCI, in September 1965, Julian Feldman, the head of the school of information and computer sciences, asked me what I was working on. When I described my ideas about a theory of warrant valuation and hedging, he said that another member of the new faculty, an economist named Sheen Kassouf (1928–2005), had written his PhD thesis on the subject. Feldman introduced us and I learned that Kassouf had discovered the same concepts in 1962 and had already been shorting overpriced warrants and hedging them, doubling his initial $100,000 in just three years.

I realized that if we worked together we could develop both the theory and the techniques for hedged investment more rapidly than by working alone. At the weekly meetings I proposed, we roughly determined the fair price for a warrant, finding quite a few that were substantially overpriced. The way to profit was to sell them short. To sell a security short you borrow the desired quantity through your broker from someone who owns it, sell it in the marketplace, and collect the proceeds. Later you have to repurchase it at whatever price then prevails to meet your contractual obligation to return what you borrowed. If your buy-back price is below your earlier sale price, you win. If it is higher, you lose.

Short selling overpriced warrants was profitable on average but risky. The same was true for buying stocks. The two risks largely canceled each other when we hedged the warrants by purchasing the associated common stock. In a historical simulation our optimized method made 25 percent a year with low risk, even during the great 1929 stock market crash and its aftermath. As we worked on theory, Kassouf and I were investing for ourselves in warrant hedges, which also made 25 percent per year.

We explained our methods for investing and presented the actual results from our hedges in *Beat the Market,* finished in late 1966 and published by Random House in 1967. There we extended our approach to include the much larger area of convertible bonds. Just as in blackjack, I was willing to share our discoveries with the public for several reasons. Among them was the awareness that sooner or later, others would make the same discoveries, that scientific research ought to be a public good, and that I would continue to have more ideas.

Having somewhat different ideas about how to set up our hedged investments, Kassouf and I ended our collaboration after we finished *Beat the Market.* As an economist, Sheen felt that he understood the companies well enough to deviate from a neutral hedge. A neutral hedge gives balanced protection against loss whether the market moves up or down. Sheen, however, was willing to modify the long and short pro-portions in the hedge to favor either a rise in the price of the underlying stock or a fall, depending on his analysis. Given my bad experiences in picking stocks and my lack of background in analyzing companies, I wanted to do hedges that were as protected as possible against changes in the stock price, no matter in which direction. I continued to work on the theory and to invest on my own.

A major theoretical breakthrough came to me in 1967. I used Oc-cam's razor—the principle that given more than one explanation, you should begin by choosing the simplest one—and plausible reasoning to arrive at a neat formula for determining the "correct" price of a warrant. Armed with this I could tell when they were mispriced and by roughly how much. That same year I began using the formula to trade and hedge over-the-counter warrants and options and, a little later, convertible bonds. An option to buy a stock is similar to a warrant, the principal difference being that warrants are typically issued by the company itself and options are not. Convertible bonds are like ordinary bonds but with the additional feature that they can be exchanged for a fixed number of shares of the issuing company's stock if the holder so desires.

Having the formula further increased my confidence and returns. This, along with the fact that the available investment opportunities were much larger than I could exploit with my modest capital, led to the next step. I began to manage hedged portfolios for friends and acquain-tances.

*Chapter 12*

# BRIDGE WITH BUFFETT

A s my reputation as an investor quietly spread around UC, Irvine, friends and members of the university community asked me to manage money for them. Using the warrant hedging techniques in *Beat the Market,* I took on several accounts with a minimum investment of $25,000. Among my new clients was Ralph Waldo Gerard, dean of the graduate school at UCI, and his wife, Frosty, so-called because of her crown of white hair. Ralph, a distinguished medical researcher and biologist, was a member of the select National Academy of Sciences. Courtly, curious, and widely informed, he enjoyed discussing big ideas with me, as he had with one of his relatives, the great stock market theorist and philosopher Benjamin Graham. Graham and Dodd's *Security Analysis,* first published in 1934, was the landmark book for the fundamental analysis of common stocks, revised and updated several times. Through Graham, Gerard had met Warren Buffett and was an early investor in one of his investment vehicles, Buffett Partnership, Ltd.

Warren, who would become Graham's greatest student and arguably the most successful investor of all time, started his first investment partnership, Buffett Associates, Ltd., in 1956 at the age of twenty-five with $100,100. He told me with a laugh that the $100 was his contribution. After starting ten more partnerships he merged them all into Buffett Partnership, Ltd., early in 1962. During the twelve years from 1956 to 1968, these funds Buffett managed compounded at a rate of 29.5 percent, before he took his fee of one-fourth of the gain in excess of 6 percent. He had no down years, whereas large company stocks and small company stocks each fell in four of those years. After Buffett's fee, Gerard's investment was growing at 24 percent a year, surpassing the typical stock market investor's experience, as measured by small-company stocks, which compounded at 19 percent per year, and large-company stocks, which returned 10 percent. Before taxes, $1 for Buffett's limited partners grew to $16.29. Each of Warren's own dollars, growing without the deduction of his fees, became $28.80.

So why were the Gerards interested in moving their money from the thirty-eight-year-old Buffett, who had been investing since he was a child and with whom they were netting 24 percent a year, to the thirty-six-year-old Thorp, who had been investing for only a few years and from whom they could expect, on the basis of past performance, to net just 20 percent a year? It was because, after the upward spike in stock prices in 1967, when holders of large-company stocks gained 38 percent on average over the two-year period and small-company stocks were up a manic 150 percent, Warren Buffett said it was too tough to find undervalued companies. Over the next couple of years he would be liquidating his partnership. His investors could cash out or, along with Warren himself, take some or all of their equity as shares in two companies owned by the partnership, one of which was a troubled little textile company called Berkshire Hathaway. Buffett himself now owned $25 million of the $100 million partnership, as a result of his management fees and their growth through reinvestment in the partnership.

The Gerards chose to take their distribution entirely in cash and were looking for a new home for it. Ralph liked the analytic approach in *Beat the Market* and my other writings, and he wanted not only to check me out himself but, as I realized later, to get a reading from the great investor with whom he had done so well. Thus it happened that in the summer of 1968 the Gerards invited Vivian and me to their home for dinner with Susie and Warren Buffett.

From their home in the Harbor View Hills section of Newport Beach, the Gerards enjoyed looking at Newport Harbor, the Pacific Ocean, and the spectacular evanescent sunsets behind Catalina Island to the west. After we sat down for dinner, Ralph's wife, Frosty, asked each person at the table to introduce themselves. Susie Buffett told us about her ambitions to be a nightclub singer and how Warren was encouraging her. She also discussed her activities in organizations that helped people, such as Fair Housing, and the National Conference of Christians and Jews.

Warren was a high-speed talker with a Nebraska twang and a stream of jokes, anecdotes, and clever sayings. He loved to play bridge and had a natural liking for the logical, the quantitative, and the mathematical. As the evening went on, I learned that he focused on finding and buying into undervalued companies. Over a period of several years, he expected each of these investments to substantially outperform the market, as represented by an index such as the Dow Jones Industrial Average (DJIA) or the Standard & Poor's 500 (S&P 500). As his mentor Ben Graham did before him, Warren also invested in warrant and convertible hedging and merger arbitrage. It was in this area that his and my interest overlapped, and where Buffett, unknown to me, was vetting me as a possible successor to manage investments for the Gerards.

As we chatted about compound interest, Warren gave one of his favorite examples of its remarkable power, how if the Manhattan Indians could have invested $24, the value then of the trinkets Peter Minuit paid them for Manhattan in 1626, at a net return of 8 percent, they could buy the land back now along with all the improvements. Warren said he was asked how he found so many millionaires for his partnership. Laughing, he said to me, "I told them I grew my own."

Then Warren asked me if I knew about three oddly numbered dice. He had recently heard about them and, in the years to come, would enjoy using them to baffle one smart person after another. Like standard dice, each face has a number between one and six, but unlike normal dice some numbers can be the same. In fact, for the dice Warren asked me about, each die has no more than two or three different numbers.

These dice are used to play a gambling game: You pick the "best" of the three dice, then from the remaining two I pick the "second best." We both roll and the high number wins. I can beat you, on average, even though you chose the better die. The surprise for nearly everyone is that there is no "best" die. Call the dice A, B, and C. If A beats B, and B beats C, it seems plausible that since A was better than B and B was better than C, A ought to be much better than C. Instead C beats A.

This puzzles people, because they expect things to follow what mathematicians call the transitive rule: If A is better than B and B is better than C, then A is better than C. For example, if you replace the phrase *better than* by any of the phrases *longer than, heavier than, older than, more than,* or *larger than,* the rule is true. However, some relationships don't follow this rule. For instance, *is an acquaintance of* and *is visible to* do not. And, if we replace *better than* by *beats on average,* these dice don't follow the transitive rule. So they're called nontransitive dice. The childhood game of Rock, Paper, Scissors is a simple example of a nontransitive rule. Rock beats (breaks) Scissors, Scissors beats (cuts) Paper, and Paper beats (covers) Rock.

Another nontransitive example with great practical impact is voting preferences. Often a majority of voters prefer candidate A over candidate B, candidate B over candidate C, and candidate C over candidate A. In these elections, where voting preference is nontransitive, who gets elected? It depends on the structure of the election process. Mathematical economist Kenneth Arrow received the Nobel Prize in Economics for showing that no voting procedure exists that satisfies an entire list of intuitively natural desirable properties. A *Discover* magazine article on this subject argued that, with a more "reasonable" election procedure, based on voter comparisons of all the major Democratic and Republican candidates, in 2000 John McCain would have received the Republican nomination and then been elected president instead of George W. Bush.

Back in Newport Beach, the die was being cast. I passed Warren's test when I told him if the dice are numbered as A = (3, 3, 3, 3, 3, 3), B = (6, 5, 2, 2, 2, 2) and C = (4, 4, 4, 4, 1, 1) then calculations show that, on average, A beats B two-thirds of the time, B beats C five-ninths of the time, and C beats A two-thirds of the time. Other sets of nontransitive dice are

possible as well. I have entertained people by marking a set of three dice
like this and letting my opponent pick his die first. After trying all three
dice in turn and losing each time, people are typically stumped.

Warren invited the Gerards and me to join him another time for an
afternoon of bridge at his house in Emerald Bay. This upscale gated
community of the very rich at the north end of Laguna Beach, California, had its own magnificent private beach and ocean views. As Warren
and I talked, the similarities and differences in our approaches to investing became clearer to me. He evaluated businesses with the aim of buying shares in them, or even the entire company, so cheaply that he had an
ample "margin of safety" to allow for the unknown and the unantici-
pated. In his view, such opportunities arose from time to time when investors became excessively pessimistic about an individual company or
about stocks in general: "Be fearful when others are greedy and greedy
when others are fearful." His objective was to outperform the market in
the long run and so he judged himself largely on his performance relative to the market.

In contrast, I didn't judge the worth of various businesses. Instead I
compared different securities of the same company with the object of
finding relative mispricing, from which I could construct a hedged position, long the relatively undervalued, short the relatively overvalued,
from which I could extract a positive return despite stock market ups
and downs. Warren didn't mind substantial variations in market prices
over months or even a few years because he believed that in the long run
the market would be up strongly and by regularly beating it during its
fluctuations his wealth would grow over time much faster than the overall market. His goal was to accumulate the most money. I enjoyed using
mathematics to solve certain interesting puzzles, which I found first in
the world of gambling, then in the world of investing. Making money
confirmed my theories by showing that they worked in the real world.
Warren began to invest while still a child and spent his life doing it remarkably well. My discoveries fit in with my life path as a mathematician and seemed much easier, leaving me largely free to enjoy my family
and pursue my career in the academic world.

Warren's house in Emerald Bay became newsworthy later on during

Arnold ("The Terminator") Schwarzenegger's successful 2003 campaign to become governor of California. Initially, Buffett was a supporter and an economic adviser to Arnold. One campaign issue was how to cut California's budget deficit. The problem was caused largely by the anti-tax measure Proposition 13, adopted by California voters in 1978. This limited the tax on real estate to 1 percent of the assessed valuation with a cap of 2 percent per year on any revaluation upward. With California's soaring prices, the tax on houses that weren't traded fell over time to a small fraction of 1 percent of their current value, thus sharply eroding the tax base and expanding the budget deficit. A house was reassessed at the current market price only when it was resold. As a result, taxes on comparable houses varied greatly, depending on when they last changed ownership. This led to major inequities in the taxes paid by different homeowners. In addition, by drastically lowering the overall effective tax rate on residences, Proposition 13 reduced the annual expense of homeownership, which in turn fueled the excessive rise in California home prices.

Businesses did even better than homeowners. They created companies to hold properties. Instead of selling a particular property, they sold the company that owned it. By keeping the same "owner," this scheme could preserve forever the original low valuation of the individual properties a particular company owned rather than increasing the tax based on a new, higher and more realistic sales price. The revenue the state lost would have been enough to eliminate all the California budget deficits from 1978 until now, and to make unnecessary all the cuts in funding for education and law enforcement, provided of course that politicians, seeing no deficits as a result, restrained themselves from adding foolish or wasteful new expenditures.

Buffett, aware of the economic harm to the state, publicly advised Schwarzenegger to shift to a fair and equitable property tax. He pointed out that by virtue of Proposition 13 the property tax on his Emerald Bay house, which he purchased in the 1960s and was now worth several million dollars, was substantially less than on his house in Omaha, currently valued at $700,000. The governor-to-be, expecting to lose votes if he followed this advice, said, "I told Warren that if he mentions Proposition

13 again he has to do five hundred sit-ups." Warren quietly discontinued advising Schwarzenegger.

Afterward, when I was thinking about Buffett, his favorite game—bridge—and the nontransitive dice, I wondered whether bidding systems at bridge might be like those dice. Could it be that no matter which bidding system you use, there will always be another system that beats it, so there's no best system? If so, the inventors of new "better" bidding systems could be chasing their tails forever, only to have their systems beaten by still newer systems, which in turn might then lose to old previously discarded systems.

Could one find the answer to this question? Possibly when computers can play bridge and bid at the expert level. How? By letting the computer play large numbers of hands, pitting various bidding systems against one another, and keeping track of how they do.

Suppose it turned out that no bidding system is best. Then your best strategy would be to ask the opponents to disclose their bidding system, as they are required to do, then choose the most lethal counter to it. When the opponents catch on and demand that your team chooses its bidding system first, this leads to an impasse that might have to be resolved by a lottery to see who chooses first, or by some kind of random assignment of bidding systems.

Bridge is what mathematicians call a game of imperfect information. The bidding, which precedes the play of the cards, gives some information about the four concealed hands held by the two pairs of players who are opposing each other. As the cards are played, players use the bidding and the cards they have seen so far to make inferences about who has the remaining unplayed cards. The stock market also is a game of imperfect information and even resembles bridge in that both have their deceptions. As in bridge, you do better in the market if you get more information sooner and put it to better use. It's no surprise that Buffett, arguably the greatest investor in history, is a bridge addict.

Impressed by Warren's mind and his methods, as well as his record as an investor, I told Vivian that I believed he would eventually become the richest man in America. Buffett was an extraordinarily smart evaluator of underpriced companies, so he could compound money much faster than the average investor. He also could continue to rely mainly on his own talent even as his capital grew to an enormous amount. Warren furthermore understood the power of compound interest and, clearly, planned to apply it over a long time.

My prediction came true for a few months in 1993, at which time he was the richest man in the world, until he was passed by Bill Gates and, later, a few other dot-commers. Buffett regained the world's top spot in 2007 only to trade places with his bridge buddy Gates again in 2008. By then, time spent with Warren had become a commodity of great value. In a vigorous auction on eBay, an Asian investor bid $2 million, to be donated to charity, for the privilege of having lunch with him.

Ralph Gerard gave me copies of Buffett's letters to his partners and his partnership document, a simple two-page affair. It was clear from this that the ideal plan would be to pool my investing for myself and others in a single limited partnership just as Warren had eventually done.

At the time, I was managing a total of about $400,000. At 25 percent a year, the accounts were grossing $100,000, and as my performance fee was 20 percent of the profits, I was earning at the rate of $20,000 a year, roughly the same as my salary as a professor. With the assets of the accounts pooled into a single account, I could manage more with less effort. A particular warrant hedge only had to be set up and managed once, rather than replicated individually for each managed account.

While I was deciding on my next steps, I got a phone call from a young stockbroker in New York named Jay Regan, who had read *Beat the Market* and told me he wanted to get into the investing business using a limited partnership to implement my convertible hedging approach. Thinking he might be able to handle the business aspects of running a hedge fund while I focused on choosing the investments and on doing further research into the markets, I arranged to meet him at my office in the UCI Math Department one day in 1969.

Ten years younger than I and of medium height, the twenty-seven-year-old Regan had thinning reddish hair, freckles, and the social skills of a promoter. A Dartmouth graduate in philosophy, he quickly took in the principles on which I based my investment methods.

We seemed to make a natural team. I would generate most of the ideas but he would bring suggestions and trading possibilities from "the Street." I would do the analysis and compute orders for him to execute through various brokers. He was to handle taxes, accounting, and most of the legal and regulatory paperwork, things I wished to avoid so I could focus on research and development.

We shook hands that day and agreed to create and manage together a new investment partnership based on the ideas in *Beat the Market.* Newport Beach was to be the think tank and trade generator, and New York the business office and trading desk. Discussing how much capital we needed to start with, we set $5 million as our target. If we made 20 percent net of expenses and charged 20 percent of that as a performance-based fee each year, we'd share 4 percent of $5 million, or $200,000, more than my remuneration as a professor of mathematics and what I was making from my smaller pool of managed accounts.

Our operation was an example of what had come to be known as a hedge fund. A hedge fund in the United States is simply a private limited partnership managed by one or more general partners (each of whom risks the loss of their entire net worth should things go badly wrong) and a group of investors, or limited partners, whose loss is limited to the amount they commit. The investors are primarily passive, with no role in the management of the partnership or in its investments. At the time, such funds were only lightly regulated, provided there were no more than ninety-nine partners and they did not solicit the general public. Hedge funds based overseas, called offshore, may also be structured as corporations or trusts.

Although hedge funds were few in number at that time, they were not a new concept. Jerome Newman and Buffett's mentor, Benjamin Graham, had started one as early as 1936. Under skilled managers whose interests were more or less aligned with the investors through the incentive of profit sharing, investors hoped for substantially better returns. The name *hedge fund* probably came about when the journalist Alfred Winslow Jones, inspired by what he learned after researching an article he was writing about investments, started a partnership in 1949. In addition to buying stocks he believed were cheap, he attempted to limit, or "hedge," risk by also selling short shares he believed were overpriced. The short seller profits if the price falls and loses if the price rises. Short selling allows an investor to profit in a down market; a fund like Jones's can, potentially, have more stable returns. Though Jones's idea didn't receive wide attention at first, a 1966 article in *Fortune* magazine by Carol Loomis, "The Jones Nobody Keeps Up With," announced that Jones's hedge fund had beaten all of the several hundred mutual funds over the last ten years and the possibilities became widely apparent.

I knew that finding investors was not going to be easy. Just as 1967–68 had been a manic two years for the markets and for the few existing hedge funds, 1969 was a major downer. Large-company stocks lost an average of 9 percent, and small-company stocks were crushed by an alarming 25 percent. Most hedge funds suffered severe losses and were closing down. Though we explained we were to be market-neutral and hedged, thus protecting principal, our ideas were new and people were scared. We finally signed up fourteen limited partners plus ourselves, each for $50,000 or more. My individual investors were among our first partners; Regan found more money by going to the courthouse, getting lists of limited partners from documents that had been filed by other hedge funds, and cold calling. I flew to New York to meet prospects, explain our methods, and add cachet with my books and academic position. By late October we had managed to get only $1.4 million in commitments but we decided to move ahead anyhow. We'd simply grow through profits, and these would attract more capital later from both current and new investors. Convertible Hedge Associates (later renamed Princeton Newport Partners) opened its bicoastal doors on Monday, November 3, 1969. An article in the *Wall Street Letter* announced our start, setting it in the context of that year's widespread market rout and the closing down of several hedge funds.

MONEY ON THE MOVE. As some hedge funds break up in the aftermath of sour performances this year, new investment partnerships continue to be formed. One of the newest is Convertible Hedge Associates, whose general partners are Ed Thorp and Jay Regan. Thorp is the fellow who developed a computerized system for beating the blackjack tables in Las Vegas, before they changed the rules on him, and wrote the book *Beat the Dealer*. He's turned his computer talents to money management and has a book out called *Beat the Market*. Regan has been with Butcher & Sherrerd, Kidder, Peabody and White, Weld. Among their limited partners are Dick Salomon, chairman of Lanvin-Charles of the Ritz; Charlie Evans (formerly of Evan-Picone) and Bob Evans (Paramount Pictures), and Don Kouri, president of Reynolds Foods, Ltd.

We completed our first two months of operation with a 4 percent profit, or $56,000. The S&P 500 Index was down 5 percent in the same two months. My $5,600 share of the general partner's fee exceeded my university income for the same period.

It was clear that I was at a crossroad. I could use my mathematical skills to develop strategies for hedging and possibly become rich; or I could compete in the academic world for advancement and distinction. I loved university-level teaching and research, and decided to stay with it as long as I could. My best quantitative financial ideas would be saved for our investors, not published, and over time would be rediscovered by and credited to others.

Buffett's report on me to the Gerards must have been favorable, since they joined us and their trust fund retained an investment in the partnership until after the deaths of Ralph and then Frosty. The time I spent with him had two major effects on my life: It helped move me along the path to my own hedge fund, and it later led me to make a very profitable investment in the company he transformed, Berkshire Hathaway.

*Chapter 13*

# GOING INTO PARTNERSHIP

rinceton Newport Partners (PNP) was a revolutionary idea when we set it up in 1969. We specialized in the hedging of convertible securities—warrants, options, convertible bonds and preferreds, and other types of derivative securities as they were introduced into the markets. Hedging risk was not new but we took it to an extreme never before tried. To begin with, we designed each of our hedges, which combined the stock and convertible securities of a single company, to minimize the risk of loss whether the stock fell or rose. We invented hedging techniques to further protect our portfolio against changes in interest rates, changes in the level of the overall market, and the catastrophic losses that can occasionally occur from enormous unexpected changes in prices and volatility. We managed this with mathematical formulas, economic models, and computers. This nearly total reliance on quantitative methods was unique, making us the earliest of a new breed of investors who would later be called quants, and who would radically transform Wall Street.

I could see from the beginning how our wealth could grow. But when I told friends and colleagues what I was up to, Vivian was almost the only one who got it, despite what I had already done in gambling. Although she wasn't a scientist or mathematician, she shared two qualities with the best of them: She asked the right questions, and she grasped the essentials. She had spent hours helping me film spinning roulette balls so I could make a machine to predict which number would come up, just as she had dealt thousands of blackjack hands so I could practice counting cards. And she helped me edit my books about gambling and the stock market and negotiate the contracts.

My initial plan for Princeton Newport Partners, which for the first five years we called Convertible Hedge Associates, was to find pairs of closely related securities that were priced inconsistently with respect to each other, and use them to construct investments that reduced risk. To form these hedges, we simultaneously bought the relatively underpriced security while offsetting the risk from adverse changes in its price by selling short the comparatively overpriced security. Since the prices of these two securities tended to move in tandem, I expected the combination to reduce risk while capturing extra returns. I identified these situations using the mathematical methods I had worked out for judging the proper price of a warrant, option, or convertible bond versus the common stock of the same company.

Betting on a hedge I had researched was like betting on a blackjack hand where I had the advantage. As in blackjack, I could estimate my expected return, estimate my risk, and choose how much of my bankroll to bet. Instead of a $10,000 bankroll I now had $1.4 million, and instead of a $500 maximum bet, the Wall Street casino had no limit. We started betting $50,000 to $100,000 per hedge.

To search for opportunities, early every afternoon after the market closed in New York, UC, Irvine students whom I hired went to the offices of two brokerage firms with which I traded. They collected the closing prices for hundreds of warrants, convertible bonds, convertible preferreds, and their associated common stocks. A preferred stock typically pays a regular dividend, whereas a common stock may or may not pay a dividend and, if it does, will generally vary over time. A preferred stock's dividend is paid first—in preference—before any payments due to the common stock. In the typical case, where the dividend amount is fixed, the preferred is like a bond but more risky because the dividend payments and the claim on assets upon liquidation are only paid after the corresponding bond payments. A so-called convertible preferred is one that can be exchanged for a specified number of shares of the common. So a convertible preferred is like a convertible bond but less secure, as it is paid only if there is enough money to do so after the bondholders receive their interest. At that time they gave us numerous investment possibilities.

I started by running the business from our house in 1969, and the house itself showed how much our circumstances had already changed. Eight years earlier when we arrived at New Mexico State University we rented a single-story nine-hundred-square-foot house with four tiny bedrooms, all of which were soon needed. Our second daughter, Karen, was born a few months later, followed by our son, Jeff, the next year. Soon thereafter, gambling winnings and book royalties not only allowed me to pay for my stock market education, but also to buy our first house. When we moved to UC, Irvine a couple of years later, we found a larger and nicer two-story home in Newport Beach, where the West Coast operations of Princeton Newport Partners began.

Vivian and I hired a contractor to add an outside staircase and a large second-story room to accommodate the business. In the new room the data was plotted on mathematical diagrams that I invented. These revealed favorable situations and let me quickly specify the appropriate trades. Each day's closing prices for a convertible and its stock were plotted as a color-coded dot on that particular convertible's diagram. The diagrams were prepared with curves that were drawn by a computer from my formula and showed the "fair price" of the convertible. The beauty of this was that I could immediately see from the picture whether we had a profitable trading opportunity. If the dot representing the data was above the curve it meant the convertible was overpriced, leading to a possible hedge: Short the convertible, buy the stock. A data point close to or on the curve indicated the price was fair, which meant liquidate an existing position, do not enter a new one. Below the curve meant buy the convertible, short the stock. The distance of the dot from the curve showed me how much profit was available. If we thought it met our target, we tried to put on the trade the next day. The slope of the curve near the data point on my diagram gave me the hedge ratio, which is the number of shares of common stock to use versus each convertible bond, share of preferred, warrant, or option.

After suffering for a few months with the distractions from the bee-hive of activity at the house, Vivian made me lease an office. Moving to the second floor of a small office building, I bought computers and hired more people. I developed printed tables for trading each hedge. These tables listed the prices of the stock versus the convertible needed to achieve our target return. Besides the new hedges we wanted to add, the tables told us how to adjust existing positions that needed the hedge ratio changed (so-called dynamic hedging) because the stock price had moved or that should be closed because we reached our objective.

Our computers used so much electricity that the office was always hot. We left the windows open and blew out the heat with fans, even during the coolest part of the California winter. Our landlord didn't charge tenants for utilities, instead paying it from his lease revenues. When the heat got my attention, I calculated that the cost of the electricity we used was more than our rent. We were getting paid to be there.

Each day after the market closed, I called Jay Regan in New York with trading instructions for the next day. He had given me the results from our trades earlier during the day, from which I had already updated my position records. The next day he executed the trades I recommended, reported the results, and the whole process was repeated.

To inform our limited partners as well as potential new partners, we periodically issued updated versions of our Confidential Private Placement Memorandum, which explained such things as the operations and objectives of the partnership, the fee structure, and the potential risks. We included simplified schematic descriptions of a few of our actual investments, without the mathematical formulas, diagrams, and calculations.

One of these trades could have been right out of the pages of *Beat the Market*. In 1970 the American Telephone and Telegraph Company

(AT&T) sold warrants to purchase thirty-one million shares of common stock at a price of $12.50 per share. Proceeds to the company were some $387.5 million, at the time the most ever for a warrant. Though it was not sufficiently mispriced then, the history of how warrant prices behaved indicated this could happen before it expired in 1975. When it did we bet a significant part of the partnership's net worth.

We were guided in this trade and thousands of others by a formula that had its beginnings in 1900 in the PhD thesis of French mathematician Louis Bachelier. Bachelier used mathematics to develop a theory for pricing options on the Paris stock exchange (the Bourse). His thesis adviser, the world-famous mathematician Henri Poincaré, didn't value Bachelier's effort, and Bachelier spent the rest of his life as an obscure provincial professor. Meanwhile a twenty-six-year-old Swiss patent clerk named Albert Einstein would soon publish in his single "miraculous year" of 1905 a series of articles that would transform physics. One of these initiated the Theory of Relativity, which revolutionized the theory of gravitation and led to the nuclear age. The second paper, on the particle nature of light, helped launch the Quantum Theory. But it is yet another of Einstein's articles that connects with my story.

In that paper Einstein explained a baffling discovery made in 1827 by the botanist Robert Brown. Brown used his microscope to observe pollen particles suspended in water. When illuminated, their tiny points of reflected light displayed a ceaseless irregular random motion. Einstein realized that this was caused by the bombardment of the pollen particles by molecules of the surrounding liquid. He wrote down equations that correctly predicted the statistical properties of the random motion of the particles. Until that time no one had ever seen a molecule or an atom (molecules are groups of atoms of various types bound together by electrical forces), and their existence had been disputed. Here was the final proof that atoms and molecules were real. This article became one of the most widely cited in all of physics.

Unknown to Einstein, his equations describing the Brownian motion of pollen particles were essentially the same as the equations that Bachelier had used for his thesis five years earlier to describe a very different phenomenon, the ceaseless, irregular motion of stock prices. Bachelier employed the equations to deduce the "fair" prices for options on the underlying stocks. Unlike Einstein's work, Bachelier's remained generally unknown until future Nobel laureate (1970) Paul Samuelson came across it in a Paris library in the 1950s and had it translated into English. Bachelier's paper appeared in 1964 in *The Random Character of Stock Market Prices,* edited by Paul Cootner and published by the MIT Press. Part of my early self-education in finance, this collection of articles applying scientific analysis to finance strongly influenced me and many others.

Bachelier had assumed that changes in stock prices followed a bell-shaped curve, known as a normal or Gaussian distribution. This didn't match real prices well, especially for periods longer than a few days. By the 1960s, academics had improved on Bachelier's work by using a more accurate description of stock price changes. Even so, these newer formulas for fair option prices, which applied as well to warrants, were not useful for trading because they included two quantities that could not be estimated satisfactorily from data. One of these was a growth rate for the stock between "now" and the warrant's expiration date. The other was a discount factor that was applied to the warrant's uncertain payoff at expiration in order to obtain its present value.

This discount factor, or markdown, accounted for the fact that investors tend to value an uncertain payoff less than if it was a sure thing. For example, if you toss a fair coin—which by definition has equal chances of coming up heads or tails—an investor who is paid $2 for heads and nothing for tails has an average but uncertain return of $1. This value is found by multiplying each payoff by the number of ways it occurs (one, in this example) and dividing by two, the number of possible outcomes. Most investors would rather be paid $1 for sure. For two investments with the same expected return, the less risky one tends to be preferred. Influenced by having been born during the Great Depression and by my early investment experiences, I made reducing risk a central feature of my investing approach.

Back in 1967, I had taken a further step in figuring out how much a warrant was worth. Using plausible and intuitive reasoning, I supposed that both the unknown growth rate and the discount factor in the existing warrant valuation formula could be replaced by the so-called riskless interest rate, namely that which was paid by a US Treasury bill maturing at the warrant expiration date. This converted an unusable formula with unknown quantities into a simple practical trading tool. I began using it for my own account and for my investors in 1967. It performed spectacularly. In 1969, unknown to me, Fischer Black and Myron Scholes, motivated in part by *Beat the Market,* rigorously proved the identical formula, publishing it in 1972 and 1973. This launched the development and widespread use of so-called derivative securities throughout the financial world. For their contributions, Myron Scholes and Robert Merton received the Nobel Prize in Economics in 1997. The Nobel committee acknowledged Fischer Black's (1938–95) contributions, and it is generally agreed that he would have shared in the prize had he not died earlier from throat cancer.

Powered largely by the formula, Princeton Newport Partners prospered. In our first two months, November and December 1969, our investors gained 3.2 percent while the S&P 500 lost 4.8 percent, an 8 percent edge. In 1970 we were up 13.0 percent versus 3.7 percent for the S&P. In 1971 the score was 26.7 percent to 13.9 percent, which was almost 13 percent better for our limited partners. In 1972 the S&P finally did better, making 18.5 percent compared with our 12 percent. Does this mean we did badly? No. It showed we were doing exactly what we intended to do, produce steady high returns in both good times and bad times. The hedges protected us against losses but at the expense of giving up some of the gains in big up-markets. The variation in our returns from year to year was mostly due to fluctuation in the quantity and quality of hedged investments, rather than the ups and downs of the market. Our first severe test came with the big bear market of 1973–74. The downturn was driven in part by the Arab oil embargo. The resulting record oil prices, adjusted for inflation, were never surpassed until the great run-up to $140 a barrel, reached in 2008.

In 1973 the S&P fell 15.2 percent and we were up 6.5, with our partners beating the market by over 20 percent. Stock market investors were hurt even more in 1974. The S&P plummeted 27.1 percent and our partners made 9.0 percent, a gap of more than 36 percent in our favor. Over that two-year cycle, limited partners in PNP saw each $1,000 increase to $1,160, whereas investors in the S&P 500 saw their $1,000 shrink to $618. Moreover, PNP made money every month in its first six years except for one in early 1974, when it declined less than 1 percent. From the peak on January 11, 1973, to the bottom on October 3, 1974, the drop in the stock market was a savage 48.2 percent, the worst since the Great Depression. Even Warren Buffett said then that it was a good thing for his partners he'd closed down when he had.

Existing partners were adding money and prospective new partners were learning about us through word of mouth. Partnership capital had grown from the initial $1.4 million to $7.4 million, and the general partners' compensation increased proportionately. Since the Investment Company Act limited us to ninety-nine partners, each investor's stake would have to average over $1 million in order for our pool to reach $100 million. Therefore we wanted high-net-worth individuals and institutional investors who would make an initial investment in PNP that would be substantial for us but a small part of their overall funds. We also liked that high-net-worth investors tended to be more knowledgeable, more experienced, and better able to judge the risks of the partnership, as well as having their own advisers. To increase the amount of new capital we could get from the dwindling number of spots available for new partners, we raised the minimum to join from our initial $50,000 to $100,000, then $250,000, $1,000,000, and eventually $10,000,000. We admitted new partners only after a careful check of their backgrounds. This was generally easy to do, as they often had careers about which there was public information, or they were personally known to us.

We modified our performance fee of 20 percent of the profits, billed annually, by including a "new high water" provision. This meant that if we had a losing year, we carried forward the losses and used them to offset future profits before we were paid more fees. This helped align our economic interests with those of the limited partners. As it happened, we never had a losing year, or even a losing quarter, and this calculation was never invoked.

PNP's offices in Manhattan and Newport Beach expanded as we hired more employees. I found talent at the nearby University of California, Irvine, where I still was a professor of mathematics. Now I had to learn how to choose and manage employees. Figuring this out for myself, I evolved into the style later dubbed management by walking around. Instead of the endless schedule of formal meetings I abhorred in academia, I talked directly to each employee and asked them to do the same with their colleagues.

I explained our general plan and direction and indicated what I wanted done by each person, revising roles and tasks based on their feedback. For this to work, I needed people who could follow up without being led by the hand, as management time was in short supply. Since much of what we were doing was being invented as we went along, and our investment approach was new, I had to teach a unique set of skills. I chose young smart people just out of university because they were not set in their ways from previous jobs. Better to teach a young athlete who comes fresh to his sport than to retrain one who has learned bad form.

Especially in a small organization, it was important that everyone work well together. As I was unable to tell from an interview how a new hire would mesh with our corporate culture, I told everyone that they were temporary for the first six months, as were we for them. Sometime during that period, if we mutually agreed, they would become regular employees.

I revised our policies as I gained experience. When my secretary signed out sick every other Friday, and I discreetly asked one of her friends in the office why, I was told she had a standing hair appointment and also caught up on accumulated personal business. She drew from her annual allotment of paid sick days because they would be lost if not used. With that system, people who used their sick leave got more days off with pay and were rewarded over those who didn't use it. I removed this instance of what economists call a perverse incentive by giving everyone a single pool of paid leave days that accumulated based on the number of hours worked and covered paid holidays, vacations, days off, and illness. Employees could use this time in any of these ways, subject only to the limitation that time off not interfere with essential job responsibilities.

In order to attract and keep superior staff, I paid wages and bonuses well above the market rate. This actually saved money because my employees were far more productive than average. The higher compensation limited turnover, which saved time and money otherwise used to teach my one-of-a-kind investment methodology. At the higher levels, it kept people from breaking off and going into business for themselves.

Investment opportunities were expanding, too, notably in April 1973 when the new Chicago Board Options Exchange (CBOE), created and managed by the long-established Chicago Board of Trade, began trading options. Before this, options were traded only over the counter (OTC), meaning that would-be buyers or sellers had to use brokers to search on their behalf for someone to take the other side of the trade. It was inefficient, and the brokers charged the customers high fees. The CBOE offered a wide range of options, with standardized terms, which were bought and sold on its trading floor, much like stocks traded on the New York Stock Exchange. Costs to buyers and sellers dropped dramatically, and trading volume skyrocketed.

In preparation for this, I programmed our Hewlett-Packard 9830A computer using my 1967 formula to calculate theoretical fair values for these options. The computer, a beautifully crafted quality device the size of a large dictionary, instructed a plotter of the type Hewlett-Packard was famous for, using ink-filled pens to represent the results as multicolored diagrams. For each option, correct pricing according to theory was represented by a curve. Each point on one of these curves represented a possible stock price and the corresponding fair price for the option. When we plotted the actual market prices of the stock and the option as a color-coded dot, we compared its location with the curve. If the point was above the theoretical curve, the option was overpriced so it was a candidate. to sell short while at the same time buying stock to hedge the risk. The distance of the point from the curve showed the amount of the mispricing. In the same way, a point below the curve showed that the option was underpriced, and by how much. This meant it was a candidate for the opposite type of hedge, long the option, short the stock. The slope of our theoretical curve at any point automatically gave the proper amounts of stock versus options for establishing a hedge that minimized risk.

The theoretical fair-value curve of option prices versus all possible stock prices was produced by the computer from the formula. This, in turn, used data such as the volatility of the stock (a measure of the recent daily percentage changes in the stock price), US Treasury interest rates, and any dividends paid by the stock during the life of the option.

A couple of months before the CBOE opened, I was ready to trade with the formula for pricing options that I thought no one else knew. Princeton Newport was going to clean up. Then I received a letter and a prepublication copy of an article from someone I hadn't heard of named Fischer Black. He said he was an admirer of my work and that he and Myron Scholes had taken a key idea from *Beat the Market,* known as delta hedging, a step further and derived an options formula. I scanned the article and saw it was the same formula I was using. The good news was that their rigorous proof verified that the formula I had discovered intuitively was correct. The bad news was that the formula was now public knowledge. Everyone was going to be using it. Fortunately, this took a while. When the CBOE opened for business we appeared to be the only ones trading from the formula. Down on the floor of the exchange it was like firearms versus bows and arrows.

To exploit price aberrations as quickly as possible, before others could and before they faded, we asked the options exchange to let our traders use programmed hand calculators on the floor. Our request was denied. The newcomers were not to have an advantage over the established old-time traders. We then asked for the next best thing, to be allowed to communicate by walkie-talkies with our floor traders. Denied. It reminded me a bit of what I had run into in Las Vegas with card counting. We then supplied our floor traders with printed trading tables that covered the ever-growing number of listed options. These were run off overnight on our high-speed printers and express-mailed to our offices in Princeton and Chicago. That served nearly as well as hand calculators would have.

Since we needed the tables in both offices as well as for traders spread over the floor of the exchange, we ran five copies. Using z-fold paper interspersed with layers of carbon paper, our Printronix Corporation machines ran all night, every night. The hedging instructions and target prices, which covered every situation likely to arise over the next few days, ran several hundred pages. Each table was a handful, with pages about eleven inches by seventeen, stacked a couple of inches deep. Much of this was described in a 1974 front-page article in *The Wall Street Journal*. Later, when established traders felt they could compete, hand calculators programmed to value options were allowed and became a basic tool for the industry.

While I was totally engaged with the university and the business, Vivian did most of the raising of our three preteen children. Yet she found time to help reelect a decent local congressman. When she opened a campaign office in Corona del Mar, party hacks tried and failed to stop her. She raised money for the campaign, found her own volunteers, and launched a large telephone-calling campaign. When the congressman was reelected, two party hacks took credit for her entire operation and moved themselves up the party ladder. Vivian was in it for results, though, not personal advancement or plaudits. In fifty-five and a half years of marriage I don't ever remember her bragging. The closest she came was when I would admire the way she matched the hues of her outfits or furnished our household with a designer's eye. She would look at me and matter-of-factly explain, "I have a good eye for color."

She also quietly organized and ran a large phone bank that helped elect the first black man to a California statewide office. She influenced people one-on-one as well. A lady she met complained about "those Jews." Vivian had lost several relatives in Nazi World War II prison camps. When she told us about meeting the woman, we expected to hear how she tore her to shreds. Explaining why she did not, Vivian pointed out that the woman would have learned nothing and simply would have become an enemy. Vivian patiently educated this basically good person, and they became friends for the rest of their lives.

Vivian's insights helped me cope with the cast of characters I was meeting in the investment world, many of whom seemed to be lacking a moral compass. She was fascinated by people. It had become second nature to take the bits and pieces someone told her about themselves and build a unified life story, which she analyzed and checked for consistency. As a result my wife was an almost unerring judge of character, motives, and expected future behavior. I was repeatedly amazed when she applied this to business and professional people I introduced her to for the first time.

She did this easily, based on so little evidence I couldn't believe it. But over and over again, Cassandra-like if I didn't listen, she was right.

After meeting one of the characters, she said, "He's greedy, insincere, and you can't trust him."

"How do you know this?" I asked.

She said, "You can see he's greedy from the way he drives. The insincerity comes out when he smiles. His eyes don't really smile, too; they mock you. And his wife has a sad look in her eyes that doesn't add up. The face she sees at home isn't the one he shows the world."

Years later, this "friend" Glen, as I'll call him, was running a hedge fund in which we were investors. The fund had lost $2 million in one of its investments, partly through fraud. When lawyers eventually recovered $1 million of the losses, Glen allocated the money to his current partners, most of whom were not among the former partners who had suffered the original loss. As he would be deriving future economic benefit from his current partners but none from the former partners, he would gain by this injustice. When I confronted him, he claimed not to be able to locate the twenty or so former partners. I had a list and told him I had current information on all but three and knew how to find those through mutual friends. Then he said he wouldn't pay and that, under the terms of the partnership, each partner had to go to arbitration separately. The amounts averaged $50,000 or so each, which he knew were not worth pursuing after lawyers' fees, personal time, inconvenience, and stress. He refused my request that he agree to a single arbitration to settle this for the entire group. He suggested slyly that maybe we should try a few individual arbitrations and if he lost them all, he might change his mind. When I asked his lawyer associate how he could ratify such unethical behavior, he said, "They don't teach ethics in law school."

As Princeton Newport Partners prospered, I was meeting interesting people. Curiously it wasn't our investment performance but a wrinkle in the tax code that led to a meeting with Paul Newman. The code lagged behind in its treatment of listed options as there were, until a few years later when the law was changed, transactions that made it possible to substantially reduce federal and state taxes. To explore this I was invited to join Paul and his tax lawyer for lunch on the set for the movie *The Towering Inferno,* at Twentieth Century–Fox in Los Angeles.

The studios were adjacent to Beverly Hills High School, the only Southern California high school with an oil well on campus. When I arrived, Paul was in blue jeans with a shirt and jacket to match, long before this was chic. I am reminded of the clean but faded Levi's that I generally wore in the 1940s for want of money and how I was astonished fifty years later when stylish people paid up for intentionally tattered and hole-filled jeans in far worse condition than my high school pants.

I was struck by Newman's remarkable blue eyes, even more intense in person than on film. Reserved, even shy when meeting someone for the first time, he looked me over, didn't say anything at first, then said, "You want a beer?" I said, "Sure," and he relaxed, deciding I was a regular guy. Over lunch, as I ate a special sandwich he recommended, he asked about my blackjack card counting system and how much I thought I could make at it full-time. Mastering disguises and playing alone, instead of running a team, I estimated $300,000 per year. "Why aren't you doing it?" he asked. I said I expected to do better running my hedge fund. As he was making six million taxable dollars that year, which was the reason for our lunch, he appreciated the answer. Nothing came of the meeting. Paul's lawyer believed that the ideas I presented for reducing his taxes were sound but new and thus likely to be challenged. His lawyer advised Paul, a high-profile progressive Democrat, not to risk being embroiled with a Republican IRS.

We had other interactions with Hollywood. Two of our early limited partners were Robert Evans and his brother, Charles. Bob was a relatively unknown actor and producer until 1966 when the conglomerate Gulf and Western took over Paramount and picked Evans as head of production. During the next eight years Evans returned Paramount to success with hits including *The Odd Couple, Rosemary's Baby, Love Story, Chinatown,* and *The Godfather.* In the 1997 movie *Wag the Dog,* Dustin Hoffman plays a character based in detail on Evans's appearance, habits, and mannerisms.

One day in 1971 or 1972 I went to Bob's villa in Beverly Hills to attempt to explain the types of trades that we were doing in the partnership. While he and Charles bobbed around in the backyard pool, protected with sunglasses and hats, I sat at the edge explaining the basic ideas behind convertible hedging. At the time Robert was married to his third (of seven) wives, the actress Ali MacGraw. Of course, I hoped she would make an appearance to question me about the intricacies of the market, but she was traveling. Ali had been nominated for an Academy Award for Best Actress in 1970 for her role in the movie *Love Story* and, even twenty years later when she was fifty-two years old, *People* magazine chose her as one of the fifty most beautiful people in the world.

Screenwriter Charles A. Kaufman (1904–91), whose screenplay for *Freud* was nominated for an Oscar in 1963, became a limited partner and regularly referred people to us, which may have indirectly caused certain other prospective partners to call us. Kaufman had a Los Angeles–based accountant who also did the books for some of the big casinos in Las Vegas. The Kaufmans gave a dinner party for Vivian and me and the accountant and his wife. The point was for me to answer questions both on partnership trading strategies and our accounting practices. When the conversation turned to blackjack and I mentioned what I knew about casino cheating, skimming, and a double set of books, the accountant acted disbelieving and astonished. His wife, a beautiful and outspoken former showgirl, would have none of it and told us they knew otherwise. The accountant may have been more connected than he let on, because shortly after this dinner, I received inquiries about investing in the partnership from then famous and highly connected Las Vegas figures like "Moe" Dalitz (1899–1989) and Beldon Katleman (1914–88). Jay Regan quickly agreed with me that we didn't have any available openings.

One of my stories that particularly put the accountant in denial began in the summer of 1962, when I was contacted by a special agent from the US Treasury. The Treasury was investigating possible tax fraud in the Nevada casino industry, believing that certain operators were removing large quantities of cash, which they were not declaring on their tax returns. Part of a secret undercover team, "John" resembled the actor Mike Connors, best known for starring in two television series around that time, *Mannix* and *Tightrope,* as well as several movies. We met for lunch regularly at the Hamburger Hamlet in Westwood Village, adjacent to the UCLA campus. John came as the character he played to fool the casinos, wearing a broad-brimmed Stetson, cowboy clothes and identification verifying that he was a wealthy Texan named C. Cash Anderson (a little Treasury humor). He drove a new red Cadillac convertible, its white top rolled down.

In Las Vegas, he bet big at the blackjack tables, an act that got him into the rooms where the casinos counted the money from the collection boxes that had been sealed and brought in from the blackjack tables. He reported seeing two sets of books, along with corresponding adding machines, one showing the real cash totals and the other the lesser amount that was reported to the government. On behalf of the government team, John was consulting me on how to improve their play at high-stakes blackjack and thereby keep down the cost to the Treasury while they pretended to be unskilled high-rollers.

As the partnership prospered, so did Vivian and I. When we started back in 1969 I forecast how quickly my wealth and Regan's would grow. On a yellow legal pad, with plausible assumptions about our company's rate of return, the rate of growth of our partnership's net worth, and taxes, I predicted that by 1975 we would be millionaires. I sent a copy to Regan.

Sure enough, in 1975, we were indeed both millionaires and the money was changing our families' lives. Vivian and I had extensive additions and improvements made to our home. Back in 1964 I bought a used red Volkswagen in Las Cruces from one of my students. A decade later, in 1975, I drove a new red Porsche 911S. Vivian's inexpensive utilitarian wardrobe was evolving into coordinated designer outfits with fashionable handbags and shoes. Our vacations, which used to be low-budget trips to professional meetings, were being augmented and replaced by cruises and stays in high-end overseas hotels.

We were now living beyond the means of most of our faculty friends. This had the unintended consequence of distancing us somewhat from the smart, funny, and educated people with whom we felt the most rapport. On the other hand, we hadn't yet made many new friends in the wealthy Orange County business community, because most of our business partners were scattered across the United States. As Vivian remarked, "We're neither fish nor fowl."

My shifting mathematical interests were also distancing me professionally from my colleagues in the department at UCI. As is generally true in universities, the research emphasis was on pure mathematics. Loosely speaking, this is the development of abstract mathematics, or theory for its own sake.

My PhD thesis was in pure mathematics and this continued to be my focus for the next fifteen years. But with the analysis of gambling games, I also developed a strong interest in applied mathematics, which uses mathematical theories to solve real-world problems. The financial world was presenting me, and Princeton Newport Partners, with an endless array of such puzzles to solve for fun and profit. I was becoming an applied mathematician again, and in a department of pure mathematics I was professionally neither fish nor fowl.

At the same time, the Math Department was headed for serious trouble. Both the levels of grant money for research and funds from the state of California to support the university had declined. This led to fierce struggles among various factions in the department for what was left. To mediate the infighting, an outsider was brought in as a chairman. He was forced out after three turbulent years. For want of anyone else who might be acceptable to the warring groups, and against my better judgment, I was persuaded by the administration to act as temporary chairman.

The assignment was worse than I thought. I found that one assistant professor had stopped showing up to teach, dividing his time between his girlfriend four hundred miles to the north in the San Francisco Bay

Area and the casinos in Reno and Lake Tahoe. A card counter, he even called me with blackjack questions! Another assistant professor was running up departmental phone bills of $2,000 per month versus a total of $200 for the other twenty-five professors combined. When I confronted him he claimed it was mathematical research. A review of the bills showed almost all the charges were for calls to two numbers in New York City. I dialed each, speaking in turn to his mother and to a store that sold musical recordings. He was enraged at me and not at all embarrassed when exposed.

Meanwhile, a full professor had stolen the confidential employment records of another full professor from the department files. When I discovered this and confronted him, he refused to return it. It turned out that the file contained a very nasty letter that he had written about his enemy. He feared that if I, as chairman, learned what he had done, I would expose him. When I asked the administration to initiate disciplinary action against these incorrigibles, they declined to act. I was stunned and stymied.

One problem in large bureaucracies is that many of the members decide it is better not to cross people, instead of standing on principle. I asked a good friend, whom I had helped to get an appointment in our department, to become my vice chairman and help me. Although he was now a full professor with tenure, he declined, saying, "I have to live in the same cage with these monkeys." I did understand his point. On the other hand, I was not confined to the cage. I had PNP. I thought, *Why try to fix this if no one will even back me up?* I was in the Math Department by choice, not by necessity. It was time to move on.

Initially, I transferred to UCI's Graduate School of Management, where I enjoyed teaching courses in mathematical finance. But I found factionalism and backstabbing as bad there as it had been in the Math Department. Both had endless committee meetings, petty squabbles over benefits, people who wouldn't pull their weight and couldn't be dislodged, and the dictum of publish or perish. I decided it was time to leave academia. Even so, it was not an entirely easy decision. I had heard more than one person say that what they wanted most in life was to be a tenured professor at the University of California. It had been my dream, too. Over the years I hired students and former staff from UC, Irvine but only one faculty member, one without tenure, was willing to take a chance and join my operation. The others found it a very scary notion. Of course, a few had regrets later.

Gradually reducing my teaching load from full-time, I finally resigned my UCI full professorship in 1982. I loved teaching and research and felt a sense of loss upon giving up a position I expected to enjoy for a lifetime, but it turned out to be for the best. I took what I liked with me. I kept my friends and continued my research collaborations. Free to do anything I wished, my childhood dream come true, I continued to present my work at meetings, as well as publish it in the mathematical, financial, and gambling literature.

I intensified my focus on competing with the wave of mathematicians, physicists, and financial economists who were now flocking to Wall Street from academia.

*Chapter 14*

# FRONT-RUNNING THE QUANTITATIVE REVOLUTION

W hen Black and Scholes published their formula, the same one I was already using, I knew that to maintain PNP's trading edge I would have to develop my tools for valuing warrants, options, convertible bonds, and other derivative securities rapidly enough to stay ahead of future marching legions of PhDs hungry for academic advancement through publication. Though I had to keep important results secret for the benefit of our investors, I could publicize lesser ideas that I thought would soon be found by others.

Before the work of Black and Scholes, I had moved beyond their basic formula, having generalized it to include cases where short-sale proceeds were withheld by the broker (to his benefit, since he got the use of the money) until the short sale was closed. Once they published, I presented these at a meeting of the International Statistical Institute in Vienna, where I was speaking. I also had extended the model to include dividend-paying stocks, since I was trading call options and warrants on many such stocks. Then the CBOE announced it would start trading put options sometime in the following year, 1974. These options, like the call options we were already trading, were called American options, as distinguished from European options. European options can be exercised only during a short settlement period just prior to expiration, whereas American options can be exercised anytime during their life.

If the underlying stock pays no dividends, the Black-Scholes formula, which is for the European call option, turns out to coincide with the formula for the American call option, which is the type that trades on the CBOE. A formula for the European put option can be obtained using the formula for the European call option. But the math for American put options differs from that for European put options, and—even now—no general formula has ever been found. I realized that I could use a computer and my undisclosed "integral method" for valuing options to get numerical results to any desired degree of accuracy for this as-yet-unsolved "American put problem." In a productive hour in the fall of 1973 I outlined the solution, from which my staff programmed a computer to produce precise calculated values. My integral method also had another advantage over the Black-Scholes approach. Whereas the latter was based on one specific model for stock prices, one with limited accuracy, my technique could value options for a wide range of assumed distributions of stock prices.

In May 1974 I had dinner with Fischer Black in Chicago, where he had invited me to give a talk at the semiannual CRSP (Center for Research in Security Prices) meeting at the University of Chicago. Then in his thirties, Fischer was trim and tall, with combed-back black hair and "serious" glasses. Focusing intently on whatever finance topic was being discussed, he spoke articulately, logically, and concisely. His notes, compact and ultra-legible, reflected this. He would go on to become one of the most innovative and influential figures in academic and applied finance. Since a computational method for pricing American puts had been easy for me, I brought it to show Fischer and to learn from him how others had solved it. I laid the answer on the table between us but before I could speak Fischer began telling me about his approach to the problem and the difficulties that had so far stopped him. Earlier, I had explored his approach and believed it would work but, as my integral method was so easy, I used it. If Fischer Black didn't know the answer, no one else did. Owing it to my partners to preserve our competitive advantage, I unobtrusively returned my work to my briefcase. Two other computational methods for finding American put prices were eventually published in scholarly journals in 1977.

As with my method for valuing American puts, my associates and I continued to solve problems for valuing so-called derivatives before the discovery and publication by academics. From 1967 until PNP closed at the end of 1988, this gave us a significant edge in trading the expanding array of new financial instruments.

Some of our trades were easy to explain to partners without using theory. One of these involved warrants issued by the Mary Carter Paint Company. Founded in 1958 as the successor to a 1908 company, it started as an acquirer of other paint companies, then evolved into a resort and casino developer in the Bahamas. Changing its name to Resorts International, it divested itself of the paint business and name. In 1972 the company had warrants that sold for 27 cents when the stock traded at $8 a share. The warrants were so cheap because they were worthless unless the stock traded above $40 a share. Fat chance. Since our model said the warrants were worth $4 a share, we bought all we could at the unbelievable bargain price of 27 cents each, which turned out to be 10,800 warrants at a total cost, after commissions, of $3,200. We hedged our risk of loss by shorting eight hundred shares of the common stock at $8. When the stock later fell to $1.50 a share, we bought back our short stock for a profit of about $5,000. Our gain now consisted of the warrants for "free" plus about $1,800 in cash. The warrants were trading close to zero but below the tiny amount the model said they were worth, so I decided we should put them away and forget them.

Six busy years passed. Then in 1978 we started getting calls from people who wanted to buy our warrants. The company had purchased property in Atlantic City, New Jersey, after which it successfully lobbied, along with others, to bring casino gambling to the state, limited to Atlantic City. On May 26, 1978, Resorts opened the first US casino outside Nevada. Having received early approval, they had no competition and reaped windfall profits until other casinos opened late in 1979. With the stock now trading at $15 a share, ten times its earlier lowest price, and the warrants trading between $3 and $4, the model said they were worth about $7 or $8. So, instead of selling and reaping a $30,000 to $40,000 profit, I bought more warrants and sold stock short to hedge the risk of loss. As the stock broke through the $100 mark, we were still buying warrants and shorting stock. We finally sold the 27-cent warrants and others for above $100 each. We ultimately made more than $1 million. At the same time, blackjack teams using my methods were exploiting the casino boom in Atlantic City with its temporary friendly environment and reasonable blackjack rules. Ironically, as they were extracting millions of dollars from the blackjack tables at Resorts and elsewhere, I was profiting from Resorts' securities.

In the three years and ten months from the start of 1973 through October 1976, limited partners in PNP gained 48.9 percent. During this time, ordinary investors had a wild ride in the stock market. The S&P Index fell 38 percent in the first two years and then surged 61 percent from 1975 through October 1976, for a net gain of just 1 percent. Meanwhile, Princeton Newport gained in every quarter.

That the market's good years have to be better than its bad years just to come out even is a general rule. As an extreme example to make the point, using only month-end values throughout, the S&P 500 fell by 83.4 percent from its peak at the end of August 1929 to the close in June 1932. A dollar invested was reduced to 16.6 cents. For this 16.6 cents to become $1 again, the index needed to become 6.02 times as large, an increase of 502 percent. The wait was over eighteen years, until the end of November 1950. The rate of growth per year during this long recovery period was 10.2 percent, near the long-term historical average.

During the 1970s, the range and sophistication of our investments expanded. Companies came with families of securities, which included convertible bonds and preferreds, warrants, and put and call options. These derived most of their value from that of the underlying stock and were called derivatives. They proliferated in number, type, and quantity in the decades to follow, as so-called financial engineers invented new ones to possibly decrease risk and certainly increase fees. I used my methodology to price these derivatives and the others that followed. This enabled Princeton Newport Partners to price convertible bonds more accurately than anyone else. Hedging with derivatives was a key source of profits for PNP during its entire nineteen years. Such hedging also became a core strategy for many later hedge funds like Citadel, Stark, and Elliott, which each went on to manage billions.

Convertible bonds today may have complex terms and conditions. However, the basic idea is simple. Consider the hypothetical XYZ 6s of 2020. Each bond was originally sold for approximately $1,000 on July 1, 2005, to be redeemed by the company for exactly $1,000, the "face amount," on July 1, 2020. The bond promises to pay 6 percent of the face amount in interest for each year of its life, in two semiannual installments of 3 percent, or $30, payable to holders of record on January 1 and on July 1. So far these are like the terms of a typical ordinary bond. However, the convertible has one more feature. At the option of the owner, it can be converted into twenty shares of XYZ common stock anytime until bond maturity on July 1, 2020. So this bond combines the features of both an ordinary bond and an option. The market price of the bond can be thought of as the sum of two parts. The first is the value of a comparable bond without the conversion feature, which will fluctuate with the level of interest rates and the financial soundness of the company. This sets a "floor" to the price.

The second part is the option value of the conversion feature. In our example, if the stock is at $50, the bond can be exchanged for twenty shares of stock, worth $1,000, which the bond is worth anyhow when it matures so there is no benefit from the conversion feature. However, if the stock were to rise at any point to $75, twenty shares of stock would be worth $1,500. The bond, which can be exchanged immediately for this amount of stock, should trade in the market then for at least that amount.

Why do companies issue such bonds? Because the value of the extra option or conversion feature, which gives the buyer a lottery ticket on the company's future, allows the company to reduce the interest rate they need to pay on the bonds in order to sell them.

Just as PNP used option valuation methods to build models for pricing convertible bonds, it did the same with other derivatives. Our hedges individually had low risk. Of two hundred that I tracked in the early 1970s, 80 percent were winners, 10 percent ended approximately even, and 10 percent lost. The losses were considerably smaller on average than the gains.

To produce even steadier returns, we hedged the overall risk from our entire collection of hedges by neutralizing the impact on our portfolio of shifts in interest rates (across the spectrum of quality and maturity). We also offset the danger to the portfolio from sudden large shifts in overall stock market prices and in the volatility level of the market. From the 1980s on, some of these techniques came into usage by modern invest- ment banks and hedge funds. They also adopted a notion we rejected, called VaR or "value at risk," where they estimated the damage to their portfolio for, say, the worst events among the most likely 95 percent of future outcomes, neglecting the extreme 5 percent "tails," then acted to reduce any unacceptably large risks. The defect of VaR alone is that it doesn't fully account for the worst 5 percent of expected cases. But these extreme events are where ruin is to be found. It's also true that extreme changes in securities prices may be much greater than you would expect from the Gaussian or normal statistics commonly used. When the S&P 500 Index fell 23 percent on October 19, 1987, a leading academic fi- nance professor said that if the market had traded every day for the thirteen-billion-year life of the universe, the chance of this happening even once was negligible.

Another tool used today is to "stress-test" a portfolio by simulating the impact of major calamitous events of the past on the portfolio. In 2008, a multibillion-dollar hedge fund managed by a leading quant used ten-day windows from the crash of 1987, the First Gulf War, Hurricane Katrina, the 1998 Long-Term Capital Management crisis, the tech- induced market drop in 2000–02, the Iraq War, and so forth. All this data was applied to the fund's 2008 portfolio and showed that these events would have led to losses of at most $500 million on a $13 billion portfolio, a risk of loss of no more than 4 percent. But they actually lost over 50 percent at their low in 2009, brought to the brink of ruin before finally recovering their losses in 2012. The credit collapse of 2008 was different in kind from the past worst cases for which they tested, and their near-extinction reflects the inadequacy of simply replaying the past.

We took a more comprehensive view. We analyzed and incorporated tail risk, and considered extreme questions such as, "What if the market fell 25 percent in one day?" More than a decade later it did exactly that and our portfolio was barely affected. When, with our expanding range and size of trades, we moved our account to Goldman Sachs as our prime broker, one of the questions I asked was: "What happens to our account if Goldman Sachs New York is destroyed by a terrorist nuclear bomb smuggled into New York Harbor?" Their reply was: "We have duplicate records stored underground in Iron Mountain, Colorado."

There is another kind of risk on Wall Street from which computers and formulas can't protect you. That's the danger of being swindled or defrauded. Being cheated at cards in the casinos of the 1960s was valuable preparation for the far greater scale of dishonesty I would encounter in the investment world. The financial press reveals new skulduggery on a daily basis.

With inflation approaching double digits and a spike in commodity prices, precious metals and options to buy or sell them were a booming business. Back in my office, I compared the XYZ Corporation's prices to the "correct" model prices we used at PNP when we sold large amounts of such options to a major dealer.

To my astonishment, I found that XYZ Corp was offering to sell me options at less than half my expected payoff! After I collected financial statements from my friendly salesman and examined them, I discovered that when XYZ Corp sold an option it counted the proceeds as income, but did not set aside any reserve to pay off the options if and when they were cashed in by the buyer. Since the correct reserves on each option they sold should have been more than twice what they were being paid, proper accounting would show their net worth becoming more negative every time they sold another option.

It was clear that they had to sell more and more options, using the increasing cash flow to pay off any early "investors" who might cash in. Classic Ponzi, and bound to end badly. What to do?

I decided on a little educational experiment. After reviewing the scanty information available on sales, options outstanding, and early redemption rates, I estimated the company would survive for at least eight more months. It turned out to be ten. Buying $4,000 worth of six-month options, I doubled my money in four months and cashed out. A few months later the offices were shuttered, the operators gone, and another fraud investigation was under way.

The next big test of PNP's investment approach came soon afterward. From 1979 through 1982 there were extreme distortions in the markets. Short-term US Treasury bill returns went into double-digit territory, yielding almost 15 percent in 1981. The interest on fixed-rate home mortgages peaked at more than 18 percent per year. Inflation was not far behind. These unprecedented price moves gave us new ways to profit. One of these was in the gold futures markets.

At one point, gold, for delivery two months in the future, was trading at $400 an ounce and gold futures fourteen months out were trading for $500 an ounce. Our trade was to buy the gold at $400 and sell it at $500. If, in two months, the gold we paid $400 for was delivered to us, we could store it for a nominal cost for a year, then deliver it for $500, gaining 25 percent in twelve months. There were a variety of risks, which we fully hedged, and several "kickers"—scenarios where we would make a higher—(often much higher) rate of return. We did similar trades in silver and copper and they worked as expected, with one tiny exception. After we took delivery of our copper, some of it was stolen from the warehouse our broker used and there was a short delay while we were reimbursed from the warehouse company's insurance.

As the era of high interest rates unfolded, savings and loan companies began to lose massive amounts of money. Here's why. Savings and loans borrowed money for a short term from depositors and lent much of it out long-term for home mortgages at fixed rates of interest. As short-term rates shot up, the cost of money to the S&Ls went up rapidly, whereas their revenue from the existing mortgage loans they had made earlier to homeowners at much lower fixed rates did not. This mismatch in interest rates between their short-term borrowing and their long-term lending would lead to the ruin of many S&Ls in the 1980s and a bailout cost to taxpayers of several hundred billion dollars.

The possible collapse of the S&Ls could have been predicted and prevented by suitable regulation, but wasn't. The great financial crises that came later shared this characteristic.

Meanwhile, Princeton Newport Partners was expanding into new types of investments.

# Chapter 15

# RISE . . .

On November 1, 1979, ten years after we started Princeton Newport Partners, the annualized return for the S&P 500, including dividends, was 4.6 percent and for small-company stocks 8.5 percent, both with far more volatility than Princeton Newport. We were up 409 percent for the decade, annualizing at 17.7 percent before fees and 14.1 percent after fees. Our initial $1.4 million had grown to $28.6 million. We ended 1979 with a grand dream for the 1980s: to expand our expertise into new investment areas. For me this meant more interesting problems to solve in quantitative finance. For the partnership it could lead to an increase in the amount of capital we could invest at high rates of return.

I called our first effort the Indicators Project. The object was to study the financial characteristics of companies, or indicators, to see if they could be used to forecast stock returns. The prototype was Value Line, an investment service that launched a program in 1965 using information such as surprise earnings announcements, price-to-earnings ratios, and momentum to rank stocks into groups from I (best) to V (worst). A stock is said to have positive momentum if its price has recently been trending strongly up, and negative momentum if strongly down.

The head of our indicators project was Dr. Jerome Baesel, a talented and articulate young economist whom I met when we were both teaching finance in what is now the Paul Merage School of Business at UC, Irvine. Also crucial to this project and virtually all the others, then and later, was Steven Mizusawa. Steve and I met in 1972 when he and another UCI student asked to do a special mathematics summer project under my direction exploring an aspect of card counting in blackjack. They did an excellent job, and so, when in 1973 I needed someone with computer skills, Steve was available. With degrees in both computer science and physics, Steve has been in charge of our computer operations and much of the associated research. He became a general partner of Princeton Newport Partners and an invaluable friend.

The project relied on two vast securities databases and the computing power to process them, both of which had recently become available. Daily historical prices of stocks, the dates and amounts of any cash dividends paid, and other data were marketed by CRSP, the University of Chicago's Center for Research in Security Prices. The Compustat database provided historical balance sheet and income information. Of the scores of indicators we systematically analyzed, several correlated strongly with past performance. Among them were earnings yield (annual earnings divided by price), dividend yield, book value divided by price, momentum, short interest (the number of shares of a company currently sold short), earnings surprise (an earnings announcement that is significantly and unexpectedly different from the analysts' consensus), purchases and sales by company officers, directors, and large shareholders, and the ratio of total company sales to the market price of the company. We studied each of these separately, then worked out how to combine them. When the historical patterns persisted as prices unfolded into the future, we created a trading system called MIDAS (multiple indicator diversified asset system) and used it to run a separate long/short hedge fund (long the "good" stocks, short the "bad" ones). The power of MIDAS was that it applied to the entire multitrillion-dollar stock market, with the possibility of investing very large sums.

Two professors of finance, Bruce Jacobs and Kenneth Levy, had independently been thinking along the same lines as I learned when they presented their work to the UC–Berkeley program in finance in the fall of 1986. Our system operated successfully until we closed it along with Princeton Newport Partners at the end of 1988. Jacobs and Levy went on to manage several billion dollars using this method.

By 1985 our offices in Newport Beach, California, and Princeton, New Jersey, had each grown to about forty employees. I managed the Newport Beach office and Jay Regan the Princeton office. We were now trading in markets all over the world. London was five time zones ahead of New York, so our traders arrived early, updated our positions across the Atlantic, and were ready for New York when it opened at 9:30 A.M. along with multiple US options markets (Chicago Board Options Exchange, AMEX, Pacific Coast, Philadelphia). In Newport Beach, three hours behind Princeton, the action began around 6 A.M. as we put the latest prices into our computers to generate new trading advice for the East Coast office. In addition, the Asian markets were open when most people in the United States were asleep. Trading warrants and convertibles in Tokyo was especially important. Phone traffic between Newport and Princeton began about 6 A.M., became very heavy for most of the day, and finally tapered off in the late afternoon.

We expanded into new types of trades, several of which we pioneered. One of these was a huge onetime-only transaction proposed to us by Goldman Sachs in late 1983. It resulted from the government-mandated breakup of the American Telephone and Telegraph Company monopoly. AT&T was being divided into a new company also to be known as AT&T plus the so-called seven sisters, which would be new regional telephone companies. Under the terms of the deal, each ten-share lot of old AT&T would be exchanged for ten shares of new AT&T plus one share in each of the seven sisters. The aggregate price of the new securities, trading "when issued" (which means you could contract "now" to buy or sell them but didn't have to put up the cash in the case of purchase, or get paid in case of sale, until they were actually issued) was greater than the price of the old AT&T by enough to make this trade attractive.

Princeton Newport bought five million shares of old AT&T at about $66 a share for $330 million. We paid for most of this with term financing, which was a special loan from our broker just for this deal, to be paid off from the proceeds when the position was closed out. Meanwhile, we offset the risk of owning old AT&T by simultaneously selling short the shares we were going to receive in exchange for our shares of old AT&T. These so-called when-issued shares consisted of five million shares of new AT&T and five hundred thousand shares of each of the new seven sisters. We did the trade through Goldman Sachs by taking half of each of two successive five million share blocks of about $330 million apiece. I have a gold-colored plaque, a so-called deal toy, on my desk commemorating the December 1, 1983, block as then being the largest dollar amount for a single trade in the history of the New York Stock Exchange. In two and a half months, PNP netted $1.6 million from the AT&T trade after all costs.

Meanwhile, an army of PhDs, following our path, greatly expanded the theory of derivatives and implemented the revolution in quantitative finance on Wall Street. They helped direct investing at hedge funds, investment banks, and other institutions. Driven in part by the sell side—the sales force that finds and sells new products—these quants invented new derivative securities that the salespeople then pushed. These products undermined the world financial system in a series of increasingly grave crises. The first of these surprised almost everyone.

On Friday, October 16, 1987, the market, as measured by the Dow Jones Industrial Average, fell about 4 percent. Since a daily move typically averages about 1 percent, this was large, but not cause for panic. However, the market had been declining somewhat and was becoming more volatile.

On the following Monday morning we watched the market continue to fall. By the time I left for my usual lunch with Vivian it was off 7 percent, more than half as large as the two record 13 percent and 12 percent down days of October 28 and 29, 1929, which together signaled the start of the Great Depression. As the market dropped further, my office called me at the restaurant, telling me with alarm that the Dow Jones Index was down four hundred points, or 18 percent, already the worst day ever, amid widespread panic. Vivian wondered whether I needed to skip the rest of our lunch and race back. PNP and we personally could be suffering massive losses. I told her there was nothing I could do in the markets that day. Our investments were either safe, thoroughly protected by hedging as I believed them to be, or not. "What will you do?" she asked. I told her that first we would relax and finish lunch. Then, after a brief visit to the office, I was coming home to think.

When I returned to my desk, the market had closed, having fallen 508 points, or 23 percent, by far the worst single day in history. One quarter of the US stock market value was "gone." The nation had lost 5 percent of its net worth in one day, and the shock ripped through markets around the world. Fear reigned. For most academic theorists, this was as close to impossible as anything can be. It was as though the sun suddenly winked out or the earth stopped spinning. They described stock prices using a distribution of probabilities with the esoteric name *lognormal*. This did a good job of fitting historical price changes that ranged from small to rather large, but greatly underestimated the likelihood of very large changes. Financial models like the Black-Scholes formula for option prices were built using the lognormal. Aware of this limitation in academia's model of stock prices, as part of the indicators project we had found a much better fit to the historical stock price data, especially for the relatively rare large changes in price. So even though I was surprised by the giant drop, I wasn't nearly as shocked as most.

Though there was no major outside event to explain this one-day collapse, when I thought it through that evening I asked myself, *Why did this happen? Will the disaster continue tomorrow? Will there be profit opportunities created by the chaos?* I believed the cause was a new financial product called portfolio insurance. Had I paid closer attention earlier to the vast expansion in its use, I might have foreseen the disaster. This investment technique was largely created and marketed by the quant firm of Leland, O'Brien and Rubinstein. Suppose a company pension and profit-sharing plan with a broad portfolio of equities wants to protect itself against a sharp drop in the market. It sets up a program, either in-house or by a portfolio insurance specialist, to switch from equities into US Treasury bills as the market falls. This is done in stages: For each drop of, say, a couple of percent, part of the stock portfolio is sold and the proceeds used to buy T-bills. If the market later rises, the process is reversed until, once again, the portfolio is fully invested in equities.

At the time of the crash $60 billion or so of equities were insured by this technique and implemented largely by computers. When the market fell 4 percent on Friday the insurance programs placed orders, to be executed at Monday's opening, to sell stock and buy Treasury bills. When trading began on Monday, these sales drove stock prices down further, triggering more selling from portfolio insurance programs. As prices continued to plummet, investors panicked and added their selling to the deluge. This "feedback loop" continued throughout the day, building to a devastating climax. Portfolio insurance was designed to protect investors from large market declines. Ironically, the cure became the cause.

To understand what I did next, a little background is needed. It is relatively expensive for portfolio insurance programs continually to sell equities as the market drops, then buy them back when it rises due to commissions paid to brokers to execute the trade and because of the impact on the market price from the sale or purchase.

The institutions using portfolio insurance, even though they paid lower rates on commissions than smaller investors, cut trading costs even more by using, instead of the underlying stocks, contracts to buy (or sell) at a specified future date the basket of stocks that made up the S&P 500 Index. These so-called futures contracts traded on exchanges along with those for future delivery of other assets, including bonds, currencies, metals, oil and gas, and agricultural products such as corn, wheat, and pork bellies. These contracts have standardized amounts and delivery dates, such as the one for one hundred troy ounces of gold to be delivered during a specified period in September 2017. The exchange stands as an intermediary between buyer and seller, each of whom must post collateral with the exchange as a guarantee they will honor their side of the contract. Known as margin, these funds are a fraction of the total contract amount. Since the futures contract will be exchangeable for the underlying asset, the two prices tend to track each other closely. The stage was set for disaster.

By October 1987, futures contracts on the S&P 500 Index had been trading for a few years and were a popular way either to gain exposure to the market (buy, or "go long") or to shed it (sell or "go short") quickly and cheaply. Normally, the prices of these futures contracts were very close to the price of the S&P 500 Index itself. That was because large enough deviations let arbitrageurs capture a profit with a nearly riskless hedge through simultaneously buying the cheaper of the index and the index futures, and selling short the other. Ordinarily, this kept the price spread narrow. We had been capturing profits this way since the first day in 1982 that these futures traded on the Chicago Mercantile Exchange.

After thinking hard about it overnight I concluded that massive feedback selling by the portfolio insurers was the likely cause of Monday's price collapse. The next morning S&P futures were trading at 185 to 190 and the corresponding price to buy the S&P itself was 220. This price difference of 30 to 35 was previously unheard of, since arbitrageurs like us generally kept the two prices within a point or two of each other. But the institutions had sold massive amounts of futures, and the index itself didn't fall nearly as far because the terrified arbitrageurs wouldn't exploit the spread. Normally when futures were trading far enough below the index itself, the arbitrageurs sold short a basket of stocks that closely tracked the index and bought an offsetting position in the cheaper index futures. When the price of the futures and that of the basket of underlying stocks converged, as they do later when the futures contracts settle, the arbitrageur closes out the hedge and captures the original spread as a profit. But on Tuesday, October 20, 1987, many stocks were difficult or impossible to sell short. That was because of the uptick rule.

The rule was part of the Securities Exchange Act of 1934 (rule 10a-1). It specified that, with certain exceptions, short-sale transactions are allowed only at a price higher than the last previous different price (an "uptick"). This rule was supposed to prevent short sellers from deliberately driving down the price of a stock. Seeing an enormous profit potential from capturing the unprecedented spread between the futures and the index, I wanted to sell stocks short and buy index futures to capture the excess spread. The index was selling at 15 percent, or 30 points, over the futures. The potential profit in an arbitrage was 15 percent in a few days. But with prices collapsing, upticks were scarce. What to do?

I figured out a solution. I called our head trader, who as a minor general partner was highly compensated from his share of our fees, and gave him this order: Buy $5 million worth of index futures at whatever the current market price happened to be (about 190), and place orders to sell short at the market, with the index then trading at about 220, not $5 million worth of assorted stocks—which was the optimal amount to best hedge the futures—but $10 million. I chose twice as much stock as I wanted, guessing only about half would actually be shorted because of the scarcity of the required upticks, thus giving me the proper hedge. If substantially more or less stock was sold short, the hedge would not be as good but the 15 percent profit cushion gave us a wide band of protection against loss.

I went through a detailed explanation of my outside-the-box analysis of why this trade was a windfall opportunity. But this day was beyond anything our trader had ever seen or imagined. Gripped by fear, he seemed frozen. He refused to execute the trades. I told him to do it for PNP and do it now, or else I wanted him to do it for my account. If that was his choice, I told him I would later tell all the other partners how the profit I made would have, but for him, belonged to the partnership rather than to me.

Here was my reasoning. If, because of the uptick rule, only about half the shorts got off, then we would be properly hedged and make about $750,000. If none got off (extremely improbable), we were buying the futures at an enormous discount—the index itself would have to fall more than another 13 percent before we began to lose. At the other extreme, especially in a market panic, there was virtually no chance all the shorts would go off. Even if all the orders to sell short were completed, the market would have to rise more than 14 percent for us to lose money. To protect against this possibility, I told my head trader that when we filled close to half the short-sale orders, he should cancel the rest. After he finally complied with my request and completed the first round, I ordered a second round of the same size. In the end we did get roughly half our shorts off for a near-optimal hedge. We had about $9 million worth of futures long and $10 million worth of stock short, locking in $1 million profit. If my trader hadn't wasted so much of the market day refusing to act, we could have done several more rounds and reaped additional millions.

We ended October "flat" for the month (approximately zero net gain or loss) whereas the S&P Index was down 22 percent. During the surrounding five-month period, from August through December, the index also fell 22 percent whereas Princeton Newport Partners gained 9 percent.

In its first decade of operation, 1969–79, PNP rose from a $1.4 million partnership to being perhaps the most mathematical, analytic, and computer-oriented firm on Wall Street. In the next eight years and two months, from November 1, 1979, through January 1, 1988, our capital base expanded from $28.6 million to $273 million, at which point we had investment positions totaling $1 billion. Partnership capital earned an annual rate of 22.8 percent before fees, and limited partners saw their wealth grow at 18.2 percent. The S&P 500 compounded at 11.5 percent, and small-company stocks annualized at 17.3 percent. We were much less risky than either of these, as industry statistics confirmed. We had no losing years or losing quarters.

We added extraordinary investment products that could expand our capital base to billions.

They included:

1. State-of-the-art convertible, warrant, and option computerized analytic models and trading systems. With this we had already become the biggest player in the Japanese warrant market.
2. Statistical arbitrage, which was a computerized analytic model and trading system for common stocks using a real-time feed of the ticker into our $2 million computer center, where we generated automated electronic orders and sent them to the floor. From one eight-by-eight cubicle we traded between one and two million shares a day, which was then 1 or 2 percent of NYSE daily volume.

3. A group of experts on interest rates joined us from Salomon Brothers. While there, they made $50 million for that firm in just eighteen months.

4. MIDAS: This indicator-driven stock prediction system was to be our entry into the broader money management business.

5. OSM Partners: a "fund of hedge funds" that invested in other hedge funds.

But all this was destined to come to an end.

## Chapter 16

# . . . AND FALL

In the middle of the day on Thursday, December 17, 1987, about fifty armed men and women burst out of the third-floor elevators to raid our office in Princeton, New Jersey. They were from the IRS, the FBI, and the postal authorities. Our employees were searched before they were free to leave the building. They were not allowed to return. The invaders impounded several hundred boxes of books and records, including Rolodexes. They dug through contents of wastebaskets and crawled through the ceiling spaces. It went on into the early-morning hours of the next day.

This was part of a campaign by Rudolph Giuliani, US Attorney for the Southern District of New York, to prosecute real and alleged Wall Street criminals. As a prosecutor later told a defense attorney, Giuliani's real objective in attacking individuals in our Princeton office was to get information to further his case against Michael Milken at Drexel Burnham and Robert Freeman at Goldman Sachs. My partner Jay Regan knew them both well and spoke to them often. Freeman had even been a roommate of Regan's at Dartmouth. Giuliani believed that Regan could help him bring them down. Regan refused to cooperate.

The government used evidence from the raid and testimony from a disgruntled former employee to develop their case. Ironically, when this man was being considered for a job as a trader by the Princeton office, they flew him to Newport Beach to get our opinion. We said emphatically that he was not suitable. However, it was our practice for each office to have the last word in the areas of the business for which it was primarily responsible. The Princeton office hired him. The five top people there were indicted and tried on sixty-four charges of stock manipulation, stock parking, tax fraud, mail fraud, and wire fraud. The defendants, in addition to Jay Regan, were our head trader, head convertible trader, the CFO and his assistant, and a Drexel Burnham convertible trader.

Neither I nor any of the forty or so other partners and employees in the Newport Beach office had any knowledge of the alleged acts in the Princeton office. We were never implicated in, or charged with, any wrongdoing in this or any other matter. Our two offices, more than two thousand miles apart, had very different activities, functions, and corporate cultures.

The key to the government's case was a few conversations they discovered on three old trading room audiotapes that had been saved years earlier, then misplaced and forgotten. They were originally created because it was the normal business practice in the Princeton office, as it was elsewhere on Wall Street, to temporarily record all telephone conversations in the trading room. A major purpose for this was to quickly resolve disputes with counterparties over trading orders and executions. With our volume of eighteen billion shares a year, mistakes were inevitable. One such trade, part of a gigantic Japanese warrant hedge executed through a firm I'll call Enco, was based on what they told us about the terms of the warrant. Our traders said Enco repeatedly assured us that the information they gave us was correct. In fact it wasn't. Our proof was on those tapes.

The resulting mistake in the quantities of securities used for our hedge position cost us $2 million. Ordinarily the tapes ran continuously, keeping the last four days of conversations, writing over the oldest as they recorded the newest. But pending a resolution, our traders saved the tape covering the disputed trade. Later, since Enco refused to admit the error was theirs, our traders prepared for arbitration or litigation by initiating and recording two more conversations in which Enco again told our traders the original information they had given us was correct. This meant two more tapes, including eight more days of conversations, were set aside for evidence. We then showed management at Enco how the facts contradicted what their staff had told us, and asked for compensation. Normally, the erring broker compensates the other party. Enco refused and said that if we litigated, they would no longer do business with us. We knew that all of the big four Japanese brokerage firms, which controlled the market in Japanese warrants and convertible bonds, would follow suit. As this area was a major contributor to our profits, we accepted the $2 million loss. Though the three tapes should then have been reused as was our usual practice, they sat forgotten in a desk for a couple of years until the government seized them in the 1987 raid as part of hundreds of boxes of files and materials.

The government invoked the Racketeer Influenced and Corrupt Organizations Act (RICO), a tool designed to prosecute mobsters, for the first time ever against securities industry defendants. It was a landmark case. The defendants posted cash bonds totaling $20 million.

To pressure them further, the US attorney began contacting our limited partners and making arrangements to subpoena them to come to New York and testify (to what?) before the grand jury. As they were passive participants not involved in the operations of the partnership, these subpoenas had no conceivable value for Giuliani's case against Regan and the others, other than to disturb and upset them, perhaps enough so they would withdraw from the partnership.

One of our investors had just returned with a carload of groceries to her country home in Northern California. As she described it, it was a sunny August afternoon, with the fragrance of pines in the desert-dry air much like the unforgettable atmosphere of Lake Tahoe in the high summer. As she prepared to carry in the bags, she noticed a sedan parked across the street, dented and with badly oxidized paint. The vehicle clearly did not belong in the neighborhood and she became concerned when two scruffy men got out and approached her. They brought a subpoena from the US Attorney ordering her to come to New York and testify before the grand jury in the Princeton Newport case.

Tall, poised, and elegant, with an artistic background, our partner was part of the Bay Area social establishment. She began by asking the two men to help her carry in the groceries. As they chatted, she said she really didn't know anything about the Princeton Newport case but she'd love to help. And she always looked forward to a trip to New York. Of course they would put her up at her favorite hotel and arrange theater tickets and restaurant reservations, wouldn't they? And she would need the information on the current exhibits at the Metropolitan, the Guggenheim, and the Whitney, and could they get her the schedule of programs at Carnegie Hall?

The bemused subpoena servers shuffled off and she heard no more from Mr. Giuliani.

Not all our investors reacted with such aplomb, but every last one of our more than ninety limited partners stood fast. No one asked to withdraw. Giuliani's ploy was exposed as a bluff when no limited partner was actually called to testify. Even so, we expected him to wreck our business if Regan didn't help him convict Milken and Freeman.

Limited partners were alarmed by the threat that RICO could be extended to their partnership assets, and by the doubts the investigation raised about some of our leadership in the Princeton office. I was disturbed by this and by the fact that information about the case was not being freely supplied to me by the Princeton office. For instance, when the government made a transcript of the trading room tapes and supplied it to the defendants, I asked to see it. I was put off with promises for weeks. Meanwhile, the lawyers for PNP, the partnership, who were separate from the defense team, also obtained a copy. At my request, they properly sent a set to me. An adviser for one of the defendants, hearing of this, was enraged and asked that PNP's lawyers be fired. I could understand why I was strung along when I read through the foot-deep stack of documents. There, in black and white, were conversations that had to be extremely embarrassing for those involved.

Legal fees for the defendants were estimated at between $10 million and $20 million. There was no telling how long the case would go on or how it would end. If the defendants were found guilty they would be liable for their own legal bills whereas if they were declared innocent, the partnership would pay. To get closure, I negotiated a flat advance payout to the defendants of $2.5 million, to cover any and all responsibility the partnership had for their legal expenses. In addition to this payout, the partnership was burdened with its own considerable legal expenses.

The return for PNP during this traumatic year was a mediocre 4 percent, reduced not only by the millions in legal costs from the case but also because the team in Princeton, consumed by defending themselves, couldn't devote their usual time to partnership business. As 1988 drew to a close, I saw no good way forward for PNP. I said I was leaving. Limited partners followed and the partnership then wound down.

Rudolph Giuliani resigned as a US Attorney early in 1989 to run unsuccessfully later that year for mayor of New York, propelled by his fame and notoriety from the several years he spent first prosecuting the mafia and then Wall Street figures. He ran again for mayor four years later, this time successfully, and served two terms.

The defendants were convicted in August 1989 on multiple counts and sentenced to jail terms of three months and fines. The convictions, using RICO, were crucial in breaking the will to resist by Milken and Freeman. Both plea-bargained. But they may have acted too soon. Two months after the PNP convictions, which included racketeering counts under RICO, the US Department of Justice for a second time took "steps to rein in the tactics in racketeering prosecutions that sparked controversy during Wall Street corruption cases brought by former Manhattan U.S. Attorney Rudolph Giuliani." The PNP defendants appealed and the Second Circuit Court of Appeals threw out the convictions for racketeering and tax fraud. It upheld the charges of conspiracy for all six defendants and securities fraud for two. In January 1992, having achieved their real goal, which was to convict Milken and Freeman, the prosecutors dropped the remaining charges against four of the five PNP defendants and a related charge against the Drexel trader. Princeton's head trader and the Drexel defendant were still facing fines and three-month prison terms for their remaining counts. In September 1992, a federal judge vacated these sentences as well.

Superficially, the PNP case appears simply to be a federal prosecution of securities violators. To understand why it really happened, you need to go back to the 1970s, when first-tier companies could routinely meet their financing needs from Wall Street and the banking community, whereas less established companies had to scramble. Seizing an opportunity to finance them, a young financial innovator named Michael Milken built a capital-raising machine for these companies from within a stodgy old Wall Street firm, Drexel Burnham Lambert. Milken's group underwrote issues of low-rated, high-yielding bonds—the so-called junk bonds—some of which were convertible or came with warrants to purchase stock. The higher yield was the extra compensation investors required to offset the perceived risk that the bonds would default. Filling a gaping need and hungry demand in the business community, Milken's group became the greatest financing engine in Wall Street history.

Such innovation outraged the old line establishment of corporate America, who were initially transfixed like deer in the headlights as a horde of entrepreneurs, funded with seemingly unlimited Drexel-generated cash, began a wave of unfriendly takeovers. Many old firms were vulnerable because the officers and directors had done a poor job of investing the shareholders' equity. With subpar returns on capital, the stocks were cheap. A takeover group could restructure, raise the rate of return, and make such a company considerably more valuable. Since that company's potential was so great, the prospective new owners could pay more than the current market price.

The officers and directors of America's big corporations were happy with the way things had been. They enjoyed their hunting lodges and private jets, made charitable donations for their personal aggrandizement and objectives, and granted themselves generous salaries, retirement plans, bonuses of cash, stock, and stock options, and golden parachutes. All these things were designed by and for themselves and paid for with corporate dollars, the expenses routinely ratified by a scattered and fragmented shareholder base. Economists call this conflict of interest between management, or agents, and the shareholders, who are the real owners, the agency problem. It continues today, one example being the massive continuing grants of stock options by management to itself, already estimated by the year 2000 to have risen to 14 percent of the total value of corporate America. By 2008 the greedy incompetence of the chieftains of corporate America had helped bring on one of the greatest financial crises in history, leading to a massive taxpayer-funded federal bailout to save the US economy from ruin.

The Drexel-funded newcomers were knocking the more vulnerable managers off their horses into the mud. Something would have to be done. Government ought to be sympathetic—the old corporate establishment had most of the money and they were the most politically powerful and influential group in the country. Their Wall Street subdivision might sustain some damage, but one could expect the fall of Drexel to release, as it did, a huge honeypot of business to be taken over by everyone else.

The old establishment financiers were lucky in that prosecutors would find numerous violations of securities laws within the Milken group and among its many allies, associates, and clients. However, it is difficult to judge how relatively bad these were, compared with the incessant violations that have always been, and continue to be, endemic in business and finance, because only a few of the many violators are caught, and when they are prosecuted it may be for only a tiny fraction of their offenses. This contrasts with the case of Drexel, where the searchlight of government was focused to reveal as many violations as possible. It's like the case of the man who was cited three times in a single year for driving while intoxicated. His neighbor would also drink and drive, but was never pulled over. Who is the greater criminal? Now suppose I tell you that the caught man did it only three times and was apprehended every time, whereas his neighbor did it a hundred times and was never caught. How could this happen? What if I tell you that the two men are bitter business rivals and that the traffic cop's boss, the police chief, gets large campaign contributions from the man who got no traffic citations. Now who is the greater criminal?

The situation was a dream come true for the government's ax, Ru-

dolph Giuliani. Politically ambitious, Giuliani was aware of how an earlier US Attorney, Thomas E. Dewey, prosecuted bootleggers in the
1930s and parlayed this into the governorship of New York and almost,
the US presidency in 1948. The prosecution of securities violations and
insider trading was the perfect ladder.

What could PNP have been worth twenty-five years later, in the year
2015? How could I possibly have any idea? Amazingly enough, a
market-neutral hedge fund operation was built on the Princeton Newport model—the Citadel Investment Group. It was started in 1990 in
Chicago by former hedge fund manager Frank Meyer when he discovered the young quantitative investment prodigy Ken Griffin, who was
then trading options and convertible bonds from his Harvard dorm
room. I met with Frank and Ken, outlining the workings and profit
centers of PNP, as well as turning over cartons of documents outlining
in detail the terms and conditions of older outstanding warrants and
convertible bonds. These were valuable, because they were no longer
available.

Citadel grew from a humble start in 1990 (when I became its first
limited partner) with a few million dollars and one employee, Griffin, to
a collection of businesses managing $20 billion in capital and having
more than a thousand employees twenty-five years later, annualizing at
about 20 percent net to limited partners. Ken's net worth in 2015 was
estimated at $5.6 billion.

As Princeton Newport Partners closed I reflected on the proposition
that what matters in life is how you spend your time. When J. Paul Getty
was the richest man in the world and manifestly not fulfilled, he said the
happiest time of his life was when he was sixteen, riding waves off the
beach in Malibu, California. In 2000, *Los Angeles Times Magazine,* speaking of new multibillionaire Henry T. Nicholas III of Broadcom Corporation, said, "It's 1:30 a.m. He's just turned 40—at his desk, in a dimly lit
office. He hasn't seen his wife and children, 'my reason for living,' for
several days. 'The last time we talked, [Stacey] told me she missed the
old days, when I was at TRW and we lived in a condo. She told me she
wants to go back to that life.' But they can't go back because he can't let
up." (They later divorced.)

I initially thought that I might continue on my own with a PNP-style partnership. But if I did that, then, in addition to the fun parts, I would be responsible for things I didn't enjoy. I changed my mind and gradually wound down our PNP office in Newport Beach, finding good jobs in the securities industry for some of our key people at places like the giant hedge fund D. E. Shaw, the financial engineering firm Barra, and the investment group running the multibillion-dollar pension and profit sharing plan at Weyerhaeuser. Then I called Fischer Black, who was now at Goldman Sachs, after hearing that he wanted to build a computerized analytic system for trading warrants and, especially, convertible bonds. Our proven state-of-the-art system was for sale, so he flew out and spent two days with Steve and me learning how it worked. He took detailed notes but finally said that it would be too costly to convert the code to run on their computers.

## Chapter 17

# PERIOD OF ADJUSTMENT

Joseph Heller and Kurt Vonnegut were at a party given by a billionaire when Vonnegut asked Heller how it felt to know that their host might have made more money in one day than Heller's *Catch-22* since it was written. Heller said he had something the rich man could never have. When a puzzled Vonnegut asked what that could be, Heller answered, "The knowledge that I've got enough."

When Princeton Newport Partners closed, Vivian and I had money enough for the rest of our lives. Though the ending of PNP was traumatic for us all, and the future wealth destroyed was in the billions, it freed us to do more of what we enjoyed most: spend time with each other and the family and friends we loved, travel, and pursue our interests. Taking to heart the lyrics of the song "Enjoy Yourself (It's Later than You Think)," Vivian and I would make the most of the one thing we could never have enough of—time together. Success on Wall Street was getting the most money. Success for us was having the best life.

It was by chance during this time that I discovered the greatest of all financial frauds. On the afternoon of Thursday, December 11, 2008, I got the news I had been expecting for more than seventeen years. Calling from New York, my son, Jeff, told me Bernie Madoff confessed to having defrauded investors of $50 billion in the greatest Ponzi scheme in history. "It's what you predicted in . . . 1991!" he said.

On a balmy Monday morning in the spring of '91, I arrived at the New York office of a well-known international consulting company. The investment committee hired me as an independent adviser to review their hedge fund investments. I spent a few days examining performance histories, business structures, and backgrounds of managers, as well as making onsite visits. One manager was so paranoid when I interviewed him at his office that he wouldn't tell me what kind of personal computers they used. When I went to the restroom he escorted me for fear that I might acquire some valuable crumb of information en route.

I approved the portfolio, with one exception. The story from Bernard Madoff Investment didn't add up. My client had been getting regular monthly profits ranging from 1 percent to more than 2 percent for two years. Moreover, they knew other Madoff investors who had been winning every month for more than a decade.

Madoff claimed to use a split-strike price strategy: He would buy a stock, sell a call option at a higher price, and use the proceeds to pay for a put option at a lower price.

I explained that, according to financial theory, the long-run impact on portfolio returns from many properly priced options with zero net proceeds should also be zero. So we expect, over time, that the client's portfolio return should be roughly the same as the return on equities. The returns Madoff reported were too large to be believed. Moreover, in months when stocks are down, the strategy should produce a loss—but Madoff wasn't reporting any losses. After checking the client's account statements I found that losing months for the strategy were magically converted to winners by short sales of S&P Index futures. In the same way, months that should have produced very large wins were "smoothed out."

Suspecting fraud, I asked my client to arrange for me to visit the Madoff operation on the seventeenth floor of the famous Lipstick Building on Third Avenue in Manhattan. Bernie was in Europe that week, and as we now know, likely raising more money. His brother, Peter, head of compliance and of computer operations, said that I would not be allowed through the front door.

I asked my client who it was that did the accounting and annual audits for the Madoff fund. I was told it was handled by a one-man shop run by someone who had been a friend and neighbor of Bernie's since the 1960s. Now on high alert for fraud, I asked when the client received confirmations of trades. The answer was that they came by mail in batches every week or two, well after the dates they supposedly occurred. At my suggestion, the client then hired my firm to conduct a detailed analysis of their individual transactions to prove or disprove my suspicion that they were fake. After analyzing about 160 individual options trades, we found that for half of them no trades occurred on the exchange where Madoff said that they supposedly took place. For many of the remaining half that did trade, the quantity reported by Madoff just for my client's two accounts exceeded the entire volume reported for everyone. To check the minority of remaining trades, those that did not conflict with the prices and volumes reported by the exchanges, I asked an official at Bear Stearns to find out in confidence who all the buyers and sellers of the options were. We could not connect any of them to Madoff's firm.

I told my client that the trades were fake and Madoff's investment operation was a fraud. My client had a dilemma. If I was right and he closed his accounts with Madoff he would protect his money, save his reputation, and avoid a legal mess. He argued that if I were wrong, he would needlessly sacrifice his best investment. I answered that I could not be wrong: I had proven from public records that the trades never happened. He was being sent make-believe trade slips. I made the point that to ignore this could put his job at risk. That clinched it. He closed his accounts with Madoff and got his money back. Over the next eighteen years, he watched other Madoff investors seem to get rich. I wonder how often he regretted hiring me.

In my attempt, via "networking," to find out how much other money was invested with Madoff I repeatedly heard that all his investors were told not to disclose their relationship, even to one another, on threat of being dropped. Even so, I asked around, located half a billion dollars, and concluded that the scheme had to be much larger. One investor's track record showed gains every month back to 1979, annualizing at 20 percent, and I was told the record was similar stretching into the late 1960s. The scheme had already been operating for more than twenty years!

Having shown that Madoff was posting made-up trades to my client's accounts, and that he was apparently doing so to several other investors with whom I spoke, I had the smoking gun that proved fraud. I warned people in my network, forecasting an ever-expanding Ponzi scheme that one day would end disastrously. Ponzi schemes fake profits to investors. They use the money the investors put in but eventually need more, which they get by recruiting new investors. These new investors also have to be paid, leading the Ponzi operators to sign up still more. The longer it went undetected the bigger it would grow and the worse it would be when it collapsed.

At this time Madoff was a major figure in the securities industry, serving as chairman of NASDAQ, running one of the largest "third market" (off the exchanges) stock trading firms in the country, consulted by government, and routinely checked out by the SEC.

Would the establishment have believed charges of wrongdoing? The story of Harry Markopoulos gives the answer. Challenged by his boss in 1999 to explain why Madoff, with a supposedly similar strategy, could produce much better and steadier returns, Markopoulos concluded that it was impossible on the basis of quantitative financial reasoning, just as I had done before I began my investigation that proved fraud. Though he didn't establish that the individual trades were faked, even without that smoking gun his arguments were overwhelmingly persuasive. For the next ten years Markopoulos attempted to get the SEC to investigate, but it brushed him aside repeatedly, cleared Madoff after superficial investigations, and quashed a request from the Boston office, prompted by Markopoulos, to investigate Madoff Investment as a possible Ponzi scheme.

In a remarkable 477-page document, "Investigation of Failure of the SEC to Uncover Bernard Madoff's Ponzi Scheme—Public Version," August 31, 2009, Report No. OIG-509, the SEC investigates and documents its own repeated failures, beginning in 1992 and continuing until Madoff confessed in 2008, to follow up on obvious clues, pointed complaints, and clear violations of securities laws. Yet the SEC continued to destroy documents through at least July 2010, relating not only to Madoff, but to major financial institutions like Goldman Sachs and Bank of America, as well as SAC Capital Advisors, during a continuing investigation of the latter. Charged with insider trading, SAC Capital agreed to a record $1.8 billion fine in late 2013 and closed itself to outside investors.

Ten years after I discovered the Madoff fraud, at a hedge fund investing conference sponsored by *Barron's,* a weekly publication by *The Wall Street Journal* presenting financial data and in-depth stories, the headline article was about the investment manager who wasn't there, the manager with the best record of all—Bernie Madoff. Better yet for investors, he didn't charge the typical hedge fund fees of 1 percent of assets per year plus 20 percent of any new net gains. Supposedly he made his money from charging small fees on the huge trading volume that was flowing through his brokerage firm from the orders he placed on behalf of his investment clients.

Even with the well-publicized doubts expressed in the *Barron's* story, and the suspicions of fraud now being voiced by many, the regulators slept on. So did Madoff's thousands of investors and the fiduciaries they paid to protect them. How did the fraud end? When it became clear that there wouldn't be enough money to keep paying investors, which is how all Ponzi schemes end, Bernie Madoff (pronounced *MADE-off,* as in "with your money") turned himself in on December 11, 2008. Probably to protect his associates, he came up with the improbable story that he was the sole conspirator in the scheme. This man who was virtually ignorant about computer systems claimed to have single-handedly directed the whole secure seventeenth-floor computerized operation, along with some twenty or so employees generating—supposedly unknowingly—a daily torrent of billions of dollars of fake trades for thousands of accounts.

On August 11, 2009, exactly eight months later, Frank DiPascali, Jr., the man who supervised Madoff's operations day-to-day, was charged by the SEC in the US District Court, Southern District of New York. At this point the SEC knew that Bernard Madoff Investment Securities (BMIS) "managed investor accounts as far back as the 1960s . . ." However, the SEC complaint said the split-strike price strategy dated from 1992, whereas I had reviewed client records showing that it was in place years earlier. Pleading guilty, Madoff told the judge that he began stealing money in the early 1990s. But his criminal empire was already big then and had started at least twenty years earlier. Madoff claimed his brother, Peter, and sons, Mark and Andrew, all principals in the firm, and the detail-oriented hands-on wife, Ruth, were totally innocent and unaware of any complicity in the massive forty-year fraud. In addition to supposedly running his swindle single-handedly, Madoff was vacationing at his various residences, traveling abroad to raise ever more money, shuffling massive funds internationally among banks, and paying large fees to "fiduciaries" who brought him investments, while the complex scheme somehow ran like clockwork during his many absences.

Bernie Madoff, in his allocution to the judge, said, contrary to fact, that he thought his swindle began about 1991, whereas I discovered then that the scheme had already been running for decades. The SEC's complaint against Frank DiPascali—presumably using information from DiPascali—that the fraud was computerized and the split-strike price strategy had begun in 1992, was also contradicted by the client reports I had reviewed from 1989 through 1991. Peter Madoff, DiPascali, and several other employees later pled guilty and were sentenced to fines and jail.

Madoff gave the size of the scam at $50 billion, though based on the amount of fake equity investors believed they had in their accounts at the end it was later estimated at $65 billion. To equitably distribute any remaining money, the bankruptcy trustee has to determine how much money each victim put in, what was paid out, and to whom. Several "handlers," who each collected billions from the investors for whom they claimed to have thoroughly verified the legitimacy of Madoff's strategy, skimmed off hundreds of millions in fees. Powered by this cash flood, they rose among the politically and socially connected superrich. One individual reportedly withdrew over $5 billion more than he put in! The fact that Madoff was letting others collect huge sums in management fees, all the while settling for much less in trading commissions, should itself have been enough to alert investors, advisers, and regulators.

The government released a list of more than thirteen thousand past and present Madoff account holders, ranging from hundreds of not very rich Florida retirees to celebrities, billionaires, and nonprofits such as charities and universities. If these legions of investors were easily gulled, often for decades, what does this swindle (and others) say about the academic theory that markets are "efficient," with its claims that investors quickly and rationally incorporate all publicly available information into their selections?

Among the thousands of Madoff investors on the list was a well-known financial adviser who had been present at the meetings in 1991 where I exposed the Madoff scam. At that time I had known Ned, as I'll call him, for many years so I made sure he understood every detail. Although we lost touch in the mid-1990s, I was astonished in 2008 to find that he and his family were on the government's list of Madoff's investors. Moreover, a mutual acquaintance told me that Ned, who had made hundreds of millions advising clients, was still directing investors to Madoff the same week that the latter confessed.

Having once known Ned well, I thought back to get more insight into why he believed in Madoff. In my opinion Ned was not a crook. Instead, I think he suffered from so-called cognitive dissonance. That's where you want to believe something enough that you simply reject any information to the contrary. Nicotine addicts will often deny that smoking endangers their health. Members of political parties react mildly to lies, crimes, and other immorality by their own but are out for blood when the same is done by politicians in the other party.

I also learned early that when I gave Ned my opinion on anything, no matter how careful or reasoned, it didn't have much impact. Others had the same experience. To make a decision, Ned would simply poll everyone he knew for their opinion and then go with the majority view. Once I figured this out, I stopped wasting my time sharing my thoughts with him.

The Ned polling method works remarkably well in certain situations, like guessing the number of beans in a barrel, or the weight of a pumpkin. The average of all the guesses by the crowd is typically much better than most of the individual guesses. This phenomenon has been called the wisdom of crowds. But like most simplifications, this has a flip side, as in the Madoff case. Here there were just two answers, fraudster or investment genius. The crowd voted for investment genius and got it wrong. I call the flip side to the wisdom of crowds the lunacy of lemmings.

By 1991, I had simplified to a staff of four people. Steve Mizusawa was hedging Japanese warrants, with some assistance from me. I was also managing a portfolio of hedge funds for myself, with help from Judy McCoy. She was in charge of tax and financial reporting, helped Steve, and backed up our office manager.

Enjoying life and ambivalent about returning to the investment hubbub, I tried to find a time-efficient way to cash in on our statistical arbitrage knowledge. After discussions with Steve, who would be crucial in implementing any such venture, I went shopping for a partner to whom we could license our software for royalties.

I contacted Bruce Kovner, a successful commodities trader whom I knew from Princeton Newport days. Kovner started with the Commodities Corporation in the 1970s, then went on to run his own commodities hedge fund, eventually making billions for himself and his investors.

Along with Jerry Baesel, the finance professor from UCI who joined me at PNP, I spent an afternoon with Bruce in the 1980s in his Manhattan apartment discussing how he thought and how he got his edge in the markets. Kovner was and is a generalist, who sees connections before others do.

About this time he realized large oil tankers were in such oversupply that the older ones were selling for little more than scrap value. Kovner formed a partnership to buy one. I was one of the limited partners. Here was an interesting option. We were largely protected against loss because we could always sell the tanker for scrap, recovering most of our investment; but we had a substantial upside: Historically, the demand for tankers had fluctuated widely and so had their price. Within a few years, our refurbished 475,000-ton monster, the *Empress Des Mers,* was profitably plying the world's sea-lanes stuffed with oil. I liked to think of my part ownership as a twenty-foot section just forward of the bridge. Later the partnership negotiated to purchase what was then the largest ship ever built, the 650,000-ton *Seawise Giant.* Unfortunately for the sellers, while we were in escrow their ship unwisely ventured near Kharg Island in the Persian Gulf, where it was bombed by Iraqi aircraft, caught fire, and sank. The *Empress Des Mers* operated profitably into the twenty-first century, when the saga finally ended. Having generated a return on investment of 30 percent annualized, she was sold for scrap in 2004, fetching almost $23 million, far more than her purchase price of $6 million.

Kovner referred me to a hedge fund in which he was a major investor, and I proposed to the manager of the fund that we would supply the software for a complete statistical arbitrage operating system and license it for 15 percent of his gross income from the use of the product. We would train their employees and provide continuing counsel. Our license fee would decline over time to adjust for improvements they might add, and for the obsolescence of the original system. However, every time we agreed on a deal, the GP insisted on making yet another change in his favor. After we had agreed to some of these, it became apparent that they were endless. I terminated negotiations.

Most of us who have dealt with used-car dealers or rug merchants, or who have bought and sold real estate, are familiar with a negotiation process perhaps best described as haggling. To illustrate, suppose a house you want is priced at $300,000. You offer $250,000. The seller counters at $290,000. You counter at $265,000, and so forth. Finally you agree to buy at $275,000. This stylized dance may involve cajolery, trickery, and deceit. Wouldn't it be simpler and more satisfying for the seller to state his price and have the buyer take it or leave it? After all, that's how it's done in most stores in the United States. How could you shop if the prices you compare aren't firm?

Yet in business deals haggling is common, just as it was with the fund manager who haggled with me. What's going on here? In our house example, suppose the seller's real lowest price is $260,000 and that the highest price the buyer is really willing to pay is $290,000. (The seller might find out, for instance, that the buyer will really pay $290,000 by reporting that he has another offer at $289,000, at which point the first buyer offers $290,000.) Thus any price between $260,000 and $290,000 is acceptable to both parties, even though neither party knows this at the time. So $30,000 is "up for grabs." The objective of the haggle is to capture as much of this $30,000 as possible for one side or the other.

On the other hand, if instead the buyer is willing only to go to $270,000 and the seller's (secret) lowest price is $280,000, there is no overlap, no price both will accept, and there will be no deal.

Where my family and I lived for over two decades was determined by just such a haggler. We had decided to build a new house and had located a lot with a spectacular view high on a hill in Newport Beach. In the depressed 1979 real estate market it was offered at $435,000. We started at $365,000; after a series of offers and counteroffers, we eventually came back with $400,000, which was countered at $410,000. We countered at $405,000, our absolute limit. Rejected. We walked. A few days later the seller relented and offered to meet our $405,000 price. But we didn't accept. Why not?

At our absolute limit, we were almost indifferent as to whether we did the deal or not. Meanwhile the seller had now alienated us, and we preferred not to have any further dealings with him. Consequently his deal was less attractive, and our top price now dropped below $405,000. Meanwhile we considered alternatives. We soon bought a better lot, built a new house, and spent twenty-two happy years there. The haggler's lot remained unsold for another decade.

Coincidentally, when we sold this house, we had another example of the losing haggle. After it had been on the market a year, we suddenly got two offers the same weekend. We were asking $5,495,000 and expected to get about $5,000,000. One offer was at $4.6 million, and the prospective buyer used his aggressive business partner to open negotiations. The partner's in-your-face style and nitpicking criticism of the house was designed to beat down the price. He alienated us and our agent. The other offer was for $5 million from an agreeable family who loved the house "as is." We accepted, upon which the other buyer begged us to reconsider, indicating he would meet or exceed the other price, and wouldn't use Mr. in-your-face to close the deal. Too bad. Lesson: It doesn't pay to push the other party to their absolute limit. A small extra gain is generally not worth the substantial risk the deal will break up.

Knowing when to haggle and when not to is valuable for traders. In the days of Princeton Newport our head trader used to crow about how, by regularly holding out for an extra eighth or quarter, he saved us large amounts of money. Here's the idea. Suppose we want to buy 10,000 shares of Microsoft (MSFT), currently trading at, say, 71 bid for 50,000 shares, and 71¼ asked for 10,000 shares. We can pay 71¼ now and buy our 10,000 shares. Or, as our trader would do, we can offer to buy our 10,000 shares at 71⅛ and see if we have any takers. If this works—and it does most of the time—we'll save $⅛ × 10,000 or $1,250.

This sounds good. Is there any risk? Yes. By trying to save $⅛ per share we may miss a big winner if the stock always trades at 71¼ or higher for however long we're trying to buy. Those stocks we miss, which run away to the upside, would have given us windfall profits. Put simply, you might scalp $⅛ twenty times but lose $10 once. Do you like that arithmetic? I don't.

I asked our trader how he could tell whether his repeated scalping for an eighth of a point offset his losses from missed opportunities. He could not make a case for what he was doing. I asked other traders around the street the same question and didn't find anyone who could clearly show that they gained more than they lost by doing this.

Markets are basic to modern economics, and trading is a fundamental activity. Modern financial theorists have, therefore, intensively analyzed how markets work, both by examining data and by developing theories to explain what they observe. They note that trades are initiated, sometimes by a buyer and other times by a seller, for a variety of reasons. Some participants have no edge—no special advantageous information—probably including most of the people who do think they have an edge. Examples of these so-called noise traders might include an index fund selling a company because it was dropped from the index,

or buying a stock that was added to its index, or an estate liquidating to
pay taxes, or a mutual fund buying or selling in response to cash additions and withdrawals. Of course, to the extent worthwhile information
is used in these trades, such examples are imperfect.

The other type of trade is initiated by traders who do have an edge.
Examples might be the illegal insider trades made famous by the prosecutions of Ivan Boesky and others in the 1980s—despite which such activities continue to this day; or the legal trades made by those who are
the first to act on public information like an earnings announcement, a
takeover, or an interest rate change.

Does all this really matter? What's an eighth of a dollar a share? For
our statistical arbitrage program that was trading one and a half billion
shares a year, it would amount to almost $200 million annually. As Sen-
ator Everett Dirksen was once quoted as saying about congressional
spending, a billion dollars here, a billion dollars there, and pretty soon
you're talking about some real money.

What the hagglers and the traders do reminds me of the behavioral psychology distinction between two extremes on a continuum of types: sat-
isficers and maximizers. When a maximizer goes shopping, looks for a
handyman, buys gas, or plans a trip, he searches for the best (maximum)
possible deal. Time and effort don't matter much. Missing the very best
deal leads to regret and stress. On the other hand, the satisficer, so-called
because he is satisfied with a result that is close to the best, factors in the
costs of searching and decision making, as well as the risk of losing a
near-optimal opportunity and perhaps never finding anything as good
again.

This is reminiscent of the so-called secretary or marriage problem in
mathematics. Assume that you will interview a series of people, from
which you will choose one. Further, you must consider them one at a
time, and having once rejected someone, you cannot reconsider. The optimal strategy is to wait until you have seen about 37 percent of the prospects, then choose the next one you see who is better than anybody

among this first 37 percent that you passed over. If no one is better you are stuck with the last person on the list.

This idea rescued me back in my graduate student days at UCLA, shortly after I had changed from the PhD program in physics to that in mathematics. My thesis adviser, Angus Taylor, decided that I, like other doctoral candidates, should deliver a mathematical talk for students. With my then comparatively skimpy mathematical background, I was stumped for a topic that would interest the mathematically knowledgeable people who would attend and also attract new faces from outside the department. At the last minute I came up with the title "What Every Young Girl Should Know" and refused to tell anyone what I was going to say about it. The room was packed, with attendance beyond anything previously seen. Most agreeably, in addition to the usual mostly male audience, there were lots of pretty coeds. From their questions and their expressions afterward, my listeners weren't disappointed. I had talked about the solution to the so-called marriage problem and had made the math behind it understandable.

*Chapter 18*

# SWINDLES AND HAZARDS

hen shifting my focus from beating gambling games to analyzing the stock market, I naïvely thought that I was leaving a world where cheating at cards was problematic and entering an arena where regulation and the rule of law gave investors a fair playing field. Instead, I learned that bigger stakes attracted bigger thieves. Bernie Madoff's Ponzi scheme was only the largest of the many exposed in 2008 and 2009, as a sharply falling market cut the supply of new money flowing into the swindles. These ranged in size from an $8 billion bank scam to swindles involving hundreds of millions of dollars each (including several hedge funds), and multimillion-dollar real estate, mortgage, and annuity scams. Swindles likely follow a simple mathematical law describing how their number increases as their economic size decreases.

The rise of the Internet and electronic connectivity created new opportunities for fraud. On Friday, August 25, 2000, my niece Dana, who was getting interested in stocks, called me after the market closed.

"Do you know anything about a stock called Emulex?" she asked.

"No, why?"

"Well, I own some, and shortly after it opened today it crashed from 113 [dollars per share] to 45 and then they suspended trading!"

"What's the news about it?" I asked.

"I don't know."

"Well, my advice is to do nothing. I'd say there's a good chance it's another Internet fraud and that the company is just as sound as it was yesterday."

We soon learned what had happened. A twenty-three-year-old college student had sent a report to the electronic news service Internet Wire for which he formerly worked, purporting to be an official news release from Emulex (EMLX). The report claimed that the company's president was resigning, good positive earnings for the last two years were being corrected to show large losses, and the SEC was to investigate. This fake information spread quickly and the stock was down 56 percent by the time NASDAQ halted trading. The hoaxer had earlier lost $100,000 selling Emulex short and managed to regain this plus a $250,000 profit before he was apprehended the following week. In the process, at the worst point, he had knocked the market capitalization of EMLX from $4.1 billion to $1.6 billion, a loss of $2.5 billion. Though the stock recovered most of its loss later in the day, it still closed down 7.31 at 105.75, a fall of 6.6 percent or $270 million in market value. The damage was much greater for those who sold during the drop. Eleven days after the hoax was exposed, and after the hoaxer was caught, the stock closed at 100.13, down 11.4 percent, never having fully recovered in the interim.

According to the theory of efficient markets (the EMH), the market sets prices so that they accurately reflect all available information. How does the collapse of 60 percent in fifteen minutes in response to false information represent the rational incorporation of information into the price? I also ask believers in the EMH to explain why the stock failed to recover in the eleven days after the hoax was exposed. The news for EMLX was good. So . . . ?

Supporters of the efficient market view have slowly accepted minor deviations from the theory. They might acknowledge the market's response to the EMLX hoax as one of these; but as the press pointed out,

the Internet is rife with such attempts, notably in chat rooms, and EMLX was just one in a series of large-scale spectacular attempts to fool the public in order to gain a profit.

Shortly afterward, on September 21, 2000, a front-page headline in *The New York Times* read "SEC Says Teenager Had After-School Hobby: Online Stock Fraud." The fifteen-year-old New Jersey high school student collected $273,000 in eleven trades. He would first buy a block of stock in a thinly traded company, then flood Internet chat rooms with messages that, say, a $2 stock would be trading at $20 "very soon." The text here was about as valuable as the message in a fortune cookie. Dr. EMH's rational all-knowing investors promptly bid up the price, at which point young Mr. Lebed sold. He had opened his brokerage accounts in his father's name. Lebed settled with the SEC, repaying $273,000 in profits plus $12,000 in interest. It's not apparent from the stories that any of this money was used to compensate the defrauded investors, whose identity or degree of injury may in any case be impossible to determine. The father's comment? "So they pick on a kid."

In the early 1980s, a decade before coming across Madoff, I learned of a remarkable investment manager. This foreign exchange trader was racking up returns of 1 percent, 2 percent, 3 percent, and even 4 percent a month. He seemed never to lose. I asked George Shows, an associate in my Newport Beach office, to make an onsite visit to J. David Dominelli in nearby La Jolla. George came back with the amazing track record and "advertising" literature but could find no evidence of any actual trading activity. Our requests for audited financial statements, proof of assets, and proof of trades were smoothly deflected. I suspected a Ponzi scheme, and we didn't invest. Two years later Dominelli's scam collapsed in 1984, wiping out $200 million and defrauding one thousand investors, including many of the social, political, and financial elite of the San Diego area.

In 1984, I came across an innovative company with a new high-tech computerized product for the financial community. They were seeking more capital to finish research and development and to market their product. The story was persuasive, the business plan made sense, and my computer expert, Steve Mizusawa, gave a thumbs-up to their plans.

I and several friends invested alongside the principals, paying them what was then the typical hedge fund fee of 20 percent of profits. The first year's financial statements showed no income, only substantial expenses for research and development. Nonetheless, the principals declared a profit and paid themselves 20 percent of it! But there was no profit, only expenses. How did the principals justify pocketing our money? They claimed that the money spent for research and development produced a value greater than the amount spent, and they treated this alleged excess value as if it were cash in the bank! We eventually managed to get them to give our money back.

Mismanaged, the company then dissipated their clear technological edge, and competitor Michael Bloomberg passed them with a similar product that became ubiquitous, making billions from it. A few years later, two of the principals opened a hedge fund, and knowing their characters, I warned against investing in it. In 2008 they were charged with misappropriating several hundred million dollars of their investors' capital in yet another Ponzi scheme.

The frauds, swindles, and hoaxes, a flood reported almost daily in the financial press, have continued unabated during the more than fifty years of my investment career.

But then, hoaxes, scams, manias, and large-scale financial irrationalities have been with us from the beginnings of the markets in the seventeenth century, long before the Internet. Yet the repeated exposés are not processed by the EMH true believer. Former UCI professor Robert Haugen, a vocal academic critic of the EMH and the author of several books arguing against the EMH, got an extreme response. During a UCLA conference, The Market Debate: A Break from Tradition, after Haugen delivered a paper on market inefficiency, he reported that Eugene Fama, father of the EMH and future co-recipient of the 2013 Nobel Prize in Economics, "... pointed to me in the audience and called me a criminal. He then said that he believed that GOD knew that the stock market was efficient. He added that the closer one came to behavioral finance, the hotter one could feel the fires of Hell on one's feet."

In the last few years, so-called high-frequency traders (HFTs) have used computers to extract money from the market by inserting themselves between buyers and sellers, gaining on average a small profit on each transaction. These predatory programs depend on extreme quickness to get ahead of everyone else, with times measured in microseconds. Policed by the laws of nature, electrical signals to the exchanges travel no faster than light, a speed limit of about one thousand feet per microsecond. Location matters, and firms have paid expensively to house their computers as physically close as possible to the exchange. Recent reports say that a majority of trades involve these programs, generating $21 billion a year in annual profits. This was 0.1 percent of the market value of all US equities. A large investment house told my son, Jeff, that they have "guys with a few million of capital that clear through them and trade hundreds of millions per day." I've wondered whether the frequent odd trading prices in Berkshire Hathaway, such as the one of $89,375.37 reported for the A shares, come from one of these trading programs.

Though many details of these schemes are either complex or not yet public knowledge, one of the mechanisms is. Some exchanges, such as NASDAQ, let HF traders peek at customer orders ahead of everyone else for thirty milliseconds before the order goes to the exchange. Seeing an order to buy, for instance, the HF traders can buy first, pushing the stock price up, then resell to the customer at a profit. Seeing someone's order to sell, the HF trader sells first, causing the stock to fall, and then buys it back at the lower price. How is this different from the crime of front-running, described in Wikipedia as "the illegal practice of a stock broker executing orders on a security for its own account while taking advantage of advance knowledge of pending orders from its customers"?

Some securities industry spokesmen argue that harvesting this wealth from investors somehow makes the markets more efficient and that "markets need liquidity." Nobel Prize–winning economist Paul Krugman disagrees sharply, arguing that high-frequency trading is simply a way of taking wealth from ordinary investors, serves no useful purpose, and wastes national wealth because the resources consumed create no social good.

Since the more the rest of us trade the more we as a group lose to the computers, here's one more reason to buy and hold rather than trade, unless you have a big enough edge. Although it's politically not likely, a small federal tax, averaging a few cents a share on every purchase, could eliminate these traders and their profits, possibly saving more for investors than the extra tax, and adding cash to the US Treasury. If this cut a trading rate of about $30 trillion a year for equities by half, a 0.1 percent tax (3 cents a share on a $30 stock) would still raise about $15 billion.

Routine financial reporting also fools investors. "Stocks Slump on Earnings Concern" cried a *New York Times* Business Day headline. The article continued, "Stock prices fell as investors continued to be concerned about third-quarter results." A slump? Let's see. "The Dow Jones Industrial Average (DJIA) declined 2.96 points, to 10,628.36." That's 0.03 percent, compared with a typical daily change of about 1 percent. Based on the historical behavior of changes in the DJIA, a percentage change greater than this happens more than 97 percent of the time. The Dow is likely to be this close to even on fewer than eight days a year, hardly evidence of investor concern.

The DJIA is calculated by adding the prices of the thirty stocks that currently make up the average, then multiplying by a number that continually is readjusted to incorporate the effects of dividends and stock splits. The current multiplier was a little over five, meaning that if just one of the thirty stocks had closed an additional point and a quarter higher, the closing DJIA number would have been over six points larger, for a rise of over three points, or 0.03 percent. DJIA stocks reportedly would have jumped, not slumped. The S&P 500 Stock Index was down a mere 0.04 percent, a lack of change almost as tiny as that of the Dow. The only real move was in the NASDAQ composite, which fell 32.8 points, or 0.9 percent. Even this volatile index was having larger daily changes two-thirds of the time.

What's going on here? The story said stocks with earnings that didn't meet expectations had been penalized the previous day. But the impact on the indexes was so small as to be meaningless. The reporter had made two errors. First, he thought statistical noise meant something. Second, he missed the other half of the story—the one about the stocks that must have gone up, and why they did—as they must have done to offset the effect of the ones that dropped.

Offering explanations for insignificant price changes is a recurrent event in financial reporting. The reporters often don't know whether a fluctuation is statistically common or rare. Then again, people tend to make the error of seeing patterns or explanations when there aren't any, as we've seen from the history of gambling systems, the plethora of worthless pattern-based trading methods, and much of story-based investing.

*Chapter 19*

# BUYING LOW, SELLING HIGH

I t's the spring of 2000 and another warm sunny day in Newport Beach. From my home six hundred feet high on the hill I can see thirty miles across the Pacific Ocean to Wrigley's twenty-six-mile-long Catalina Island, stretched across the horizon like a huge ship. To the left, sixty miles away, the top of the equally large San Clemente Island is just visible above the horizon. The ocean starts two and a half miles from where I sit, separated by a ribbon of white surf from wide sandy beaches. An early trickle of boats streams into the sea from Newport Harbor, one of the world's largest small-boat moorings, with more than eight thousand sail and power vessels, and some of the most expensive luxury homes in the world. Whenever I leave on vacation I wonder if I have made a mistake.

As I finish breakfast the sun is rising above the hills behind me, illuminating the financial towers to the west in the enormous business and retail complex of Fashion Island. By the time the skyscrapers are in full sunlight I drive three miles to my office in one of them. The statistical arbitrage operation that Steve and I restarted in 1992 has been running successfully now for eight years.

Our computers traded more than a million shares in the first hour and we are ahead $400,000. Currently managing $340 million, we have purchased $540 million worth of stocks long and sold an equal amount short. Our computer simulations and experience show that this portfolio is close to market-neutral, which means that the fluctuations in the value of the portfolio have little correlation to the overall average price changes in the market. Our level of market neutrality, measured by what financial theorists call beta, has averaged 0.06. When beta is zero for a portfolio, its price movements have no correlation with those of the market, and it is called market-neutral. Portfolios with positive beta tend to move up and down with the market, more so for larger beta. The beta of the market itself is chosen to be 1.0. Negative beta portfolios tend to fluctuate oppositely to the market. Our risk-adjusted excess return, the amount by which our annualized return has exceeded that from investments of comparable risk and called alpha by finance theorists, has averaged about 20 percent per year. This means that our past annual rate of return (before fees) of 26 percent can be thought of as the sum of three parts: 5 percent from Treasury bills with no risk, about 1 percent due to our slight correlation to the market, plus the remaining 20 percent, the amount by which our return exceeds investments with comparable risk.

Using our model, our computers calculate daily a "fair" price for each of about one thousand of the largest, most heavily traded companies on the New York and American stock exchanges. Market professionals describe stocks with large trading volume as "liquid"; they have the advantage of being easier to trade without moving the price up or down as much in the process. The latest prices from the exchanges flow into our computers and are compared at once with the current fair value according to our model. When the actual price differs enough from the fair price, we buy the underpriced and short the overpriced.

To control risk, we limit the dollar value we hold in the stock of any one company. Our caution and our risk-control measures seem to work. Our daily, weekly, and monthly results are "positively skewed," meaning that we have substantially more large winning days, weeks, and months than losing ones, and the gainers tend to be bigger than the losers.

Scanning the computer screen, I see the day's interesting positions, including the biggest gainers and the biggest losers. I can see quickly if any winners or losers seem unusually large. Everything looks normal. I walk down the hall to Steve Mizusawa's office, where he is watching his Bloomberg terminal, checking for news that might have a big impact on one of the stocks we trade. When he finds events such as the unexpected announcement of a merger, takeover, spin-off, or reorganization, he tells the computer to put the stock on the restricted list: Don't initiate a new position and close out what we have.

Steve has just persuaded the broker where we do most of our business to cut our commissions by 0.16 cents per share. The savings are big. Our entire holding of stocks, long and short, turns over about once every two weeks, or twenty-five times per year. At current levels this means we sell $540 million of stocks held long and replace them with $540 million of new stocks, a total value traded of $1.08 billion. We do the same with our shorts, for another $1.08 billion worth of trades. Trading both sides twenty-five times a year means we do $54 billion, or 1.5 billion shares annually. When famed hedge fund manager Michael Steinhardt retired, he astonished many by announcing he had traded a billion shares in one year.

The reduction Steve negotiated saves us $1.6 million a year. Even after this, our brokers are collecting $14.3 million per year from us. Our broker was smart to stay competitive.

Why is statistical arbitrage so-called? *Arbitrage* originally meant a pair of offsetting positions that lock in a sure profit. An example might be selling gold in London at $300 an ounce while at the same time buying it at $290 in New York for a $10 gain. If the total cost to finance the deal and to insure and deliver the New York gold to London were $5, it would leave a $5 sure profit. That's an arbitrage in its original usage.

Later the term was expanded to describe investments where risks are expected to be largely offsetting, with a profit that is likely, if not certain. For instance, in what is called merger arbitrage, company A trading at $100 a share may offer to buy company B, trading at $70 a share, by exchanging one share of company A for each share of company B. The market reacts instantly and company A's shares drop to, say, $88 while company B's shares jump to $83. Merger arbitrageurs now step in, buying a share of B at $83 and selling short a share of A at $88. If the deal closes in three months, the arbitrageur will make $5 on an $83 investment or 6 percent. But the deal is not certain until it gets regulatory and shareholder approval, so there is a risk of loss should the negotiations fail and the prices of A and B reverse. If the stocks of A and B returned to their preannouncement prices, the arbitrageur would lose $12 = $100 – $88 on his short sale of A and $13 = $83 – $70 on his purchase of B, for a total loss of $25 per $83 invested, or 30 percent. The arbitrageur won't take this lopsided risk unless he believes the chance of failure to be small.

Our portfolio has the risk-reducing characteristics of arbitrage but with a large number of stocks in the long side and in the short side of the portfolio, we expect the statistical behavior of a large number of favorable bets to deliver our profit. This is like card counting at blackjack again, but on a much larger scale. Our average trade size is $54,000 and we are placing a million such bets per year, or one bet every six seconds when the market is open.

As I walk back to my office, I think about how our statistical arbitrage venture came to be. While teaching finance in the UCI Graduate School of Management, I had many stimulating discussions with Dr. Jerome Baesel, the professor in the next office. I invited him to work full-time at Princeton Newport Partners. A major responsibility for him was to direct the indicators project, a research program I conceived. Neither Jerry nor I believed the efficient market theory. I had overwhelming evidence of inefficiency from blackjack, from the history of Warren Buffett and friends, and from our daily success in Princeton Newport Partners. We didn't ask, *Is the market efficient?* but rather, *In what ways and to what extent is the market inefficient?* and *How can we exploit this?*

The idea of the project was to study how the historical returns of securities were related to various characteristics, or indicators. Among the scores of fundamental and technical measures we considered were the ratio of earnings per share to price per share, known as the earnings yield, the liquidation or "book" value of the company compared with its market price, and the total market value of the company (its "size"). Today our approach is well known and widely explored but back in

1979 it was denounced by massed legions of academics who believed market prices already had fully adjusted to such information. Many practitioners disagreed. The time was right for our project because the necessary high-quality databases and the powerful new computers with which to explore them were just becoming affordable.

By luck, one of our researchers almost immediately found the basic idea behind statistical arbitrage. He ranked stocks by their gain or loss over the previous two weeks. The stocks that had gone up the most did worse as a group than the market in the next few weeks, and the stocks that were the most down did better. Historically, the annualized return was 20 percent from buying the one-tenth of stocks that had fallen most and selling short the tenth that had risen most. We called the system MUD, as it was constructed from the "most-up, most-down" stocks. As UCI mathematician William F. Donoghue would joke, "Thorp, my advice is to buy low and sell high." The portfolio of long stocks tracked the market and the short portfolio did the opposite, so the two sides together mostly canceled the movement of the market. This gave us what we liked, a market-neutral portfolio. But that portfolio still had larger fluctuations in value than our usual investments, so we put statistical arbitrage aside for the time being.

Unknown to us, a couple of years later an ingenious researcher at Morgan Stanley invented a product similar to ours but with substantially less variability. Trading probably began in 1983. With experience, his confidence increased and his investments expanded. Statistical arbitrage had become a significant profit center at Morgan Stanley by 1985 but the credit for its discovery, and the rewards from the firm, did not attach to the discoverer, Gerry Bamberger. While his boss Nunzio Tartaglia continued to expand the operation, a dissatisfied Bamberger handed in his notice.

As part of our plan to add diversified profit centers, Princeton Newport Partners was seeking to bankroll people who had successful quantitative strategies. Bamberger, now out of a job, contacted us. He described his strategy as high-turnover, market-neutral, and low-risk, with at any one time a large number of stocks held long and a large number held short. It sounded very much like our statistical arbitrage strategy, so even though we knew only the general characteristics of the portfolio and none of the details of how trades were chosen, we followed up. Once I gave my word that I would tell no one else unless either he okayed it or the information entered the public domain by some other route, I met with Gerry and he told me how his strategy worked.

Gerry Bamberger was a tall, trim Orthodox Jew with an original way of looking at problems and a wry sense of humor. We worked together for several weeks in Newport Beach to test his system exhaustively. If I was satisfied, we would bankroll a joint venture with Gerry. He brought a brown bag for lunch, and it always contained a tuna salad sandwich. I finally had to ask, "How often do you have a tuna salad sandwich for lunch?" Gerry said, "Every day for the last six years." He was a heavy smoker and I'm extremely sensitive to tobacco smoke—to the extent that we did not hire smokers or allow smoking in our office—so we negotiated how to handle this. We compromised. Whenever Gerry needed a cigarette he would step outside our ground-floor garden office. This is not the ordeal in Southern California that it could have been during an East Coast winter.

The source of gain in the Bamberger version of statistical arbitrage was the most-up, most-down effect we had discovered in 1979–80. We hedged market risk but Gerry reduced risk even more by trading industry groups separately. To measure the historical performance of his system and to simulate real-time trading, we used Princeton Newport's 1,100-square-foot computer room filled with $2 million worth of equipment. Inside were banks of gigabyte disk drives as large as washing machines, plus tape drives and central processing units, or CPUs, the size of refrigerators. All this sat on a raised floor consisting of removable panels, under which snaked a jungle of cables, wires, and other connectors.

The room also had its own safety system. In case of fire, the air was automatically replaced by noncombustible halogen gas within eighty seconds. Once this happened the room had too little oxygen for fire to burn or for people to breathe. We practiced how to get out in time and to trigger the halogen manually, if necessary.

Our facility was high-tech in the mid-1980s, but with the enormous increase in computer miniaturization, speed, and cheapness, now even

The author at age five.

The author with lab equipment. This photo was taken in Lomita, a town in Southern California where he lived and attended Narbonne High School.

*Lomita News* (this newspaper has since folded)

The wearable computer that beat roulette. Completed in June 1961 by Claude Shannon and Edward Thorp and used successfully in Vegas. It is now in the MIT Museum.

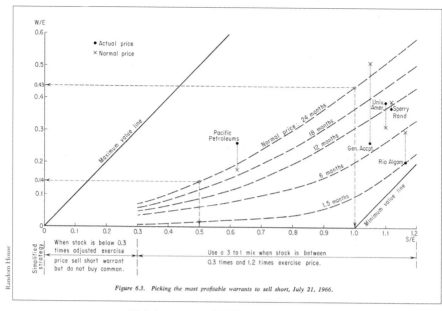

Figure 6.3. *Picking the most profitable warrants to sell short, July 21, 1966.*

Hedging warrants, 1966. From *Beat the Market.*

A simple mechanical device for counting cards and calculating the advantage, built in 1964.

Counting cards at the Tropicana Hotel, 1964.

Working with my PhD thesis students Dorothy Daybell and
David Arterburn, New Mexico State University, 1964.

George Kew, *Life* magazine

Don Cravens, *Life* magazine

Chairing a session at a mathematics meeting, 1964.

A standard European single zero roulette. Our wearable computer is on display in the background.

Playing blackjack at Lake Tahoe, Nevada, 1981, with Stanford Wong (left) and Peter Griffin (right).

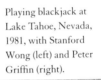

Claude Shannon.

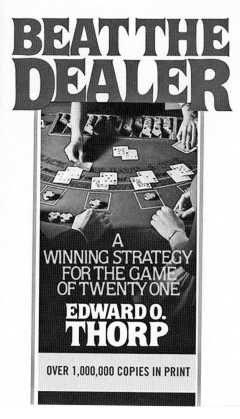

A *NEW YORK TIMES* BESTSELLER

# BEAT THE DEALER

A WINNING STRATEGY FOR THE GAME OF TWENTY ONE

EDWARD O. THORP

OVER 1,000,000 COPIES IN PRINT

The cover of
*Beat the Dealer.*

Vivian and Edward Thorp at home, 2004.

cellphones store many gigabytes. The room was chilled to a constant
sixty degrees Fahrenheit by its own cooling system and had sealed doors
and dust filters to keep the air clean. Since smokers strongly emit tiny
particles for an hour or more after even a single cigarette, Gerry agreed,
with a lot of good-natured kidding, that the computer room was off
limits.

When I was totally satisfied, we set up a joint venture, funded by
PNP and run in New York by Gerry as a turn-key operation. We called
it BOSS Partners, for "Bamberger (plus) Oakley Sutton Securities"—
the latter an entity created by us to assist PNP. On capital ranging from
$30 million to $60 million, BOSS earned between 25 and 30 percent in
1985. Returns gradually declined to 15 percent or so by 1988. The wan-
ing profitability and the mounting Giuliani attack on our Princeton office discouraged Gerry from continuing in the securities industry. He
elected to retire a millionaire.

Meanwhile, I took the statistical arbitrage concept a step further.
Trading started with my improved approach in January 1988, thus by
chance missing the crash of 1987. How would we have done? Despite a
22 percent drop in the S&P 500 Index, BOSS made 7 percent for October
1987. Computer simulations showed our new statistical arbitrage product would also have had a good day and a record month. This was a ship
for riding out cataclysms.

To control risk further, I replaced Bamberger's segregation into industry groups by a statistical procedure called factor analysis. Factors are
common tendencies shared by several, many, or all companies. The most
important is called the market factor, which measures the tendency of
each stock price to move up and down with the market. The daily returns on any stock can be expressed as a part that follows the market
plus what's left over, the so-called residual. Financial theorists and practitioners have identified a large number of such factors that help explain
changes in securities prices. Some, like participation in a specified industry group or sector (say, oil or finance) mainly affect subgroups of stocks.
Other factors, such as the market itself, the levels of short-term and
long-term interest rates, and inflation, affect nearly all stocks.

The beauty of a statistical arbitrage product is that it can be designed to offset the effects of as many of these factors as you desire. The portfolio is already market-neutral by constraining the relation between the long and short portfolios so that the tendency of the long side to follow the market is offset by an equal but opposite effect on the short side. The portfolio becomes inflation-neutral, oil-price-neutral, and so on, by doing the same thing individually with each of those factors. Of course, there is a trade-off: The reduction in risk is accompanied by limiting the choice of possible portfolios. Only those that are market-neutral, inflation-neutral, oil-price-neutral, et cetera, are now allowed, and so the attempt to reduce risk also tends to reduce return.

We called the new method STAR, for "STatistical ARbitrage." At the request of one of our investors we sent a trading history to Barra, a world leader in researching and developing financial products. They tested STAR with their model E2, which had fifty-five industry factors and thirteen macroeconomic factors. They found that our returns were essentially factor-neutral, and did not appear to result from lucky bets.

It was good that we advanced beyond the Bamberger model because, in simulation, its returns continued to fall. Moreover, after finishing with a good 1987, Morgan Stanley reportedly expanded their investment in it to $900 million long and $900 million short, which had to drive down returns for everyone using the method. The rumor was that they lost between 6 percent and 12 percent, leading to the winding down of the product.

People at Morgan Stanley began leaving the quantitative systems group that was in charge of statistical arbitrage. Among those to depart was David E. Shaw, a former professor of computer science at Columbia University. He had been wooed to Wall Street to use computers to find opportunities in the market.

In the spring of 1988, Shaw spent the day in Newport Beach. We discussed his plan to launch an improved statistical arbitrage product. PNP was able to put up the $10 million he wanted for start-up, and we were impressed by his ideas but decided not to go ahead because we already had a good statistical arbitrage product. He found other backing, creating one of the most successful analytic firms on Wall Street, and later would become a member of the president's science advisory committee.

Using statistical arbitrage as a core profit center, he expanded into related hedging and arbitrage areas (the PNP business plan again), and hired large numbers of smart quantitative types from academia. In 2014, *Forbes* ranked him as the 134th richest American, at $3.8 billion. One of his hires was Jeff Bezos, who, while researching business opportunities in 1994 for Shaw, got the idea for an online bookstore and left to start a company called Amazon.com. At $30 billion in 2014, Bezos was the fifteenth richest American.

As PNP began winding down in late 1988, despite the stress we developed yet another approach to statistical arbitrage that was simpler and more powerful. But as PNP phased out, I wanted simplicity. We focused on two areas that could be managed by a small staff, Japanese warrant hedging and investing in other hedge funds. Both went well.

I had no immediate plans to use our new statistical arbitrage technique and I expected that continuing innovations by investors using related systems would, as is the way of things, gradually erode its value. Four years passed, and then, my friend and former partner Jerry Baesel came to me with tales of extraordinary returns from statistical arbitrage. Besides D. E. Shaw & Company, the practitioners included former Morgan Stanley quants who were starting their own hedge funds, and some of my past PNP associates. I asked the former Morgan Stanley people if they knew how statistical arbitrage started at their firm. No one did. A couple had heard rumors of a nameless legendary "discoverer" of the system, who of course, was Gerry Bamberger—so thoroughly had recognition for his contribution been erased.

If our statistical arbitrage system still worked, Jerry Baesel told me that one of our former investors, a multibillion-dollar pension and profit sharing plan that was his current employer, wanted most or all of the capacity. Every stock market system with an edge is necessarily limited in the amount of money it can use and still produce extra returns. One reason is that buying undervalued securities tends to raise the price, reducing or eliminating the mispricing, and selling short overpriced securities tends to lower the price, once again shrinking the mispricing. Thus, opportunities for beating the market are limited in size by how trading them affects market prices.

Since our statistical arbitrage method was mostly computerized, Steve and I could run the managed account with help from our small office staff. It would let me have time to enjoy life. We decided to go ahead. The venture began auspiciously. Our software ran smoothly, first in simulation and then with real money, starting in August 1992.

I also wanted to invest my own money. I could do this efficiently and profitably by creating a new investment partnership. This led to the launching of Ridgeline Partners in August 1994 to trade alongside our institutional account. Limited partners gained 18 percent per year over its eight and a quarter years of operation.

Appendix E shows results for the large managed account, which for confidentiality I call XYZ. The annualized return of 7.77 percent and the annualized standard deviation of 15.07 percent for the S&P 500 during this period are somewhat below its long-term values. The unlevered annualized return for XYZ before fees, at 18.21 percent, is more than double that of the S&P; the riskiness, as measured by the standard deviation, is 6.68 percent. The ratio of (annualized) return to risk for XYZ at 2.73 is more than five times that of the S&P. Estimating 5 percent as the average three-month T-bill rate over the period, the corresponding Sharpe ratios are 0.18 for the S&P versus 1.98 for XYZ.

The graph in Appendix E, XYZ Performance Comparison, displays two major "epochs." The first, from August 12, 1992, to early October 1998, shows a steady increase. The second epoch, from then until September 13, 2002, has a higher rate of return, including a remarkable six-month spurt just after the collapse (after four years) of the large hedge fund called, ironically, Long-Term Capital Management. Following the spurt during the last quarter of 1998 and the first quarter of 1999, the growth rate reverts for the rest of the time to about what it was in the first epoch. However, the variability around the trend is greater.

One cause for this greater variability might be the delayed and disputed election of George W. Bush. We also had an economic sea change from budget surpluses to massive deficits as a result of increased spending and tax rate reductions. More uncertainty came with the collapse of the dot-com bubble and the horrors of 9/11.

We charged Ridgeline Partners 1 percent per year plus 20 percent of net new profits. We voluntarily reduced fees during a period when we felt disappointed in our performance. We gave back more than $1 million to the limited partners. Some of today's greedy hedge fund managers might say our return of fees was economically irrational, but our investors were happy and we nearly always had a waiting list. Ridgeline was closed a large part of the time to new investors, and current partners were often restricted from adding capital. To maintain higher returns, we sometimes even reduced our size by returning capital to partners.

Unlike some hedge fund managers who also had a waiting list, we could have increased our fees by raising our share of the profits or adding more capital, thereby driving down the return to limited partners. Such tactics by the general partner to capture nearly all the excess risk-adjusted return, or "alpha," rather than share it with the other investors are what economic theory predicts. Instead, I preferred to treat limited partners as I would wish to be treated in their place.

In August 1998, the hedge fund Long-Term Capital Management (LTCM), a pool of $4 billion, lost nearly all its money. Highly leveraged, it threatened to default on something like $100 billion in contracts. Some claimed that the world financial system itself was threatened. The Federal Reserve decided LTCM was "too big to fail" and brokered a bailout by a consortium of brokers and banks, each of whom had a financial self-interest in saving LTCM. At about the same time several Asian economies got sick, and Russia defaulted on its debt.

The combination of events greatly increased volatility in the financial markets. Would these disruptions increase our potential rate of return or would they thwart our statistical arbitrage system? Hedge funds were suffering in multiple ways. Owners of Asian securities lost heavily. Financial institutions suddenly were less willing to extend credit, and leveraged hedge funds were forced to liquidate positions. We heard that large statistical arbitrage positions were being closed out. This seems likely because they are liquid and can be sold quickly to raise cash. This deleveraging and liquidity crisis foreshadowed a similar and far greater global rerun in 2008.

If there was such a large movement out of statistical arbitrage positions, we would expect our portfolios to lose while that was happening, because if others sell the stocks we own this drives the price down and our long positions show a loss. Similarly, if they have sold short the same stocks we have and they buy them back, this bids up the price of the stocks we are still short and we show a loss. Once the liquidation of portfolios winds down, we would expect a rebound. What actually happened was that after a small dip in the last four days of September, October began with six straight losing days during which our portfolio lost 4.2 percent, the sharpest blow we had ever experienced. Since this was just after the end of the quarter, I suspect it was due to involuntary liquidation of statistical arbitrage positions to raise cash to satisfy creditors. Fortunately we had just finished September with our best month ever.

Though October began badly, we recovered all our losses and continued the winning streak that started in September. It went on for six amazing months, through February 1999. During this time we made 54.5 percent. The result for the twelve months ending with August 1999 was that Ridgeline's limited partners made 72.4 percent. This was from a market-neutral product using leverage of 2:1 or less. Several of our limited partners asked if we had ever seen anything like this. I told them that in thirty-five years of market-neutral investing I never had, but not to get used to it, as we were unlikely to repeat this performance.

Between Ridgeline and XYZ we managed as much as $400 million in statistical arbitrage and another $70 million in other strategies, whereas PNP's peak was $272 million. Compared with PNP's maximum of eighty employees, only six of us at Ridgeline faced our formidable competitors. Several of those had hundreds of employees, including scores of PhDs in mathematics, statistics, computer science, physics, finance, and economics. We were a highly automated, lean, and profitable operation.

We decided to close down in the fall of 2002. Returns, although respectable, had declined in 2001 and 2002. I believed this was due to the huge growth in hedge fund assets, with a corresponding expansion of statistical arbitrage programs. I had seen this happen before in 1988 when Morgan Stanley's expansion of statistical arbitrage seemed to have a negative effect on our returns. The declining rate of return in statistical arbitrage seemed to be confirmed by the experience of most other hedge funds operating in the "space."

The most important reason to wind down the operation was that time was worth more to me than the extra money. Vivian and I wanted to enjoy our children and their families, and to travel, read, and learn. It was time once again to change course in life.

And I had investments that remained interesting, such as the mutual savings and loan conversions in which my son, Jeff, and I began participating way back in 1990.

*Chapter 20*

# BACKING THE TRUCK UP TO THE BANKS

One day in 1990 my entrepreneurial son, Jeff, called to advise me to open passbook savings accounts at mutual savings and loan associations. Why would I want to tie up money at 5 percent when I was earning 20 percent? Jeff answered, "How would you like a little piece of a few billion dollars of value no one owns?" I said, "Keep talking." And he explained how it worked.

There were at that time a couple of thousand mutual savings and loan associations around the country. They began as associations formed by depositors who pooled their money, allowing the members to borrow as needed, meanwhile paying interest on their loans to those who had money in the pool. The depositors owned the association "mutually," which meant that the business value that built up during operation was also "owned" by the depositors. As time passed, depositors came and went, but upon leaving they left their share of the business behind. No mechanism existed for extracting this value.

The giant slow-motion collapse of the US savings and loan industry, starting in the late 1970s and continuing through the 1980s, created a need for capital to buoy weakened institutions, capital to exploit the new opportunities to fill the void left by failed institutions, and capital to compete with the new larger consolidated savings and loans that were appearing.

The mutuals could raise capital only by attracting more depositors, a slow and uncertain process, but their rivals, the "stock" savings and loans, were corporations owned by shareholders. They could get more capital from the marketplace, as they needed it, by selling shares. Facing such competition, some of the more entrepreneurial managers of mutuals decided to "convert" to stock companies, and this began the process of extracting billions of dollars that no one could previously claim.

Here's how it is done. Imagine a hypothetical mutual savings and loan, which we'll call Magic Wand S&L, or MW, with $10 million in liquidation or book value, and net income of $1 million per year. If MW were a stock bank with one million shares outstanding, each share would have a book value of $10 and earn $1 per share, which is 10 percent of book value. Suppose that if there were such a thing as MW stock, it would, as is typical, trade at one times book value, or $10 per share.

Management decides to "convert" MW to a stock savings and loan and issue for the first time one million shares of stock at $10 per share, for proceeds of $10 million. After this initial public offering, or IPO, MW has $10 million in new cash plus the $10 million in equity previously owned by the depositors, for a new total of $20 million in equity. Each share now has a book value of $10 cash plus $10 in contributed equity, for a total of $20.

What will the new shares sell for in the marketplace? The contributed equity ought to be worth $10 based on the current market price of comparable stock S&Ls and the $10 in cash ought to be worth another $10, so once the public understands this, we expect the new stock to trade at about $20.

Buy a $20 stock for $10. Who loses? No one, but those depositors who do not purchase enough stock on the offering to capture their share of the pre-IPO equity they "owned" give up some of the gains to the others, who then are able to get more. Fortunately, the IPOs are generally structured so depositors have priority over other classes in applying for stock. Usually only one class has still higher priority. Who? You guessed it!

The insiders: officers, directors, and employee stock option and benefit plans. This allows the insiders to capture some of the depositors' value, which provides a powerful motivation for management to convert.

Suppose we had the foresight to become a depositor in Magic Wand S&L before the deadline for eligibility to participate in the IPO. Sometime after the eligibility deadline, the bank announces its intention to convert, chooses an investment banker to manage the stock offering, and gets regulatory approval. Magic Wand creates a temporary department called the conversion center, which issues a package of documents including a prospectus with the terms of the conversion and information including which groups can participate, their level of priority, and background data including the financial statements of the bank for the last few years. The stock order form in the package allows us to apply for up to 1 percent of the one million shares offered, or ten thousand shares, at $10 a share. We wire $100,000 to the conversion center, hoping to get our full allotment of ten thousand shares but knowing from experience that anything between zero and ten thousand shares is possible. A couple of weeks later we learn that we bought nine thousand shares. We get a stock certificate in the mail and deposit it in our brokerage account. We also get a check for $10,191.78, $10,000 of which is a refund for the one thousand shares we requested but didn't get, and $191.78 for interest earned during escrow at, in this example, 5 percent on our $100,000 while waiting fourteen days for the deal to close.

What happens to the price of our stock? It opens at $12 and over the next few weeks slowly moves up to $16, still below the $20 per share paid for comparable stocks that have traded for a while in the market.

It doesn't quite make it to $20. Why not? First, the net cash to Magic Wand is a little less than $10 per share because the underwriters get a few percent of the proceeds, so the new book value is a little less than $20, perhaps $19.30 per share. Second, the market price of S&Ls fluctuates and the group has been a little weak lately. The price has dropped a couple of points below book value. Third, it will take management time to put the new cash to work, so earnings won't reach $2 per share for a year or two. Even so, we made 60 percent in a few weeks.

Many of the players in this game, so-called flippers, take their profit in the first few days and move on. On the other hand, I will hold a well-managed company for months or years. If the stock continues its rise toward book value, this gives further gains. Also, waiting more than a year to sell gives a long-term capital gain, with less tax to pay.

Overall, S&L IPOs have been profitable for the buyers, but most deals aren't as good as MW. The short-term profit has been in the 10 to 25 percent range, with a few small losses.

Services are available to help you analyze deals and avoid the poorer ones. Or you can judge them yourself.

Jeff and I each opened hundreds of savings accounts. Some of this was done by mail, but much of it had to be done in person. Whenever we went on a business trip we checked our database to see which S&Ls we should visit.

In one case, a very large S&L looked ripe for conversion so the IPO would be big. The bank required that accounts be opened in person, rather than by mail, which reduced the competition. Jeff urged my son-in-law Rich and me to fly to Dallas for the day.

When we arrived, sitting next to us also waiting to open accounts were a thirtysomething hotshot from Beverly Hills and his girlfriend. Acting obviously secretive, like an incompetent CIA agent, Mr. Sunglasses chatted us up, learned we were from out of town, and wondered if we were playing the S&L game like he, the expert, was. We acted naïve, and he importantly gave us a business card. Amused, I saved it, and, a few months later when a financial piece about me appeared in *Newsweek,* mailed him a copy with a note saying I enjoyed meeting him at the bank. A year later, I was $85,000 better off from spending the day in Dallas.

I visualized opening accounts as planting acorns in the hope of getting a crop of oak trees. Only these were strange acorns. They could lie dormant for months or years, perhaps forever; but once in a while, at random, a mighty tree of money would explode out of the ground. Was this "farm" worth operating?

Our hundreds of accounts took capital away from other investments. Paid low interest rates on our passbooks and certificates of deposit (CDs), we sacrificed an expected 10 to 15 percent differential to maintain our accounts. We also had expenses and the so-called opportunity cost. Fortunately, Judy McCoy in my office managed the project competently and efficiently.

The harvest from our crop of S&L accounts sometimes netted a million dollars in a year. The game has slowly wound down over the last two decades. Mutual S&Ls have converted, leaving fewer opportunities.

The gain has also diminished because more people have opened accounts, thus spreading the profits among more players. Investors also have posted larger balances in CDs, savings accounts, and checking accounts in the hope of being allocated more shares in a future conversion. Tying up more capital increases the cost to stay in the game. Our profits have been dwindling. Currently we're keeping our old accounts but are spending less effort in trying to open new ones. Even so, a quarter of a century after we began opening accounts, 2014 was a good year.

Meanwhile, my other investments have done well. One of them is Buffett's Berkshire Hathaway.

## Chapter 21

# ONE LAST PUFF

After twelve successful years, with the stock market vastly overpriced in his opinion, Warren Buffett outlined the windup of Buffett Partnership, Ltd., in October 1969. Partners would get a payout consisting of at least 56 percent cash, possibly some scraps of stock in assorted companies, and an estimated 30 to 35 percent, for those who chose not to have them sold for cash, in two companies—Diversified Retailing and a New England textile company called Berkshire Hathaway. He added the discouraging, "For the first time in my investment lifetime, I now believe there is little choice for the average investor between professionally managed money in stocks and passive investment in bonds."

As I reread Buffett's letter today I see no clue now, nor did I then, that Berkshire Hathaway would become the successor to Warren's partnership. Ralph Gerard, a longtime investor with Buffett and the man who introduced us, never did, either. Of the $100 million distributed to partners, about $25 million was Buffett's. He eventually ended up with nearly half of Berkshire's stock.

Berkshire was what Buffett and his mentor Benjamin Graham called a cigar butt—you can pick it up cheaply and get one last puff. As *Forbes* said in 1990, in its characteristic shorthand, "[Buffett] bought Berkshire Hathaway textile mills 1965 ($12/share), dissolved partnership 1969 after thirty-fold growth, decided to use Berkshire Hathaway as prime investment vehicle. Textile business floundered (ceased operations in 1985) but investment business boomed."

Focused on Princeton Newport, I lost track of Warren after 1969. Then in 1983, I heard about the remarkable growth of a company called Berkshire Hathaway. Not knowing it was to become Warren's investment vehicle, I had stopped paying attention to it back in 1969. The stock price then was $42 a share, if you could find anyone to trade with. It was now publicly trading at over $900. I knew at once what this meant. The "cigar butt" had become a humidor of Havanas. Despite its having increased by a multiple of more than 23 in fourteen years, I made my first purchase at $982.50 a share and continued to accumulate stock. By contrast, in 2004 I was talking to a bank president in San Francisco when he mentioned that his mother had been a limited partner in Buffett Partnership, Ltd., and received some Berkshire stock as part of her distribution when the partnership closed. "That's wonderful," I said. "At today's prices [then $80,000 a share or so] she must be very rich." "Sadly," he said, "she sold at $79 for a several hundred percent profit."

If asked for advice, I recommended the stock to family, friends, and associates with the understanding that it was a long-term holding with a possibly volatile future. I didn't suggest it to those who couldn't understand the reasoning behind the purchase and who would be scared by a big drop in price. The response was sometimes frustrating.

In 1985 our divorced house cleaner, Carolyn, got $6,000 as a settlement from an automobile accident. She wanted to invest it to send her children, aged five and six, through college. Week after week she pleaded with me to advise her, but as she knew absolutely nothing about securities or investing, I declined. Urged on by her fortune-teller, who told her that I would double or even triple her money, she persisted. In a weak moment I relented, provided that if she bought the stock I recommended, she would never sell before checking with me. I arranged low commissions for her, as a favor to me by a broker friend, and she bought two shares of Berkshire Hathaway (BRK) for $2,500 each. She later left housecleaning for office work and we lost touch with her. Meanwhile BRK rose to about $5,000 a share just before the October 1987 crash. I learned later from the broker that Carolyn had sold near the post-crash bottom at $2,600 a share. Sixteen years later, in the first quarter of 2003 at the time her children might have been finishing college, the stock ranged between about $60,000 and $74,000 a share.

My wife and I, our oldest daughter, Raun, and her husband, Brian, their daughter Ava, and my son, Jeff, decided, at Jeff's suggestion, to go to the May 2003 annual meeting held, as always, in Warren's hometown of Omaha, Nebraska. I wrote Warren ahead of time, mentioning that we were coming and that seven-year-old Ava, also a shareholder, had questions for him. Although we hadn't been in contact since 1969, he remembered our meetings fondly and said to tell Ava that he would "bone up" so he'd be ready for her questions.

The shareholders' meeting was on a Saturday morning and we flew in the previous Thursday, expecting to leave, variously, on Sunday and Monday. The small annual shareholder meetings of thirty years earlier had grown into a huge multiday celebration featuring "Berkshire millionaires" and informally known as "Woodstock for capitalists."

We began by sampling from the array of Berkshire companies including Dairy Queen (a chain of ice cream confection stores), Borsheims jewelry (the largest independent jewelry store) and its special "annual meeting weekend" rates for shareholders, Nebraska Furniture Mart (the largest independent furniture store), and of course See's Candies, a California favorite. Every Berkshire company employee whom we encountered—and they were many and diverse—seemed competent, courteous, and well trained, a remarkable fact, the learning of which in itself (considering the size of our stake) made the trip worthwhile. Friday night we went to Gorat's Steak House, Buffett's favorite, and had a large and delicious T-bone with trimmings for . . . $18.95. Buffett and his business partner, Charlie Munger, were scheduled to eat there Saturday night at a special shareholders' dinner, so we booked that, too.

Saturday's meeting began at 7:30 A.M. with a video for the early arriv-
als. We slept in and ambled over to the Omaha Civic Auditorium just
before 9:30, when Warren and Charlie would take the stage. On the way
we passed several incoherently screaming protesters—a first?—wearing
signs accusing Warren and the company of supporting infanticide. They
displayed bloody photos of aborted fetuses and incorrectly accused the
company of being pro-abortion. The ironic consequences are reported
below.

Finding the Omaha Civic Auditorium full with a crowd of fourteen
thousand, we joined two thousand more in an overflow room. Warren
and Charlie presented a concise account of Berkshire's previous year,
seen by us on a big-screen TV, and then answered questions. There were
ten microphone stations with long sign-up lists at each. Ava was ninth
on the shortest list we could find. After an hour, the slow pace of the
questions and answers made it evident that her turn would never come.
On the way out we visited the extensive product exhibits by various
Berkshire companies. You could buy See's Candies, sets of encyclope-
dias, and for $8 have your picture taken with a cardboard cutout of War-
ren. As Vivian said, "They're not giving anything away."

Berkshire has evolved from the simple stock-picking days of the
1960s into a conglomerate with three major parts. First there are common stockholdings in companies like Coca-Cola, Gillette, and *The
Washington Post*. Second, there are wholly owned or controlled companies such as Wesco Financial, World Book Encyclopedia, and Clayton
Homes. The 2003 annual report lists some sixty-six of these, with 172,000
employees, orchestrated by Warren and Charlie from a corporate office
that has "swollen" to sixteen employees. Third and perhaps most important is the insurance segment consisting mostly of GEICO and the
reinsurance company General Re.

We headed for lunch and the NetJets exhibit at the local airport. Saturday night we were back at Gorat's. The price of the T-bone dinner we
had Friday was, as a "special for shareholders," now $3 more. Charlie
Munger reluctantly worked the room we were in and I mentioned to
him a tale I'd heard about his youth. Charlie had gone to Harvard Law

School and, when my friend Paul Marx got his degree there a few years later, he found that Charlie was a legend—with many saying he was the smartest person ever to have attended. As a first-year student Charlie was reported to have regularly intimidated professors. In a famous interchange, the professor called upon Charlie, who had not read the case at hand, to answer questions about it. Charlie's immediate response was, "Sir, you tell me the facts and I'll tell you the law." While autographing my menu, Charlie said sadly, "That was a long time ago . . . a long time ago."

Omaha turned out to be a surprising treat. A Midwest town that had peaked early in the last century, much of the city had migrated to the suburbs, leaving a quiet and spacious downtown. Sunday we visited Omaha's fine art museum, featuring a spectacular photographic exhibit by Warren's son Howard. Also interesting was the zoo, which had two large and distinct domed walk-through habitats. Sunday afternoon, tornado warning sirens sounded and everyone in the hotel was directed to the gym in the basement. As we waited out the storm, I exercised on the machines while my son-in-law Brian Tichenor went to the fourth floor and looked outside to see the horizontal counterweighted arms of multistory construction cranes spinning freely on their vertical supports. This protected them from being demolished by the tornado. Alternating waves of lower and higher pressure caused the soda in his hand to repeatedly fizz excessively, then not at all. The tornado wandered randomly through town, doing minor sporadic damage. The tornado belt, a region of mid-America from Omaha to Dallas, terrorizes residents with an average of eighty tornadoes a year, more than anywhere else in the world.

Flights out of Omaha were canceled. With thirty thousand people who had come for the Berkshire weekend missing flights and wanting to leave as soon as possible, it looked as if we would be delayed at least two days. We held a family conference and within an hour Jeff had chartered a private jet for us. The next morning we took a ten-minute ride to the local airport and boarded in minutes—no wait, no lines, no luggage hassle, no TSA body scans and searches. We had two engines, two pilots, a flight attendant, and a good lunch. Seven-year-old Ava spoke for everyone when she declared she never wanted to fly any other way again. Whereas it took ten hours to reach Omaha from Newport Beach, California, including hours of delay in Dallas due to thunderstorms, we got home in two hours.

For many years Berkshire had a shareholder-directed charitable contribution program. Each year the company allowed each A shareholder to donate $X, where $X was $1 a share at the start and gradually increased to something like $18 a share. Shareholders allocated their amounts to charities chosen by them, not management, and Berkshire sent the money. As a result of the antiabortion protests at this annual meeting and the related boycott of a Berkshire company, the program was discontinued. The antiabortion protesters succeeded in eliminating not only shareholder contributions supporting family planning, but those to other charities as well, including organizations the demonstrators themselves favored.

To decide whether to buy Berkshire one can do a little analysis. Berkshire, as remarked earlier, has three major parts. First are the positions in publicly traded companies like Coca-Cola, *The Washington Post,* and Gillette. The securities markets price these every day. Is this Buffett portfolio worth more than, less than, or the same as its market price? Should one add a premium for Buffett's market timing and stock-picking prowess?

Second are numerous wholly owned companies such as See's Candies, Clayton Homes, and NetJets. We can value these by applying the principles of security analysis to the balance sheets, and by considering the growth rates of the companies, their "franchise value," and the quality of management.

The third component is the insurance group, with GEICO the most important. To value these non-public companies we use, in addition to security analysis as above, the value of the "float." This is money paid as premiums that is currently being held to pay off future claims. Buffett invests this and has made a profit well in excess of the projected cost of claims. To the extent Warren makes superior returns on the float, as well as follows his practice of selling insurance when prices are high and step-ping aside when competition drives prices down, the value of Berkshire is greater. For a few years prior to 2008 Berkshire had an uninvested cash surplus of as much as $40 billion, as Buffett found stocks generally overpriced. This "cash drag" slowed the price increase of Berkshire during that period. When the market collapsed in 2008, he put this money to work.

As Berkshire has grown, Buffett's gain over the S&P 500 has dimin-ished, as he predicted. Table 2, which covers my experience, shows this. The edge dropped in each new period. Beating the index in the future will be ever more difficult. There is also price risk arising from the un-certainty when Buffett ceases to manage Berkshire. Despite the likeli-hood that his replacements will be unusually talented, the stock price may fall sharply, perhaps for an extended time.

Not long after buying Berkshire, I began putting some of my PNP profits into other hedge funds. Networking with some of the smartest and richest people on Wall Street, sharing information and investment opportunities, I also gained the benefits of diversifying my personal portfolio.

**Table 2: Total Return of Berkshire Hathaway A Stock Compared to Total Return of S&P 500 for Four Successive Periods**

| Date | Price of BRKA | BRKA Annualized Return | S&P 500 Annualized Return | BRKA Edge Per Year |
|---|---|---|---|---|
| 12/31/1980 | 425 | — — — | — — — | — — — |
| 12/31/1990 | 6,675 | 31.70 % | 13.93 % | 17.77 % |
| 12/29/2000 | 71,000 | 26.67% | 17.46 % | 9.21 % |
| 12/31/2010 | 120,450 | 5.42 % | 1.41 % | 4.01 % |
| 12/30/2016 | 244,121 | 12.50 % | 12.47 % | 0.03 % |

BRKA historical prices from Yahoo, BRK-A.
S&P 500 Total Return from Ibbotson SBBI 2014 Classic Yearbook and from Yahoo ^SP500TR for last period.

*Chapter 22*

# HEDGING YOUR BETS

Hedging your bets supposedly protects against catastrophic losses. But when the 2008 recession hit, many investors in hedge funds lost heavily. The worldwide collapse in credit and in asset prices was worse than any downturn since the Great Depression. Housing prices tumbled, the S&P 500 fell 57 percent from its October 9, 2007, high, and US private wealth declined from $64 trillion to $51 trillion. Small investors like my niece and my house cleaner, watching the equity index funds in their IRAs plunge, asked me if they should dump their stocks. Many investors had to sell, including the wealthiest university endowment fund in the country, Harvard's, valued at $36.9 billion in early 2008 but now desperate for cash.

Hedge funds, which were supposed to protect investors against such declines, dropped an average 18 percent. Even so, the most highly compensated hedge fund manager, James Simons of Renaissance Technologies, made $2.5 billion. The top twenty-five managers collected $11.6 billion, down from $22.5 billion in 2007.

It was now twenty years after the end of Princeton Newport Partners, and hedge funds had proliferated until there were ten thousand worldwide, with total equity estimated at $2 trillion. Their worldwide pool of wealthy investors is a mix of private individuals, trusts, corporations, pension and profit-sharing plans, foundations, and endowments. The 2008 crash dealt a massive blow to the hedge fund industry. Four hundred billion had been swept away. This triggered worldwide requests for withdrawals by investors who were angered by losses that weren't supposed to happen. They were shocked when many funds refused to return their remaining money.

As the economy slowly recovered and the market bounced back to new highs, investors forgot what happened to them in 2008–09. By 2015 hedge fund assets reached a new high of $2.9 trillion. Management fees ranging between 1.5 and 2 percent delivered $50 billion to the operators. Their percentage of the profits added perhaps another $50 billion. This $50 billion in performance fees supposedly represents 20 percent of the profits after all other charges. But investors as a group actually pay a larger percentage. To see why, suppose there are two funds that start the year at $1 billion each. One fund nets $300 million and the other loses $100 million. At 20 percent of profits, the first fund collects a $60 million performance fee and the second collects none. Pooling the results from the two funds, we see that investors pay $60 million on a profit of $200 million, a rate of 30 percent of the combined gains and losses.

With Princeton Newport, growth from new capital came slowly and was earned by performance. Over forty years this battle for funding changed dramatically. So-called alternative investments became the hottest new frontier for what to do with your money. Beginning in the late 1990s, you could, in effect, just put up a sign saying HEDGE FUND OPENING HERE, and a line of investors would quickly extend around the block. A modest-sized $100 million hedge fund earning a gross return of 10 percent per year ($10 million) may pay the manager or general partner a management fee of 1 percent of $100 million—$1 million. In addition, the manager gets 20 percent of the remaining $9 million in profit, or another $1.8 million, as a performance fee, for a total of $2.8 million per year. Some of this, perhaps $1 million, pays expenses, leaving a net of $1.8 million a year in pretax income. The investors, or limited partners, get the remaining $7.2 million for a 7.2 percent annual return.

The general partners in a similar billion-dollar hedge fund—and there are scores of them—might share ten times as much, or $28 million a year. Even a little $10 million hedge fund would, with proportionate fees, expenses, and returns, provide a single general partner with $280,000 a year. It's clear from this that you can get very rich running a hedge fund. With these rewards, we shouldn't be surprised to find many of the (believed to be) best investors in the business running hedge funds.

The consensus of industry studies of hedge fund returns to investors seems to be that, considering the level of risk, hedge funds on average once gave their investors extra return, but this has faded as the industry expanded. Later analyses say average results are worse than portrayed. Funds voluntarily report their results to the industry databases. Winners tend to participate much more than losers. One study showed that this doubled the reported average annual return for funds as a group from an actual 6.3 percent during 1996–2014 to a supposed 12.6 percent.

The study goes on to point out that if returns over the years are given weights that correspond to the dollars invested, then the returns are "only marginally higher than risk-free [US Treasury Bonds] rates of return." Another reason that reports by the industry look better than what investors experienced is that they combine higher-percentage returns from the earlier years, when the total invested in hedge funds was smaller, with the lower-percentage returns later, when they managed much more money.

It's difficult to get an edge picking stocks. Hedge funds are little businesses just like companies that trade on the exchanges. Should one be any better at picking hedge funds than we are at picking stocks?

Hedge fund investors also suffer major disasters. In the spring of 2000, after severe losses, one of the biggest collections of hedge funds in the world, run by Julian Robertson, which included the flagship Tiger Fund, announced that it was closing. From small beginnings in 1980, Robertson's funds had grown to $22 billion before the demise. At the end, a combination of market losses and investor withdrawals chopped the pool to $7 billion, with more withdrawals pending. Robertson, claiming to be a value investor, blamed irrational crazed high-tech markets. As Shakespeare might advise, "The fault is not in our markets, but in ourselves . . ."

A couple of months later, another of the world's biggest hedge fund groups, managed by George Soros and associates, including his flagship Quantum Fund, announced heavy losses, followed by withdrawal of most investor funds. Drastically downsized from a peak of over $20 billion, Soros's operation was restructured and converted into a vehicle to manage his own money. Soros and his principal associate, Stanley Druckenmiller, had taken the opposite posture to Robertson: They had bet on tech stocks. At about the same time, Van Hedge Fund Advisors, in an article titled "Good Year for Hedge Funds," announced that the preceding year, 1999, was the best year for their hedge fund index since they began it in 1988: +40.6 percent in the United States and +37.6 percent offshore. Soros later resurged. In 2008 he personally made $1.1 billion, an amount that was good for only fourth place among hedge fund managers that year.

Should you invest in hedge funds? First you need to determine if you're economically qualified. Though such funds typically require a minimum investment of $250,000 or more, some start-ups will relax this to $50,000 or $100,000 when they first raise money. The original reason to require a substantial minimum investment was historical. In order to qualify for certain exemptions from securities regulations, and thereby gain the freedom to make a wide range of investments, hedge funds had to limit themselves to fewer than one hundred partners. But then, in order to have a pool of tens or hundreds of millions of dollars, the fund had to avoid filling their quota of partners with small investors.

The SEC later raised the limit to five hundred partners in certain circumstances. Many hedge funds only admit accredited investors; in the case of individuals, that means those who jointly with their spouse have a net worth of at least $1 million or have had an income of at least $200,000 in each of the last two years and expect to repeat that figure in the current year. This leaves plenty of candidates. In 2013, among more than one hundred million US households, the number having a net worth of $1 million or more was estimated at between five and eight million.

Next you need to determine whether either you, or an agent you choose to act for you, are knowledgeable enough. As the $65 billion Ponzi scheme perpetrated by Bernard Madoff showed, thirteen thousand investors and their advisers didn't do elementary due diligence because they thought the other investors must have done it. The issue here is the same as for those buying stocks, bonds, or mutual funds. You need to know enough to make a convincing, reasoned case for why your proposed investment is better than standard passive investments such as stock or bond index funds. Using this test, it is likely you will rarely find investments that qualify as superior to the indexes.

Another issue is taxes. US domestic hedge funds, like most active investment programs, are tax-inefficient. Their high turnover tends to produce short-term capital gains and losses taxed at a higher rate than securities owned for more than one year.

For tax-exempt investors, US hedge funds that borrow money (but not their clones based outside the United States) trigger taxes for the otherwise tax-exempt entity to the extent the realized gains, losses, and income are generated by the loans. This is called unrelated business taxable income (UBTI).

If you have an area of expertise, look for funds that your knowledge can help you evaluate. Hedge fund data services typically list more than a thousand or so funds from the several thousand that currently exist. These services, along with Internet sources like Wikipedia, classify hedge funds by asset types. Another way to sort is by methodology, such as: fundamental, using economic data as opposed to technical, using just price and volume data; or quantitative (using computers and algorithms) compared with non-quantitative; or bottom-up (analyzing individual companies) versus top-down (focusing on broader economic variables). Other important characteristics are the fund's expected returns, risks, and how the payoffs correlate with those from other asset classes. For instance, the returns from funds that exploit trends in the prices of commodity futures often are not correlated significantly with the market. This can make them useful in reducing the fluctuations in the value of your overall portfolio. There are equity long-only funds, short-only funds, and long/short funds. Market-neutral funds (like PNP and Ridgeline) attempt to have returns uncorrelated with the market.

Funds also may specialize by geographic area or by a country's level of financial and economic development such as so-called emerging markets, or by economic sector such as biotechnology, gold, oil, or real estate.

You can also choose a "fund of funds," which is a hedge fund that invests in a portfolio of other hedge funds—much the way mutual funds invest in a collection of stocks—and whose management is in the business of evaluating hedge funds. In addition to what the hedge funds charge directly, the fund of funds manager collects a second layer of fees, typically 1 percent per year plus 10 percent of the profits.

A class of people as smart as hedge fund managers can hardly be expected to overlook the advantages of deception. In fact, hedge funds frequently start out small and build spectacular records, later turning ordinary as they grow.

One method that leads to this has also been used to launch new mutual funds. Fund managers sometimes start a new fund with a small amount of capital. They then stuff it with hot IPOs (initial public offerings) that brokers give them as a reward for the large volume of business they have been doing through their established funds. During this process of "salting the mine," the fund is closed to the public. When it establishes a stellar track record, it is opened to everyone. Attracted by the amazing track record, the public rushes in, giving the fund managers a huge capital base from which they reap large fees. The brokers who supplied the hot IPOs are rewarded by a flood of additional business from the triumphant managers of the new fund. The available volume of hot IPOs is too small to help returns much once the fund gets big, so the track record declines to mediocrity. However, the fund promoters can use more hot IPOs to incubate yet another spectacularly performing new fund; and so it goes on.

The SEC finally acted in 1999, when for the first time it brought about the firing of one well-known fund manager for playing this game.

The manager's growth fund, best in its category for 1996 but closed to the public, reportedly had only a few hundred thousand dollars in capital at that point and got more than half its first-year gain of 62 percent from thirty-one hot IPOs! The manager opened the fund to the public in February 1997, to a flood of money, but failed to disclose the use of IPOs to inflate the track record.

Of course there are many reasons, other than salting the mine, for a decline to mediocrity. For a manager to get major investor attention he typically needs a decent initial record, or a persuasive case based on factors like a prior reputation, or even a business plan. Sometimes, just simple sales hype is enough. Some managers are lucky when they start—perhaps starting a "growth fund" in the late 1990s and buying a few Internet stocks like AOL or Amazon.com. With time, lucky managers tend to fade.

Hedge fund operators have ways of ending up with far more than the 20 percent of profits typically specified as their management fee. One of these I call "Heads we win, tails you lose." To see how this works, go back to 1986 when I was interviewing a wealthy hedge fund manager to see if my fund of hedge funds, OSM Partners, should invest with him. Times were good, his flock of hedge funds was prospering, and he invited me to leave PNP, bring my expertise and employees, and join him. I'd get half the management fee on a much larger pool of money. No, thanks.

The following year the crash of October 1987 hit his funds with losses varying from 30 percent to 70 percent. Performance fees would not be paid to him again until these losses were recovered. It might take years. If he's down 50 percent, for example, he has to double the money, making 100 percent, just to get even again. Facing no performance fees for years, he chose to terminate his hedge funds, leaving himself rich and his investors with losses. The net result was that he made off with all the profits. In less than a year he launched a fresh set of hedge funds, from which he could have the chance to immediately collect performance fees.

Cherry-picking, as I call it, is another way some hedge fund managers milk their limited partners. I first came across this in the late 1970s. It

was a lackluster decade for equities. A guru had been picking undervalued companies and making 20 percent or so per year before his fee. After
friends recommended I invest, I did some digging and learned he had
another pool that was making 40 percent. That was just for himself, his
family, and close friends. That pool got its fill of the best situations. The
rest went to the 20 percenters. I don't invest with bad people, so I passed.
Hedge fund documents, drawn up by lawyers hired and instructed by
the general partner, typically permit these conflicts of interest.

Improperly charging expenses to the partnership is another way that
the limited partners get less than they should. The list of issues goes on,
the point being that hedge fund investors don't have much protection
and that the most important single thing to check before investing is the
honesty, ethics, and character of the operators.

The hedge fund Long-Term Capital Management was launched in
1994 with a dream team of sixteen general partners, led by the legendary
former Salomon Brothers trader John Meriwether and two future (1997)
Nobel Prize winners in economics, Robert Merton and Myron Scholes.
The group included other former Salomon traders, more distinguished
academics, and a former Federal Reserve vice chairman. Investors included the central banks of eight countries, plus major brokerages,
banks, and other institutions.

The principals of a financial engineering group I knew, who were
coincidentally doing work for LTCM at that time, asked if I had an interest in investing in the fund. I declined because Meriwether had a history at Salomon of being a major risk taker and the partnership's
theorists were, I believed, lacking in "street smarts" and practical investment experience. Warren Buffett says, "Only swing at the fat pitches."
This did not look to me like a fat pitch.

The annual percentage return to LTCM investors was in the 30s and
40s, but this was based on enormous leverage, reportedly varying between 30:1 and 100:1. Without leverage, returns would be just a fraction
of a percent over the cost of money. They had hundreds of billions long
and hundreds of billions short. They expanded to $7 billion in capital
before giving back $2.7 billion, which increased both the risk and the
return on the remaining capital. Later, when adverse market conditions

created fairly small losses in percentage terms, the leverage magnified the impact and nearly wiped them out. After losing 90 percent of their capital in weeks, and with total ruin imminent, the fact that they were "too big to fail" led to a rescue effort encouraged by the Federal Reserve. The fund was liquidated in an orderly fashion and investors recovered a small percentage of their stake.

Not long after, Meriwether and four others of the sixteen partners started a new hedge fund similar to LTCM, but using less leverage. Nobelists Scholes and Merton chose not to join him again. Investors, including some of the losers from LTCM, soon put up $350 million. Growth and new capital increased it further. Then his "flagship" fund was reported to have ended the year 2008 down 42 percent, losing more than $300 million. It closed in 2009. In 2010 Meriwether started yet another hedge fund. Merton became a consultant to J. P. Morgan & Co., while retaining his teaching position at Harvard. Scholes returned to his faculty position at Stanford, became a financial consultant, and later launched another hedge fund.

The lessons we should have learned about excess leverage from the collapse of Long-Term Capital Management were ignored. Ten years later, history repeated on a worldwide scale when loose regulation and high leverage led to the near-collapse of the entire financial system in 2008. As part of the overall meltdown, hedge fund assets fell from $2 trillion to $1.4 trillion from losses and withdrawal of capital. Hedge funds were now a mature asset class. I predicted to *The Wall Street Journal* that any edge for investors would gradually disappear.

Meanwhile, the superrich, buttressed with government bailout billions, bounced back from the Great Recession. By 2012 they were richer than ever.

## Chapter 23

# HOW RICH IS RICH?

While chatting long-distance with a financial entrepreneur in London, I asked, "How much wealth would you need today to retire and live comfortably for the rest of your life?" "I know my exact number," he replied. "It's $20 million." I said, "According to my calculations, each year you can withdraw the equivalent of 2 percent of that amount, or $400,000 in today's dollars, with only a small probability of ever using up your fortune." In his early forties, married and with three small children, he said this sounded good to him. But everyone has a different number.

The famous American fiction writer John D. MacDonald characterized levels of wealth in 1970 in his Travis McGee series. As I remember, his economist co-hero Meyer said $100,000 was "adequate" and $250,000 "comfortable," whereas $1,000,000 was "substantial." To have $5,000,000 was "impressive." Since inflation has cut the real buying power of the dollar, MacDonald's corresponding year 2015 numbers would be six times as large, with $600,000 as adequate, $1,500,000 as comfortable, $6,000,000 as substantial, and $30,000,000 as impressive.

Dinesh D'Souza gave the following classification, which I have adjusted for inflation.

**Table 3: Classifications of Wealth**

| | Income | Wealth |
|---|---|---|
| Superrich | $15 million+ | $150 million+ |
| Rich | $1.5–15 million | $15 million–150 million |
| Upper-middle | $112,000–1.5 million | $750,000–15 million |
| Middle | $50,000–112,000 | $82,000–750,000 |
| Lower-middle | $22,000–50,000 | $15,000–82,000 |
| Poor | $0–22,000 | $0–15,000 |

US household wealth was estimated at $83 trillion at the end of 2014, mainly stocks, bonds, real estate, and personal property. What if we divided it up so everyone had the same amount? With 320 million people participating, each would have about $270,000. However, such estimates of national wealth and of the distribution of wealth and income are problematic. It depends on what's counted and how it's counted, and much data is not available.

It's also true that this increasing national wealth has become more unevenly distributed. The median wealth of a US household fell 36 percent, after inflation, from 2003 to 2013, declining from $88,000 to $56,000. In contrast, a household at the 97.5 percentile was 12 percent better off, with its net worth moving from $1.19 million up to $1.36 million.

A million dollars still sounds like real money, even though it doesn't buy nearly what it once did. In fact, it would take $20 million today to match the buying power of $1 million a century ago. How many in the United States have a net worth of $1 million? No one knows exactly, because comprehensive information on personal wealth is difficult to collect. Much of it is not available, not reported, or deliberately hidden to avoid taxes, theft, or criminal prosecution, or simply for personal privacy. Most of the available information applies to household units, of which there are about 125 million. Some households consist of only one person and most of the rest have a single economically dominant individual, so counting wealthy households probably gives a good estimate for the number of wealthy individuals.

The number of households worth at least $1 million was thought to be about ten million in 2015. With so many millionaire households, the goal of becoming one of them looks within reach. To see what might be done, imagine you're an eighteen-year-old blue-collar worker with no savings and no prospects. What if, somehow, you could save $6 a day and buy shares in the Vanguard S&P 500 Index Fund at the end of each month? If that investment grows in a tax-deferred retirement plan at the long-term average for large stocks of about 10 percent, then after forty-seven years you can retire at age sixty-five with $2.4 million. But where do you find an extra $6 a day? The pack-and-a-half-a-day smoker who kicks his drug habit saves $6 each day. If the construction worker who drinks two $5 six-packs of beer or Coke each day switches to tap water he can save $10 a day, $6 of which he puts in an index fund and $4 of which he spends on healthy food to replace the junk calories from the beer or Coke.

Most of us, with greater opportunities to redirect our expenditures, can expect to do better than our poor, young, blue-collar worker. An article titled "Budget Basics: 25 Things You Can Do to Trim Yours Today" began with the excellent suggestion "Write down everything you spend. The waste in your daily spending should soon become apparent." Number two agrees with my advice to pay off credit card debt as soon as possible. Number four says to give up smoking. Number twenty-three suggests buying a car used rather than new because "A car is worth about ⅓ less the minute you drive it off the lot." Whether or not the immediate loss is that great, it's generally agreed that the buyer of a new car gets relatively little real useful value in return for the early years of rapid depreciation. Suppose you could settle for a $10,000 used car rather than a $20,000 new car. Invested at a hypothetical after-tax annual return of 8 percent just like the cigarette money, the $10,000 difference grows to over $100,000 in thirty years. To those who balk at changing their ways we can only ask, along with Regis Philbin, "Who wants to be a millionaire?"

Investors I dealt with typically were not just millionaires but multi-millionaires with fortunes of $5 million and up. How many households have reached these rarefied heights? The great Italian economist Vilfredo Pareto studied the distribution of income and in 1897 came up with a "power law" formula that seems then and now to describe fairly well how many top wealth holders in a modern society have reached various levels. To calibrate the formula we need just these two facts: The *Forbes* 400 cutoff for the United States, which was $1.55 billion in 2014, and the total wealth of those four hundred, an amazing $2.3 trillion. The formula gives us Table 4.

**Table 4: Estimated Numbers of Wealthiest Households, United States, Year 2014**

| Wealth Level W: This Amount or More | Formula Estimate of Number N of US Households Having This Much or More |
| --- | --- |
| $1 million | 9,300,000 |
| $5 million | 1,030,000 |
| $10 million | 400,000 |
| $20 million | 155,000 |
| $50 million | 44,000 |
| $100 million | 17,000 |
| $250 million | 4,900 |
| $500 million | 1,900 |
| $1 billion | 730 |
| $1.55 billion | 400 |

The formula is a good fit for only high wealth levels, giving numbers that are too large below a point somewhere in the neighborhood of $1 million.

You might wonder how the numbers corresponding to table 4 would look for your city, county, region, or state. If your area were average, you could simply multiply the estimated number for the United States by the percentage living in your area. Orange County, California, where I live, had just over three million people in 2014, or 1 percent of the total US population, so the numbers were easy. Just move the decimal point two steps to the left in table 4, getting a table for Orange County, and giving a total of forty-nine people worth a quarter of a billion dollars or more, for example. But the distribution of the rich varies widely. Areas like Redmond, Washington, home of Microsoft, or Silicon Valley, California, a center of the dot-com revolution, or Manhattan, New York, the self-proclaimed financial capital of the universe, have far more than their share, while other regions consequently are underrepresented.

Some of the superrich call $100 million a "unit" and, when they have their first unit, proudly announce that "the first unit is the hardest." Our table estimates seventeen thousand households were in this select group in 2014. With 125 million American households, the politically controversial 1 percent are the wealthiest 1,250,000. The cutoff is around $4 million. However, as we'll discuss, it's the top 0.01 percent of all households, a mere 12,500, that run our society. Members of this group are worth at least $125 million.

At the top of the ladder was William F. (Bill) Gates, the co-founder and largest shareholder of the Microsoft Corporation (MSFT), whose fortune at one point made him the first human ever to achieve a net worth of more than $100 billion, an amount which then exceeded 1 percent of the entire gross national product of the United States. Gates— even after giving a large part of his fortune to his charitable foundation—once again led the 2014 *Forbes* list of the richest people in the US at $81 billion.

To see where you stand on the ladder of wealth, estimate your or your household's net worth. List the value of what you own, your assets, and what you owe, your debts or liabilities. The difference is your net worth. To get a quick start, don't do any research, don't consult any records. When you don't know exact numbers, just guess. If you're uncertain, put in a low value for what you own and a high value for what you owe, leading to a conservative value for what you're worth. Table 5 is an example, for someone just at the threshold of the top 1 percent, based on a hypothetical composite of several wealthy people I know.

**Table 5: Estimating a Household's Net Worth**

| Assets (Thousands) | | |
|---|---|---|
| **Real estate** | | |
| Principal residence | 875 | |
| Vacation home | 220 | |
| | Subtotal | 1,095 |
| **Personal property** | | |
| Auto 1 | | 35 |
| Auto 2 | | 21 |
| Furniture | | 30 |
| Art | | 10 |
| Jewelry | | 35 |
| | Subtotal | 131 |
| **Securities, publicly traded** | | |
| Stocks | | 1,400 |
| Bonds | | 830 |
| Mutual funds | | 775 |
| Other | | 25 |
| | Subtotal | 3,030 |
| **Securities, privately held** | | |
| Start-up technology company | | 10 |
| Limited Partnership interest (hedge fund) | | 715 |
| **Cash** | | |
| Checking | | 11 |
| Savings/money market account | | 23 |
| | Subtotal | 759 |
| | TOTAL ASSETS | 5,015 |
| **Liabilities (Thousands)** | | |
| **Real estate** | | |
| Mortgage, principal residence | | 750 |
| **Other loans** | | |
| Credit cards | | 2 |
| Brokers, margin accounts | | 55 |
| Taxes owed but not yet paid | | 22 |
| | TOTAL LIABILITIES | 829 |
| **Net Worth (Thousands)** | | |
| Assets | | 5,015 |
| Liabilities | | 829 |
| | NET WORTH | 4,186 |

This quick assessment gives you an idea of where you stand. Later you will want to make a more accurate balance sheet, which I do about once a year. The difference in balance sheet net worth from one year to the next shows the change in your total wealth after income, expenses, gains and losses. This series of annual balance sheets shows how your wealth is changing over the years.

In the asset section, for each item list the amount of cash you feel sure it would sell for in a reasonably short time. That car you bought new a year ago for $45,000 might have a replacement cost of $39,000 now, but you might be able to sell it for only $35,000. Put down $35,000. Recent sales of houses comparable with yours might range from $925,000 to $950,000, but after all sales and closing costs, you might net only $875,000. Put down $875,000. What you owe on the mortgage will be deducted in the liabilities section.

Unlike liquid listed securities, the current market prices for property such as cars, houses, art, and jewelry are not continuously displayed, but the analogy to securities prices is useful for understanding the impact of commissions on profits and losses. Just as each security has a current price for which you can buy it, the asking price, and a somewhat higher cost to you after paying commissions, we can imagine an all-inclusive "asking" price that we would have to pay for a piece of property identical to what we now own. Call this the replacement cost. And just as each security has a current price someone will pay for it, called the bid price, and a somewhat lower net proceeds to us after commissions, we also can imagine the highest net proceeds we might receive after selling costs for a piece of property. This is the liquidation value that we are listing in the asset section.

This spread between replacement value and liquidation value may be high for real property—often as much as 10 to 20 percent. For instance, I buy a $100,000 painting and pay $7,000 more in sales taxes, for a total of $107,000. The next day I change my mind and sell it for the same price of $100,000, paying $10,000 in commissions, for net proceeds of $90,000. The spread was $90,000 to $107,000, a difference of $17,000 or 17 percent of the "base" price of $100,000. This is what is lost in a round of buying and selling. It's that way with houses, cars, art, and jewelry. In contrast, the cost to trade listed securities is typically only a small fraction of a percent—which, along with their liquidity, makes them more appealing stores of wealth.

*Wealth,* which I use synonymously with the accountants' term *net worth,* shows how rich you are now, whereas *income* measures how much money your wealth, labor, and ingenuity are currently generating. A major part of aggregate wealth increase, especially at the higher wealth levels, comes from investments such as stocks, bonds, real estate, and collectibles. Wealth, not income, is the measure of how rich someone is now. However, examples like the movie star who leaps to fame and starts making $20 million per year show that income may lead to future large increases in wealth.

It's that increase in net worth from year to year that takes you up the ladder of wealth. To measure your increase in wealth from one year to the next, compare the yearly balance sheets. Divide the difference by the beginning wealth to get your percentage change for the year. This gives you an idea of how fast you are compounding. If you also construct an income statement for the period, the net income after expenses should match your change in net worth.

Balance sheets are snapshots that tell you where you are at a particular time. The income statement tells you what happens between two balance sheets. To appreciate the income statement without bothering to look anything up, jot down a list of all the sources that added to, or subtracted from, your wealth during the last twelve months. Do this "rough and dirty"; focus on the ideas rather than details and precision. Here are some categories to check:

A. Income, taxable and nontaxable:
   1. Earned income such as wages and salaries.
   2. Unearned income such as interest and dividends.
   3. Realized capital gains and losses.
   4. Royalties, honoraria, all other taxable receipts.
   5. Tax-free interest, such as municipal bonds.

B. Nontaxable gains and losses:
   1. Appreciation or depreciation of property such as real estate, art, and autos.
   2. Unrealized capital gains or losses in securities.

C. Expenses (all money paid out for "costs"—that is, not saved):
   1. Living expenses, consumption.
   2. Income taxes.
   3. Gifts.
   4. Any other money earned but not saved.

Category A is what most people call income. Reduced by deductions and nontaxable income, it is what you'll pay income tax on. Category B is less tangible and psychologically less appreciated or understood, but it adds to your wealth equally, and because taxes on it are deferred or never paid, the money works longer for you. Thus this type of gain is more desirable. Ironically, most people during the last century focused on income such as dividends and interest. As the folly of paying unnecessary taxes dawned on investors, the dividend rate paid by companies in the last part of the twentieth century dwindled and stock prices soared, shifting returns away from income and toward capital gains.

Category C is everything you spend or consume that doesn't contribute to your wealth. Think of your wealth at the start of the year as liquid partly filling a huge measuring cup. The balance sheet tells you how much is there. During the year categories A and B tell how much you add and category C tells you how much you take out. The difference, A + B − C, is how much you added or subtracted during the year. This is net economic gain and, as an investor, it's what you want to maximize. The balance sheet at the end of the year corresponds to the liquid left in the measuring cup.

The income statement shows that your taxable income may be very different from your economic income. Statistics for economic incomes are not available, being mostly unknown and not reported. However, though the disparities between economic income and taxable income may vary wildly from taxpayer to taxpayer and from year to year, we do know how taxable incomes are distributed among households. For instance, those American households that paid the most income tax in 2007, the top 0.01 percent, numbering fifteen thousand, each paid taxes on $11.5 million or more. Their 6.04 percent of the entire country's declared income was then the highest percentage ever. It totaled $557 billion, an average $37 million each.

The journal *Tax Notes* said the top 0.01 percent of American households expanded their inflation-adjusted income from 1973 to 2007 by 8.58 times whereas the bottom 90 percent gained about $8 per year! This inequality increased further in the next decade.

One of the keys to reaching such great wealth at the top is compound growth.

*Chapter 24*

# COMPOUND GROWTH: THE EIGHTH WONDER OF THE WORLD

For those who want to climb the ladder of wealth, it is helpful to appreciate the unusual arithmetic by which money grows. Compound interest, described in a phrase of disputed origin, is "the eighth wonder of the world." Wonder or trick, it has built great fortunes, and you can use it to get richer.

In 1944, the fifty-one-year-old IRS estate auditor Anne Scheiber left the organization that rewarded her for twenty-three years of distinguished service by never promoting her. Then she invested her savings of $5,000 in the stock market. Living frugally and studying companies, she continually reinvested her dividends. Her portfolio continued to grow until she died in 1995 at age 101. When her lawyer, Ben Clark, tried to meet with officials of Yeshiva University to tell them about a bequest she had left to the school, they had never heard of Anne Scheiber and wondered how to avoid wasting their time. But when the meeting was finally held, they learned that Ms. Scheiber was leaving them $22 million for the benefit of women students.

Were Anne Scheiber's choices unusually lucky? How would an average investor have done? Taking the period from the start of 1944 until the end of 1997, allowing a couple of years for the settlement of the estate and the delivery of securities to Yeshiva, $5,000 invested in a large stock index grew to a mere $3.76 million; but the same amount invested in small stocks grew, on average, to $12.31 million. Starting with a little more than Anne, investing $8,936 instead of $5,000, the average small stock investor would have achieved her $22 million result.

Compound interest, or more accurately compound growth, is the process Anne Scheiber used, accumulating wealth by reinvesting her gains. An easy way to think about compound growth, and also about the ladder of wealth, is in terms of doubling and redoubling. Consider two investors, Sam Scared and Charlie Compounder. Suppose Sam Scared starts with $1; each time it doubles, he puts his $1 profit in a sock instead of reinvesting it. After ten doublings, Sam has a profit in the sock of $1 × 10 plus his original $1 for a total of $11. Charlie also starts with $1 and makes the same investments but lets his profit ride. His $1 becomes $2, $4, $8, et cetera, until after ten doublings he has $1,024. Sam's wealth grows as $1, $2, $3 . . . $11. This is called simple growth, arithmetic growth, or growth by addition. Charlie's increases as $1, $2, $4 . . . $1,024. This is known variously as compound, exponential, geometric, or multiplicative growth. Over a sufficiently long time, compound growth at a small rate will vastly exceed any rate of arithmetic growth, no matter how large! For instance, if Sam Scared made 100 percent a year and put it in a sock and Charlie Compounder made only 1 percent a year but reinvested it, Charlie's wealth would eventually exceed Sam's by as much as you please. This is true even if Sam started with far more than Charlie, even $1 billion to Charlie's $1. Realizing this truth, Robert Malthus (1766–1834), believing that population grew geometrically and resources grew arithmetically, forecast increasingly great misery.

Politicians, dimly aware of the awesome power of compound growth, have in many jurisdictions passed laws against perpetuities to prevent the enormous concentrations of wealth that might arise from investments compounding without limit. On the other hand, some states and counties welcome perpetual trusts, being more interested in deriving revenue from them now.

The population of the world increased from 2.5 billion in 1930 to

7.3 billion in 2015, a growth rate of about 1 percent a year. It's expected to reach 9.7 billion by 2050. Everyone knows that this can't keep up; the carrying capacity of the earth—the amount of humanity the earth can support as limited by the available solar energy for food, and by other scarce resources—has been estimated as up to one hundred billion people. But what if we could somehow keep growing at, say, a rate of 1 percent a century? A calculation shows that in 1.2 million years we would be a solid sphere of flesh with a radius almost as large as that of our galaxy, expanding at the speed of light!

How fast do ordinary investments grow? The best simple long-term choice has been a broad common-stock index fund. At the average past growth rate of about 10 percent a year, such an investment has doubled in about 7.3 years. Historically, inflation offset about 3 percent of this, stretching to a little over a decade the average time required to double real buying power. Taxable investors in an index fund, which generates dividends and some realized capital gains, pay government another percent or so annually, delaying the doubling time to about twelve years.

To get quick approximate answers to compound interest problems like these, accountants have a handy trick called "the rule of 72." It says: If money grows at a percentage R in each period then, with all gains reinvested, it will double in 72/R periods.

Example: Your money grows at 8 percent per year. If you reinvest your gains, how long does it take to double? By the rule of 72, it takes 72 ÷ 8 = 9 years, since a period in this example is one year.

Example: The net after-tax return from your market-neutral hedge fund averages 12 percent a year. You start with $1 million and reinvest your net profits. How much will you have in twenty-four years?

By the rule of 72, your money doubles in about six years. Then it doubles again in the next six years, and so forth, for 24 ÷ 6 = 4 doublings. So it multiplies by 2 × 2 × 2 × 2 = 16 and becomes $16 million. For more on the rule of 72, see appendix C.

The rule of 72 can expose outrageous claims. My personal trainer went to a stock market seminar where the operators were pitching a method called "rolling stocks." Selecting common stocks that would supposedly oscillate between two levels, they advised the investor to repeatedly buy low and sell high. The operators claimed the suckers could make 22 percent a month. Why would they bother to share their secret when, by putting $2,000 in a tax-deferred IRA and reinvesting their gains, they would have more than $46 trillion in ten years?

Suppose you invest time and energy to add $1,000 to your wealth. Will you sacrifice as much to make another $1,000? And another? Economic theorists believe that most people won't and that we typically put less value on each successive $1,000 increase in our net worth. We feel this way about all scarce useful items, or so-called economic goods. We value each additional unit less than the last.

I apply this to the trade-offs among health, wealth, and time. You can trade time and health to accumulate more wealth. Why health? You may be stressed, lose sleep, have a poor diet, or skip exercise. If you are like me and want better health, you can invest time and money on medical care, diagnostic and preventive measures, and exercise and fitness. For decades I have spent six to eight hours a week running, hiking, walking, playing tennis, and working out in a gym. I think of each hour spent on fitness as one day less that I'll spend in a hospital. Or you can trade money for time by working less and buying goods and services that save time. Hire household help, a personal assistant, and pay other people to do things you don't want to do. Thousand-dollar-an-hour New York professionals who pay $50 an hour for a car and driver so they can work while they commute understand clearly the monetary value of their time.

To get an idea of what your time is worth, take a moment now to think about how much you work and the income you get from your effort. Once you know your hourly rate you can identify situations where buying back some of your time is a bargain and other situations where you want to be selling more of your time. As you get used to thinking this way, I predict that you will often be surprised at how much you can gain.

Most people I've met haven't thought through the comparative values to them of time, money, and health. Think of the single worker who spends two hours commuting forty miles from hot and smoggy Riverside, California, to a $25-an-hour job in balmy Newport Beach. If the worker moves from his $1,200-a-month apartment in Riverside to a comparable $2,500-a-month apartment in Newport Beach, his rent increases by $1,300 a month but he avoids forty hours of commuting. If his time is worth $25 per hour he would save $1,000 ($25 × 40) each month. Add to that the cost of driving his car an extra sixteen hundred miles. If his economical car costs him 50 cents a mile or $800 a month to operate, living in Newport Beach and saving forty hours' driving time each month makes him $500 better off ($1,000 + $800 – $1,300). In effect he earned just $12.50 per hour during his commute. Does our worker figure this out? I suspect he does not, because the extra $1,300 a month in rent he would pay in Newport Beach is a clearly visible cost that is painfully and regularly inflicted, whereas the cost of his car is less evident and can be put out of mind.

Americans supposedly spend an average of forty or more hours a week watching television. Those who do have plenty of "junk time," which they can use instead for an exercise or fitness program. Five hours a week for this can add five years of healthy life.

Undervaluing such a deferred benefit is a widespread investment error and seems to be part of our basic psychological makeup. A psychologist experimenting with four-year-olds offered each child one marshmallow, promising a second marshmallow if the first was still there when the experimenter returned to the room in twenty minutes. Left to their own devices, two-thirds of the children promptly ate their marshmallow and one-third waited to get two. Evaluating the children eight years later at age twelve, the testers found that the two-marshmallow children were markedly higher achievers than the one-marshmallow children. If you're a one-marshmallow child who grew up to buy on credit at crushing rates of 16 percent to 29 percent annualized, and you ask me where to invest some free cash, the first thing I recommend is paying off your credit card debt. The interest is nondeductible and the saving is certain, so you're earning a risk-free after-tax rate of 16 to 29 percent. The second thing I recommend is that you start investing some of your marshmallows, in order to enjoy more of them later, instead of gobbling them all immediately.

## Chapter 25

# BEAT MOST INVESTORS BY INDEXING

The easiest way to outperform most investors and grow your wealth is based on a simple concept that all investors should understand, both as a tool for investing and as an example of logical thinking about the markets. Consider a mutual fund that buys every stock trading on a major US stock exchange, investing in each company a percentage equal to that company's percentage of the total value of all the US stocks. Thus the fund behaves like the entire market, with the same daily percentage price changes and dividend payouts. This means if the oil giant Exxon has a market value, computed as share price times number of shares outstanding, of $400 billion and the total market value of all stocks is $10 trillion, then the index fund puts 4 percent of its net worth in Exxon, and so on for all the other stocks. A mutual fund like this that replicates the composition and investment results of a specified pool of securities is called an index fund, and investors who buy such funds are known as indexers.

Call any investment that mimics the whole market of listed US securities "passive" and notice that since each of these passive investments acts just like the market, so does a pool of all of them. If these passive investors together own, say, 15 percent of every stock, then "everybody else" owns 85 percent and, taken as a group, their investments also are like one giant index fund. But "everybody else" means all the active investors, each of whom has his own recipe for how much to own of each stock and none of whom has indexed. As Nobel Prize winner Bill Sharpe says, it follows from the laws of arithmetic that the combined holdings of all the active investors also replicate the index. Although this idea is well known, and I'm not sure where it first appeared, I first heard it from him and he has given the clearest exposition I've seen. I'll call it Sharpe's Principle.

I met Bill Sharpe in 1968 or 1969, when we were both young professors at UCI. Highly regarded, he had already completed the work for which he was awarded the Nobel Prize in 1990. Unfortunately he was in UCI's School of Social Sciences and I didn't really get to know him before he was recruited by Stanford just two years after his arrival. Had he still been at UCI after Princeton Newport Partners was well under way, might we have collaborated? He contributed a key simplification for understanding options, the binary model, and I might have been able to convince him that markets have significant inefficiencies—in other words, opportunities for abnormal risk-adjusted returns. Discussing this in 1975 when I invited him to lecture at UCI, Bill argued that my rewards from PNP didn't demonstrate market inefficiency, because you could argue that I and my associates were simply getting paid according to our worth. Had we turned our talents to other areas of economic endeavor we could expect the same.

Before costs, each passive investor gets the same return as the index. This is also true for the active investors as a group but not for each one individually. Holding a larger percentage than the index in some stocks and less in others, they may do better or worse than the index in various periods. Although the results (before costs) for the entire group of active investors matches the return on the index, their individual returns are statistically distributed around it with most fairly close and some quite different.

They have more risk without the expectation of more return. Reducing risk through diversification is one reason to buy an index, but an even more important one is reducing the costs that investors bear. Index funds trade infrequently, with stocks turning over just a few percent a year as the "keepers" of the index occasionally add and remove stocks, or because cash flows into or out of the fund. On the other hand, active investors as a group have been trading more than 100 percent of their portfolio per year. This imposes a substantial cost on them from commissions and by their impact on market prices.

To illustrate the losses from market impact, suppose XYZ stock has a "true" price of $50 a share. Assuming for simplicity that it trades in 10-cent increments, between trades there will be buyers bidding for various amounts at $49.90, $49.80, $49.70, and so forth. Similarly, sellers will be asking $50.10, $50.20, et cetera. Someone who places an order to buy at whatever price is available in the market, called a market order and one of the most common types, will pay $50.10, a little above the true price. This 10-cent difference between the price paid and the "true" price is called market impact. Market impact increases with order size since, to continue our example, a large market order may clean out not only the offering at $50.10 but also stock offered for sale at higher prices, resulting in an average purchase price above $50.10 and a market impact greater than 10 cents per share.

When Steve Mizusawa and I operated Ridgeline Partners, we reduced these costs by dividing large orders into smaller ones of $20,000 to $100,000, and waiting a few minutes between transactions to allow the market price to recover. We know the "true" price is somewhere at or between the highest bid price (the Bid) and the lowest asking price (the Offer), but not exactly where. On average, it is about halfway between the two. To see that market impact is a real cost, suppose in our example that just after buying stock at $50.10 the buyer wants to sell it at market. He gets $49.90, for an immediate loss of 20 cents or about 0.4 percent.

Investors who don't index pay on average an extra 1 percent a year in trading costs and another 1 percent to what Warren Buffett calls "helpers"—the money managers, salespeople, advisers, and fiduciaries that permeate all areas of investing. As a result of these costs, active investors as a group trail the index by 2 percent or so, whereas the passive investor who selects a no-load (no sales fees), low-expense-ratio (low overhead and low management fee) index fund can pay less than 0.25 percent in fees and trading costs. From the gambling perspective, the return to an active investor is that of a passive investor plus the extra gain or loss from paying (on average) 2 percent a year to toss a fair coin in some (imaginary) casino. Taxable active investors do even worse, because a high portfolio turnover means short-term capital gains, which currently are taxed at a higher rate than gains from securities, the sales of which have been deferred for a year. For instance, if $1,000 is invested at 8 percent and gains are taxed when realized, table 6 compares the result of paying the tax every year versus paying only at the end of a certain number of years. I used 35 percent for short-term capital gain taxes and 20 percent for long-term capital gains. Actual rates will vary with the investor's tax bracket and changes in the law.

Influential private equity and hedge fund managers have persuaded their friends in Congress to grant them the benefits of deferring taxes on their overseas income for many years and, even better, then paying the tax not at the rates for ordinary income that are paid by wage earners, but rather at much lower long-term capital gains rates. The difference between the first and last columns of table 6 indicates the magnitude of the benefits.

Table 6: With an Investment Making 8%, Paying Tax Every Year at 35%, at 20%, and Paying 20% at the End

| Investment Ends at Year | Value of Investment | | |
| --- | --- | --- | --- |
| | Pay 35% Tax Every Year | Pay 20% Tax Every Year | Pay 20% Tax at End |
| 0 | 1,000 | 1,000 | 1,000 |
| 1 | 1,052 | 1,064 | 1,064 |
| 10 | 1,660 | 1,860 | 1,927 |
| 20 | 2,756 | 3,458 | 3,929 |
| 30 | 4,576 | 6,431 | 8,250 |

If the index beats the pool of active investors by 2 percent each year, does that mean it also beats most equity mutual funds? Widely publicized, year-end annual reports show the S&P Index of 500 stocks beating a majority of mutual funds most years but not always. Why? For one thing, we're comparing apples and oranges: The S&P 500 Index isn't the whole market—if our universe is the total stock market index then it's an active investor, although one with low costs—since it doesn't include most small companies, so the assets of a mutual fund that are not part of the S&P 500 are not subject to Sharpe's Principle as applied to that index. The S&P 500 stocks are selected by the Standard & Poor's Corporation, with occasional deletions and additions. Although these five hundred large companies account for roughly 75 percent of the market value of all publicly traded stocks, it omits some very large companies, notably, before 2010, Berkshire Hathaway, one of the ten largest US companies by market value. In fact, the compound annual return on small companies for the eighty-two years from 1926 through 2007 was 12.45 percent, compared with 10.36 percent for large companies. Yet the extra boost for mutual funds from having had some of their assets in smaller stocks still hasn't offset their extra costs.

Another aspect of the apples-and-oranges comparison is the impact of cash balances. Since fund investors continually add or withdraw money, funds are partly invested in fluctuating cash balances. When the market rises strongly, the interest on this cash doesn't keep up and the fund return lags the return on the equity portion of its holdings. Conversely, when the market is down sharply, the losses on the fund's equity position are reduced to the extent it is in cash and by the interest it gets on that cash. The impact of this cash drag is generally small.

Also, non-index mutual funds are only part of the total pool of active investors. Conceivably, their managers could be relatively skilled, in which case the mutual fund group would outperform the rest of the active investors. In this case, though the active investors lagged overall, the mutual fund group might excel compared with the others. However, academic studies of the historical returns of mutual funds show little evidence of such managerial skill on the part of mutual funds. Third, it is not the number of active investors that must lag the index, according to Sharpe's Principle. Instead, it is the return on the total pool of actively managed assets invested in the index that must underperform.

Morningstar, which tracks mutual fund performance, does periodic studies comparing fund performance with indexes. The 2009 results are typical. After adjusting for risk, size, and investment category, only 37 percent beat their benchmark over the previous three years, with similar results for five and ten years.

The benefits from indexing are shown in table 7. Here I have used historical returns on large stocks, like those in the S&P 500, with my assumed costs. More details are given in appendix B. After costs and inflation, tax-exempt passive investors gained 6.7 percent annually compared with 4.7 percent for the actives, over two-fifths better. After taxes it is 2.0 percent for the actives and 4.8 percent for the indexers, more than double.

Table 7: Comparison of Passive Versus Active Investing

|  | Index | Passives | Actives |
|---|---|---|---|
| Before costs | 10.1% | 10.1% | 10.1% |
| After costs | — | 9.7% | 7.7% |
| After inflation | 7.1% | 6.7% | 4.7% |
| Tax-exempt after inflation | — | 6.7% | 4.7% |
| After taxes | — | 4.8% | 2.0% |

If you index, select a fund with annual expenses less than 0.2 percent. Reject funds that add management fees, sales loads, or other charges. The one charge you can ignore is a penalty for selling before a short holding period, such as thirty days, which funds introduced to prevent costly large-scale rapid in-and-out trading by certain investors.

Each year, typically at the end of October, US equity mutual funds assign the year-to-date taxable gains or losses to their current investors. If you were to make an investment shortly before this in a year when the fund had a lot of gain, you could experience the inequity of paying taxes on an amount far larger than your real economic gain. On the other hand, in a year when the fund allocated large losses, a purchase shortly before the time to receive the losses could let investors reduce their tax bill without having had a corresponding economic loss.

Tax-exempt investors such as IRAs, 401(k)s, employee benefit plans, and foundations ought to consider swapping their active investments in equities into a broad no-load index fund, unless they have strong reasons to believe their current investments give them a significant edge. In my experience, superior stock-picking ability is rare, which means almost everyone should make the switch.

Taxable investors need to review their holdings on a case-by-case basis. For instance, in 2015, with a cost basis of about $1,000 a share, a market price of $225,000 a share, and a combined federal and state tax rate of, say, 30 percent, I would net about $157,800 per share after a sale of my Berkshire Hathaway Class A stock. An index fund purchased with this smaller amount would have to do about 43 percent better than Berkshire in the future for me to catch up. This seems extremely unlikely.

Like me with Berkshire, investors who don't trade, and use no advisers, will avoid the usual expenses paid by active investors. In fact, their costs may be even less than those of indexers. If such a buy-and-hold investor were, for instance, to choose stocks at random, purchasing an amount of each proportional to its market capitalization, we could show, by reasoning like that used to prove Sharpe's Principle, that the expected return is the same as for the index from which the stocks were chosen minus the presumably small costs of acquiring the stocks.

The main disadvantage to buy-and-hold versus indexing is the added risk. In gambling terms, the return to buy-and-hold is like that from buying the index then adding random gains or losses by repeatedly flipping a coin. However, with a holding of twenty or so stocks spread out over different industries, this extra risk tends to be small. The threat to a buy-and-hold program is the investor himself. Following his stocks and listening to stories and advice about them can lead to trading actively, producing on average the inferior results about which I've warned. Buying an index avoids this trap.

For another way to look at index investing, suppose the same percentage of each US stock were put into a low-cost index fund and all the rest went into a giant pool actively managed by the world's best managers. Then a clerk managing the index fund with a computer to do the book-keeping would beat the team of the best managers on earth, by the amount of their extra commissions and fees. In contests promoted by journalists, random portfolios of stocks selected using chance devices such as darts, dice, or (figurative) chimpanzees hold their own against the experts.

## Chapter 26

# CAN YOU BEAT
# THE MARKET?
# SHOULD YOU TRY?

W hen I first became interested in blackjack, everyone said there was no way to beat it. Winning systems, often involving complicated ways of varying the amounts wagered, were proven mathematically to be impossible for many of the classical gambling games. Besides, if someone could beat the casinos, the rules would be changed to stop them. When I became interested in the stock market, I heard the same claims about investing. Academics had developed a series of arguments known as the efficient market hypothesis (EMH). Using financial market data, they showed that tomorrow's prices looked like random fluctuations around today's prices, therefore they were not predictable.

Besides, if a price change were predictable, somebody would immediately trade on this until it was no longer so. This notion gave rise to an apocryphal story that all finance students have heard. Eugene Fama, father of EMH, was strolling across the University of Chicago campus with a graduate student. Looking down, the student exclaimed, "Look, there is a $100 bill on the ground." Without a glance down or a break in stride, Fama replied, "No, there isn't. If there were, someone would have picked it up already."

The cards dealt at blackjack also seem to appear at random but not if you "track the shuffle," which is a way to beat the game by watching the order in which the discarded cards are stacked, then mathematically analyzing the particular shuffling technique being used, leading to a partial prediction of the new ordering of the cards for the next deal. The likelihood of any card being the one that is dealt next is not random if you count the cards. What appears random for one state of knowledge may not be if we are given more information. Future prices are not predictable and no one can beat the market, but only when market prices "truly" fluctuate randomly.

Supporters of the efficient market hypothesis, really a collection of related hypotheses, generally believe that securities markets in advanced developed countries respond quickly and almost completely to new information. True believers originally held that most investors were rational and well informed over the decades. However, they have reluctantly yielded to the overwhelming evidence to the contrary, but they still say the collective impact of investors generally keeps current market prices close to the best possible estimate of the value, averaged over all future scenarios. Since the 1960s, academics in economics and finance have defended the various versions of the efficient market hypothesis as they churned out tens of thousands of articles, thousands of PhDs, and hundreds of books.

The classic view of the correct price of a common stock is that it is derived from the value of all the future earnings. These earnings are uncertain and subject to unknowable factors. Could anyone have known beforehand how to allow for the impact of 9/11 on the future earnings, hence on the then current market price, of firms headquartered in the Twin Towers of the World Trade Center? These future payoffs are discounted to a present value reflecting their various probabilities and risks. If the market does a good job of using today's public information to set current prices, then the only investors who have an edge are those with material private information. The high-profile prosecution of investors in the 1980s for illegal trading on inside information makes the point.

The EMH is a theory that can never be logically proved. All you can argue is that it is a good or not-so-good description of reality. However, it can be disproven merely by providing examples where it fails, and the more numerous and substantive the examples, the more poorly it describes reality.

So far I've shown how markets were beaten in the past with examples from gambling, from the trading and results of Princeton Newport Partners, Ridgeline, and other hedge funds, and from the story of Warren Buffett and Berkshire Hathaway. Doing better than the market is not the same as beating it. The first is often simply luck; the second is finding a statistically significant edge that makes sense, then profiting from it. To illustrate, PNP did this in the 1980s when it exploited the large discounts to liquidation value that frequently appeared among closed-end funds.

Closed-end funds start out by selling shares to investors. They are called closed because this sale of shares happens one time only, at the launch of the fund. Management then invests the money in a stated category of securities, such as high-tech, Korean, junk bonds, green energy, or biotech. To illustrate how such a fund might work, suppose we're in the midst of a precious metals boom. The promoters sell shares of stock in the "Pot of Gold" (POG) closed-end fund through brokerage firms, paying 8 percent of the proceeds to these firms and their sales forces. Investors buy ten million shares at $10 a share, for proceeds of $100 million less 8 percent, netting $92 million, which the managers of POG invest in listed gold stocks. Each share, originally costing $10, now represents $9.20 worth of stock, which is its net asset value (NAV) per share. The "sell side," the Wall Street promoters, have just captured 8 percent of the money. Notice that an investor could have bought gold stocks directly and, for each $10, owned $10 worth of stock.

The shares of POG begin trading in the marketplace. Investors who are optimistic about the skills of management could bid these shares up to $11, $12, or even more, despite the NAV remaining at $9.20. Over time both the market price of POG shares and their NAV (the value per share of the underlying assets held by POG) will fluctuate. Any price for POG above NAV is called a premium to NAV and any price below NAV is a discount. One more thing—NAV represents the liquidation value of POG shares but, as long as management controls the fund, they are worth substantially less. That's because management collects fees and incurs expenses, thereby reducing the benefits of ownership for the shareholders, compared with an investor who owns the underlying portfolio directly.

Because of management's costs and fees, closed-end funds typically trade at a discount to net asset value. If management's fees and expenses tend to run at, say, 15 percent of the wealth being created by the underlying portfolio, then the shareholders might expect 85 percent of the future stream of benefits, so a fair price to pay ought to be 85 percent of NAV, or a discount of 15 percent. In the case of POG, the first investors pay $10 per share. Wall Street's selling charges cut this to $9.20. Then management takes 15 percent of future earnings, which reduces the value to the investor by another 15 percent, leaving a value per share for him of 85 percent × $9.20 or $7.82. He's immediately lost $2.18 of his $10 or 21.8 percent of his investment to his helpers. It's like having a brand-new car depreciate as soon as you drive it off the lot. As time passes, the market price, as a percentage of NAV, fluctuates and the pattern varies from fund to fund and with overall market conditions. I've seen discounts of 50 percent and premiums of 80 percent. To exploit this, an investor can seek to buy funds at deep discounts, relative to their histories and to that of comparable funds.

You can also sell short shares of funds trading at a high premium. Depending on their makeup, the long and short funds in your portfolio might hedge each other to some extent, with futures and options providing additional risk-offsetting possibilities. The returns from such a strategy can be fairly steady, but the long "workout" periods, during which premiums or excessive discounts tend to disappear, can make them modest. I once invested for a few years in an intelligently managed hedge fund that used this approach. Because of the slowness with which the mispricings diminished, our annualized return was 10 percent instead of the 15 percent we hoped for.

If POG was trading at a 40 percent discount with shares at $6 each and an NAV of $10, we could attempt to buy enough shares to force and win a vote to convert the fund to an open-end mutual fund, allowing shareholders to redeem at net asset value. Then we pay $6 a share and cash out at $10 a share, for a profit of $4 or 67 percent on our $6. A closed-end fund trading at a big discount was an opportunity for Princeton Newport. Despite fierce opposition from entrenched management, we succeeded in doing deals of this type profitably.

The differences between the market price and the net asset value of closed-end funds leave nowhere to hide for those who believe the market does a good job of setting prices correctly. Why do investors sometimes pay $1.80 for $1 of assets and other times offer to sell $1 worth of securities for 50 cents? It can't be lack of information, since NAVs and calculated percentage price deviations are published regularly, along with actual portfolio holdings.

An unusual opportunity to buy assets at a discount arose during the financial crash of 2008–09, in the form of certain closed-end funds called SPACs. These "special purpose acquisition corporations" were marketed during the preceding boom in private equity investing. Escrowing the proceeds from the initial public offering (IPO) of the SPAC, the managers promised to invest in a specified type of start-up company. SPACs had a dismal record by the time of the crash, their investments in actual companies losing, on average, 78 percent. When formed, a typical SPAC agreed to invest the money within two years, with investors having the choice—prior to the SPAC buying into companies—of getting back their money plus interest instead of participating.

By December 2008, panic had driven even those SPACs that still owned only US Treasuries to a discount to NAV. These SPACs had from two years to just a few remaining months either to invest or to liquidate and, before investing, offer investors a chance to cash out at NAV. In some cases we could even buy SPACs holding US Treasuries at annualized rates of return to us of 10 to 12 percent, cashing out in a few months. This was at a time when short-term rates on US Treasuries had fallen to approximately zero!

For those who still believe that the market always prices securities properly, here's a profit opportunity that arose because investors couldn't even do arithmetic.

To see what happened, first picture two car dealers with stores side by side. The first dealer offers new Ford sedans for $9,000, plus a $2,000 rebate payable in six months. The second dealer offers the identical new Ford sedans for $14,850. Everyone who drives up can see both prices on huge signs. The higher-priced dealer has balloons flying over his lot and a band playing. The lower-priced dealer does a brisk business but the higher-priced dealer is mobbed. Most of our "rational" investors prefer to pay too much. Nuts? Not possible? It happens often. For instance, in the next example the $9,000 Ford plus a $2,000 rebate is like 100 shares of 3Com and the identical Ford for $14,850 is like 135 shares of PalmPilot. Now for the details.

Famous for its PalmPilot handheld personal organizer, the company 3Com, with stock market ticker COMS, announced that it was spinning off its PalmPilot division as a separate company. Some 6 percent of PalmPilot, ticker PALM, was offered to the public in an initial public offering at a price of $38 per share on Thursday, March 2, 2000. By the end of the day the 23 million shares that had been issued changed hands more than one and a half times, for a one-day trading volume of 37.9 million shares. The price peaked at $165 before closing at $95. The portion of PalmPilot sold in the IPO was deliberately set well below demand and led to a buying frenzy and price spurt typical at the time for tech stock IPOs. So far, this just repeated what we had often seen during the previous eighteen months of the tech stock boom.

Now for the market inefficiency. At Thursday's closing the market priced PalmPilot at $53.4 billion, yet it valued 3Com, which still owned 94 percent of PalmPilot, at "only" $28 billion. But that means the market valued 3Com's 94 percent of PalmPilot at $50 billion, so it valued the rest of 3Com at negative $22 billion! Analysts, however, estimated the value of the rest of 3Com at between $5 billion and $8.5 billion. And within six months or so, 3Com intended to distribute these PalmPilot shares to its shareholders. Anticipating this, my son, Jeff, had called me a few days earlier to mobilize capital for this possible opportunity. You could buy PALM directly in the IPO (to get IPO stock you had to be "connected") or at wildly gyrating, much higher prices in the "aftermarket," when it began trading. Or you could buy PALM indirectly by buying COMS and waiting a few months to get 1.35 shares of PALM for each share of COMS owned. Moreover, you would also have a share in the post-spin-off business of 3Com, which was profitable and would have $8 cash per share. Jeff estimated the stock would then have had a value of $15 to $25.

Analyst's note: Jeff's estimate of 135 shares of PALM to be distributed for each 100 shares of COMS was deliberately conservative—a "worst-case" choice—compared with the typical "street" estimate of 150 shares. Thus the street's estimate makes the disparity look even wider than what we assumed. The uncertainty arose because the number of shares of PALM to be distributed to COMS shareholders depended on how many shares of COMS were outstanding at the time, and that would depend on how much dilution occurred in the interim from—for instance—outstanding options.

When Jeff and I were discussing strategy on the first day, at one point the prices were $90 per share for 3Com and $110 per share for PalmPilot. Buying 135 shares of PalmPilot outright cost $14,850, but if we paid $9,000 for 100 shares of 3Com we got both 135 shares of PalmPilot and 100 shares of the 3Com "stub" company. (Think of each 100 shares in 3Com as a ticket having two parts, one labeled 135 SHARES OF PALMPILOT and the other piece or stub labeled 100 SHARES OF 3COM POST-SPIN-OFF.) If you buy the hundred shares of 3Com you pay $9,000 and get $14,850 worth of PalmPilot and a 3Com stub with a current estimated value of between $1,500 and $2,500. Sell this for, say, $2,000 and the 135 PalmPilot shares only have a net cost of $7,000.

I challenge efficient market theorists to answer these questions: Why were people willing to pay $14,850 for 135 shares of PALM when they could have paid $7,000, and why were some investors buying PALM stock at a price that set a value of $53 billion for the company instead of acquiring it at a price of less than half as much by buying it via 3Com stock? It's not a question of information. The terms were simple, public, and known in advance.

How could Jeff and I exploit this? One approach was to buy 3Com, wait six months or so, then sell off both the PalmPilot shares we would get from 3Com and the remaining 3Com stub. But what if 3Com and PalmPilot were both substantially overpriced now and their prices fell drastically by then? There was reason to believe this might happen. First, COMS had run from about $50 two months earlier to over $100 just before the IPO, in anticipation of the spin-off. Second, we believed tech stocks were in a speculative bubble driven by a large pool of irrational investors, many of them in the new day-trading "casinos." We were right about the speculative bubble. The NASDAQ reached its all-time high at this time, then lost 75 percent in less than three years. Sixteen years later it still hadn't fully recovered.

We could borrow and then sell short 135 shares of PALM at $110 for proceeds of $14,850, which would be held in escrow by our broker until we returned the borrowed shares. We could also buy a hundred shares of COMS at $90 for a cost of $9,000, setting up a nearly riskless hedge for an almost sure profit. In six months or so we would get 135 shares of PALM from our 100 shares of COMS and deliver it to clear our short position. Then the $14,850 short-sale proceeds would be released to us from escrow, leaving us with a net profit of $5,850 in cash and a hundred shares of the 3Com stub. If this were currently priced at $15 per share we could sell it for an additional $1,500, making a total gain in six months of $7,350 on a $9,000 investment, or 82 percent.

Such profits for ourselves and other arbitrageurs were limited by the amount of PALM our brokers would lend us to sell short. One of our friends, who runs a $2.7 billion convertible hedge fund, was able to short two hundred thousand shares of PALM and had previously bought COMS at a much lower price, anticipating the pre-IPO run-up.

As *The Wall Street Journal* pointed out, in the few days when arbitrageurs (hedgers) could borrow more shares of PALM, they might have been able to reduce the disparity if they sold short PALM and bought 3Com, as in our example. Here we see clearly a mechanism of market inefficiency, namely the different behavior of the "dumb" or irrational PALM buyers and the savvy arbitrageurs. The *Journal* went on to point out that a similar pricing disparity arose in mid-February when IXnet,

Inc., was spun off from IPC Communications Inc. Even though IPC still owned 73 percent of IXnet, it was valued by the "efficient" market at less than half of IXnet. Jeff hedged this one, too.

Like members of the Flat-Earth Society, efficient market believers have no problem with the 3Com-PALM example. A leading advocate of the EMH explained that arbitrageurs couldn't correct the price disparity because there wasn't enough PALM available to sell short, and if there had been, the arbitrageurs (hedgers) would have brought the prices into a relationship consistent with the relative values. This is true. I and others would have bet a major part of our net worth if we could have borrowed the stock. However, the buyers of PALM could and should have corrected the mispricing themselves and by doing so substantially increased their holdings of PALM at no cost, simply by selling their PALM and reinvesting the proceeds in 3Com. Yet widespread public explanations of this, including a front-page story in *The New York Times* the day following the offering, had little immediate impact. Investors not only couldn't do arithmetic, they apparently didn't know anyone who could.

With the PALM/COMS example in mind, let's take another look at the efficient market theory.

For a perfectly efficient market, one you can't beat, we expect:

1. All information to be instantly available to many participants.
2. Many participants to be financially rational—for example, they will always prefer more money to less money, other things being equal.
3. Many participants to be able instantly to evaluate all available relevant information and determine the current fair price of every security.
4. New information to cause prices immediately to jump to the new fair price, preventing anyone from gaining an excess market return by trading at intermediate prices during the transition.

Note: Supporters of this theory realize, in varying degrees, that some or all of these conditions are unrealistic, but claim that they hold well enough to make it a good approximation.

Now let's see how markets really operate, so we can understand how better to invest.

In our odyssey through the real world of investing, we have seen an inefficient market that some of us can beat where:

1. Some information is instantly available to the minority that happen to be listening at the right time and place. Much information starts out known only to a limited number of people, then spreads to a wider group in stages. This spreading could take from minutes to months, depending on the situation. The first people to act on the information capture the gains. The others get nothing or lose. (Note: The use of early information by insiders can be either legal or illegal, depending on the type of information, how it is obtained, and how it's used.)

2. Each of us is financially rational only in a limited way. We vary from those who are almost totally irrational to some who strive to be financially rational in nearly all their actions. In real markets the rationality of the participants is limited.

3. Participants typically have only some of the relevant information for determining the fair price of a security. For each situation, both the time to process the information and the ability to analyze it generally vary widely.

4. The buy and sell orders that come in response to an item of information sometimes arrive in a flood within a few seconds, causing the price to gap or nearly gap to a new level. More often, however, the reaction to news is spread out over minutes, hours, days, or months, as the academic literature documents.

Our portrait of real markets tells us what it takes to beat the market. Any of these can do it:

1. Get good information early. How do you know if your information is good enough or early enough? If you are not sure, then it probably isn't.

2. Be a disciplined rational investor. Follow logic and analysis rather

than sales pitches, whims, or emotion. Assume you may have an edge only when you can make a rational affirmative case that withstands your attempts to tear it down. Don't gamble unless you are highly confident you have the edge. As Buffett says, "Only swing at the fat pitches."

3. Find a superior method of analysis. Ones that you have seen pay off for me include statistical arbitrage, convertible hedging, the Black-Scholes formula, and card counting at blackjack. Other winning strategies include superior security analysis by the gifted few and the methods of the better hedge funds.

4. When securities are known to be mispriced and people take advantage of this, their trading tends to eliminate the mispricing. This means the earliest traders gain the most and their continued trading tends to reduce or eliminate the mispricing. When you have identified an opportunity, invest ahead of the crowd.

Note that market inefficiency depends on the observer's knowledge. Most market participants have no demonstrable advantage. For them, just as the cards in blackjack or the numbers at roulette seem to appear at random, the market appears to be completely efficient.

To beat the market, focus on investments well within your knowledge and ability to evaluate, your "circle of competence." Be sure your information is current, accurate, and essentially complete. Be aware that information flows down a "food chain," with those who get it first "eating" and those who get it late being eaten. Finally, don't bet on an investment unless you can demonstrate by logic, and if appropriate by track record, that you have an edge.

Whether or not you try to beat the market, you can do better by properly managing your wealth, which I talk about next.

# Chapter 27

# ASSET ALLOCATION AND WEALTH MANAGEMENT

P rivate wealth in the industrially advanced countries is spread among major asset classes such as equities (common stocks), bonds, real estate, collectibles, commodities, and miscellaneous personal property. If investors choose index funds for each asset class in which they wish to invest, their combined portfolio risk and return will depend on how they allocate among asset classes. This also is true for investors who don't index. Table 8 gives a rough overview of the asset categories. Investment assets held by mutual funds, hedge funds, foundations, and employee benefit funds are not included, since their underlying assets have already been counted. Derivative securities, which include warrants, options, convertible bonds, and many later complex inventions, derive their value—as we have seen—from that of an "underlying" security such as the common stock of a company. Instead of listing them separately, they're understood to be included as part of their underlying asset class.

How are your assets divided among the categories in table 8? The big three for most investors are equities, interest rate securities, and real estate. Each accounts for about a quarter of the total net worth of US households, though the proportions fluctuate, particularly when an asset class experiences a boom or a bust.

**Table 8: Major Asset Classes and Subdivisions**

**EQUITIES**
- Common Stock
- Preferred Stock
- Warrants and Convertibles
- Private Equity

**INTEREST RATE SECURITIES**
- Bonds
  - US Government
  - Corporate
  - Municipal
  - Convertibles
- Cash
  - US Treasury Bills
  - Savings Accounts
  - Certificates of Deposit
- Mortgage-Backed Securities

**REAL ESTATE**
- Residential
- Commercial

**COMMODITIES**
- Agricultural
- Industrial
- Currencies
- Precious metals

**COLLECTIBLES (Art, gems, coins, autos, etc.)**

**MISCELLANEOUS (MARKETABLE) PERSONAL PROPERTY**
- Motor vehicles, planes, boats, jewelry, etc.

Investors who chase returns, buying asset classes on the way up and selling on the way down, have had poor historical results. The tech bubble that ended in 2000, the inflation in real estate prices that peaked in 2006, and the sharp drop in equity prices in 2008–09 were especially costly for them. On the other hand, the buy-low/sell-high investors, whom you might think of as "contrarian" or "value" investors, have tended to outperform by switching some funds between asset classes.

The tables in appendix B show that stocks and commercial real estate have provided the best long-run results for investors. Interest rate investments have been roughly break-even after taxes and inflation, and only modestly positive for nontaxable investors. However, though equities have performed best in the long run, they have had extended periods when they have been in drawdown, meaning that they were below their previous all-time high. Real estate fell sharply in the financial crisis of 2008–09.

Assuming that the risks and returns for asset classes in the twenty-first century will be similar to what they were in the twentieth, long-term passive investors are likely to do best in common stocks and income-producing commercial real estate, though the data is sketchier for the latter. Diversifying between the two may reduce risk and increase overall return.

Many investors do not want the level of risk involved in common stocks or real estate, where the high overall returns are interrupted by savage reductions in wealth.

A retired couple I knew had investments worth $6 million, which they planned to use as their means of support for the rest of their lives. Spending 4 percent of this per year, with the unspent part invested in "something safe that keeps up with inflation," this couple could enjoy the inflation-adjusted equivalent of about $240,000 pretax per year for the twenty-five remaining years at least one of them might live. They chose to put half in tax-free municipal bonds and the rest in equities. They feared a replay of the Great Depression.

I thought this plan suited them. As neither husband nor wife was interested in learning about finance and investing, they should remain passive investors. Even my suggestion, in the early 1990s, to put about $500,000 in Berkshire Hathaway, then trading at $12,000 per share, was too much for them to think about. It would have been worth $9 million in 2016 when the husband, who had outlived his wife, finally passed away. Having half their money in relatively safe and stable municipal bonds would likely preserve enough wealth to ride through adversity.

The years passed. Although their market value varied inversely with interest rates, the municipal bonds paid an average of 4 percent or so, tax-free, or about $120,000 annually. Overall, US equity investments increased four or five times on average (before taxes, investment adviser fees, and other costs), and Berkshire Hathaway advanced from $12,000 to almost $150,000, fell to $75,000 during the crisis, then rose above $200,000 per share in 2016. When the crisis of 2008 struck, equities lost half their value before rebounding. As tax receipts shriveled, the massive deficits of the US government were echoed at state and local levels. The safety of municipal bonds no longer seemed so assured. However, although they would have done better in equities, they still had enough money and, feeling safe, didn't worry as they would have done watching the ups and downs in the value of a stock portfolio.

Another investor I know structured his portfolio of a few million dollars to produce income at the level he wished to spend. Accordingly, his portfolio consists mostly of short- and intermediate-term bonds, on which he pays a significant income tax. Curiously, he thinks he can only spend income, in the form of dividends and interest, and he views capital appreciation as something less real. I tried, and failed, to convince him that higher total return (after tax) means more money to spend and more money to keep, no matter how it divides between realized income and unrealized capital gains or losses. To own a stock like Berkshire Hathaway, which has never paid a dividend, and therefore produces no "income," would be unthinkable for him. This investor's costly preference for realized income rather than total return (economic income) is common.

The investor who is willing to do a little thinking, along with the investing work that follows, has many ideas to check. For instance, there has been a strong inverse relationship between the last few years' average price/earnings ratio of the stock indexes like the S&P 500 and the total return on the index over the next few years. Put simply, a high P/E ratio suggests stocks are overpriced and are likely to underperform, whereas a low P/E indicates the opposite. An investor who is diversified among asset classes might exploit this by decreasing his allocation to stocks when P/Es have been historically higher and shifting more into stocks when the P/Es have been lower.

I prefer to think in terms of the inverse of P/E, or earnings divided by price, sometimes known as E/P but perhaps better described as earnings yield. When the P/E is 20, for example, the earnings yield is 1/20, or 5 percent. An investor who owns the S&P 500 Index could think of it as a low-grade long-term bond, comparing the earnings yield of this "bond" to the total return from some benchmark for actual bonds, such as long-term Treasuries or corporates of a particular quality grade. When the earnings yield on the stock index is historically high relative to the bond benchmark, the investor sells some of his bonds and buys stocks. When bond yields are high compared with stocks, he shifts money from stocks back to bonds.

Stories sell stocks: the wonderful new product that will revolutionize everything, the monopoly that controls a product and sets prices, the politically connected and protected firm that gorges at the public trough, the fabulous mineral discovery, and so forth. The careful investor, when he hears such tales, should ask a key question: At what price is this company a good buy? What price is too high? Suppose, after doing your analysis of the company's financial statements, management, business model, and prospects, you conclude that it's worth buying at $40 a share, at which price you expect not only a satisfactory excess risk-adjusted return but have a margin of safety in case your analysis is flawed. Suppose you also conclude that the expected return at $80 is substandard, so the stock is likely overpriced. Typically you'll avoid investing in stocks when they are trading above your buy price but, if you follow many companies carefully, from time to time some will be attractive purchases. The range between your "buy" price and the "likely overpriced" level, in this case from $40 to $80, is likely to be narrower for better, more experienced investors, enabling them to participate in more situations and with greater confidence.

The value of the US stock market at the end of 2014 was a little over a third of the world total. The sales pitch for investing in stocks of more than one country is to win the usual benefit of diversification—lower risk for a given level of return. The results have been mixed: excellent for 1970–86 and mediocre from 1987 through 2015. In recent years, especially in crises, world markets, reflecting the increasing globalization of information through technology, have tended to move much more in tandem with the US market, limiting the amount by which diversification overseas reduces risk.

A majority of American households own their own home. For many it is a large part of their wealth. How good an investment has it been? In 1952, one of my uncles and his wife paid $12,000 for a small one-story wood-and-stucco home in the working-class community of Torrance, California. In 2006, he sold his house near the peak of the real estate bubble, which was especially extreme in California. Despite the deterioration of his neighborhood into a borderline gang area, and the advanced age of his house, he netted about $480,000 after taxes and commissions. His investment multiplied forty times in fifty-four years, for a compound annual return of 7 percent. Also, his expenses of a few percent a year in property taxes and maintenance were less than what he would have paid to rent a similar property.

Although stories like this abound, my uncle was lucky. According to economist Robert Shiller, average US home prices after inflation increased from 1890 to 2004 by about 0.4 percent a year, with the rate being about 0.7 percent in the later 1940–2004 period. It follows from this that making a profit should not be a primary reason for owning your home. You can rent instead and do about as well financially. However, you may want, as I do, the non-quantified benefits of homeownership: You are your own boss, able to make changes and improvements at will without prior approval from a landlord. If you have a fixed-rate loan or have paid for your house in full, you have the security of knowing that your future monthly costs are controlled.

As I've noted, taxable investors share their profits with government, which on average sharply reduces their wealth compared to a nontaxable investor with the same portfolio. They do have a chance to offset this in whole or in part using the well-known idea of tax-loss selling.

In its simplest form, investors sell losing stocks before the end of the current year, realizing losses that reduce the year's income taxes. This behavior contributes to the so-called January effect where selling pressure in December further depresses the stock prices of the year's losers, followed by a rebound and excessive performance in January. The impact is greater for smaller companies. Investors used to realize a tax loss by selling a loser and buying it back immediately, with little risk of economic loss (or gain). To inhibit this loss of tax revenue by making it risky, the US government introduced the "wash sale rule," which says that anyone who sells a stock at a loss and buys it back within thirty-one days may not recognize the loss for tax purposes. The rule is worded also to thwart savvy investors inclined to swap into an "equivalent" stock to get around this.

The flip side of tax-loss selling is tax-gain deferral, where an investor who wishes to sell a security with a large gain waits until after the end of the year, deferring the tax due on it by one year. The money can be used for an additional year before being turned over to the government.

Though laws change, generally the tax rate on long-term capital gains, which are those from positions held for more than a year before being sold, has been substantially less than the rate paid on short-term capital gains. Thus, an investor with a profit may benefit by waiting for more than a year to sell. On the other hand, short-term losses are first used to offset short-term gains in the tax calculation, so they are often more valuable than long-term losses, which means that it is often better to sell losers before you have owned them for over a year.

Princeton Newport Partners reduced or deferred much of the partners' taxable gains at a time when tax laws were different from what they are now. Nonetheless, interesting possibilities still exist.

Tax-loss selling can be organized to yield greater benefits. Suppose you are a taxable investor who is happy buying and holding a stock index fund. If instead you buy a "basket" of twenty or thirty stocks that are chosen to track the index, you may be able to harvest increased tax benefits. That such a small number of stocks can, together, act like an index is shown by the Dow Jones Industrial Index, a basket of just thirty stocks. It has historically moved in concert with the S&P 500, even though the two indexes are chosen by entirely different methods and the very similar price behavior of the two was not planned. To do index arbitrage, PNP developed techniques in the mid-1980s for finding baskets of stocks that did a particularly good job of tracking an index. We used this very profitably the day after "Black Monday," October 19, 1987, to capture a spread of over 10 percent between the S&P 500 Index and the futures contracts on it. Quants have honed this to a fine art and, through their trading, generally keep the price discrepancy very small.

To cut taxes, start with a tracking basket and, each time a stock drops, say, 10 percent, sell the loser and reinvest the proceeds in another stock or stocks chosen so the new basket continues to track well. If you want only short-term losses, which is usually best, sell within a year of purchase. I advise anyone considering doing this in a serious way to study it first with simulations using historical databases.

When making an investment, it is important to understand how easy it might be to sell later, a feature known as liquidity. The lack of liquidity in hedge funds and in real estate would prove costly for investors in the 2008–09 recession.

After closing Ridgeline Partners in 2002, I watched with growing concern as deficits expanded and the prices of houses and equities soared. Meanwhile, hedge funds were changing their terms to lock up investors, making it increasingly difficult to withdraw capital. Allowed withdrawal dates went from monthly to quarterly, annually, or worse. Notices had to be given further in advance: thirty days became forty-five, sixty, or ninety days. Funds imposed limits known as throttles on the amount that could be withdrawn on any one date. The SEC played right into this with a new requirement that managers of hedge funds with over $100 million become registered investment advisers, unless they locked up initial investments for at least two years. Many funds joyously tied up their investors' money, avoiding registration in the process— a win–win for the funds, to the disadvantage of the investors the SEC was meant to be protecting.

In the spring of 2008 I realized that the collapse in housing prices was going to have much wider repercussions, so I issued partial withdrawal notices to several hedge funds in which I was invested. Unfortunately, these once fairly liquid investments were no longer so. The financial crisis of 2008 intensified sharply in September, before most of my withdrawals were scheduled to be paid, by which time the fund values had declined significantly. Many funds faced a crisis with their imprudently leveraged assets. The failure to anticipate the financial collapse by repositioning themselves led to sharp losses for their investors. Hedge funds, supposedly profitable in down markets, fell 18 percent for the year, while large stocks were off 37 percent and equity real estate investment trusts dropped over 40 percent. The new generation of hedge fund managers, carried away by the credit and asset bubble, either didn't know how to hedge or didn't think it was worth the cost.

The largest university endowments, such as Harvard, Yale, Stanford, and Princeton, also with substantial hedge fund investments, had even less flexibility, since they had long favored illiquid alternative investments, such as private-equity funds, commodities, and real estate. After leading the pack for years with returns in the high teens, they now gave back much of their accumulated edge, with percentage losses in the mid-20s, compared with 18 percent for the median large endowment.

Because you can't get out in time when trouble is coming, the excess returns you expect from illiquid investments may be offset by the economic impact of unforeseen future events.

The boom and bust in residential and commercial real estate that occurred in the first decade of this century introduced millions of homeowners to the dangers of leverage. Encouraged by the industry's promotional myth that prices only went up, homeowners borrowed 80 percent, 90 percent, and even 100 percent to buy their houses. As prices did rise, millions retained this high leverage by refinancing or taking on second mortgages and home equity loans. When in 2006 prices peaked and then fell, selling by homeowners who were now underwater (meaning that they owed more than the current market price), along with those who bought more house than they could handle and couldn't keep up with their payments, depressed prices further, triggering new selling. The lesson of leverage is this: Assume that the worst imaginable outcome will occur and ask whether you can tolerate it. If the answer is no, then reduce your borrowing.

My understanding of how to use leverage began with my experience in the casinos. When I deployed my card counting system for blackjack, it made intuitive sense to bet more when the expected gain, or edge, was greater. The question was, how much? The answer was in a 1956 article by Bell Labs physicist John L. Kelly, who some said was the smartest person there, after Claude Shannon. In his fascinating history of the topic, *Fortune's Formula,* William Poundstone points out that for a favorable bet that pays odds of $A for a bet of $1, the optimal Kelly bet is the percent of your capital equal to your edge, divided by the odds, A. In blackjack, the typical favorable edge was usually between 1 and 5 percent and the odds, or payoff per dollar bet, averaged a little more than 1. So, following the criterion when the card count was good, I bet a percentage of my bankroll that was a little less than my percent advantage. Kelly's criterion is not limited to two-value payoffs but applies generally to any gambling or investing situation in which the probabilities are known or can be estimated.

What happens if you do this? Kelly showed mathematically that the wealth of someone following his system would, with increasing likelihood, exceed the fortune of a competitor using an essentially different betting scheme. From blackjack, I went on to use Kelly's formula to manage bets in baccarat and to allocate money among investments.

Some key features of the Kelly Criterion are: (1) The investor or bettor generally avoids total loss; (2) the bigger the edge, the larger the bet; (3) the smaller the risk, the larger the bet. The Kelly Criterion, not having been invented by the old-line academic economists, has generated considerable controversy.

Bill Gross, co-founder of PIMCO, who learned about the Kelly Criterion in the summer of 1969 when he played blackjack in Nevada, is still influenced by it in making investment decisions. As he told *The Wall Street Journal,* "Here at PIMCO, it doesn't matter how much you have, whether it's $200 or $1 trillion. You'll see it throughout our portfolio. We don't have more than 2 percent in any one credit. Professional blackjack is being played in this trading room from the standpoint of risk management, and that's a big part of our success."

Three caveats: (1) The Kelly Criterion may lead to wide swings in the total wealth, so most users choose to bet some lesser fraction, typically one-half Kelly or less; (2) for investors with short time horizons or who are averse to risk, other approaches may be better; (3) an exact application of Kelly requires exact probabilities of payoffs such as those in most casino games; to the extent these are uncertain, which is generally the case in the investment world, the Kelly bet should be based on a conservative estimate of the outcome.

As I pointed out in *Wilmott* magazine, Warren Buffett's thinking is consistent with the Kelly Criterion. In a question and answer session with business students at Emory University, he was asked, in view of the popularity of *Fortune's Formula* and the Kelly Criterion, to describe his process for choosing how much to invest in a situation. He and his associate Charlie Munger, when managing $200 million, put most of it into just five or so positions. Sometimes he was willing to bet 75 percent of his fortune on a single investment. Investing heavily in extremely favorable situations is characteristic of a Kelly bettor.

In a typical life cycle, prior to adulthood we consume more than we produce. As we acquire education and training, we contribute more to society than it takes to support us. During this period, a prudent or fortunate investor will accumulate wealth from which to draw upon later as he ages and reduces his income from work.

At this point, to support yourself entirely from your savings, how much can you spend each year without running short? There is no one answer, of course, because of the differences in our individual needs, desires, and circumstances. One retiree I know has $10 million. He lives well and believes that if his investments keep up with inflation, he can spend $400,000 a year for the next twenty-five years before he runs out, and that's plenty for his purposes. This is the most "conservative" way to look at the problem: Invest in something like short-term US Treasury bonds, which have little risk and keep up with inflation, divide what you have by the greatest number of years you may live, and that is what you can safely spend each year.

What if you want the payouts to continue "forever," as you might for an endowment? Computer simulations showed me that with the best long-term investments, such as stocks and commercial real estate, annual future spending should be limited to the inflation-adjusted level of 2 percent of the original gift. This surprisingly conservative figure assumes that future investment results will be similar in risk and return to US historical experience. In that case, the chance that the endowment is never exhausted turns out to be 96 percent.

The 2 percent spending limit is so low because, if the fund is sharply reduced in its early years by a severe market decline, a higher spending requirement might wipe it out.

## Chapter 28

# GIVING BACK

In 2003, Vivian and I offered to endow a chair in mathematics at the University of California, Irvine. We were guided by what we had learned from the charitable giving we had done over several decades. One principle was to make the gift transformative, with an impact well beyond what you'd expect from the monetary amount. We also wanted to fund projects that wouldn't happen without our support. These conditions were met.

A new chairman had transformed the Math Department in the 1990s, quelling the strife, marginalizing the bad actors, and bringing in talented new faculty. Though there were endowed chairs on the campus, math had none. By creating one, we could attract a star and raise the department to a still-higher level. We stated our objectives as (1) to support the research of an individual mathematician of exceptional talent; and (2) using an unusual investment and distribution policy, to cause the principal to increase through compound growth so that the chair eventually becomes one of the most richly endowed in the world, thereby attracting extraordinary mathematical talent to UCI.

To meet our first objective, the endowment is to be used only to supplement the research activities of the chair holder. These funds are in addition to, not instead of, the standard faculty salary and support from the university. If the university is not willing to hire someone, neither are we. This arrangement is to remain unchanged even if, as we expect, the distribution from the endowment one day grows far beyond the salary paid by the campus to the chair holder.

Funds used for general departmental, campus, or university budgets, or for any purpose not directly in support of the research activities of the chair holder, are limited to 5 percent of the annual money drawn. We specified a distribution rate of 2 percent annually, which means 0.1 percent covers administration and 1.9 percent goes to the chair. We knew that limiting the annual draw from the endowment to 2 percent was crucial to our long-term compounding objective.

We donated appreciated Class A shares of Berkshire Hathaway, which eliminated a possible long-term capital gain for us if, instead, we kept the shares and someday sold them. Stock is to be sold only as needed to fund the chair. However, just one Berkshire A share would create far more cash (over $200,000 in 2016) than the annual payment from the endowment. Therefore, when money is needed, we asked that an A share first be exchanged for fifteen hundred B shares, the specified conversion ratio. Worth about $140 each in mid-2016, the B shares could then be sold in precise amounts to create funds when required. The point is to keep the endowment fully invested in stock until cash is needed. When we are no longer alive, remaining shares will be exchanged for a broad, no-load, US stock index fund with a very low expense ratio, such as the Vanguard S&P 500 or the Vanguard Total US Stock Index.

What kind of growth in the value of the endowment might we expect? Over the last two hundred years, a broad US stock index has grown about 7 percent faster than inflation. No one knows whether the future will be equally good, but even if the increase exceeded inflation by only 5 percent, the net annual growth in purchasing power would be 3 percent. Doubling on average every twenty-four years, after a century the endowment and its annual payouts would have grown over nineteen times in today's dollars. In two hundred years this rate of growth would

increase it to 370 times what is was worth when the chair was funded in
2003. If the United States continues to prosper, if the university continues to exist, and if our investment and distribution policies continue to
be implemented, the power of compounding may well lead to an endowment fund for our chair in mathematics that, valued in today's dollars, exceeds that of the current endowment for any other chair that now
exists in the world.

For those who wonder how likely this is to come to pass, we remind
them of a similar plan by Benjamin Franklin to, in the words of biogra-
pher H. W. Brands, make a bequest that "would be immediately useful,
yet it would gain in philanthropic power with passing years."

Upon his death in 1790, Franklin set aside two special revolving funds
of 1,000 pounds each. One went to Boston, and the other to Philadelphia.
They were to be lent in small portions at 5 percent per annum to help
"young married artificers." Franklin expected each fund compounding
at 5 percent per annum to increase in a century to over 130,000 pounds,
at which point 100,000 pounds was to be used for public works. In the
second hundred years Franklin thought the remainder could, at 5 percent, increase to more than 4 million pounds, which then was to be divided between the cities and their states. In actuality, the Boston fund
had grown to $4.5 million by 1990 and the Philadelphia fund to $2 million.

How have we done so far? In the first thirteen years, the principal
of the endowment more than doubled after spending and despite the
2008–09 market collapse. Regarding the future existence of the university, former University of California chancellor Clark Kerr observed
that "since 1520, only about 85 institutions have remained continuously
in existence . . . about 70 . . . [of these] . . . are universities . . . few things
last longer or are more resilient than universities."

Political fads and fashions come and go. Special-interest groups attempt to advance their agendas by seeking preferences or handicaps for
particular subgroups. The history of mathematics through the ages
shows contributions from an enormous diversity of cultures, beliefs, and
social systems. We specify that there is to be neither preference given nor
discrimination against any candidate on the basis of his or her race, reli-

gion, national origin, gender, or beliefs, and that mathematical merit and future potential, as well as the will and ability to implement them, be the criteria for selection.

We hope we have planned well and that our gift, like Ben Franklin's, will accrue to the benefit of many generations.

Another charitable opportunity that fit our criteria arose in 2004. The George W. Bush administration had severely restricted the allowed federal funding of stem cell research. Further, labs doing proscribed research had to be absolutely separate from federally funded facilities. Theoretically, if a pencil paid for by government funds was used for forbidden work, the entire federal grant could and would be revoked.

The nation faced a delay in the development of lifesaving therapies, a massive brain drain as our scientists moved overseas to continue their work, and the loss of our lead in stem cell technology. California voters stepped in, approving a $3 billion bond issue to create CIRM, the California Institute for Regenerative Medicine. The purpose was to provide ten years of support for stem cell research freed from the Bush restrictions.

CIRM intended to fund five or six centers at university campuses throughout the state, each one of which would eventually get hundreds of millions of dollars. The money would help construct research facilities entirely separate from any federal funding, as well as fund grants for faculty to develop new stem cell treatments for diseases. UCI already had an important group of stem cell experts and was strategically placed in biotech-rich Orange County. However, to qualify, the campus had to complete building the research center in two years, and significant portions of the funding had to come from both the university and private donors. Who in Orange County was rich enough and willing to be the lead private donor?

The next part of the story begins back in 1966 when a senior at Duke University had a horrible automobile accident. He lost his scalp and most of his blood. Fortunately a state trooper found the scalp and it was reattached. It took a long time for his body to heal. While spending much of his senior year in the hospital, he read *Beat the Dealer*. That summer, between graduation and an upcoming three-year enlistment in the navy, he ignored his mother's advice to the contrary and went to Las Vegas as one of the early card counters.

Using *Beat the Dealer* as a guide, he brought a bankroll of $200 and ran it up to $10,000. It took four months. The grueling days at the green felt tables often lasted sixteen hours. It was a hard way to earn money but the real value, as with so many before and after him, was in what the young man learned. As he later said, "I had no clue that my four months at the tables in Las Vegas were to lay the foundation for a successful career in Wall Street. [It] taught me several important principles that I've employed for the past twenty-five years . . ."

Returning from Vietnam in 1969, the card counter went to UCLA to get a master's degree in business. He read about convertible bonds in *Beat the Market,* which influenced him to write his master's thesis on that topic. Graduating two years later in 1971, he found that jobs for MBAs were scarce. But when he answered an ad for a junior credit analyst at Pacific Mutual, they liked both the man and the thesis topic.

In the subsequent decades, he co-founded Pacific Investment Management Company, which would one day manage almost $2 trillion. The Duke senior had become a billionaire known worldwide as William H. Gross, the Bond King. Bill and his wife, Sue, had already donated tens of millions for medical causes, so a group at UCI arranged a lunch meeting with Bill to see if he and Sue would give $10 million and become the lead donors for a new CIRM-subsidized stem cell research center.

In the course of the conversation, I mentioned that a $10 million gift would lead to as much as $600 million in the years to come, leveraging their donation sixty times. I saw an instant flash in Bill's eyes and thought: *Bill and Sue must value the chance to make an impact far greater than the value of the amount donated, just as Vivian and I do.* After careful consideration, they said yes.

So far, so good. But CIRM also required, as evidence of community support, that significant gifts come from several private donors, not just one. Along with others, Vivian and I added our own contribution.

CIRM followed through with $30 million in 2008 and the $70 million facility was completed in less than two years, under budget and ahead of schedule.

The University of California also met another test Vivian and I used when considering a contribution. We wanted at least 90 percent of the amount we gave to be spent directly on our target purpose, rather than on fundraising and administration. You can check this percentage for any nonprofit organization from its annual financial statements by looking at the ratio of money spent on the target to the amount of money spent overall.

Vivian and I were indebted to the University of California system for giving us a quality education that we could not have afforded otherwise. It was also where we met. We enjoyed saying thank you.

The timing for funding the Sue and Bill Gross Stem Cell Research Center was fortunate. The economic climate was about to change drastically for the worse.

*Chapter 29*

# FINANCIAL CRISES: LESSONS NOT LEARNED

On October 9, 2007, the S&P 500 reached an all-time closing high of 1,565. Led by home prices, which began to fall from their inflated 2006 peak, it drifted downward, then accelerated to a low of 676 on March 9, 2009, a decline of 57 percent. A million dollars' worth of the index at the high fell to $430,000 at the low. Single-family homes declined 30 percent. One bright spot was bonds. Borrowing declined and interest rates fell, pushing US government and higher-quality corporates up strongly. Despite an offset from this rise in bond prices, the net worth of US households, which peaked in June 2007 at $65.9 trillion, fell to $48.5 trillion during the first quarter of 2009, a loss of 26 percent. It was the worst blow to national wealth since the Great Depression eighty years earlier.

The lessons learned then by our grandparents were forgotten after two generations. The stock market collapse that triggered that calamity was the climax to a speculative bubble. As stock prices rose in the 1920s, "investors" (mostly gamblers) came to believe that they would continue ever upward. A leading economist of the day encouragingly declared that stocks had permanently reached a new high plateau. But the key to the disaster that followed was easy money and leverage. Investors could buy stocks on as little as 10 percent margin, meaning that they could put up only 10 percent of the purchase price and borrow the other 90 percent. It sounds eerily familiar because it is. The 2008 collapse in housing prices had the same cause: unlimited unsound loans to create highly leveraged borrowers.

Here's how it worked in the stock market in 1929. If shares trading for $100 each were purchased for $10 down and a $90 loan per share and subsequently went to, say, $110, the happy investor then had $20 per share of equity, equal to $110 minus the $90 he originally borrowed from his broker. He doubled his money on a mere 10 percent rise in the stock. He can now borrow 90 percent against this $10-per-share profit to buy an additional $90 worth of stock, bringing the total value of his stock to twice what he originally bought. If the investor repeats this each time his stock goes up another 10 percent, both his equity and his loan will double again at each step. After five such increases of 10 percent over the previous price, the stock will trade at $161 per share, a 61 percent gain. Meanwhile our pyramiding investor will have doubled his equity five times, to thirty-two times the starting amount. Ten thousand dollars becomes $320,000. After ten steps up of 10 percent, during which the investor's stake undergoes ten doublings, the stock will be at $259 and from the original purchase of $10,000 worth of stocks using only $1,000, the investor now has $10,240,000 of the same security. His equity is 10 percent of this. He's a millionaire. Such is the hypnotically enticing power of leverage.

But what happens if the stock price then drops 10 percent? Our giddy investor loses his entire equity and his broker issues a margin call: Pay off the loan—which is now more than $9 million—or be sold out. As stock prices rose in 1929, investors leveraged themselves in this way to buy more, driving prices higher. The positive feedback loop led to an average total return on large-company stocks of 193 percent from the end of 1925 to the end of August 1929. A purchase of $100 on no borrowing grew to $293, and our 10 percent down investor who pyramided might have doubled his money more than ten times, gaining more than a thousand times his original investment. However, as prices eased in

September and October 1929, the equity of the most highly leveraged investors vanished. When they were unable to meet margin calls, their brokers sold their stock. These sales drove prices down, wiping out investors who hadn't been quite as leveraged, triggering a new round of margin calls and sales, driving prices down further. As the equity bubble burst, the greatest stock market decline in history began. Large-company stocks eventually dropped by 89 percent, to one-ninth of their earlier peak prices.

As waves of leveraged investors were ruined, bank and brokerage firms, saddled with bad debts, were wiped out, in turn ruining other institutions to whom they owed money. As the contagion spread, economic activity declined sharply, US unemployment reached 25 percent, and a worldwide depression ensued. It was only in January 1945—after more than fifteen years and most of World War II—that, on a month-end basis, large-company stocks finished above their August 1929 all-time high. Again, an investment in corporate bonds more than doubled on average over this period and long-term US government bonds almost did so, showing that diversification into asset classes other than equities, though possibly sacrificing long-term return, can preserve wealth in bad times.

To prevent a repeat of 1929, the Securities Exchange Act of 1934 empowered the board of governors of the Federal Reserve System to prescribe the part of the purchase price the investor has to put up to purchase a listed security. He may borrow any or all of the remainder. Since 1934 this has varied between 40 percent and 100 percent. A 100 percent margin means all purchases must be fully paid for with cash. In 2009, initial margin was 50 percent. Stock exchanges specify the minimum amount of margin that must be maintained as prices fluctuate, the so-called maintenance margin. For instance, at the maintenance margin rate of 30 percent, when the net worth of an investor's account is less than 30 percent of the value of the stocks he owns, his broker calls for cash to pay off enough of the loan to bring the investor's equity back to the 30 percent level. Otherwise, the broker will sell off stock until this is accomplished.

The collapse of the banking system was fueled in part by depositors, who, seeing some banks fail, rushed to withdraw their money from the others while there was still time. To dispel such panics in the future, the Banking Act of 1933 (the second Glass-Steagall Act), separated commercial and investment banking in an effort to limit the impact of speculation. It also established the Federal Deposit Insurance Corporation (FDIC), which covered losses up to a certain limit. (In 2015 the amount insured was $250,000 per account.) This safety net was severely tested in the 1980s, when the savings and loan collapse cost the Federal Deposit Insurance Corporation—that is, US taxpayers—$250 billion, about $1,000 for every man, woman, and child in the country.

Beginning in the 1980s, government, including presidents, Congress, and the Federal Reserve, gave us three decades of reduced regulation of the financial industry. Leverage, easy money, and "financial engineering" then brought a series of asset bubbles and threats to the stability of the financial system itself.

The first worldwide shock was the crash of October 1987, when the US market fell 23 percent in a single day. The cause was a massive feedback event driven by the recently invented quant product of portfolio insurance, leveraged through the new financial futures markets. Fortunately, equities and the economy recovered quickly. Unfortunately, little was learned about the perils of excess leverage.

A second warning came in 1998 with the collapse of the hedge fund Long-Term Capital Management (LTCM). Run by a high-rolling trader and two winners of the Nobel Prize in Economics, this so-called dream team of the best traders and academic financial theorists in the world was on the verge of losing the fund's entire $4 billion of net worth. In the deregulatory environment of the time, they were leveraged between thirty and one hundred times. Profits of less than 1 percent annualized were magnified with borrowed money into yearly returns of 40 percent or so. As long as the world of asset prices was normal, all was well, but just as in 1929 when investors on 10 percent margin were wiped out by a small reversal in prices, so LTCM, with its margin ranging from 1 to 3 percent, was ruined by a sea change in markets.

As Nassim Taleb points out eloquently in his book *The Black Swan,* apparent excess returns like those for LTCM in normal times may be illusory as they may be more than offset by infrequent large losses from extreme events. Such "black swans" can be bad for some and good for others. Ironically, having passed in 1994 on the chance to invest in LTCM and temporarily get rich, I made money in 1998 by exploiting the distorted market prices left in the wake of their collapse. LTCM's loss was our gain in Ridgeline Partners.

LTCM's collapse threatened to put $100 billion or so of bad assets on the books of other institutions. This would bankrupt some banks, brokerage houses, or hedge funds, in turn spreading around more bad assets and bankrupting more institutions. If allowed to happen, this domino effect might have led to a worldwide financial collapse, but a Federal Reserve–inspired consortium intervened, took over LTCM, supplied more funding, and conducted an orderly liquidation.

Nothing appears to have been learned from this. Spearheaded by Congress, the banking industry got what it wanted. The first Glass-Steagall Act, enacted in the Great Depression to separate commercial and investment banking, was repealed in 1999. This allowed big institutions to take on more risk with less regulation through the trading of massive amounts of unregulated derivative securities. When Commodity Futures Trading Commission chairperson (1996–99) Brooksley Born wanted to regulate the derivatives that would later be a major cause of disaster, the PBS program *Frontline* detailed how she was blocked in 1998 by the triumvirate of Federal Reserve chairman Alan Greenspan, US Treasury Secretary Robert Rubin, and Deputy US Treasury Secretary Lawrence Summers, all of whom would later advise government on the 2008–09 bailout. Nassim Taleb asked why, after a driver crashes his school bus, killing and injuring his passengers, he should be put in charge of another bus and asked to set up new safety rules.

The brief era of government surpluses, where revenues exceeded expenses, ended. More tax cuts reduced revenue in 2001. Expenses increased with wars, the military budget, and the cost of entitlements. Deregulation continued. Americans spent more than they earned, consumed more than they produced, and borrowed abroad to pay for it. The administration and Congress, pushed by a powerful real estate lobby, promoted an expansion of homeownership to millions who couldn't afford it. When my niece, who worked in the mortgage industry, declined to approve unsound loans, management sent them to another underwriter for approval. Homes, which allegedly always appreciate, were bought with little or no money down and low introductory teaser interest rates to lower the initial payments. Liar loans, where the buyer supplies false financial information, were easy to get and became common.

The mortgage industry sold the loans to Wall Street, where they were securitized, which means that they were packaged into pools to back a variety of bonds. These were then rated by agencies such as S&P, Moody's, and Fitch, which—in a blatant conflict of interest—were paid by their customers, the same ones whose securities they were supposedly rating objectively. High ratings made the securities easier to sell, but when home prices began to decline from their inflated peak in 2006, many of these securities, including those that these agencies gave the very highest rating of AAA, turned out to have little value.

As prices for residential real estate in 2006 climbed to heights never before seen, many owners turned their houses into piggy banks. Having borrowed almost 100 percent of market value in many cases, they were underwater as soon as prices declined slightly. They then owed more than their houses were worth.

The vast expansion of credit that fueled the housing bubble was based largely on securities invented by a newly arrived army of financial engineers, or quants. Combining their training in mathematics and the hard sciences with notions like the efficient market hypothesis and its relative, the belief that investors are rational, they built new products using models that supposedly mirrored reality, but didn't.

These products cost the US economy several trillion dollars in forever-lost gross national product and societal waste, and caused comparable damage worldwide. It's worth taking time to understand them.

I encountered the first of these, called CMOs, or collateralized mortgage obligations, when they were developed in the mid-1980s. It helps first to analyze the individual home mortgages that were pooled as collateral for the CMOs.

Suppose that your best friend, wanting to buy a home for $400,000, asks you to lend him 80 percent of the purchase price, or $320,000, with the other $80,000 provided by his savings. In return he agrees to repay the loan over thirty years and to pay you interest at the going rate of 6 percent annually. This is called a fixed-rate loan, because the interest will remain at 6 percent no matter how the market fluctuates. If this were an interest-only loan then your friend would pay you 6 percent of $320,000, or $19,200 a year, and would finally repay the entire principal in one balloon payment of $320,000 at the end of thirty years.

Instead you elect a level-payment scheme in which your friend pays a fixed amount at the end of each month. This payment is a little larger than the monthly interest-only payment of $1,600 ($19,200 ÷ 12) and, as computed from standard real estate formulas, turns out to be $1,918.59. The extra amount reduces the principal slightly after each payment, which in turn cuts the amount of interest charged on the next payment. Thus, as time passes, an increasing part of each payment goes toward reducing the principal. The principal declines slowly at first, but near the end of the thirty years, the loan has been mostly paid off and the interest due is small, so the payments then mainly reduce principal. Your security for the loan is your friend's house. Your contract specifies that in the event your friend defaults on the loan, you can sell the house and use the proceeds to pay yourself part of, or hopefully all of, what he owes. But you have no further recourse.

If housing prices have never gone down by much, at least not for a long time, what's your risk? Well, this question is about average prices, not those of individual houses. Your friend's neighborhood could turn into a slum. Or he might have bought the house in New Orleans shortly before Hurricane Katrina. In any case there are risks that threaten you with the loss of some or all of the money you have lent.

Life and casualty insurance companies deal with risks like this all the time. What they do is sell many insurance policies, any one of which may cost the insurance company more than it is paid in premiums—but their degree of risk, spread over the entire pool, is expected (on the basis of past experience) to leave the insurance company with a profit after it pays casualty losses and expenses.

The same idea is behind collateralized mortgage obligations. Assemble hundreds or thousands of mortgages. Four thousand mortgages at

$250,000 each creates a $1 billion pool! Collect the interest and principal payments from each of these mortgages and use them to pay people to whom you have sold shares of the pool. This stream of monthly payments is much like those from a bond, and shares of the CMO pools were priced like bonds.

However, to price them accurately we need to know how much we are going to lose on defaults. When I studied this for Princeton Newport, I learned that the practice in the financial industry was to assume that default rates would follow normal historical experience. There was no attempt to quantify and adjust for infrequent large-scale bad events like the Great Depression, and the massive increase in defaults that could occur. The models failed to incorporate Black Swan risk into the pricing.

Another problem was forecasting the rate at which homeowners might pay off their mortgages early, perhaps to refinance their existing home. A thirty-year mortgage held for the full period is much like a long-term bond. Paid off in five to ten years, it is more like an intermediate bond, and if it is retired in two or three years, the payments resemble those from a very short-term bond. Since interest rates vary, depending on the length of time until a bond is redeemed (this variation in rates is known as the term structure of interest rates), the correct price to pay for the CMO depends on how rapidly the mortgages in the pool are paid off as well as on their default rate. As I noticed back in the 1980s, the prepayment rate on fixed-rate mortgages is highly unpredictable. When the Federal Reserve's actions cause long-term rates to drop, new mortgages are cheaper than existing ones. Homeowners then pay off their mortgages early and refinance to lower their monthly payments. On the other hand, if rates rise, homeowners hang on to their fixed-rate existing loans, causing prepayment rates to plunge.

With pricing based on bad models, Wall Street used CMOs to pour credit into the housing market. Mortgage-lending companies refinanced new home mortgages, then sold them to banks and Wall Street firms, getting new cash to fund additional mortgages. The banks and Wall Street firms pooled these mortgages to back CMOs, which they sold to "investors," getting their cash back to recycle into the purchase of yet more mortgages to back new CMOs.

Everybody got rich. The mortgage origination companies collected fees from the homeowner borrowers. The banks and brokers bought the mortgages, issued CMOs, and sold them at a profit. They also had a steady income from servicing the CMOs, collecting the payments from the mortgage pools, deducting a fee, and distributing the rest to the CMO holders. How could so many fees be collected and yet leave anything that could be sold for a profit to the buyers of the CMO shares? This was done via financial magic. The CMOs were divided into tranches (French for "slices"), creating a hierarchy of CMO classes, with the most preferred being paid first and the least preferred getting what was left, if anything. The rating agencies, paid by the CMO issuers to estimate the quality of the tranches, erred substantially in the direction of optimism. Since higher-rated securities sell for more than those of lower ratings, the CMOs sold for more than they would have otherwise. The magic was that the sum of the parts (tranches) were sold for more than the cost of the whole. Politicians prospered, too, as the real estate and securities industries contributed enthusiastically to their reelection campaigns. Everyone was winning and the party was on.

The academic community made its contributions. As Nobel Prize winner Paul Krugman pointed out, macroeconomists assured us that, due to their greater understanding, catastrophic failures could no longer occur. Scott Patterson details in his book *The Quants* how all of this was facilitated by quants who, with calculations based on academic financial theory, assured everyone that their model prices were accurate and the risks small.

Hundreds of billions of dollars' worth of CMOs were sold to investors worldwide. The idea was so good that it was expanded to CDOs— collateralized debt obligations—where other kinds of debt like loans on autos or credit cards were used instead of home mortgages. Risky as these proved to be, an even more dangerous security, the credit default swap, or CDS, appeared on the scene, to the unconcern of sleeping regulators. A CDS is essentially an insurance policy that a lender can purchase to protect himself against a default by the borrower. Typically the insurance is bought for a certain number of years for a fixed annual payment. For instance, on the $320,000 loan to your home-buying friend, you might be worried about a default in the next five years so, if it were available, you might purchase insurance for the period at, say, $1,600 per year, or 0.5 percent of the initial loan amount.

Trillions of dollars' worth of these credit default swaps were issued, and began trading like any other security. To buy or sell these contracts, you didn't have to own the debt the CDS insured. That in itself wasn't the problem, since the financial markets are simply one big casino, though one with economic benefits, and all investment positions are equivalent to bets. The problem was that the issuers of CDSs could issue them with no collateral other than their "full faith and credit," meaning that if their bets lost they might not have the money to pay.

The margin (collateral set aside to assure payment) was generally small to zero. These unregulated items often were held by subsidiaries, so they wouldn't appear explicitly in the financial statement of the parent company. A case in point was American International Group (AIG), a huge worldwide insurance company, which—when the crisis hit in 2008—was threatened with collapse. During the US government handout of hundreds of billions to save the financial system, AIG was the largest single recipient—a whopping $165 billion. They had issued trillions of dollars in CDSs through a subsidiary, backed mainly by their name. As the bonds they insured dropped in price, they had to post collateral to back the (now losing) CDSs they had sold. Eventually, they couldn't pay, threatening to create hundreds of billions in losses for banks and investment houses worldwide. Not only did the US bailout of AIG help domestic companies such as Goldman Sachs, which held $10 billion of bad paper assets from AIG that was absorbed by the taxpayers, but the largesse was distributed worldwide to cover AIG's defaults.

To see how crazy this was, imagine that Joe Sixpack offered to sell you a CDS on your $320,000 loan to your friend for $1,600 a year for five years. Joe is doing well, has a million-dollar house with no debt, and is therefore "good for the money." Happy with $1,600 a year in extra income, Joe continues to sell CDSs on residential mortgages. Unregulated, he sells a thousand just like the one he sold you, and his income grows to $1.6 million a year. If these loans average $320,000 each, he is insuring a total of $320 million, all backed by his million-dollar house. You object, arguing that Joe couldn't sell this many CDSs because once he's sold a few of them people would realize there was a good chance he couldn't pay off in a crisis. Ah, but what if Joe did this in a subsidiary and didn't disclose the vast scale of his operations? Welcome to AIG.

Each CDS Joe Sixpack sells is a potential future liability. It should be carried as such on his books and will prove to be a good sale only if the premiums he receives, plus reinvestment income, are more than enough to cover the future claims against the credit default insurance he has sold. Just like the similar situation that arises for life insurance companies, Joe needs to set aside a reserve on his books to cover these future payouts, and he needs to increase those reserves as the likelihood of payouts increases. If instead Joe collects the income and doesn't put aside a reserve, then he is running a Ponzi scheme like the one I described at XYZ Corporation in the 1970s, where they sold call options on precious metals far too cheaply, called the proceeds income, and did not set aside an appropriate amount for payouts they might have to make later to the option holders. How did AIG's CDS operation differ from either Joe's scheme or XYZ's?

Between 2004 and 2008, five major investment banks—Goldman Sachs, Morgan Stanley, Merrill Lynch, Bear Stearns, and Lehman Brothers—had increased their leverage to something like 33:1, rivaling the levels that doomed the ill-fated hedge fund Long-Term Capital Management just six years earlier. With, say, $33 in assets and $32 of liabilities for each $1 of net worth, a decline of a little over 3 percent in assets would wipe out their equity. Once this happened and a bank was known to be technically insolvent, creditors would demand payment while they could still get it, triggering a classic run on the bank, just as in the 1930s.

When the crisis hit four years later in 2008, the same length of time it took excess leverage to destroy LTCM, the run on the bank threatened to destroy all five of these geared-up Goliaths. Three of these five investment banks ceased to exist as independent entities; the other two, Morgan Stanley and Goldman Sachs, were saved by government intervention plus, for Goldman, a multibillion-dollar purchase of 10 percent preferred stock and warrants by Warren Buffett's Berkshire Hathaway. Both returned to prosperity in 2009, with Goldman triumphant. Partners were on track to share near-record bonuses of between $20 billion and $30 billion. The elimination or marginalization of some rivals was not a bad thing. Appearing pixyish in his public appearances, when CEO Lloyd Blankfein was asked about the gigantic bonuses, he explained that the firm was "doing God's work." The argument is the standard academic one that more trading creates efficient capital markets, with better prices for buyers and sellers, for the benefit of all humankind. It came out later that part of God's work was bankers knowingly selling mortgage-based junk securities while at the same time making massive bets that would pay off if their clients were ruined. When you compare the pay scale for God's bankers with that for his clerics, you must conclude that the work of bankers is indeed divine.

Though there were individual personal and institutional casualties among the financial establishment, the politically connected wealthy raided the public purse for a trillion dollars to save entities that were "too big to fail." Expensive sops were disbursed to mollify and reward special-interest groups. Those who turned in a vehicle to be scrapped, and then bought another car, were paid up to $4,500 in a program known as Cash for Clunkers. Spun as good for the environment, the only requirement was that the new purchase get gas mileage of one to four miles a gallon more, depending on the category of vehicle. The environmental benefits of this small gain in mileage were more than offset by the extra pollution produced in the manufacture of a whole new automobile. Car dealers, however, cheered as the boost from replacement-car sales cleared inventory from their packed lots.

As full-time and part-time unemployment rates continued to climb, unemployment insurance was repeatedly extended. This is good to the extent it is needed, but it would seem to be in the public interest to employ as many of those idle beneficiaries as possible in doing useful work. Programs like the Works Progress Administration (WPA) and the Civilian Conservation Corps (CCC), which I remember from my childhood, built roads, bridges, and public works during the 1930s, and the improvement in our infrastructure benefited us all for decades.

The real estate industry got its political handout. First-time home-buyers got an $8,000 fully refundable tax credit—"fully refundable" means you can apply for and get the $8,000 check even if you never paid a penny of tax in your life. The deceptive language is typical of politicians. Under this poorly monitored program a four-year-old bought a house. At least it was his first time.

In some cases, unrepentant mortgage lenders accepted the tax "refund" as the down payment, requiring no additional equity from the buyer. Congress further rewarded the real estate lobby by extending the program to those who hadn't bought a house in the last three years. Inspired by Cash for Clunkers, why not pass a new program called Dollars for Demolition in which people who own run-down residences get paid a "fully refundable" tax credit of, say, $100,000 to tear down their house and build a new one? This would reenergize the construction industry—a key part of the American economy. There is no end to the possibilities.

Asset bubbles, where investor mania drives prices to extreme heights, are a recurring puzzle for investors. Can you profit? Can you avoid major losses? In my experience, it has been easy to spot a bubble after it is well under way, as prices and valuations far exceed historical norms and seem to have no economic sense. Examples include the savings and loan boom in the 1980s, the tech stock overvaluation in 1999–2000, and the great inflation in housing prices that peaked in 2006. Making a profit is trickier. Like a Ponzi scheme, it's not easy to tell when it will end. If you bet against it too early you can be ruined in the short run even though you are right in the long run. As Keynes said, the market can remain irrational longer than you can remain solvent.

What about avoiding losses? Once you spot the bubble, you simply don't invest in it. However, there is the problem of spillover damage or contagion. The collapse of housing prices from 2006 to 2010 didn't just hurt speculators and those who bought too late. Derivatives spread the damage throughout the world. In March 2009, when the S&P 500 had fallen 57 percent from its peak, I could not tell whether to buy stocks or to sell what I had. Either decision might have been a disaster. If we continued into a major worldwide depression, buying more would be costly. In the other scenario, the one that occurred, this was the bottom, and stocks rebounded over 70 percent in less than a year. Warren Buffett, who had better information and insight than almost anyone, later told *The Wall Street Journal*'s Scott Patterson that at one point he was looking into the abyss and considering the possibility that everything could go down, even Berkshire Hathaway. It was only when the US government indicated it would do whatever was necessary to bail out the financial system that he realized we were saved.

How can we prevent future financial crises driven by the systemic and scarcely regulated use of extreme leverage? One obvious step is to limit leverage by requiring sufficient collateral to be posted by both counterparties when they trade. That's what is done on regulated futures exchanges, where contracts are also standardized. This model has worked well for decades, is easy to regulate, mostly by the exchanges themselves, and has had few problems.

Institutions that are "too big to fail," and have a significant risk of doing so, should be broken into pieces that are small enough to fail without jeopardizing the financial system. As Alan Greenspan finally admitted, "Too big to fail is too big." This is a catchy sound bite but it misstates the real problem. It's not the mere size of an institution that creates the danger. It is the size of the risk to the financial system from a failure. As Paul Krugman points out, Canada's financial system was as concentrated in big institutions as was that of the United States yet Canada didn't have massive mortgage defaults, collapsing financial institutions, and giant bailouts. The difference was that Canada had strict standards for mortgages and tighter limits on bank leverage and risk.

Our corporate executives speculate with their shareholders' assets because they get big personal rewards when they win—and even if they lose, they are often bailed out with public funds by obedient politicians. We privatize profit and socialize risk.

The ability of corporate executives to capture an increasing share of public wealth is reflected in what CEOs earn. Compared with one of their average workers, CEOs in 1965 took home 24 times as much but "four decades later the ratio was 411 to 1." Another indication of increasing economic inequality is the share of national income captured by the top one-hundredth of 1 percent of all earners. In 1929 they captured 10 percent of national income. This fell to about 5 percent during the Great Depression, gradually rising again beginning in the 1980s. In the last few years the share of national income claimed by these 12,500 households broke its 1929 record of 10 percent and continues to increase. These executives claim that their compensation inspires them to be the creative engines of capitalist society, benefiting all of us. The crisis of 2008 is one of our rewards.

Studies done both before and after the 2008–09 recession showed that the larger the percentage of corporate profit paid to the top five executives, the poorer the earnings and the stock performance of the company. These superstars tended to drain their companies rather than benefit them. The executives claim that "market forces" determine their salary. However, as Moshe Adler, in his article "Overthrowing the Overpaid," points out, economists David Ricardo and Adam Smith, writing more than two hundred years ago, "concluded that what a person earns is determined not by what that person has produced but by that person's bargaining power. Why? Because production is typically carried out by teams . . . and the contribution of each member cannot be separated from that of the rest."

A wave of populist outrage has led to demands for laws to limit executive pay. A simpler and more effective solution is to empower the shareholders. They are the owners of the company and the ones looted by their officers and directors.

At present, most corporate boards run their firms like third-world fiefdoms. When shareholders vote to elect directors, generally nominated by the self-perpetuating board, they typically can vote yes or no. One yes vote can elect a director in the face of a million no votes. The company rules are deliberately designed to make it difficult or impossible for independent shareholders to nominate directors or place issues on the ballot. Instead, corporations—their legal existence already being permitted and regulated by the state—should be required to conduct democratic elections following the usual voting rules in our American democracy. Moreover, any block of shareholders that together holds some specified percentage of the shares should have the unrestricted right to nominate directors and to put issues on the ballot, including the replacement of board members and top executives.

Some companies disenfranchise shareholders by having two or more classes of shares with different degrees of voting power. Management may, for instance, own A shares with ten votes each and the public may own B shares with one vote each. How would you like to live in a country where any "insider" could cast ten votes and any "outsider" got only one? Abolish this and make it one share, one vote. Another problem arises because, currently, institutions that hold shares in custody for their owners can cast proxy votes for those shareholders who decline to vote. These proxies usually perpetuate current management and ratify its decisions. Change this so that the only votes that count are those cast directly by the shareholder; so-called proxy votes would not count.

These two measures—democratic elections and shareholder rights to put issues to a vote—would allow the owners of the company, namely, the shareholders, to exert control over the compensation of top executives, their so-called agents, and would, in my opinion, be far more effective and accurate than direct government regulation.

Our economy slowly recovered in the years following the 2008–09 crisis. However, little has been done to add safeguards to prevent a recurrence. As the philosopher George Santayana famously warned, "Those who cannot remember the past are condemned to repeat it." Though the institutions of society have difficulty learning from history, individuals can do so. Next, I share some of what I've learned.

## Chapter 30

# THOUGHTS

To end this story of my odyssey through science, mathematics, gambling, hedge funds, finance, and investing, I would like to share some of what I learned along the way.

Education has made all the difference for me. Mathematics taught me to reason logically and to understand numbers, tables, charts, and calculations as second nature. Physics, chemistry, astronomy, and biology revealed wonders of the world, and showed me how to build models and theories to describe and to predict. This paid off for me in both gambling and investing.

Education builds software for your brain. When you're born, think of yourself as a computer with a basic operating system and not much else. Learning is like adding programs, big and small, to this computer, from drawing a face to riding a bicycle to reading to mastering calculus. You will use these programs to make your way in the world. Much of what I've learned came from schools and teachers. Even more valuable, I learned at an early age to teach myself. This paid off later on because there weren't any courses in how to beat blackjack, build a computer for roulette, or launch a market-neutral hedge fund.

I found that most people don't understand the probability calculations needed to figure out gambling games or to solve problems in everyday life. We didn't need that skill to survive as a species in the forests and
jungles. When a lion roared, you instinctively climbed the nearest tree
and thought later about what to do next. Today we often have the time
to think, calculate, and plan ahead, and here's where math can help us
make decisions. For instance, are seatbelts and air bags "worth it"? Suppose we upgrade a hundred million vehicles at a cost of $300 each, a total
of $30 billion, and have five thousand fewer traffic deaths per year. If
these vehicles with their added safety features are around for ten years,
that's fifty thousand lives saved at a cost of $30 billion, or $600,000 per
life. Though many in the auto industry disagreed, we spent the money
and saved the lives.

What about the pack-a-day smoker? Forty years of this will make his
life on average seven years shorter. Each cigarette not only brings death
twelve minutes closer, but adds health problems to spoil one's remaining
years. Then there are the costs to the rest of us, namely, higher medical
costs in the final years, more sick days during the working years, and
secondhand smoke damage. But these are averages. Some smokers do
not die of smoking-related diseases, whereas others die at an early age.
It's like gambling at roulette. On average you lose 5 cents when you bet
$1. But this is an average. Some gamblers are wiped out quickly and
others may hold their own for quite a while.

One of the major public policy issues today is the trade-off between
the costs and the benefits of certain procedures. Some choices are stark.
Is it better to spend $500,000 to save the life of someone with super-drug-
resistant tuberculosis or to use the same amount to save fifty lives by
delivering fifty thousand doses of flu vaccine at $10 each to schoolchil-
dren? Statistical thinking can help us with choices like these.

I believe that simple probability and statistics should be taught in
grades kindergarten through twelve and that analyzing games of
chance such as coin matching, dice, and roulette is one way we can learn
enough to think through such issues. Understanding why casinos usually win might help us avoid gambling and teach us to limit our losses
to their entertainment value. Gambling now is largely a socially corro-

sive tax on ignorance, draining money from those who cannot afford the losses.

Most of what I've learned from gambling also is true for investing. People mostly don't understand risk, reward, and uncertainty. Their investment results could be much better if they did. For instance, years ago my homeowners' association kept their cash reserves in thirty-day US Treasury bills for absolute safety. However, they spent only about a fifth of these reserves each year. I suggested that they put a fifth of their reserves into US Treasuries maturing in the coming year, another fifth to mature the year after, and so forth. This well-known strategy, called laddering, generally pays off because longer-term US bonds, with more price fluctuation before they mature, generally yield more. Five-year bonds have beaten thirty-day T-bills by about 1.8 percent annually over the last eighty-three years. The treasurer of the association, a professional accountant, opposed the idea at first but later agreed and used it profitably.

I would like to see basic finance taught in elementary and secondary schools. If more of our citizens knew how to balance their checkbooks and to create and understand income statements and balance sheets for themselves, they might do better at choosing homes they can afford. Properly managing investments would better prepare people for retirement and make them less dependent on society during their lifetimes.

One of my great pleasures from the study of investing, finance, and economics is the discovery of insights about people and society. The physical sciences have rules such as the law of gravitation that generally hold true in the world as we know it. But human beings and the way they interact aren't covered by broad, unchanging theories and may never be. Instead I've come across more limited concepts that tie things together and serve as shortcuts to understanding.

One of these is a favorite of libertarians and free-market fans, introduced by Adam Smith back in 1776. Smith suggested that in an economy of many small buyers and sellers, each trying to increase his own profit, our collective benefit would be maximized as though guided by an "invisible hand." The notion is of limited use, because most markets are not as Smith assumed. Take computer chips: 99.8 percent of them, worldwide, are made by just two US companies, and the smaller one is fighting to survive.

An opposite concept to the magic of the invisible hand is "the tragedy of the commons," as explained in 1968 by Garrett Hardin. Imagine a natural resource that anyone can freely use, such as—once upon a time—catching fish in the ocean. In the eighteenth century, schools of cod were so vast that Benjamin Franklin was amazed when his ship plowed through them for days at a time. Now, after two centuries of overfishing, this population has collapsed. How has individual self-interest maximized social good? On a global scale we have the example of pollution. Individual humans have freely burned fossil fuels and greatly increased the amount of greenhouse gases such as $CO_2$, leading to a continuing rise in the earth's temperature over the last century. The tiny particles also emitted have caused lung diseases and deaths. But each polluter gains more individually from his own actions than he loses, so he has no direct pressure to change.

The solution for society illustrates another neat unifying concept, that of "externalities." In the arcane jargon so beloved by the economic priesthood, an externality is a cost or benefit for society that results from private economic activity. The externality is negative in the case of air pollution. The "fair" solution then becomes obvious: Estimate the damage and tax it by that amount. Externalities also can be positive. If I fireproof my house it protects my neighbors, and tends to both reduce the costs of local fire services and increase profits for my insurer. Instead of being taxed, I may be rewarded by a drop in my insurance rates.

Berkshire Hathaway's Charlie Munger presents his list of such thinking tools in the engaging *Poor Charlie's Almanack: The Wit and Wisdom of Charles T. Munger.* This multidisciplinary collection of insights includes a favorite of mine for understanding deals and relationships, namely, "Look for the incentives," which is closely related to finding "Cui bono?" or "Who gains?" Cui bono instantly explains why seven thousand US gun dealers, lining the border with Mexico from Tijuana to Corpus Christi, are allowed freely to provide nearly all the military-level arms used by the Mexican drug cartels. It explains why Congress mandated the wasteful folly of corn-based ethanol, the production of which causes almost as much pollution as it offsets and drives up food prices for every-one. If ethanol use were the goal, why was there, until the end of 2011, a 54-cent-per-gallon tariff to keep Brazilian ethanol out?

More insights come from a much bigger idea of fundamental impor-tance for all investors, the recognition that the group I call the politically connected rich are the dominant economic and political power in the United States. This is a key concept for understanding what happens in our society and why it happens. They are the ones who buy politicians, using campaign contributions, career opportunities, investment profits, and more. As owners of wealth who also control power, they run the country and will continue to do so. We saw how they used the govern-ment to bail them out of the financial crisis of 2008–09.

Let me be clear. I don't object to some people being richer, even much richer, than others. I object to gain of wealth through political connec-tions rather than earning it by merit. If a basketball franchise pays my neighbor Kobe Bryant $20 million a year because it takes that much to get him, fine. But if hedge fund managers bribe politicians to put a clause in the laws cutting the tax rate on much of their income to a fraction of the percentage the average worker pays, I object.

Simplistically, there are two types of rich, those who use government to tilt the playing field in their favor and those who don't. The former pay taxes at a rate well below the middle class and the latter pay at sub-stantially higher rates. The blended rate of the two groups is similar to that paid by the upper middle class. But the politically connected rich typically point to the higher rates paid by their nonconnected rich fel-lows as a cover to demand still more tax breaks for themselves. The power in this group resides mostly in those who are in the upper 0.01 percent of wealth holders, currently worth $125 million or more.

Another theme for dealing with public policy issues is to simplify rules, regulations, and laws. Get government out of the business of mi-cromanaging. For example, California and many other states have their own income tax code, which resembles the federal tax code but is differ-ent enough so that a resident must complete and file a state return that is as detailed and complex as his federal return. Here's my solution. Let the state tax for individuals simply be a fraction of the federal tax, to be set by the legislature, and chosen to raise the same total revenue as the current tax. The return would fit on a postcard, saving hours for each taxpayer and freeing several thousand unproductive state employees for useful work in the private sector. Eliminating three thousand state of California employees at a cost of $100,000 each, including salaries, benefits, and overhead, would save the hard-pressed state $300 million a year, not to mention all the time and money saved by citizens. So we have a revenue-neutral proposal that is a net gain for the state.

Even greater benefits come when we apply this approach to the federal tax code. Tax rates are high because the loophole-riddled regulations allow many to pay less or even nothing. A revenue-neutral flat tax could make the tax code simple and fair, and would catch those who currently are getting a free ride from the rest of us. All income would be taxed equally, with an exemption set at, say, one and a half times the poverty level. Those below this cutoff would pay no tax. As this entire group has only a small part of national income, the impact of these exemptions would be minor. Because much currently untaxed income would be taxed, the estimated revenue-neutral rate would be 20 percent or so. Again, we could have an enormous benefit to society. Hundreds of thousands of government employees, tax lawyers, accountants, and tax preparers would be freed to make (hopefully) a productive contribution to society. The value-added tax is another proposal that recaptures those who have escaped taxation and cuts the top tax rate in half.

Having an idea that benefits society is the first step. The hardest part, more often than not, is passing laws to implement it. This has become harder, as the political clash between the parties in the United States has become extreme. Politics, once called the art of the possible, is becoming the art of the impossible. Gridlock between uncompromising factions was one cause of the fall of the Roman Empire.

History, arguably, has had just two great superpowers, the Roman Empire after the defeat of Carthage, and the United States after the fall of the Soviet Union. Of great importance for long-term investors is whether the US will be the dominant world power in the twenty-first century, or whether we have peaked, dissipating our strength in costly foreign wars, financial mismanagement, and domestic strife. The first scenario could lead to another century of equities returning 7 percent a year after inflation. The other outcome could be far less pleasant. I reassure the pessimists by noting that we're still rich, still innovating, and besides, Rome wasn't destroyed in a day. Nations that were once among the most powerful, such as Britain, France, Italy, Spain, the Netherlands, and Portugal, are still among the most developed and civilized of countries. To the optimists I mention the obvious: endless deficits, massive wastage of lives and wealth in wars, political subsidies (pork, bailouts, corporate welfare, paying the able-bodied not to work), and destructive partisanship in all three branches of government. Meanwhile, the rise of China is transforming the geopolitical and economic landscape.

One of the most ominous and underappreciated threats to our future is in education and technology. My own state of California is a leader in the race to the bottom. The anti-tax movement has starved the state of revenue, especially the educational system. The ten campuses of the University of California, once among the finest public systems of higher education in the world, raised tuition to $12,000 a year by 2015. When I was a student in 1949 it was $70, which is like $700 today, adjusting for inflation. A good education was available to any qualified student. The university's graduates went on to lead the technological revolution; but by 2014 the state contributed only about 10 percent of the total cost of all campus operations.

If the UC system doubled tuition and fees it could drop state support altogether and go private! Since out-of-state and foreign students are charged three times the tuition paid by California residents, individual deans and administrators are raising more money by replacing the latter by the former. Meanwhile gifted foreign students, many of them Chinese, receive advanced degrees in the United States and return home, rather than struggle for postdoctoral funding and permission to become residents. Talented American-born scientists and engineers are joining them in a reverse brain drain. Economists have found that one factor has explained a nation's future economic growth and prosperity more than any other: its output of scientists and engineers. To starve education is to eat our seed corn. No tax today, no technology tomorrow.

*Epilogue*

———

reud said that once we have the basic necessities of food, clothing, shelter, and health, then what we seek is wealth, power, honor, and the love of men and women. For financial titans who aggressively continue to seek tens of millions, hundreds of millions, and sometimes billions, you can ask, "Is the winner really the one who dies with the most toys?" How much is enough? When will you be done? Often the answer is "Never."

To preserve the quality of my life and to spend more of it in the company of people I value and in the exploration of ideas I enjoy, I chose not to follow up on a number of business ventures, although I believed that they were nearly certain to become extremely profitable. Once I worked out the major concepts in a subject and proved them in action, I liked new mental challenges, moving on from gambling games to the investment world, with warrants, options, convertible bonds and other derivatives, then statistical arbitrage. Starting as a university professor, I expected to spend my life teaching, doing research, and talking to smart like-minded people; but from childhood I was intrigued by the power of abstract thinking to understand and direct the natural world. When I later saw how physics could predict roulette outcomes through the fog of chance, and mathematics could tip the odds in blackjack, I was drawn into a lifetime of adventure.

It was my good fortune to share most of this journey with a remarkable companion. From childhood, my wife, Vivian, loved books and was a voracious reader. One year we kept a journal about the books we read. In twelve months she cruised through more than 150 books at seven hundred words or more per minute. I know that because one day when we were both reading, I couldn't believe how fast she was turning the pages, so, without her knowing, I timed her for an hour. She passed on her love of books and her extraordinary facility with the English language to our children and grandchildren.

She mastered bridge, studied art and art history, learned to prepare quality healthy meals, completed a master's degree in library science, inspired her family to focus on personal fitness and health, and supported causes and charities. She was also one of the rare people known as super-recognizers. She could casually recognize people she'd met decades before, even though they had been transformed—in my opinion often beyond recognition—by age, style, carriage, shape, and size. When most of us remember the past, the memories fade over time and the "facts" may shift closer to the heart's desire. When it had to do with people, Vivian's memory was both extraordinarily accurate and unchanging over time.

After she died from cancer in 2011, we celebrated her life with a memorial service. When I think of our lives together, I remember what her brother said then: "Nobody can take away the dance you have danced."

Life is like reading a novel or running a marathon. It's not so much about reaching a goal but rather about the journey itself and the experiences along the way. As Benjamin Franklin famously said, "Time is the stuff life is made of," and how you spend it makes all the difference.

Best of all is the time I have spent with the people in my life that I care about—my wife, my family, my friends, and my associates. Whatever you do, enjoy your life and the people who share it with you, and leave something good of yourself for the generations to follow.

## Appendix A

# THE IMPACT OF INFLATION ON THE DOLLAR

This table indicates how the buying power of a dollar has changed. To see what my $11,000 win at blackjack in 1961 with Manny Kimmel and Eddie Hand was equal to in 2013, we multiply $11,000 by the 2013 index and divide by the 1961 index: $11,000 × 233.0 ÷ 29.9 = $85,719. To convert dollars in year A to dollars in year B, multiply by the index for B and divide by the index for A.

Overall, the index has increased by about 3.6 percent a year, but there are some unusual variations. The index falls (deflation!) after the 1929 crash and stays at a reduced level for the next decade. Then it increases rapidly during World War II and the first postwar years.

Although inflation has been moderate in the United States and in most first-world countries most of the time, it is occasionally catastrophic. During the German hyperinflation of 1919–23, the currency declined to one hundred billionth of its starting value (divide by 100,000,000,000). Debtors were freed and lenders were ruined. This level of inflation would reduce the $18 trillion or so US national debt of 2015 to the equivalent of $180. In 2009, the African nation of Zimbabwe experienced a hyperinflation comparable to the German one, with Z-one-trillion bills commonplace.

From its peak in 1929, the S&P 500 total return index (dividends reinvested) had, at its low in 1932, fallen by 89 percent. However, these were deflationary times, so the nation had the cold comfort of knowing that after adjusting for inflation, the index had lost only 85 percent.

**Table 9: Consumer Price Index**

| Year | Index | Year | Index | Year | Index |
|------|-------|------|-------|------|-------|
| 1913 | 9.9 | 1934 | 13.4 | 1955 | 26.8 |
| 1914 | 10.0 | 1935 | 13.7 | 1956 | 27.2 |
| 1915 | 10.1 | 1936 | 13.9 | 1957 | 28.1 |
| 1916 | 10.9 | 1937 | 14.4 | 1958 | 28.9 |
| 1917 | 12.8 | 1938 | 14.1 | 1959 | 29.2 |
| 1918 | 15.0 | 1939 | 13.9 | 1960 | 29.6 |
| 1919 | 17.3 | 1940 | 14.0 | 1961 | 29.9 |
| 1920 | 20.0 | 1941 | 14.7 | 1962 | 30.3 |
| 1921 | 17.9 | 1942 | 16.3 | 1963 | 30.6 |
| 1922 | 16.8 | 1943 | 17.3 | 1964 | 31.0 |
| 1923 | 17.1 | 1944 | 17.6 | 1965 | 31.5 |
| 1924 | 17.1 | 1945 | 18.0 | 1966 | 32.5 |
| 1925 | 17.5 | 1946 | 19.5 | 1967 | 33.4 |
| 1926 | 17.7 | 1947 | 22.3 | 1968 | 34.8 |
| 1927 | 17.4 | 1948 | 24.0 | 1969 | 36.7 |
| 1928 | 17.2 | 1949 | 23.8 | 1970 | 38.8 |
| 1929 | 17.2 | 1950 | 24.1 | 1971 | 40.5 |
| 1930 | 16.7 | 1951 | 26.0 | 1972 | 41.8 |
| 1931 | 15.2 | 1952 | 26.6 | 1973 | 44.4 |
| 1932 | 13.6 | 1953 | 26.8 | 1974 | 49.3 |
| 1933 | 12.9 | 1954 | 26.9 | 1975 | 53.8 |
| 1976 | 56.9 | 1989 | 124.0 | 2002 | 179.9 |
| 1977 | 60.6 | 1990 | 130.7 | 2003 | 184.0 |
| 1978 | 65.2 | 1991 | 136.2 | 2004 | 188.9 |
| 1979 | 72.6 | 1992 | 140.3 | 2005 | 195.3 |
| 1980 | 82.4 | 1993 | 144.5 | 2006 | 201.6 |

| Year | Index | Year | Index | Year | Index |
|------|-------|------|-------|------|-------|
| 1981 | 90.9  | 1994 | 148.2 | 2007 | 207.3 |
| 1982 | 96.5  | 1995 | 152.4 | 2008 | 215.3 |
| 1983 | 99.6  | 1996 | 156.9 | 2009 | 214.5 |
| 1984 | 103.9 | 1997 | 160.5 | 2010 | 218.1 |
| 1985 | 107.6 | 1998 | 163.0 | 2011 | 224.9 |
| 1986 | 109.6 | 1999 | 166.6 | 2012 | 229.6 |
| 1987 | 113.6 | 2000 | 172.2 | 2013 | 233.0 |
| 1988 | 118.3 | 2001 | 177.1 | 2016 | 240.0 |

US Department of Labor
Bureau of Labor Statistics
Washington, DC 20212
Consumer Price Index
All Urban Consumers—(CPI-U)
US City Average
All Items
1982–84=100
*Note: Index values are averages for the year.

*Appendix B*

---

# HISTORICAL RETURNS

Table 10: Historical Returns on Asset Classes, 1926–2013

| Series | Compound Annual Return* | Average Annual Return** | Standard Deviation | Real (after inflation) Compound Annual Return* | Sharpe Ratio† |
|---|---|---|---|---|---|
| Large Company Stocks | 10.1% | 12.1% | 20.2% | 6.9% | 0.43 |
| Small Company Stocks | 12.3% | 16.9% | 32.3% | 9.1% | 0.41 |
| Long-Term Corporate Bonds | 6.0% | 6.3% | 8.4% | 2.9% | 0.33 |
| Long-Term Government Bonds | 5.5% | 5.9% | 9.8% | 2.4% | 0.24 |
| Intermediate-Term Government Bonds | 5.3% | 5.4% | 5.7% | 2.3% | 0.33 |
| US Treasury Bills | 3.5% | 3.5% | 3.1% | 0.5% | - - - |
| Inflation | 3.0% | 3.0% | 4.1% | - - - | - - - |

\* Geometric Mean
\*\* Arithmetic Mean
† Arithmetic

From: Ibbotson, *Stocks, Bonds, Bills and Inflation,* Yearbook, Morningstar, 2014. Siegal's *Stocks for the Long Run* gives US returns from 1801. Dimson et al. give returns for sixteen countries and an analysis. The return series depends on the time period and on the specific index chosen. I've used Ibbotson as my standard because detailed annually updated statistics have been readily available.

**Table 11: Historical Returns (%) to Investors, 1926–2013**

| Series | Compound Annual Return* | Deduct Management Costs | | Before Tax; Deduct Trading Losses | | After Tax | | Real (After Inflation) Tax-Exempt | | Taxable | |
|---|---|---|---|---|---|---|---|---|---|---|---|
| | | Passive | Active | Passive | Active | Passive | Active | Passive | Active | Passive | Active |
| Large Company Stocks | 10.1 | 9.9 | 8.9 | 9.7 | 7.7 | 7.8 | 5.0 | 6.7 | 4.7 | 4.8 | 2.0 |
| Small Company Stocks | 12.3 | 12.1 | 11.1 | 11.9 | 9.9 | 9.5 | 6.4 | 8.9 | 6.9 | 6.5 | 3.4 |
| Long-Term Corporate Bonds | 6.0 | 5.8 | 5.3 | 5.7 | 5.0 | 3.7 | 3.3 | 2.7 | 2.0 | 0.7 | 0.3 |
| Long-Term Government Bonds | 5.5 | 5.3 | 4.8 | 5.2 | 4.5 | 3.4 | 2.9 | 2.2 | 1.5 | 0.4 | -0.1 |
| Intermediate-Term Government Bonds | 5.3 | 5.1 | 4.6 | 5.0 | 4.3 | 3.3 | 2.8 | 2.0 | 1.3 | 0.3 | -0.2 |
| US Treasury Bills | 3.5 | 3.3 | 2.8 | 3.2 | 2.7 | 2.1 | 1.8 | 0.2 | -0.3 | -0.9 | -1.2 |
| Inflation | 3.0 | - | - | - | - | - | - | - | - | - | - |

* Geometric Mean

From: Ibbotson, *Stocks, Bonds, Bills and Inflation,* Yearbook, Morningstar, 2014. Siegal's *Stocks for the Long Run* gives US returns from 1801. Dimson et al. give returns for sixteen countries and an analysis. The return series depends on the time period and on the specific index chosen. I have again used Ibbotson as my standard.

**Table 12: Schedule of Assumed Costs Which Reduce Historical Returns (%)**

| | Stocks | | Bonds | | Bills | |
|---|---|---|---|---|---|---|
| | Passive | Active | Passive | Active | Passive | Active |
| Management Costs | 0.2 | 1.2 | 0.2 | 0.7 | 0.2 | 0.7 |
| Trading Costs | 0.2 | 1.2 | 0.1 | 0.3 | 0.1 | 0.1 |
| Estimated Tax Rate on Remainder | 20.0 | 35.0 | 35.0 | 35.0 | 35.0 | 35.0 |

**Table 13: Annual Returns (%), 1972–2013**

|  | Compound Annual Return* | Average Annual Return** | Standard Deviation |
|---|---|---|---|
| Equity REITs | 11.9 | 13.5 | 18.4 |
| Large Company Stocks | 10.5 | 12.1 | 18.0 |
| Small Company Stocks | 13.7 | 16.1 | 23.2 |
| Long-Term Corporate Bonds | 8.4 | 8.9 | 10.3 |
| Long-Term Government Bonds | 8.2 | 8.9 | 12.4 |
| Intermediate-Term Government Bonds | 7.5 | 7.7 | 6.6 |
| US Treasury Bills | 5.2 | 5.2 | 3.4 |
| Inflation | 4.2 | 4.3 | 3.1 |

\* Geometric Mean
\*\* Arithmetic Mean

Comparative historical returns from investing in income-generating real estate are indicated in table 13, which lists total returns from publicly traded Real Estate Investment Trusts for the period 1972–2013.

From: Ibbotson, *Stocks, Bonds, Bills and Inflation,* Yearbook, Morningstar, 2014. Siegal's *Stocks for the Long Run* gives US returns from 1801. Dimson et al. give returns for sixteen countries and an analysis. The return series depends on the time period and on the specific index chosen.

*Appendix C*

# THE RULE OF
# 72 AND MORE

The rule of 72 gives quick approximate answers to compound interest and compound growth problems. The rule tells us how many periods it takes for wealth to double with a specified rate of return, and is exact for a rate of 7.85 percent. For smaller rates, doubling is a little quicker than what the rule calculates; for greater rates, it takes a little longer. The table compares the rule in column 2 with the exact value in column 3. The "exact rule" column shows the number that should replace 72 to calculate each rate of return. For an 8 percent return, the number, rounded to two decimal places, is 72.05, which shows how close the rule of 72 is. Notice that the number in column 4 for the exact rule should equal the column 1 return per period multiplied by the corresponding values in column 3 (actual number of periods to double), but that the column 4 figures don't quite agree with this. That's because the numbers in columns 3 and 4 are rounded off from the exact figures, correct to two decimal places.

The mental calculator may notice that the exact rule changes by about one-third for each 1 percent change in the return per period; so an easy approximation to the exact rule is 72 + (R–8%)/3. For 1 percent this gives 69.67 compared with the exact 69.66, and for 20 percent we get 76.00 compared with the exact 76.04. The formula fits well for the rest of the table, too.

**Table for the Rule of 72**

| Return Per Period | Number of Periods to Double | | |
|---|---|---|---|
| | By Rule of 72 | Actual | Exact Rule |
| 1% | 72 | 69.66 | 69.66 |
| 2% | 36 | 35.00 | 70.01 |
| 3% | 24 | 23.45 | 70.35 |
| 4% | 18 | 17.67 | 70.69 |
| 5% | 14.4 | 14.21 | 71.03 |
| 6% | 12 | 11.90 | 71.37 |
| 7% | 10.29 | 10.24 | 71.71 |
| 8% | 9 | 9.01 | 72.05 |
| 9% | 8 | 8.04 | 72.39 |
| 10% | 7.2 | 7.27 | 72.73 |
| 12% | 6 | 6.12 | 73.40 |
| 15% | 4.8 | 4.96 | 74.39 |
| 20% | 3.6 | 3.80 | 76.04 |
| 24% | 3 | 3.22 | 77.33 |
| 30% | 2.4 | 2.64 | 79.26 |
| 36% | 2.0 | 2.25 | 81.15 |

The idea behind the rule works for other wealth multiples. For instance, to get a rule for multiplying by 10, divide all the numbers in the table by 0.30103 (which is $\log_{10} 2$). Thus for 8 percent we get approximately 240, so we have a "rule of 240" for multiples of 10. We conclude that a return of 8 percent multiplies wealth by 10 in about $240 \div 8 = 30$ years.

When Berkshire Hathaway offered to buy Shaw Industries for about $2 billion in cash, one manager mentioned that their earnings were up ten times from sixteen years before. By the rule of 240, we quickly find an approximate growth rate of $240 \div 16 = 15\%$. The actual figure is 15.48 percent.

# PERFORMANCE OF PRINCETON NEWPORT PARTNERS, LP

**Table 14: Annual Return in Percent**

| Period Beginning and Ending | Princeton Newport Partners, LP (1) | Princeton Newport Partners, LP (2) | S&P 500 Index (3) | 3 Month US T-Bill Total Return |
|---|---|---|---|---|
| 11/01/69—12/31/69 | +4.0 | +3.2 | -4.7 | +3.0 |
| 01/01/70—12/31/70 | +16.3 | +13.0 | +4.0 | +6.2 |
| 01/01/71—12/31/71 | +33.3 | +26.7 | +14.3 | +4.4 |
| 01/01/72—12/31/72 | +15.1 | +12.1 | +19.0 | +4.6 |
| 01/01/73—12/31/73 | +8.1 | +6.5 | -14.7 | +7.5 |
| 01/01/74—12/31/74 | +11.3 | +9.0 | -26.5 | +7.9 |
| 01/01/75—10/31/75* | +13.1 | +10.5 | +34.3 | +5.1 |
| 11/01/75—10/31/76 | +20.2 | +16.1 | +20.1 | +5.2 |

| Period Beginning and Ending | Princeton Newport Partners, LP (1) | Princeton Newport Partners, LP (2) | S&P 500 Index (3) | 3 Month US T-Bill Total Return |
|---|---|---|---|---|
| 11/01/76– 10/31/77 | +18.1 | +14.1 | -6.2 | +5.5 |
| 11/01/77– 10/31/78 | +15.5 | +12.4 | +6.4 | +7.4 |
| 11/01/78– 10/31/79 | +19.1 | +15.3 | +15.3 | +10.9 |
| 11/01/79– 10/31/80 | +26.7 | +21.4 | +32.1 | +12.0 |
| 11/01/80– 10/31/81 | +28.3 | +22.6 | +0.5 | +16.0 |
| 11/01/81– 10/31/82 | +27.3 | +21.8 | +16.2 | +12.1 |
| 11/01/82– 10/31/83 | +13.1 | +10.5 | +27.9 | +9.1 |
| 11/01/83– 10/31/84 | +14.5 | +11.6 | +6.5 | +10.4 |
| 11/01/84– 10/31/85 | +14.3 | +11.4 | +19.6 | +8.0 |
| 11/01/85– 10/31/86 | +29.5 | +24.5 | +33.1 | +6.3 |
| 11/01/86– 12/31/87** | +33.3 | +26.7 | +5.1 | +7.1 |
| 01/01/88– 12/31/88 | +4.0 | +3.2 | +16.8 | +7.4 |
| Total Percentage Increase[1] | 2,734% | +1,382% | 545% | 345% |
| Annual Compound Rate of Return[1] | 19.1% | 15.1% | 10.2% | 8.1% |

* Fiscal year changed to November 1 start date from January 1 start date.
** Fiscal year changed back to January 1 start date.
[1] These figures are for the period from inception through 12/31/88.
The period 01/01/89 through 05/15/89 is omitted because:
    (a) the partnership was liquidating and distributing its capital in a series of payments,
    (b) it was no longer engaged in its traditional business and the return on capital was complex to calculate,
    (c) available figures are estimates.
The partnership was originally called Convertible Hedge Associates and changed its name to Princeton Newport Partners as of 11/01/75.
(1) Before allocation to general partners, including managing general partners
(2) Net to limited partners
(3) Including dividends

Table 15: Princeton Newport Performance Comparison

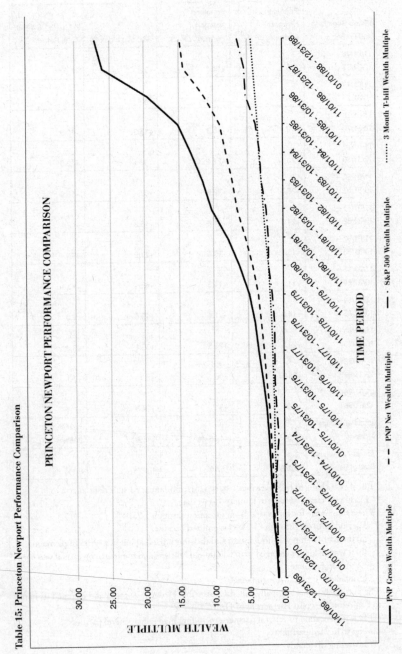

PRINCETON NEWPORT PERFORMANCE COMPARISON

# OUR STATISTICAL ARBITRAGE RESULTS FOR A FORTUNE 100 COMPANY

The table XYZ Performance Summary gives basic statistics for just over ten years. These results are without the use of leverage and before fees. The actual returns were better for the investor because gains from using leverage exceeded the fees we charged.

The graph XYZ Performance Comparison shows the cumulative wealth relatives for XYZ, the S&P 500, and T-bills + 2 percent. From the end of 1994 until about August 1, 2000, we see one of the great bull markets of all time. The S&P 500 exploded at an average rate of 26 percent per year, multiplying wealth by 3.7 during those 5.6 years.

The graph indicates a distinct increase in variability from August 1, 1998, through the middle of February 2002. Some contributors may have been the LTCM disaster, which began in August 1998; the dot-com collapse in March 2000; and the destruction of the Twin Towers of the World Trade Center on September 11, 2001.

**Table 16: XYZ Statistical Arbitrage Results**

| | Start Date | 08/12/1992 | |
| | End Date | 09/13/2002 | |
| | Months Traded | 122 | |
| | **XYZ** | | **S&P 500** |
| Annualized Rate of Return | 18.2% | | 7.77% |
| Annualized Standard Deviation (Risk) | 6.68% | | 15.07% |
| Return/Risk | 2.73 | | 0.52 |
| One Dollar Becomes | 5.48 | | 2.14 |

**Table 17: XYZ Performance Comparison**

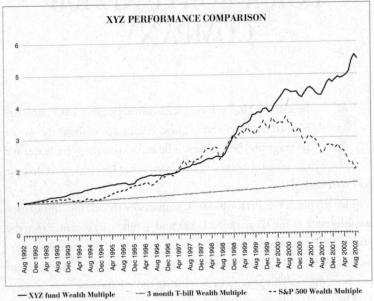

— XYZ fund Wealth Multiple    ⋯ 3 month T-bill Wealth Multiple    - - S&P 500 Wealth Multiple

# ACKNOWLEDGMENTS

"All writing is rewriting" is a claim I came to appreciate as I worked and reworked the manuscript. I received innumerable helpful comments from those who read some or all of the manuscript at various stages of its evolution. Thank you, Catherine Baldwin, Richard Goul, Judy McCoy, Steve Mizusawa, Ellen Neal, Tom Rollinger, Raymond Sinetar, Jeff Thorp, Karen Thorp, Raun Thorp, Vivian Thorp, and Brian Tichenor.

Ellen Neal turned my handwritten squiggles into typescript and cheerfully endured endless revisions. Professional editor and writer Richard Cohen and Random House editor Will Murphy, assisted by Mika Kasuga, gave extensive advice ranging from voice and content to detailed line-edits. David Halpern of The Robbins Office helped me from start to finish.

Some chapters draw upon articles I wrote for the financial magazine *Wilmott*. By giving me that forum, Paul Wilmott, the founder of the magazine, along with the magazine's editor, Dan Tudball, have contributed to this book.

I checked facts, depending on extensive files of correspondence, news clippings, and financial records. It is likely errors remain and for these I apologize. When I have withheld or changed names it was to preserve privacy or confidences, or to avoid a negative impact on the reputation of an individual or an entity.

My thanks to the many sharp-eyed readers who sent me corrections, suggestions, and edits, in particular Aaron Brown, Chris Cole, and Don Schlesinger for their extensive lists, and to Andrea Kaufman for her help with both the corrections and the audio book.

From childhood to old age, I owe any success I have had to the wonderful people who have been a part of my life: my family, friends, mentors, teachers, and the partners and associates who have worked beside me, especially my late wife, Vivian, whose love and support sustained me for almost sixty years.

# NOTES

## CHAPTER 1

3   **a single word**   Curiously, my son had the same experience. He didn't say anything until he was about the same age. His sister, about a year and a half older, was his interpreter. They would go around as a little pair and when he indicated with body language and facial expressions what he wanted, she would get it done.

4   **complete sentences**   Henriette Anne Klauser, in *Writing on Both Sides of the Brain,* Harper, San Francisco, 1997, pp. 36–38, tells a similar story of a first grader who wouldn't write no matter how she prompted him until, suddenly after seven months, he released a torrent of fluency.

4   **Great Flu Pandemic**   More people died from the Great Flu Pandemic of 1918–19 than from any other plague in history, and more than from World War I itself.

9   **the US version**   In the US and the UK, a million is one followed by six zeros. US usage adds three zeros for each step up, so a billion has nine zeros, a trillion twelve zeros, and so on. Practice in the UK adds six zeros at each stage so a billion has twelve zeros, etc.

9   **one standard deviation**   Standard deviation indicates the size of a typical fluctuation around an average value.

10   **to the news**   See Nassim Taleb's readable and insightful book *Fooled by Randomness.*

10   **quick mental estimate**   By the rule of 72, discussed later, a 24 percent annual growth rate doubles money in about $72/24=3$ years. After nine years we have three doublings, to two, then four, and finally eight times the starting value. But it actually takes about 3.22 years because the rule of 72 underestimates the doubling time more and more as rates increase beyond 8 percent.

15   **of the Alamo**   The story of this epic battle and the subsequent ordeals of those held captive by the Japanese is told by Eric Morris in *Corregidor: The American Alamo of World War II,* Stein and Day, New York, 1981, reprinted paperback, Cooper Square Press, New York, 2000.

## CHAPTER 2

24   **surgical facilities**   The horrors of life in such camps is eloquently rendered in *Three Came Home: A Woman's Ordeal in a Japanese Prison Camp,* by Agnes Keith, 1949, paperback 1985, Eland Books, London and Hippocrene Books, New York.

27   **was still running**   Edmund Scientific's *Scientifics 2000 Catalog for Science and Engineering Enthusiasts,* page 31.

27   **several thousand feet**   See *The Darwin Awards, Evolution in Action,* "Lawnchair Larry," pp. 280–81, by Wendy Northcutt, Plume (Penguin), New York, 2002.

27   **of these flares**   String soaked in potassium nitrate solution and dried.

29   **recipe and procedure**   About fifty years later, while listening to Ken Follett's novel *The Man From St. Petersburg,* I noted that the terrorist antihero's recipe and procedure for making nitroglycerine were consistent with how I made it as a boy in my mother's refrigerator.

33   **depth of 5 feet**   http://digitalcollections.lmu.edu/cdm/ref/collection/chgface/id/294.

33   **a man's hand**   As in 1 Kings 18:44.

41   **dimensional analysis**   I was familiar with the book *Dimensional Analysis* by Percy W. Bridgeman, Yale University Press, New Haven, CT, 1922.

43   **joined the rest**   In 2015, my granddaughter Claire Goul was one of three hundred semifinalists in the same contest. It was now the Intel Science Talent Search and had become more competitive, with three top prizes of $150,000 each, compared to one top prize of $10,000 back in 1949.

## CHAPTER 3

53   **standard American wheel**   European wheels had only one green number and further improvements in the odds, such as the player betting on red or black only losing half his stake if that number came up.

54   **systems must fail**   One of the most well-known examples is the Pythagorean theorem from plane geometry. It says that for a right triangle, the sum of the squares of the sides equals the square of the hypotenuse. For instance, the triangle with sides 3, 4, and 5 is a right triangle and $3^2+4^2=5^2$. Also $12^2+5^2=13^2$ for another right triangle. There are infinitely many and we could check them one at a time, but never finish. The theorem does it all at once.

58   **a rubber ring**   Feynman put the rubber ring, which was made from the same material as that used on the *Challenger,* in the ice water and showed that, when it became cold like it did during the launch of the *Challenger,* it became so brittle it was likely to fail. Feynman tells the story in *Classic Feynman,* edited by Ralph Leighton, Norton, New York, 2006.

59   **wealthy older student**   T. T. Thornton

59   **for every frame**   You can see the film at www.edwardothorp.com.

## CHAPTER 4

62   **a new strategy**   Baldwin, et al (1956).

64   **and even awe**   For the rules of blackjack and my original report of this experience, see Thorp, *Beat The Dealer*, 1962, rev. ed. 1966.

## CHAPTER 5

67   **mathematics course**   The course was measure theory, basic to probability and statistics.

68   **partially played decks**   For one fifty-two-card deck we can choose a subset by selecting 0, 1, 2, 3, or 4 Aces in five ways, similarly selecting the number of cards for values Two through Nine in each of five ways, and selecting between 0 and 16 Ten-value cards in seventeen ways for a grand total of $5 \times 5 \times \ldots 5 \times 17 - 1$ (there are nine 5s, one each for Ace, Two, . . . Nine) or a little over 33 million different total partial decks. (We subtract one to delete the case where zero cards of each value are chosen, leading to a subset with no cards in it.) For the eight-deck game the corresponding figures is $33 \times \ldots \times 33 \times 129 - 1$, or about 6 quadrillion (6 followed by 15 zeros) partial decks.

69   **to a gigantic**   For people who like to compute, suppose that each of these strategy tables was written on a separate piece of paper the size of a dollar bill. I estimate the volume of a dollar bill at 1.08 cubic centimeters so the strategy tables would occupy 37 cubic meters or 1300 cubic feet. For eight decks they would fill a space of 6.5 cubic kilometers or 1.6 cubic miles.

73   **0.21 percent**   The Baldwin group said later that their figure of 0.62 percent for the casino's edge should have been 0.32 percent. An arithmetic error caused the incorrect figure.

73   **the blackjack rules**   Casino blackjack rules have varied over time and among casinos. The rules I used for the calculations were then typical.

74    **(half the deck)**    The chance that the last twenty-six cards contain all four Aces is about 5.5 percent.

74    **type from the deck**    Later exact calculations give numbers which are a bit more favorable to the player. These results also are affected by the many variations in casino rules. For details see Thorp (1962, 1966), Griffin (1999), Wong (1994).

75    **$200 bankroll**    This book spans more than eighty years, during which the value of money has changed dramatically. For an accurate perspective the reader can convert money to current dollars using Appendix A.

76    **my mathematical work**    The discovery was an example in functional analysis, in which both Taylor and the mathematician were specialists.

77    **Shannon at noon**    Our meeting was on September 29, 1960, and I memorialized the details in a letter I wrote that same evening to a friend, mathematician Berthold Schweizer.

78    **to the academy**    Thorp, Edward O., "A Favorable Strategy for Twenty-One," *Proceedings of the National Academy of Sciences,* Vol. 47, No. 1, 1961, pp. 110–12.

78    **the program booklet**    Thorp (1960). *Fortune's Formula* also was the title of William Poundstone's 2005 book covering some of this story about blackjack, roulette, the stock market, and the Kelly Criterion.

79    *The Boston Globe*    "Can Beat Blackjack, Says Prof.," by Richard H. Stewart, *Boston Globe,* January 24, 1961, page 1.

79    **across the country**    For example, *Columbus Dispatch* (1961), *Las Vegas Sun* (1961), *Miami News* (1961), *New York Herald Tribune* (1961), *New York World Telegram* and *Sun* (1961), *Washington Post* and *Times Herald* (1961).

# CHAPTER 6

81    **ran his story**    Thomas Wolfe, *Washington Post,* January 25, 1961, page A3.

84    **offered a strand**    Paul O'Neil (*Life* magazine, 1964), in a generally accurate story, erroneously quotes me as saying of the string of pearls, "We had it appraised first thing in the morning. It was worth $16." Neither statement is correct. This was repeated by Bruck (1994) even though I told her this part of the *Life* story was wrong. A good misquote is hard to kill.

89    **the everyday gambler**    Schwartz, David G., *Roll the Bones,* Gotham Books, New York, 2006.

90    **was a characteristic**    Feller (1957), (1968).

90    **the investment worlds**    The greatest bond investor ever, William H. Gross, also learned this lesson in the casinos of Las Vegas. Motivated by *Beat the Dealer,* he went there in the summer of 1966, turning a $200 bankroll into $10,000. See *Bill Gross on Investing,* William H. Gross, Wiley, New York, 1997, 1998. He would later use the ideas in co-managing two *trillion* dollars for PIMCO.

93    **with the house**    I realized later that I would have had an advantage if I had started each deal with big bets, maintaining them if the count was good and causing the dealer to shuffle when it wasn't.

95    **a serious loss**    Why might a bigger bankroll lead to more risk of losing it all? The reasons are partly technical, partly psychological. First the technical: To exploit the larger bankroll we would be likely to make maximum bets ($500 in those days) even in situations that were just slightly favorable. This would increase the size of the fluctuations in our stake and require a longer playing time than I had available to be fairly sure of coming out ahead.

Now the psychological: X and Y didn't have my level of understanding of, and confidence in, the system. If, with a $100,000 bankroll they would in fact quit when we were down say $60,000, then I would be playing and sizing bets and taking risks as though I had a $100,000 bankroll when, unknown to anyone, I really only had a $60,000 bankroll. This subtle distinction between the ostensible bankroll and the real bankroll has contributed to the downfall of many gamblers and investors, as we shall see.

An additional psychological problem which I didn't expect was Kimmel insisting playing his "pidgeon" version of my system, betting big, losing back much of the fruits of my labor, and then excitedly refusing to stop.

96    **afternoon in Boston**    Ivi, her mother, and two sisters came to the US after World War II as refugees from Estonia.

## CHAPTER 7

97   **great mathematics centers**   Segel, Joel, *Recountings,* A.K. Peters, Ltd. Wellesley, MA, 2009, tells the story of mathematics at MIT.

98   **to stay on**   My family's relationship with MIT continued two generations later. Three of my grandchildren, fraternal triplets, entered together as freshmen. See, e.g., "Triplets Celebrate After ALL are Accepted to Prestigious MIT . . . ," *London Daily Mail,* Saturday, July 25, 2015.

98   **building the first one**   The MIT Media Lab timeline erroneously gives the year 1966 for our computer, probably because I first revealed its existence in the 1966 revised edition of *Beat the Dealer.* However, the correct year is 1961, when we completed and successfully tested it in Las Vegas, as explained in numerous subsequent publications, and verified in correspondence dated August 1961, between Shannon and me, now in the archives of the MIT Museum. The device itself also remains at the museum.

99   **few early players**   Among them were Emmanuel Kimmel (Mr. X of *Beat the Dealer*), Jesse Marcum (the "little dark haired guy from Southern California" in *Beat the Dealer*), Russell Gutting ("Junior"), Benjamin F. ("System Smitty") Smith, and Mr. F. (who I was told was Joe Bernstein, the "silver fox" in columnist Herb Caen's book *Don't Call It Frisco*). Marcum seems to have been the only one who consistently adhered to the method.

101   **fairly thorough shuffles**   Of course, seven is not a magic number. The actual number of shuffles needed varies, depending how close to "random" is specified, the type of shuffle, and how "random" is measured.

101   **in private games**   *Danger in the Cards* has been out of print for many years.

104   **William F. Rickenbacker**   For more on this trip see the letters from Thorp and Barnhart in *Blackjack Forum,* Vol. XVII #1, Spring 1997, pp. 102–104, XX #1, Spring 2000, pp. 9–30, and XX #2, Summer 2000, pp. 105–107.

104   **working for the board**   He wrote about our experience in a syndicated column titled "Even 'Honest' Vegas House Cheats."

105   **bits of publicity**   E.g., *Time,* "Games: 'Beating the Dealer,'" January 25, 1963, p. 70.

108   **"It's Bye! Bye! Blackjack" appeared**   Scherman, 1964.

108   **a nine-page story**   O'Neil, Paul. "The Professor Who Breaks the Bank," *Life,* March 27, 1964, pp. 80–91.

109   **a heart attack**   In April of 1966.

110   **thwart these card counters**   Vic Vickery, "Counting on Blackjack," *Las Vegas Style* magazine, May 1993, pp. 61, 67.

111   **Players Too Smart**   Carson City (UPI): *New York Journal-American,* April 3, 1964.

## CHAPTER 8

113   **High–Low System**   I called this the Complete Point Count in *Beat the Dealer*.

113   **pooling their bankrolls**   For the optimal trade-off between risk and return, the bet size in a given situation is proportional to bankroll. To the extent the players on a team are unsure about the current size of the group's bankroll, they will tend to reduce their bets slightly.

114   **Pacific Stock Exchange**   Google the Blackjack Hall of Fame write-ups for more on Francesco, Hyland, Uston, and others in this chapter.

114   **the blackjack community**   As the popularity of the game surged, a blackjack community evolved. Special newsletters for counters were circulated and, later, websites appeared. Stanford Wong's newsletters and websites provided cutting edge information on how and where to play for best advantage. Arnold Snyder's quarterly *Blackjack Forum* had articles from leading players and theorists over its twenty years or so of publication and gave a good informal history of the war with the casinos. Anthony Curtis's *Las Vegas Advisor* was a monthly guide to events, and to best deals on food, accommodations, and playing conditions. The Gambler's Book Store, managed by Howard Schwartz, continued to offer the latest books and systems. Richard Reid's website www .bjmath.com was a treasury of articles, workshops and discussions. The network that arose accelerated the development of new methods for advantageous play.

115   **The second line**   Later more exact calculations changed these numbers somewhat. They also vary slightly with the number of decks.

115   **nearest whole number**   Thirteen was chosen because it gave a good fit.

115   **count was to use**   The strengths of various card counting systems are thoroughly discussed in *The Theory of Blackjack* by Peter Griffin, 6th Edition, Huntington Press, 1999.

116   **in the discard tray**   An easy way to do this is by estimating how many half decks are left, as described in *Professional Blackjack* by Stanford Wong (pseud.), Pi Yee Press, 1994.

116   **the point count**   If you divide the ultimate strategy values in table 1 by eight and round off to the nearest whole number, you get the values of 0 or 1 that make up the complete point count. However the values for sevens and nines are about as close to 1 and –1, respectively, as they are to zero. Choosing them thusly gives the alternative point count I was using in Puerto Rico.

116   **"what I've got."**   The quote is from Thorp (1966), pp. 84–85.

118   **1970s, several people**   Notably, Keith Taft.

119   **a powerful advantage**   I explained the idea in Thorp, Edward O., "Non-random Shuffling With Applications to the Game of Faro," *Journal of the American Statistical Association,* pp. 842–47, December 1973. A much expanded version appears in *Gambling and Society*, edited by W. Eadington, Charles C. Thomas, Springfield, IL, 1975, as: "Probabilities and Strategies for the Game of Faro," pp. 531–60.

120   **cheating, the statutes**   N.R.S. 465.015.

120   **success much more difficult**   *Legends of Blackjack* by Kevin Blackwood and Larry Barker, Kindle eBook, April 5, 2009, tells the stories of some of the leading professionals.

120   **the Blackjack Ball**   "The Smartest Guy in the Room," by R.M. Schneiderman, *Newsweek,* February 20, 2012, pp. 56–57.

121   **in the movie *21***   Inspired by the Ben Mezrich book *Bringing Down the House.*

121   **rate the games**   Stanford Wong's monthly newsletter is thorough.

## CHAPTER 9

123   **exploitable patterns**   Pearson, Karl, *The chances of death and other studies in evolution*, London, New York, E. Arnold, 1897.

123   **sailed the Caribbean**   *Los Angeles Times*, February 27, 2003, page B12, obituary of Albert Hibbs. See also Wilson (1965, 1970).

123   **Hibbs later wrote**   Caltech obituary for Hibbs at http://pr.caltech.edu/periodicals.

123   **a thing of the past**   Decades later, professional gambler Billy Walters found and exploited effective roulette wheels, as reported in *Beating the Wheel,* by Russell T. Barnhart, Carol Publishing, New York, 1992. Walters is interviewed in *Gambling Wizards,* by Richard W. Munchkin, Huntington Press, Las Vegas, Nevada, 2002, pp. 16–18. With a plastic playing card and a few minutes at a roulette wheel, I can tell you whether any of the dividers, or frets, separating the pockets on the rotor, are high or low, loose or tight, and which numbers will be affected. For good measure I would also check to see if the wheel was level and that the rotor hung true on its spindle.

126   **odds in his . . . favor**   Thanks to Richard Cohen for supplying this.

129   **a 1956 paper**   Kelly, J. L., "A New Interpretation of Information Rate," *Bell System Technical Journal,* Vol. 35, 1956, pp. 917–26.

129   **and the stock market**   Thorp, Edward O., "Optimal Gambling Systems for Favorable Games," *Review of the International Statistical Institute,* Vol. 37, 1969, pp. 273–93; Thorp, Edward O., "The Kelly Criterion in Blackjack, Sports Betting, and the Stock Market," *Handbook of Asset and Liability Management,* Vol. 1, S.A. Zenios and W.T. Ziemba, editors. Elsevier, New York, 2006.

134   **called wearable computers**   "A Brief History of Wearable Computing" timeline—MIT Media Lab, www.media.mit.edu/wearables/lizzy/timeline.html.

134   **only one person**   O'Neil, Paul, "The Professor Who Breaks the Bank," *Life,* March 27, 1964, pp. 80–91.

134   **our roulette system**   Thorp, Edward O., *Beat The Dealer*, 2nd Edition, Vintage, New York, 1966.

134   **the details later**   Thorp, Edward O., "Systems for Roulette I," *Gambling Times*, January/February 1979; Thorp, Edward O., "Physical Prediction of Roulette I, II, III, IV," *Gambling Times,* May, July, August, October 1979; Thorp, Edward O., *The Mathematics of Gambling,* Lyle Stuart, Secaucus, New Jersey, 1984.

134   **by hardware problems**   Bass, Thomas A., *The Endaemonic Pie,* Houghton Mifflin, New York, 1985.

134  **May 30, 1985**  One of the uninformed people writing for Wikipedia claimed our computer was used to "cheat" at roulette. This is false. We and the many others who subsequently used roulette and blackjack computers could not be prosecuted under the strong anti-(player) cheating statutes already in place in Nevada. That's why the Nevada state legislature had to pass a law specifically outlawing "devices."

## CHAPTER 10

137  **thermonuclear weapons**  Ulam, S. M., *Adventures of a Mathematician,* Scribner's, New York, 1976.
138  **to a set of rules**  These rules are designed to make the casino's edge roughly the same on the two bets.
138  **for the two bets**  Thorp and Walden (1966).
138  **Walden and I proved**  Thorp and Walden (1973).
139  **is in blackjack**  Griffin (1995), Thorp (1984), Vancura (1996).
139  **so the effect**  Griffin (1995), Thorp (1984), Vancura (1996).
142  **as many tables**  Vancura (1996).

## CHAPTER 11

145  **can be ruinous**  The Kelly Criterion highlights the perils of overbetting even when you have the edge.
146  **waiting fifteen years**  The NASDAQ Composite finally exceeded its March 2000 peak in April of 2015. However, investors were still behind more than 20 percent after adjusting for inflation.
146  **weren't available yet**  *Bogle on Mutual Funds,* pp. 169–70 says "The indexing concept was . . . introduced . . . to the mutual fund industry in 1976." and in fact by the author himself, John C. Bogle.
147  **or the stock market**  According to a Fidelity Research Institute Report dated February 2007 stocks averaged about 10 percent a year, beating residential real estate by more than 4 percent a year for 1963–2005 and by more than 5.5 percent annualized over 1835–2005. Bonds also did better than residential real estate.
149  **to Mr. Market**  See *The Warren Buffett Way,* by Robert G. Hagstrom, Jr., Wiley, New York, 1994, pp. 50–51, and *The Warren Buffett Portfolio,* by Roberg G. Hagstrom, Jr., Wiley, New York, 1999, pp. 143–44.
152  **thesis on the subject**  Kassouf, Sheen T., *Evaluation of Convertible Securities,* Analytical Publishers Co., 602 Vanderbilt Street, Brooklyn, New York 11218, 1962. A brief summary of hedging with warrants and convertible bonds.
153  *Beat the Market*  You can read more about our theories and investments in *Beat the Market* at www.edwardothorp.com.

## CHAPTER 12

155  **researcher and biologist**  You can read about his remarkable scientific aptitude and career on The National Academics Press website, www.nap.edu/books, in *Biographical Memoirs* v.53 (1982), National Academy of Sciences. In 1974 Gerard, who became one of my first investors using money paid out to him by Buffett, passed away. His wife, Frosty, survived him for several years. When she died, part of their Princeton Newport investment went to support the University of California, Irvine.
155  **analysis of common stocks**  The classic 1940 second edition was reissued by McGraw-Hill in 2002.
156  **was his contribution**  Some biographies of Buffett say $105,000. My figure, which I recall from conversations with Warren, is confirmed in the definitive biography of Buffett, *The Snowball,* by Alice Schroeder, Random House, New York, 2008.
156  **a manic 150 percent**  Returns on equities are from Ibbotson Associates (2007).
157  **Peter Minuit**  Minuit, Peter (1580–1638), Dutch colonial governor in America, helped establish New Amsterdam, the settlement that became New York City. He joined the Dutch West India Company and set out for the company's settlement in America. He reached Manhattan Island in 1626 and became the first director general of the colony. Minuit purchased the island from one of

the Algonquian-speaking tribes with trinkets valued at 60 Dutch guilders, a sum later calculated at $24.

157 **with all the improvements**  From 1626 to 1968 is 342 years. Twenty-four dollars compounding at 8 percent would become $6.47 trillion, ⅛ or more of the net worth of the USA at that time. By 2013 this grows at 8 percent to $206 trillion, enough to buy half the world: estimating US 2013 net worth as $100 trillion ($77 billion for households plus $23 billion for government) and assuming the US has about 25 percent of the globe's total net worth gives an estimate of $400 trillion for the market value of the world.

158 *Discover* **magazine article**  "May the Best Man Lose," *Discover,* Nov. 2000, pp. 85–91. For more on voting paradoxes, see Poundstone, William, *Gaming the Vote: Why Elections Aren't Fair (and What We Can Do About It),* Hill and Wang, New York, 2008, and Saari, Donald G, "A Chaotic Exploration of Aggregation Paradoxes," *SIAM Review,* Vol. 37, pp. 37–52, March 1995, and *A Mathematician Looks at Voting,* American Mathematical Society, 2001.

159 **are typically stumped**  For more on nontransitive dice see Gardner, Martin, *The Colossal Book of Mathematics,* Norton, New York, 2001, and Finkelstein, Mark and Thorp, Edward, "Nontransitive Dice with Equal Means, in *Optimal Play: Mathematical Studies of Games and Gambling,* Stewart N. Ethier and William R. Eadington, editors, University of Nevada, Reno, 2007.

163 **early as 1936**  See Schroeder, loc. cit.

164 **the last ten years**  Loomis, Carol, "The Jones Nobody Keeps Up With," Personal Investing, *Fortune,* April 1966.

164 **few existing hedge funds**  The hedge fund world at the start of 1968 was tiny, almost insignificant. The combined capital in dollars was less than one one-thousandth of what it was in 2016. Back in 1968, the top twenty funds ranged in size from $80 million down to $12 million.

 Altogether, there were about 150 funds, with aggregate capital of a billion or two. This grew to more than two trillion dollars a half a century later. Since the dollar value of GNP was about a tenth of what it was forty-eight years later, hedge funds compared to GNP grew more than a hundred times from 1968 to 2016.

164 **and were closing down**  The decline is catalogued in Robertson, Wyndham and Haines, Angela, "The Hedge Funds' Dubious Prospects, A Report on Twenty-Eight Funds," Personal Investing, *Fortune,* October 1970. The group consisted of the largest hedge funds as of December 31, 1968. The big winner was Buffett Partnership, Ltd., which was closing after a spectacular twelve years because stock prices were too high compared with the underlying value of the companies. The only other fund whose assets had increased was Steinhardt, Fine, Berkowitz & Co.

164 *Wall Street Letter*  *The Wall Street Letter,* Myron Kandel, Editor, Nov. 17, 1969.

## CHAPTER 13

166 **never before tried**  The year before, Arbitrage Management Company was set up to exploit the hedging ideas in *Beat the Market.* Among others it involved Harry Markowitz, who later won a Nobel Prize in Economics, and John Shelton, a leading finance professor and warrant theorist. Though profitable, the gains were not enough to keep it from disappearing from the scene after three years.

170 **would transform physics**  For a full account see the inspiring *Annus Mirabilis: 1905, Albert Einstein and the Theory of Relativity,* by John and Mary Gribbin, Penguin, New York, 2005.

171 **of stock price changes**  See the article by Case M. Sprenkle in *The Random Character of Stock Market Prices,* Paul H. Cootner, editor, MIT Press, Cambridge, MA, 1964.

172 **riskless interest rate**  Academic economists and financial theorists have long assumed, as in the Black-Scholes formula, that US Treasury bonds and their short-term version, bills, are riskless. The argument goes that the government can always print the money it needs in order to pay the interest and to redeem them at maturity. Congressional battles over whether to raise the debt ceiling, such as the clash in 2013, exposed the fallacy. The US can pay its debts but it may choose not to. Default is possible. Since investors generally demand to be paid a higher rate of interest to purchase risky debt, this dispute over the debt ceiling has led to higher borrowing costs for the US. Thus, those opposing an increase in the debt ceiling have made the debt itself larger.

172 **warrant expiration date**  For an account of what I did, see my articles in *Wilmott* magazine, Sept. 2002, Dec. 2002, and Jan. 2003. They are also available on my website at www.edwardothorp.com.

For an introduction to the methods of plausible reasoning see *Mathematics and Plausible Reasoning,* Vols. I and II, by George Polya, Princeton University Press, 1954, and his more elementary *How to Solve It,* 2nd Edition, Doubleday, 1957.

172  **I began using it**   For a background discussion, see *Derivatives: Models on Models,* by Haug, Espen Gaarder, Wiley, New York, 2007, pp. 27–44.

172  **Beat the Market**   They acknowledge this in their famous paper, Black, F. and Scholes, M., "The Pricing of Options and Corporate Liabilities," *Journal of Political Economy,* Vol. 81, May–June 1973, pp. 637–54.

172  **the identical formula**   The fact that their formula was identical to the one I was using verified that my plausible reasoning led to the correct result.

173  **down when he had**   *Buffett: The Making of an American Capitalist,* by Roger Lowenstein, Random House, New York, 1995, page 156.

175  **customers high fees**   In a massive replay, hundreds of trillions of dollars' worth of derivatives contracts now trade Over-the-Counter (OTC). Again, the banks and brokers love the high fees and are resistant to standardizing the contracts. The OTC contracts are under-collateralized and could easily precipitate a financial collapse similar to what we saw in 2008–09. Exchange-traded standardized contracts could eliminate this threat.

176  **from the formula**   Years later I heard that one trader had consulted Black and also was using formula prices when trading began at the CBOE.

177  **The Wall Street Journal**   "Computer Formulas Are One Man's Secret to Success in Market," by Jonathan R. Laing, *Wall Street Journal,* September 23, 1974, page 1.

179  **running my hedge fund**   *Fortune's Formula,* page 172, incorrectly reports that I was making as much then as Paul Newman was.

180  **One of my stories**   *Beat the Dealer,* 1966 edition, pp. 167ff.

# CHAPTER 14

185  **where I was speaking**   "Extensions of the Black-Scholes Option Model," Thorp, Edward O., Contributed Papers 39th Session of the International Statistical Institute, Vienna, Austria, August 1973, pp. 1029–36.

186  **model for stock prices**   This is the so-called lognormal model for stock price changes. A different but important situation which it fails to cover for option valuation is the bimodal, or two-peaked, payoff distribution which arises when one company makes a tender offer for another.

186  **and applied finance**   *Fischer Black and the Revolutionary Idea of Finance* by Mehrling, Perry, Wiley, New York, 2005.

187  **were eventually published**   See "Option Pricing: The American Put," by Parkinson, Michael, *Journal of Business 1977,* v50(1), pp. 21–36, and "The Valuation of American Put Options," by Brennan, Michael J. and Schwartz, Eduardo, *Journal of Finance 1977,* v32(2), pp. 449–62.

188  **than $1 million**   Andrew Tobias used my account of this trade and several others we did in his book *Money Angles,* Simon and Schuster, New York, 1984, pp. 68–72.

188  **is a general rule**   If you make 20 percent in year one and 30 percent in year two the wealth and relatives are 1.20 and 1.30. Multiplying gives 1.56, which is the wealth relative for the two successive years, the amount a dollar grows to if reinvested. Thus the two-year gain is 56 percent, *not* 20 percent+30 percent or 50 percent. If you simply *add* the numbers in the table you get +11.7 percent for the market, which isn't nearly as bad. But to find out what a dollar invested at the start of 1973 grows to, or diminishes to, you need to *multiply* together the results for successive periods, which produces the –0.5 percent figure. The result from investing $1 for one period is called the "wealth relative" (wealth at the end of the period). For instance, if you make 12 percent during the year, the wealth relative for that twelve months is 1.12. When we *add* the numbers for the returns for PNP limited partners the result is 42.1 percent, significantly less, in this case, than the actual 48.9 percent figure obtained by *multiplying* successive wealth relatives.

188  **only month-end values**   Month-end figures for the S&P 500 are from Ibbotson. Because the Great Depression was, on average, deflationary, the results based on inflation adjusted or "real" returns are less extreme.

190  **quality and maturity**   More precisely, "duration," which is the discounted weighted average time for the payment stream.

193   **hundred billion dollars**   During the early stages of the run-up in interest rates, S&Ls were raising money by selling puts at bargain prices on Government National Mortgage Association (GNMA) bonds. Bonds usually trade in thousand-dollar denominations or "par" amount and are quoted as a percent of par, so these bonds—quoted at 98—were currently selling at $980 each. The puts we bought from the S&L which issued them gave us the right to sell the bonds to that S&L at this price for the life of the put, which in our case ranged from twelve to eighteen months. If the bonds fell, we could buy the bonds below 98 and "put them" to the bank, which was required to pay us 98 under the terms of the contract. If the bonds rose instead, the puts would expire worthless. As the price of a put tends to move in a direction opposite to that of the underlying security, we hedged the risk of loss on the put by buying GNMA ("Ginnie Mae") futures, i.e., contracts to buy GNMA bonds at a certain price and time in the future. In futures markets, contracts require daily settlement of gains and losses. If the bonds fell in price we would have temporarily to lay out cash for our losses in the futures markets, even though we would ultimately get the money back when we cashed in our puts. Since our cash and borrowing power was finite, this limited how big a hedge we could safely carry to completion. To estimate the maximum safe size for our hedge we needed to consider the lowest price anyone imagined GNMA bonds could drop to during the next eighteen months. The number was 85, a fall of 13 points. I said, let's be super-cautious and double our margin of safety to cover a collapse of 26 points, or a price of 72. This prudence was rewarded when the unexpected happened and the bonds fell as low as 68 during the duration of our trade.

## CHAPTER 15

195   **at UC, Irvine**   It was then the Graduate School of Management.

195   **were earnings yield**   Earnings yield is E/P, Where E is annual earnings (either trailing twelve months or predicted next twelve months—you choose). This is the inverse of P/E, the famous price/earnings ratio, but E/P is better because of problems in the interpretation of P/E when E is zero or negative.

196   **several billion dollars**   *Market Neutral Strategies,* Bruce I. Jacobs and Kenneth N. Levy editors, Wiley, New Jersey, 2005.

196   **when it opened**   Hours for the N.Y.S.E. were from 10 A.M. to 4 P.M. Monday through Friday, from October 1, 1974, until September 30, 1985, when the opening time changed to 9:30 A.M.

196   **of which we pioneered**   Among them were the interest rate swap (the object here was to hedge away interest rate risk in our positions), the bond cash and carry, the commodity cash and carry, capturing a profit when closed-end funds could be purchased below their liquidation value, and special deals.

198   **historical stock price data**   I learned only recently, while reading the interview of Harry Markowitz in *Masters of Finance,* IMCA, Greenwood Village, CO, 2014, page 109, that Markowitz and Usmen got the same answer for daily S&P 500 Index price changes as we did for a much larger data set of two hundred individual stocks. Their work, done sometime before 1987, and submitted before he won the Nobel Prize for Economics in 1990, was initially rejected for publication (!), appearing elsewhere only in 1996.

199   **of the impact**   Market impact refers to the fact that "market orders" to buy are, on average, filled at or above the last previous price and "market orders" to sell tend to be filled at or below the last previous price.

202   **gained 9 percent**   The accounting period with an odd length of five months arose here for PNP because the fiscal year end for PNP changed in 1987 from October 31 to December 31.

202   **statistics confirmed**   Common metrics include the Sharpe ratio, the Sortino ratio, the distribution of drawdowns, and the MAR ratio (annual return divided by maximum drawdown). See, for instance, the three-part series by William Ziemba in *Wilmott* magazine: "The Great Investors," March, May and July 2006.

202   **or losing quarters**   For comparison, the S&P 500 was down in eleven of the thirty-two full quarters and small company stocks lost in thirteen.

## CHAPTER 16

210   **associates, and clients**   *Den of Thieves* by James B. Stewart, Simon and Schuster, New York, 1991.
211   **Ken Griffin**   *The Quants* by Scott Patterson, Crown, New York, 2010.

211 **first limited partner** Conversation with Citadel's Scott Rafferty.

211 **$5.6 billion** The *Forbes* 400 list likely misses people that should be on it, the numbers are estimates, and wealth fluctuates, so the rankings are not exact. For example, Warren Buffett qualified when the list was started in 1982 but they didn't discover him until 1985! Also missing from the *Forbes* list are "The $13 Billion Mystery Angels," of the article by Zachary Mider, *Bloomberg Businessweek,* May 8, 2014. Mider reveals that a group of former PNP employees made at least $13 billion in the twenty-five years after starting their own firm in 1989, with the aid of our quantitative methods and computer algorithms.

211 **Malibu, California** For some of his thoughts, see J. Paul Getty, *How to Be Rich: The Success of a Billionaire Businessman,* Playboy Press, New York, 1965.

211 **Corporation, said** *Los Angeles Times Magazine,* January 23, 2000, pp. 10ff and page 35.

212 **D. E. Shaw** When D. E. Shaw hired one of our key employees the first thing they reportedly did was debrief him for six hours to find out everything he could tell them about PNP.

212 **convertible bonds** The program had methods for incorporating quality deterioration and credit default risk which were, I believe, unique at the time.

## CHAPTER 17

213 **I've got enough** *The New Yorker,* May 16, 2005.

215 **buyers and sellers** We chose a sample of ten option trades from the forty which we had not already proven to be fakes.

215 **a legal mess** For the classic story of a legal mess, see Jarndyce versus Jarndyce in *Bleak House* by Charles Dickens.

215 **his best investment** If Madoff is really gaining 20 percent a year and their best alternatives give, say, 16 percent a year, then they're only out 4 percent a year.

217 **to destroy documents** Rothfeld, Michael and Strasburg, Jenny, "SEC Accused of Destroying Files," *Wall Street Journal,* August 18, 2011, page C2.

217 **the headline article** Arvedlund, Erin E., "Don't Ask, Don't Tell," *Barron's,* May 7, 2001.

218 **in the early 1990s** "Bernard Madoff Gets 150 Years in Jail for Epic Fraud (Update 7), Bloomberg .com, June 29, 2009.

218 **$65 billion** News Release, "Bernard L. Madoff Charged in Eleven-Count Criminal Information," U.S. Attorney for the Southern District of New York, March 10, 2009.

218 **One individual reportedly** One Jeffry M. Picower, according to *The New York Times,* Sunday, July 5, 2009, page B2. According to a later report in *The New York Times* by Diana B. Henriques, October 2, 2009, page B5, the trustee liquidating the Madoff assets, Irving H. Picard, "reported that one Picower account had been overdrawn by $6 billion when Mr. Madoff was arrested."

220 **the individual guesses** If half of the crowd's guesses are on each side of the average it is a mathematical fact that the average will be closer to the correct value than at least half of the individual estimates. What is interesting is that the crowd consensus is often much better yet.

220 **hedging Japanese warrants** "The Money Man: A Three-time Winner," *Forbes,* November 25, 1991, pp. 96–97.

224 **so-called secretary or marriage problem** Today one might retitle it as "The Significant Other Problem."

## CHAPTER 18

228 **to gain a profit** A couple of weeks after the EMLX hoax, the *Los Angeles Times* reported that the SEC, in a "web fraud sweep," accused thirty-three companies and individuals of illegally using the Internet to make more than $10 million in profits by driving up the prices of more than seventy small thinly traded stocks, hyping them on chat rooms, websites, and in email messages.

229 **before the Internet** Two readable and entertaining accounts are the famous *Extraordinary Popular Delusions and the Madness of Crowds,* by Charles MacKay, and its more current sequel, *Ponzi Schemes, Invaders from Mars and Other Extraordinary Popular Delusions,* by Joseph Bulgatz.

229 **Hell on one's feet** See page 71 of Haugen, *The New Finance: The Case Against Efficient Markets,* Second Edition (1999).

230 **Recent reports** "Toxic Equity Trading Order Flow on Wall Street," by Arnuk, Sal and Saluzzi, Joseph, A Themis Trading LLC White Paper, www.themistrading.com, and "Algo Traders Take

$21bn in Annual Profits," by Tom Fairless of *Financial News,* quoting the research firm Tabb group.

230 **for the A shares**   Reported as of 1:22 P.M. New York time on July 24, 2009.

230 **one of the mechanisms**   "Traders Profit With Computers Set at High Speed," by Charles Duhigg, *New York Times,* Friday, July 24, 2009, Page A1, and "SEC Starts Crackdown on 'Flash' Trading Techniques," by Charles Duhigg, *New York Times,* Wednesday, August 5, 2009, Page B1. See also: (1) Patterson, Scott, and Geoffrey Rogow, "What's Behind High-Frequency Trading," *Wall Street Journal,* Saturday/Sunday, August 1–2, 2009, page B1. (2) Wilmott, Paul, "Hurrying Into the Next Panic?", *New York Times,* Wednesday, July 29, 2009, page A19.

230 **Krugman disagrees sharply**   Krugman, Paul, "Rewarding Bad Actors," *New York Times,* Monday, August 3, 2009, page A19. See also O'Brien, Matthew, "High Speed Trading Isn't About Efficiency—It's About Cheating." *The Atlantic,* February 2014.

231 **cut a trading rate**   The dollar value of all trades in U.S. equities varies from year to year, as does the portion created by the high-frequency traders.

231 **Business Day headline**   *New York Times,* September 28, 2000.

## CHAPTER 19

235 **billion shares annually**   The Medallion Fund, a hedge fund closed to new investors, run by mathematician James Simons, includes a similar and far larger trading operation than ours with a higher rate of turnover and a vast annual trading volume. Now an investment vehicle for Simons and his associates in his firm Renaissance Technologies Corporation, it is probably the most successful hedge fund in history.

237 **of our researchers**   David Gelbaum.

237 **Gerry Bamberger**   For this and much more, see *A Demon of Our Design,* by Richard Bookstaber, Wiley, New York, 2008.

239 **in the securities industry**   See the book *The Quants: How a New Breed of Math Whizzes Conquered Wall Street and Nearly Destroyed It,* by Scott Patterson, Crown, New York, 2010.

241 **and more powerful**   It was based on the statistical notion of "principal components"; We called it ETS, for "Equity Trading System."

241 **Japanese warrant hedging**   See *Forbes,* November 25, 1991, pp. 96–99, "A Three Time Winner," and the article by Shaw, Thorp and Ziemba, "Risk Arbitrage in the Nikkei Put Warrant Market of 1989–1990," *App. Math. Fin.* 2, 243–71 (1995).

242 **trend is greater**   The graph makes returns in the second epoch appear even more variable relative to the first than they really were. The proper display for comparing variability and growth rates is a so-called lognormal graph. For that graph of XYZ's performance, see Thorp, Edward O., "Statistical Arbitrage, Part VI," *Wilmott,* July 2005, pp. 34–36.

244 **had ever experienced**   Reportedly, Simons's secretive Renaissance Partners had a similar experience in August of 2008, losing 8 percent or so in a few days, then rebounding to make more than 100 percent for the year.

244 **employees, only six**   Since the six people in my office also had other responsibilities, we had only 3.5 "full-time equivalents" on the project.

244 **in statistical arbitrage**   Firms doing statistical arbitrage, such as the hedge fund group Citadel, already had in place most of the technology, talent, and expertise needed later to create and implement high frequency trading (HFT). For an account of HFT, see the book *Flash Boys* by Michael Lewis; In 2005, three years after we went out of the statistical arbitrage business, Steve and I worked with Jerry Baesel, who was then at Morgan Stanley Asset Management, to see if it was worth restarting. We concluded it was marginal because simulation showed a recent unlevered return of 10 percent or so, not attractive enough when compared to other investment opportunities then available to us. Meanwhile, we put the "shrink-wrapped" software on our shelf with a tag saying "add people and data to reactivate." Had we been running the program during the 2008–09 economic crisis, I suspect that we would have had a rerun of our "miraculous" 1998–99 results.

## CHAPTER 20

248 **or ten thousand shares**   The number of shares for which a depositor can apply varies from one offering to another, but between ¼ percent and 1 percent of the issue is common.

249 **deals aren't as good**   If, for example, the business value in the MW deal were $5 instead of $10, management helped themselves to $3 of the final enterprise value, and selling costs were $1, buyers of the IPO would get a value of $5+$10–$3–$1=$11 for their $10. The market won't recognize this value right away, so the stock will start trading below $11 a share. Meanwhile, market prices for the group of S&Ls as a whole could drop, taking the new stock's price down, too. Or, if the market sees management as greedy—$3 is a lot to take out for themselves—or not competent to put the new capital to work, the stock will decline.

250 **so-called opportunity cost**   Opportunity cost refers to the cost of the opportunity that was given up. In addition to the cost of redirecting our capital from other investments, it includes the value of whatever didn't get done because we redirected our personal time to the S&L project.

## CHAPTER 21

251 **never did, either**   After BPL closed, Buffett accumulated Berkshire stock whenever he could, often from his friends, associates, and former partners. According to Schroeder, *The Snowball*, pp. 341–42, the stock was unregistered then so it had to be traded privately.

252 **As *Forbes***   Forbes 400, October 22, 1990, page 122.

252 **growth, decided**   Quietly.

252 **made my first purchase**   Buffett was so uninformative about his plans that his own children sold their stock fairly early. I started buying about the time his daughter Susie sold off the last of hers.

253 **$74,000 a share**   "Ordinary" investors tend to switch their money from securities that drop in price to those that have gone up, a strategy sometimes described as chasing returns. An academic study of all domestic US equity mutual funds covering 1991 through 2004 showed that this behavior by the fund investors reduced their annual returns by an average of 1.6 percent; Friesen, Geoffrey C. and Sapp, Travis R.A., "Mutual Fund Flows and Investor Returns: An Empirical Examination of Fund Investor Timing Ability," *Journal of Banking and Finance,* September 2007. Summarized in "Buying High and Selling Low," Mark Hulbert, *New York Times,* July 12, 2009, Mutual Fund Report, page 18.

255 **a famous interchange**   Paul Marx told me this story.

256 **principles of security analysis**   As practiced by Graham, Dodd, Buffett, Munger, Fisher and others.

## CHAPTER 22

258 **fund in the country**   The woes of Harvard's endowment fund are chronicled in "Rich Harvard, Poor Harvard," by Nina Munk, *Vanity Fair,* August 2009, pp. 106ff.

258 **average 18 percent**   This loss figure of 18 percent is commonly cited by the industry and I use it throughout the book. However, it substantially understates the drop because some funds did not fully discount their toxic assets, others with illiquid assets reported too late to be counted, reports are voluntary so losers are less likely to respond, and the impact of funds which disappeared during the year may not have been included.

258 **billion in 2007**   *New York Times,* March 25, 2009, page B1.

259 **Management fees**   Incentive fees in 2015 averaged 17.7 percent of any profit, compared to 19.3 percent in 2008, according to *The Wall Street Journal,* September 10, 2015. Management fees had declined to an average of 1.54 percent.

260 **hedge fund returns**   The studies encountered difficulties obtaining clean long-term data and in correcting for survivorship bias: funds that died early and may not be in the database are expected to have performed more poorly. Omitting them and studying only the survivors overstates the results.

260 **Later analyses**   Dichev, Ilia D. and Yu, Gwen, "Higher risk, lower returns: What hedge fund investors really earn," *Journal of Financial Economics,* 100 (2011) 248–63; Lack, Simon, *The Hedge Fund Mirage,* Wiley, New York, 2012.

260 **One study**   *Bloomberg Businessweek,* "Buzzkill Profs: Hedge Funds Do Half as Well as You Think," August 17, 2015, reports on a study by Getmansky, Lo, and Lee. Using data from 1996 through 2014, they conclude that a reported average return of 12.6 percent was really 6.3 percent when the losers, who tend not to report, are included.

261 **As Shakespeare**   *Julius Caesar,* Act I, Scene II, lines 140–41.

261 **in an article** *International Fund Investment,* April 2000, page 64.

261 **managers that year** *New York Times,* March 25, 2009, page B1.

263 **playing this game** *New York Times,* September 9, 1999, National Edition, page C10.

264 **tend to fade** Consider the statistical phenomenon of regression toward the mean.

266 **of their stake** Numerous books and articles give accounts of what happened, including Roger Lowenstein, *When Genius Failed,* Random House, New York (2001), "Failed Wizards of Wall Street," *Business Week,* September 21, 1998, pp. 114–20, and "Hedge Fund's Star Power Lulled Big Financiers Into Complacency," by Timothy L. O'Brien and Laura M. Holson, *New York Times,* October 23, 1998. For some of my comments, see Tim O'Brien's story "When Economic Bombs Drop, Risk Models Fail" in the *New York Times,* October 4, 1998. A sensational *Nova* program on LTCM that aired in February 2000, asserted that the total LTCM contracts outstanding amounted to a trillion dollars.

## CHAPTER 23

267 **good to him** Perhaps too good. He later stole millions from his firm and fled to Brazil.

268 **following classification** *Forbes,* October 11, 1999, page 60.

268 **$83 trillion** *Orange County Register,* March 7, 2014, Business, page 3.

268 **is not available** How big is the underground economy? What's the value of privately held non-traded businesses? How much of the national wealth consisting of patents, copyrights, and innovation is being counted? Most household labor is not monetized, hence is not customarily counted in national income.

268 **$1.36 million** Source: *Money* magazine report on a University of Michigan study, the lead author being Fabian T. Pfeffer. Much of the increase in inequality comes from the fact that housing prices were about the same in 2014 as they were in 2003, whereas US stocks, as represented by the S&P 500, doubled. The rich have a higher proportion of their wealth in stocks and less in housing than poorer people.

269 **for large stocks** Ibbotson Associates yearbook.

269 **saves $6 each day** He saves more each day in later years assuming the price of cigarettes increases along with inflation.

269 **An article** http://quickenloans.quicken.com/Articles/fthbc_afford_budget.asp.

269 **$10,000 difference grows** Mentally calculated by the rule of 240 in Appendix C.

270 **The formula** Assume the power law $N = AW^{-B}$, where W is a high enough wealth level to exclude most people, and N is the number having wealth at least W, and A and B are unknowns. The two facts I used to find A and B were (1) when $N = 400$, $W = \$1.3$ billion, and (2) the total wealth of the 400 was $1.2 trillion, giving an average value of three times the cutoff. The result is $N = 400\,[(1.3\text{ billion})/W]^{4/3}$. The value 4/3 for B seems to be roughly the same from year to year, as the average wealth seems to be about three times the cutoff. So you can recalibrate the formula each year that this is true by simply replacing 1.3 billion by the current cutoff. Using 1999 data, in "How Rich Is Rich?—Part 1," *Wilmott* magazine, July 2003, pp. 44–45, I found the slightly different value 1.43 instead of 4/3. Perhaps coincidentally, the 2009 *Forbes* 400 edition offers a calculator using this formula on page 20 at forbes.com/baldwin. *Forbes,* page 20, says the formula uses the exponent 0.7, which equals 1/B and, therefore, a value for B of 1.43. Their formula inverts mine and expresses W as a function of N. For an extended discussion of formulas for estimating wealth and income, including evidence for the Pareto equation, see Inhaber and Carroll (1992) and the many further references therein as well as Scafetta, Picozzi and West, "An out-of-equilibrium model of the distribution of wealth," *Quantitative Finance,* Vol. 4 (2004) pp. 353–64.

270 **billion dollars or more** *The Orange County Business Journal* listed 36, with Lakers basketball star Kobe Bryant in 36th place at $250 million. Since I know of people they missed, the figure of 49 may be closer to the truth.

271 **$81 billion** The Gates household had as much wealth as 150 thousand average US households. In other words, one one-thousandth of *all* the private wealth in the United States.

274 **large increases in wealth** Carrying this a step further, you could guess someone's future wealth, in current dollars, by estimating the present value of their future savings, plus their current net worth. This is similar to some methods used by analysts to calculate the value of a company in

current dollars, and hence the fair price for its stock. Using an estimated future inflation rate you could then arrive at a value for their wealth on any future date.

276  **$37 million each**  *Bloomberg,* August 17, 2009, citing UC–Berkeley economics professor Emmanuel Saez, noted for his continuing studies of, and statistics on, the distribution of income and wealth in America. Note that the average of $37 million, divided by the cutoff of $11.5 million, is 3.2, very close to the result of the same calculation for the wealth distribution of the *Forbes* 400, suggesting that 2007 superrich taxable income followed the same, or nearly the same, power law as that for wealth.

## CHAPTER 24

277  **disputed origin**  The claimed sources include Benjamin Franklin, various Rothschilds, Albert Einstein, Bernard Baruch, and "unknown."

278  **$22 million result**  These figures do not include trading costs or income taxes. A buy-and-hold investor loses little to trading costs and is taxed only on dividends. Taxes, if any, vary with the investor.

280  **less than the last**  So-called decreasing marginal utility.

280  **as one day less**  Adults with the same chronological age vary widely in their fitness age. Qualifiers for the Senior Olympic Games have a functional and fitness age averaging twenty-five years less than their calendar age, as reported in "Older Athletes Have a Strikingly Young Fitness Age," by Gretchen Reynolds, in the *New York Times,* July 1, 2015. Studies of identical twins give persuasive evidence of the longevity benefits of exercise. See, for instance, "One Twin Exercises, the Other Doesn't," Gretchen Reynolds, *New York Times,* March 4, 2015.

281  **forty hours of commuting**  Assuming he works on average about twenty days a month.

281  **a month to operate**  Costs include fuel, maintenance, insurance, license fees, and depreciation, plus the owner's time spent taking care of these.

## CHAPTER 25

282  **the US stocks**  The Vanguard Total Stock Market Index Admiral Shares, ticker symbol VTSAX, does this. Actually, it invests in each stock proportionally to the market value of the so-called float, which is the estimated fraction of freely trading shares, as opposed to shares being held which are not available for trading. The difference in performance between the two methods has been negligible.

283  **it first appeared**  Justin Fox, *The Myth of the Rational Market,* page 119, reports that Ben Graham, in 1962, pointed out that investment funds as a whole shouldn't expect to beat the market "because in a significant sense they . . . *are* the market."

283  **the clearest exposition**  Sharpe, William, "The Arithmetic of Active Management," *Financial Analyst's Journal,* Vol. 47, No. 1, pp. 7–9, January/February, 1991.

284  **all areas of investing**  According to Lipper, Inc., *Wall Street Journal,* July 6, 2009, section R, the average equity mutual fund expense ratio alone was 1.22 percent in 2007, compared to 0.20 percent for Vanguard's no-load equity index funds. As the expense ratio is only a part of the fees investors pay, the "helpers" collect substantially more than 1 percent per year and, with trading costs, active investors lag passives by well over 2 percent annually.

287  **five and ten years**  Fund Track, by Sam Mamudi, *Wall Street Journal,* October 8, 2009, page C9.

287  **corresponding economic loss**  These extra taxable gains or losses will be offset later if you liquidate your investment.

288  **to catch up**  Taxes leave me with 70 percent of my sales price. To get back to $100, $70 has to increase by $30 or 42.9 percent.

## CHAPTER 26

291  **beat the market**  This sounds nonsensical at first. What it means is that no one has any information whatsoever that has predictive value.

291  **to the contrary**  They display the well-known characteristic known as cognitive dissonance.

291  **and hundreds of books**  An excellent history of these meanderings is Justin Fox's book *The Myth of the Rational Market.*

291 **all the future earnings** Interpreted as net value paid out or accumulated for the benefit of a sole owner.

292 **on inside information** As chronicled by James Stewart in *Den of Thieves*, Connie Bruck in *The Predators' Ball*, and others.

294 **this type profitably** Tobias, Andrew, *Money Angles*, Simon and Schuster, New York, 1984, pp. 71–72. Often, management would offer to redeem shares at an intermediate price, thus cashing out the dissidents and retaining an asset base of unredeemed shares which they could continue to be paid to manage.

294 **in a few months** Buying SPACs was not without risk because the assets were not protected from creditors in bankruptcy. Jeff, who discovered the strategy, researched the risks in each case before investing.

297 **or 82 percent** I have omitted details such as how the actual cash required for the investment might vary from the $9,000 of the example because of the interaction of margin regulations with the investor's preexisting portfolio, and also because of time-varying marks to the market on the short position.

297 **The Wall Street Journal** *Wall Street Journal*, March 3, 2000, page C19, "Palm Soars As 3Com Unit Makes Its Trading Debut."

298 **the EMH explained** Malkiel, Burton G., *A Random Walk Down Wall Street*, Norton & Co., New York, 2007.

298 **The New York Times** *New York Times*, March 3, 2000, page A1, "Offspring Upstages Parent In Palm Inc.'s Initial Trading."

299 **academic literature documents** It often takes weeks or months for the stock price to fully adjust after announcements of unexpected earnings, stock buybacks, and spin-offs.

# CHAPTER 27

301 **already been counted** Mutual fund management companies and hedge fund general partnership interests have a separate and often considerable market value but they have already been counted as part of the private equity subcategory.

303 **between asset classes** For a highly mathematical discussion of this effect, sometimes called "volatility pumping," see *The Kelly Capital Growth Investment Criterion: Theory and Practice*, editors Leonard C. MacLean, Edward O. Thorp, and William T. Ziemba, World Scientific, 2010.

305 **The results** For a comprehensive history of returns for world stock markets, see *Triumph of the Optimists*, by Dimson [et al].

306 **1940–2004 period** "Causes of the United States Housing Bubble," from Wikipedia, 09/16/09 version; Ziemba, William, "What Signals Worked and What Did Not 1980–2009, Parts I, II, III, *Wilmott* magazine, May, July and Sept. 2009.

306 **owning your home** On *average*, significant money in excess of inflation is made in commercial real estate but not in residential real estate. Homeowners and would-be buyers often don't understand the distinction. They also are misled by the stories of big winners at various times and in different localities. They share this error with stock market investors, which is no surprise as many are the same people. Behavioral finance theorists have analyzed this human tendency.

309 **median large endowment** "Princeton's Endowment Declines 23 percent," by John Hechinger, *Wall Street Journal*, September 30, 2009, page C3.

310 **Fortune's Formula** The title, *Fortune's Formula*, should sound familiar, as it was the title of the talk I gave on blackjack to the American Mathematical Society in 1961. Bill Poundstone considerately asked if he might use it as his title. In *Beat the Dealer* I called this, naturally enough, the Kelly Gambling System. Since 1966 I've called it the Kelly Criterion and the name has stuck.

310 **larger the bet** You can read about the details in articles I have written, most of which are available on my website at www.edwardothorp.com.

310 **considerable controversy** In addition to Poundstone's history, mathematically trained readers can study some of the burgeoning modern developments in *The Kelly Capital Growth Investment Criterion: Theory and Practice*, editors Leonard C. MacLean, Edward O. Thorp, and William T. Ziemba, World Scientific, 2010.

310 **As he told The Wall Street Journal** "Old Pros Size Up the Game," by Scott Patterson, *Wall Street Journal*, March 22, 2008, page A9. Gross left PIMCO in 2014 and went to Janus to manage money.

311 **out in _Wilmott_ magazine** See "Understanding the Kelly Criterion," by Edward O. Thorp, _Wilmott,_ May 2008, pp. 57–59, and http://undergroundvalue.blogspot.com/2008/02/notes-from -buffett-meeting-2152008_23.html.

312 **Computer simulations** The simulations were done by mathematician Art Quaife.

## CHAPTER 28

314 **stock index fund** Why not continue to hold Berkshire? One reason is that I can't foresee who will be managing the endowment in the distant future and believe it best to lock them into the well-understood mechanical approach of indexing. This avoids the waste that occurs from active investing.

315 **H. W. Brands** _Fortune,_ August 11, 2003.

315 **resilient than universities** As quoted in Sample, Steven B. and Bermis, Warren, _Los Angeles Times_ Book Review, July 13, 2003, page R9.

316 **criteria for selection** I thank Professor Ronald Stern for encouraging and facilitating the creation of the chair, Paul Marx of the University Foundation for legal help and for many insightful conversations, and my wife, Vivian, for her part in creating the conditions that made our contribution possible.

317 **early card counters** See _The Bond King,_ by Timothy Middleton, Wiley, New Jersey, 2004, and _Everything You've Heard About Investing is Wrong,_ by William H. Gross, Random House, New York, 1997, as well as the revised version _Bill Gross on Investing,_ by William H. Gross, Wiley, New York, 1997, 1998.

317 **past twenty-five years** Gross, 1997, op. cit. page 90.

317 **causes, so a group** The idea of meeting with Bill Gross started with Professor Stern, then Dean of the School of Physical Sciences, and Greg Gissendanner, who was UCI's University Advancement Officer at the School. My friend and attorney, Paul Marx, knew Bill and set up a lunch.

318 **ahead of schedule** Sue and Bill Gross later gave an additional $4 million to complete the fourth floor conference center and laboratories.

## CHAPTER 29

319 **all-time closing high** Source: www.finance.yahoo.com, daily closing prices, adjusted for splits and dividends. Figures are truncated from 1565.15 and 676.53.

319 **$48.5 trillion** The Federal Reserve, as reported in the _Los Angeles Times,_ March 12, 2010.

320 **$161 per share** The successive 10 percent increases over the previous stock price compound, moving the stock from $100 to $110, then to $121, $133.10, etc., reaching $161.05 after the fifth increase.

320 **more than ten times** Month-end returns from the end of 1925 to the end of August 1929 show no decline in the index from a previous peak of 10 percent, suggesting that conditions were encouraging for borrowing as stock prices increased.

321 **maintenance margin** For a discussion of maintenance margin, see, for instance, _Beat the Market,_ by Thorp, Edward O. and Kassouf, Sheen T., Random House, New York, 1967, Chapter 11.

322 **impact of speculation** Wikipedia.

323 **_Frontline_** _Frontline: The Warning,_ October 20, 2009, pbs.org, available on DVD.

324 **gross national product** What would have been produced by workers who are unemployed never gets "made up." Social waste included deteriorating empty untended houses and the impact on society of shattered lives.

327 **Krugman pointed out** Krugman, Paul, "How Did Economists Get It So Wrong?" _New York Times Magazine,_ September 6, 2009, pp. 36–43.

327 **in his book** _The Quants: How a Small Band of Math Wizards Took Over Wall Street and Nearly Destroyed It,_ by Scott Patterson, Crown, New York, 2010.

331 **remain solvent** He also said, on the same point, "In the long run we are all dead."

332 **anyone, later told** Patterson, Scott, _Wall Street Journal._

332 **Krugman points out** Krugman, Paul, "Good and Boring," _New York Times_ Op-Ed, February 1, 2010.

333 **411 to 1** Hiltzik, Michael, "Echoes of Bell in CEO Salaries," _Los Angeles Times,_ page 31, October 3, 2010. _Wall Street Journal_ (as reprinted in _The Orange County Register,_ May 11, 2014, Business,

page 3) says a study by the Economic Policy Institute found that for the 350 companies with the largest sales, CEOs received 18 times the pay of their workers in 1965 but were compensated 201 times as much, on average, in 2012.

333 **as Moshe Adler**   Adler, Moshe, "Overthrowing the Overpaid," *Los Angeles Times* Opinion, page A15, January 4, 2010.

## CHAPTER 30

338 **Garrett Hardin**   Hardin, Garrett, "The Tragedy of the Commons," *Science,* Vol. 162, No. 3859 December 13, 1968, pp. 1243–48.

338 **protects my neighbors**   Vaccination is a positive externality as it protects others from contracting a disease from the recipient.

338 **collection of insights**   *Poor Charlie's Almanack: The Wit and Wisdom of Charles T. Munger,* Foreward by Warren Buffett, edited by Peter Kaufman. Expanded third edition, 2008.

339 **much of their income**   Read the evolving discussion of the taxation of so-called carried interest in Wikipedia and elsewhere on the Internet. The 2012 Republican presidential candidate, Mitt Romney, was a substantial beneficiary.

340 **of national income**   The top 1 percent have about a third of taxable income, the next 9 percent have another third, and the bottom 90 percent have the remaining third.

340 **20 percent or so**   To get a simplistic feel for the numbers, government received $3.25 trillion in income in 2015 and GNP was $18 trillion. If we exempt $2 trillion for the very poorest citizens and tax the remaining $16 trillion of GNP at a single rate, the result is 3.25/16 or 20 percent.

341 **a year by 2015**   According to the UC Admissions Office, this is mitigated by the fact that more than half of undergraduates pay no tuition and more than two-thirds receive grants and scholarships averaging $16,300.

341 **of them Chinese**   My grandson Edward, while a high school senior, was taking an advanced mathematics class (partial differential equations) at UCI. Thirty-one of the thirty-six students were Chinese. As they were unaware that Edward speaks Mandarin fluently, he overheard many candid conversations.

## APPENDIX A

344 **dollar has changed**   For an insightful discussion of why the inflation index from the 1970s may be much too low as a result of a series of government revisions in the method of calculation, and the consequences to investors and consumers, see "Fooling With Inflation" by Bill Gross (June 2008) at www.pimco.com.

   For updated Consumer Price Index numbers and for month-by-month values, go to www.bls .gov/cpi or do the usual Google search.

## APPENDIX C

351 **$2 billion in cash**   *Los Angeles Times*, Thursday, September 7, 2000, page C5.

# BIBLIOGRAPHY

Bass, Thomas A. *The Eudaemonic Pie*. New York: Houghton Mifflin, 1985.

Black, Fischer, and Myron Scholes. "The Pricing of Options and Corporate Liabilities." *Journal of Political Economy* 81.3 (1973): 637–54.

Blackwood, Kevin, and Larry Barker. *Legends of Blackjack: True Stories of Players Who Crushed the Casinos*. Kindle EBook, April 5, 2009.

Bogle, John C. *Bogle on Mutual Funds: New Perspectives for the Intelligent Investor*. Burr Ridge, IL: Irwin, 1994.

Edwardothorp.com. View articles written by the author.

Feller, William. *An Introduction to Probability Theory and Its Applications*, Volume I. New York: Wiley, 1957, 1968.

Fox, Justin. *The Myth of the Rational Market: A History of Risk, Reward, and Delusion on Wall Street*. New York: Harper Business, 2009.

Griffin, Peter A. Introduction. *The Theory of Blackjack: The Compleat Card Counter's Guide to the Casino Game of 21*. Las Vegas, NV: Huntington, 1995, 1999.

Gross, William H. *Bill Gross on Investing*. New York: Wiley, 1998.

*Ibbotson SBBI 2014 Classic Yearbook: Market Results for Stocks, Bonds, Bills, and Inflation, 1926–2013*. Chicago, IL: Morningstar, 2014.

Kelly, J. L. "A New Interpretation of Information Rate." *Bell System Technical Journal* 35.4 (1956): 917–26.

Lack, Simon. *The Hedge Fund Mirage: The Illusion of Big Money and Why It's Too Good to Be True*. Hoboken, NJ: Wiley, 2012.

MacLean, L. C., Edward O. Thorp, and W. T. Ziemba. *The Kelly Capital Growth Investment Criterion: Theory and Practice*. World Scientific, 2011.

Malkiel, Burton Gordon. *A Random Walk Down Wall Street: The Time-Tested Strategy for Successful Investing*. New York: W. W. Norton, 2007.

Mezrich, Ben. *Bringing Down the House: The Inside Story of Six MIT Students Who Took Vegas for Millions*. New York: Free Press, 2002.

Munchkin, Richard W. *Gambling Wizards: Conversations with the World's Greatest Gamblers*. Las Vegas,
    NV: Huntington, 2002.
Munger, Charles T., and Peter D. Kaufman. *Poor Charlie's Almanack: The Wit and Wisdom of Charles T.
    Munger*. Foreword by Warren Buffett. Virginia Beach, VA: Donning Publishers, 2008.
O'Neil, Paul. "The Professor Who Breaks the Bank." *Life* 27 March 1964: 80–91.
Patterson, Scott. *The Quants: How a New Breed of Math Whizzes Conquered Wall Street and Nearly De-
    stroyed It*. New York: Crown, 2010.
Poundstone, William. *Fortune's Formula: The Untold Story of the Scientific Betting System That Beat the
    Casinos and Wall Street*. New York: Hill and Wang, 2005.
Schroeder, Alice. *The Snowball: Warren Buffett and the Business of Life*. New York: Bantam, 2008.
Segel, Joel. *Recountings: Conversations with MIT Mathematicians*. Wellesley, MA: A K Peters/CRC Press,
    2009.
Siegel, Jeremy J. *Stocks for the Long Run: The Definitive Guide to Financial Market Returns and Long-
    Term Investment Strategies*. New York: McGraw-Hill, 2008.
Taleb, Nassim Nicholas. *The Black Swan: The Impact of the Highly Improbable*. New York: Random
    House, 2007.
———. *Fooled by Randomness: The Hidden Role of Chance in Life and in the Markets*. New York: Ran-
    dom House, 2005.
Thorp, Edward O., and Sheen T. Kassouf. *Beat the Market: A Scientific Stock Market System*. New York:
    Random House, 1967. Available at www.edwardothorp.com.
———. *Beat the Dealer: A Winning Strategy for the Game of Twenty-One*. New York: Random House,
    1962, Rev. 1966, Rev. 2016.
———. "A Favorable Strategy for Twenty-One." *Proceedings of the National Academy of Sciences* 47.1
    (1961): 110–12.
———. "Optimal Gambling Systems for Favorable Games." *Review of the International Statistical Insti-
    tute* 37.3 (1969): 273–93.
———. "The Kelly Criterion in Blackjack, Sports Betting, and the Stock Market." *Handbook of Asset
    and Liability Management,* Volume 1, Zenios, Stavros Andrea, and W. T. Ziemba, Editors. Am-
    sterdam: Elsevier, 2006.
Wong, Stanford. *Professional Blackjack*. La Jolla, CA: Pi Yee, 1994.

# INDEX

gambling (*cont'd*):
"cheating" defined in Nevada statutes, 120
end play system, 99
Fundamental Theorem of Card Counting, 138
games of pure chance, 65
hidden computers and, 134–35
horse racing, 65
house edge, various games, 62
innovations by Harold Smith, 89
interrupted approach not affecting outcome, 102
investing as, 145
Kelly strategy, 129
Martingale system, 53
mathematical analysis of games, 65
need for an edge, 61
Nevada devices law, 134–35, 363n134
problem of winning systems, 79
profile of successful card counter, 140
roulette, 44, 53–54, 122–35
as a socially corrosive tax on ignorance, 336–37
Thorp barred from play in Las Vegas, 143
Thorp's curiosity about, 66
Thorp's publishing his blackjack strategy, 76–77
trade-off between risk and return, 58
U.S. earnings in, 65
US Treasury agent anecdote and, 180–81
*Gaming the Vote* (Poundstone), 365n158
*Gangster #2* (Stuart), 95
Garrett Hardin, "the tragedy of the commons," 338
Gates, Bill, 162, 271, 371n271
Gaussian or bell-shaped curve, 126, 171, 190
GEICO, 254, 256
Gelbaum, David, 369n237
General Re, 254
Gerard, Ralph and Frosty, 155, 251, 364n155
    Buffett and, 156, 159, 162
    Thorp managing portfolio of, 156, 165
Getty, J. Paul, 211
Gillette, 254
Gissendanner, Greg, 374n317
Giuliani, Rudy, 204, 206, 207, 208, 210–11, 239
Glass-Steagall Act, 322, 323
gold and gold futures, 192
Goldman Sachs, 191, 204, 212, 217, 329
    bailout of, 330
    bailout of AIG and, 328
    huge bonuses paid by, 330
    PNP's massive AT&T trade, 196–97
    recovery of, 330
Gorat's Steak House, Omaha, 253, 254
Goul, Claire (granddaughter), 360n43
Goul, Richard (son-in-law), 34

Government National Mortgage Association (GNMA) "Ginnie Mae," 366n193
Graham, Benjamin, 149, 155, 157, 163, 251–52, 372n283
    *Security Analysis,* 145, 155
Great Depression, ix, 6, 11–12, 25, 171, 173, 319, 366n188
    banking system collapse, 321–22
    the 1 percent, 333
    stock market crash, 197, 319, 320–21, 374n320
    unemployment, 321
    WPA and CCC, 12, 331
Great Flu Pandemic of 1918–19, 4, 359n4
Great Recession (financial crisis of 2008–2009), 210, 243, 258, 319–34, 370n257
    Berkshire Hathaway shares and, 304
    Cash for Clunkers, 330, 331
    deregulation and, 323
    derivatives and, 197, 323, 332
    economic inequality and, 333
    excess leverage and, 150, 266, 320
    expansion of credit and, 323–24
    government bailouts and, 323, 330, 339
    hedge funds and, 190–91, 258, 259, 266, 370n258
    loss in net worth of US Households, 319
    mortgage industry and, 323–24
    municipal bonds and, 304
    preventing a recurrence, 334
    real estate losses, 303, 308–9, 319
    rich get richer and, 266
    SPACs, 293
    stock market losses, 304
    tax credit for first-time homebuyers, 331
    unemployment and, 330–31
    university endowments and, 309
    warning signs, 322
*Green Felt Jungle, The,* 120
Greenspan, Alan, 323, 332
Griffin, Beverly and Robert, 113
Griffin, Ken, 211
Griffin, Peter, 119
    *The Theory of Blackjack,* 119, 363n115
Griffin Investigations, Inc., 113
Grosjean, James, 113, 120
Gross, William H. "Bill," 310, 316–17, 361n90, 374n310, 374n317
    *Bill Gross on Investing,* 361n90
    "Fooling With Inflation," 375n344
Grossman, Harvey and Llewellyn, 91
Guare, John, 127
Gutting, Russell "Junior," 99, 362n99

Hafen, Bellamia, 142
Hafen, Kay, 140–434
haggling, 221–23

stock markets and investments (*cont'd*):
laddering, 337
leverage, risk of, 150
liquidity, 308–9
liquid securities, 234
lognormal model, 198, 366n186
"lucky" streaks, 90, 361n90
margin, 199, 321
market inefficiency, 229, 236, 295, 300
market-neutral portfolio, 234, 237, 240, 263
momentum, 149
need for an edge, 61
negative or positive beta portfolios, 234
net asset value (NAV), 292–94
passive investors, 282–83, 287, 303
prediction and, 65
price/earnings ratio (P/E ratio), 304–5, 367n195
psychological errors of investors, 147, 149, 281
quants, 166
residual, 239
risk, reward, and uncertainty, 337
Sharpe's Principle, 283, 286, 288, 372n283
short selling, 153, 164, 167, 197, 200–201, 236, 237, 241, 297, 373n297
stock prices and bell curve, 171
"stress-test" of a portfolio, 190
swindles and hazards, 226–32
Table 6: With an Investment Making 8%, Paying Tax Every Year at 35%, at 20%, and Paying 20% at the End, 285
Table 7: Comparison of Passive Versus Active Investing, 287
Table 10: Historical Returns on Asset Classes, 1926–2013, 347
Table 11: Historical Returns (%) to Investors, 1926–2013, 348
Table 12: Schedule of Assumed Costs Which Reduce Historical Returns (%), 348
Table 13: Annual Returns (%), 1972–2013, 348
taxable investors, 288, 306, 307–8
tax-exempt investors, 287–88
Thorp's early investment mistakes, 144, 148–51
Thorp's formula for "correct" price, 154
Thorp's formula for trading, 170–72, 175–76, 185, 365n172, 366n172
Thorp's integral method, 186
Thorp's lesson from the blackjack tables, 88
trade-off between risk and return, 58
trading costs, 284–85
typical compounding of stocks, 156
uptick rule, 200–201
US as dominant world power and, 340–41
value investors, 302–3, 373n303
value of the US stock market (2014), 305

VaR or "value at risk" technique, 190
volatility of the stock, 176
"volatility pumping," 373n303
"wealth relative," 366n188
Stuart, Mark (*Gangster #2*), 95
Stump, Mr., 30–32, 35
Summers, Lawrence, 323
Surdez, Georges, 126
*Survey of Modern Algebra, A* (Birkhoff and MacLane), 57
Swiss banks, 150

Taft, Keith, 363n118
Taleb, Nassim, 323
*The Black Swan,* 322–23
*Fooled by Randomness,* 359n9
Tartaglia, Nunzio, 237
taxes, 373n303
on active investors, 285
on capital gains, 285, 307
carried interest, 375n339
cuts of 2001, 323
hedge funds and, 262
how to cut taxes on investments, 308
net worth, income, and, 274, 275, 276
the 1 percent and, 276, 372n276
revenue-neutral flat tax, 340
Table 6: With an Investment Making 8%, Paying Tax Every Year at 35%, at 20%, and Paying 20% at the End, 285
taxable investors, 288, 306, 307–8, 372n287, 372n288
tax-exempt investors, 287–88
tax-gain deferral, 307
tax-loss selling, 306–8
Thorp's reform ideas, 339–40, 375n339
unrelated business taxable income (UBTI), 262
value-added tax, 340
wash sale rule, 307
*Tax Notes,* 276
Taylor, Angus, 59–60, 69, 76, 225, 361n76
tech stocks, 261, 302, 331
term financing, 197
*Theory of Blackjack, The* (Griffin), 119
theory of probability, 66, 123
"$13 Billion Mystery Angels, The" (Mider), 367n211
Thornton, T. T., 59, 360n59
Thorp, Edward O.
advice on living life, 343
astronomy interest, 137
character, 5, 25, 37–38, 41, 47–48, 51, 82, 131, 342–43
charitable giving and, 313, 318
choice of futures and, 131
on education, 335–37, 341
experimentation and, ix–x, 5

PHOTO: © MARK JORDAN

EDWARD O. THORP is the author of the bestseller *Beat the Dealer: A Winning Strategy for the Game of Twenty-One* (Random House 1962, 1966). It presented the first scientific system ever devised for a major casino gambling game and revolutionized the game of blackjack. His book *Beat the Market* (Random House 1967, co-authored with Sheen T. Kassouf) helped start the derivatives revolution that transformed world securities markets. Based on his work, he launched the first market-neutral hedge fund in 1969. Dr. Thorp, with Claude Shannon, also invented the first wearable computer in 1961 to win at roulette. He has also written *Elementary Probability* (1966), *The Mathematics of Gambling* (1984), and numerous mathematical papers on probability, game theory, and functional analysis.

He completed undergraduate and graduate work at UCLA, receiving the BA and MA in physics, and the PhD in mathematics in 1958. He has taught at UCLA, MIT, and New Mexico State University, and was Professor of Mathematics and Finance at the University of California, Irvine.

edwardothorp.com
amanforallmarkets.com